ROGERS' THERAPEUTIC CONDITIONS:
EVOLUTION, THEORY AND PRACTICE

Volume

Congruence

edited by
Gill Wyatt

PCCS BOOKS
Ross-on-Wye

First published in 2001

PCCS BOOKS
Llangarron
Ross-on-Wye
Herefordshire
HR9 6PT
United Kingdom
Tel (01989) 77 07 07
website www.pccs-books.co.uk
email contact@pccs-books.co.uk

**Rogers' Therapeutic Conditions:
Evolution, Theory and Practice
Volume 1: Congruence**

ISBN 1 898059 29 2

Cover design by Old Dog Graphics
Printed by Bookcraft, Midsomer Norton, Somerset, United Kingdom

Contents

PART THREE: The Wider Context and Links to the Other Conditions

Introduction to the Series
Gill Wyatt

The concept for this series grew out of my idea to publish a book of edited papers on congruence and Pete Sanders (of PCCS Books) vision of extending this to Rogers' six conditions. We felt it crucial that all six conditions would need to be addressed in order to avoid repeating a recent pattern of emphasising the significance of what has become 'the three core conditions' i.e. congruence, empathy and unconditional positive regard. The four volumes of *Rogers' Therapeutic Conditions: Evolution, Theory and Practice*, are then,

> Vol 1 Congruence (condition three)
> Vol 2 Empathy (condition five)
> Vol 3 Unconditional Positive Regard (condition four)
> Vol 4 Contact and Perception (conditions one and six)

The editors of each of these volumes, where appropriate, have included:
- both previously published papers and newly commissioned work;
- client incongruence as it affected the theme of that volume;
- international contributors;
- the full diversity of person-centred therapy would be represented — client-centred, experiential and process-directed
- an historical review of the conceptualisation and development of the condition;
- research projects and findings;
- at least one contribution in each volume which focuses on the (re)integration of the volume condition with Rogers' other conditions.

The more experience I gain as a psychotherapist and counsellor and the more examination of theory I make, the more I realise the complex and subtle interplay of the six conditions. I used to see congruence, empathy and unconditional positive regard as the therapist conditions; client incongruence as the client's condition; and contact and the client's perception as the conditions of the relationship. It made sense on many levels. Now, however, I see all these conditions as more relational in their nature and more entwined in practice. Others have hypothesised that there may be only one therapeutic condition and that Rogers' conditions are facets of this meta-condition (Bozarth, 1998; Wyatt, 2000; Schmid, 2001, [this series Chapter 14, Vol. 1]). So although this series is in some respect separating the conditions from one another, I want the reader to understand that the spirit of this separation is in the hope that the examination of the separate parts will facilitate a deeper exploration of the inter-relationship of the conditions and how they create a whole.

ROGERS' SIX CONDITIONS

It has been suggested by many writers that Rogers' theoretical statement of 1957

The Necessary and Sufficient Conditions of Therapeutic Personality Change was the most critical event in the development of client-centred therapy — and perhaps even for psychotherapy as a whole (Barrett-Lennard 1998). In writing this paper he had set himself the task '. . . to state, in terms which are clearly definable and measurable, the psychological conditions which are both necessary and sufficient to bring about constructive personality change' (Rogers, 1957, p. 95). He hypothesised that no other conditions were necessary, if these six conditions existed and continued over time '. . . this is sufficient. The process of constructive personality change would follow' (ibid.). 'Constructive personality change' meant a change in the personality structure of the individual which would lead to 'greater integration, less internal conflict,' (ibid.) an increase in energy for living and a shift in behaviour away from what is regarded as 'immature' to behaviours regarded as 'mature'. Rogers had successfully delivered to the psychotherapy world a crucial statement that described the basic attitudes and conditions necessary for an effective therapeutic relationship for all theoretical orientation.

In 1959 Rogers published his major theoretical conceptualisation of Client-centred Therapy '*A Theory of Therapy, Personality, and Interpersonal Relationships, as Developed in the Client-Centered Framework*'. Here he writes his theory of therapy and personality change as an 'if-then' statement. If the conditions of the therapeutic process exist then a process is set in motion by these conditions and the result of this process will be 'certain' outcomes in personality and behaviour (Rogers, 1959, p. 212). In an interview with R. T. Hart (1970) Rogers explained that this theory formulation in Koch (1959) was actually written in 1953–54 and so although his 1959 paper was published after his 1957 statement it has to be seen as an antecedent for his 1957 statement. Other sources of this pivotal theoretical exposition can be found in earlier writings (1939, 1942, 1946 and 1951). In the little known 1946 paper Rogers described '. . . six "conditions" of therapist attitude and behaviour which . . . led predictably to a pattern of described qualities of therapy process and outcome.' (Barrett-Lennard, 1998, p. 66). These conditions included creating a warm, safe non-judgmental environment, to 'respond with deep understanding' of the client's emotional experience, 'to set limits on behaviour but not attitudes and feelings', and for the therapist to withhold from '. . . probing, blaming, interpreting, reassuring or persuading.' (Rogers, 1946, quoted in Barrett-Lennard, 1998, p. 66).

Then, in *Client-Centered Therapy* (1951), Rogers developed these precursors of his conditions referring to the importance of warmth (p. 41), therapist attitudes, deep understanding, and respect and acceptance; that these attitudes needed to be deeply and genuinely held by the therapist to be effective; and that the therapist should relate to the client 'in a deeply personal way' (p. 171). Within his personality theory he first coined the term 'congruence' and finally, the forerunner of condition six can be identified by Rogers giving attention to how the client perceives the counsellor (p. 42).

A wealth of research was also being carried out at the Chicago Counseling Center during the 1950s. This included The Parallel Studies Project and the research findings published by Rogers and Dymond (1954). This research revealed a surprisingly regular process during client-centred therapy, raising questions about the requirements for the occurrence of this process. (Barrett-Lennard 2001, personal communication). Looking for an answer to this brought Rogers a step closer to his 'conditions statement'.

Two other factors were part of this evolution. In 1954 Standal published his PhD thesis on *The Need for Positive Regard* in which he developed the idea of unconditional positive regard (UPR). The warmth, acceptance and respect that Rogers had referred to earlier came to fruition in Standal's concept. UPR was the term that Rogers used in his future writings. There was also an elaboration on the idea of the therapist needing to be genuine in his ability to step into the client's frame of reference and to relate 'in a deeply personal way'. Streich and Bown both accentuated the significance of the therapist being a whole person, with Bown advocated therapists allowing their (strong) emotions into the therapeutic relationship (Raskin, 1996), and Seeman wrote about the importance of the 'integration' of the therapist (1951). The therapist's congruence as one of Rogers' conditions was taking form.

Rogers 1957 conditions statement was integrative in the sense that it applied equally to all theoretical applications whereas his 1959 theoretical statement was specifically addressing client-centred therapy. There are some minor differences between Rogers' two theoretical statements of his six conditions. In 1959 he expressed them as follows and I have shown the (later) 1957 wording when different in italics. Before researching this chapter I believed the changes occurred between the 1957 paper and the 1959 paper and that the dates represented the chronological order of writing. Now we need to understand any significance of these changes in reverse. I have been unable to find any discussion of the importance of the changes, whether they were connected to the shift from a client-centred statement to an integrative statement or reflected other developments in Rogers' thinking.

1) That two persons are in *(psychological)* contact
2) That the first person, whom we shall term the client, is in a state of incongruence, being vulnerable, or anxious.
3) That the second person, whom we shall term the therapist, is congruent *(or integrated)* in the relationship.
4) That the therapist is experiencing unconditional positive regard toward the client.
5) That the therapist is experiencing an empathic understanding of the client's internal frame of reference *(and endeavours to communicate this to the client).*
6) That the client perceives, at least to a minimal degree, conditions 4 and 5, the unconditional positive regard of the therapist for him, and the empathic understanding of the therapist. *(The communication to the client of the therapist's empathic understanding and unconditional positive regard is to a minimal degree achieved).*

In the late 1950s and 1960s there was a profusion of research studies based on Rogers' Necessary and Sufficient Conditions. Barrett-Lennard developed his Relationship Inventory (BLRI) to measure the presence of the conditions in the therapeutic relationship to facilitate quantitative research. His research in 1962, although criticised later, did imply that the perceived therapist's conditions were 'involved in the generation of the associated change' of the client (Barrett-

Lennard, 1962 p. 31). Rogers, with colleagues, undertook the Wisconsin Project with hospitalised clients who were diagnosed 'schizophrenic' (Rogers, Gendlin, Kiesler and Truax 1967). This was an ambitious research project that failed to produce the hoped for results that unequivocally supported the conditions. Despite this disappointing conclusion, much more work was carried out that continued to explore the link between the therapeutic conditions and personality change for the client. The BLRI continued to be used, as were the rating scales of therapist congruence, empathy and UPR generated by Truax (Truax and Carkhuff, 1967). The results of this research, and later reviews of these studies, produced conflicting conclusions. Truax and Carkhuff (1967), Truax and Mitchell (1971), Patterson (1984), Gurman (1977) Stubbs and Bozarth (1994) reported evidence ranging from 'significant' to 'overwhelming' in support of the relationship between client-perceived therapist conditions and client outcome. On the other hand Mitchell, Bozarth and Krauft (1977), Parloff, Waskaw and Wolfe (1978), Lambert, DeJulio and Stein (1978), Watson (1984) Beutler, Crago and Arizmendi (1986) and Cramer (1990) concluded that none of the studies had been designed, (a) to deal with the complexity of all of the therapeutic conditions in determining outcome; (b) to deal with the relational nature of these conditions; (c) to address sampling difficulties or (d) to utilise accurate enough measures. These findings suggested that Rogers' therapeutic conditions had not been tested rigorously enough. Whether this is true or not, there does seem to be overwhelming evidence from this time (1950s and 1960s), and more recent reviews, which support the hypothesis that the client-counsellor relationship and client variables (factors unique to each client and their environment) are the major determinants in client outcome rather than therapist-employed techniques or the particular theoretical orientation of the therapist (Duncan and Moynihan 1994, Bozarth, Zimring, and Tausch in press).

Rogers moved to La Jolla in 1963 and established the Center for Studies of the Person in 1968. His focus during these 'California years' moved strongly away from clinical work, as he became fascinated with groups in general and the encounter movement in particular. He increasingly turned to the application of the client-centred philosophy beyond the therapeutic relationship — including education, facilitation of client-centred therapists, large groups and international cultural conflicts. He was not to return to his earlier clinical focus and so he made no further major theoretical additions to his 1957 and 1959 conditions statements

The one notable exception was a paper written by Rogers and Sanford published in 1984. In this paper the first condition concerning 'psychological' contact is dropped. The condition related to the therapist's congruence is expanded to include the therapist's communication and the last condition is extended from the therapist's empathy and UPR, to now include the therapist's 'realness' needing to be perceived minimally by the client (Rogers and Sanford 1984, p. 1382–83). Again I have been unable to trace the significance of what would appear to be a major shift from his 1957/1959 conditions statement.

There have been three developments arising from Rogers clinical research and theoretical writings: (a) Gendlin, drawing from European existential philosophy, emphasised the significance of the experiential process of the client and developed 'focusing' (and subsequent evolution into experiential psychotherapy); (b) Wexler and Rice, using cognitive learning psychology, concentrated on the client's style of information processing (developing into process-directed therapy); and (c) Truax and Carkhuff's elaboration of a skills based eclectic model of the helping relationship.

The impact of Rogers' therapeutic conditions on psychotherapy, counselling and the helping professions has been immense. Even though the mainstream psychotherapy world challenged his findings, they also publicly awarded him honours and validation during the 1950s and early 1960s. Since then there has been a decline in the appreciation of his work, particularly in the United States. This is despite the fact that most, if not all, theoretical orientations acknowledge the significance of the therapeutic relationship and the importance, particularly of empathy. Psychotherapy research over the last 10 years has been specificity-based — defining specific treatments for specific psychological problems. This, along with the ill-informed criticism that client-centred and experiential psychotherapies lack depth of theory and cannot be applied to 'disturbed' clients, has meant that Rogers and his conditions are seldom acknowledged. Furthermore, client-centred and experiential psychotherapies are often misrepresented and dismissed as valid theoretical orientations.

Over the last ten years there has been renewed interest in person-centred therapy, particularly in Britain and Europe where numerous successful training programmes for person-centred counselling and psychotherapy have been developed. There has been renewed interest in research by, among others, Tausch et al., Greenberg, Lietaer, McLeod and there has been the theoretical contributions of Prouty, (Pre-therapy), Warner (Fragile Process) and Mearns (Working at Relational Depth and Configurations of Self). These contributions may help to elevate the standing of person-centred therapy. This series is another endeavour to extend the theoretical and clinical standing of person-centred therapy so that it can take its rightful place within psychotherapy, counselling and related mental health professions.

REFERENCES

Barrett-Lennard, G.T. (1998). *Carl Rogers' Helping System: Journey and Substance*. London: Sage.

Barrett-Lennard, G. T. (1962). Dimensions of therapist response as casual factors in therapeutic change. *Psychological Monographs*, 76(43), whole 562.

Beutler, L. E., Crago, M. and Arizmendi, T. G. (1986). Research on therapist variables in psychotherapy. In S. L. Garfield and A. E. Bergin (Eds.), *Handbook of psychotherapy and behavior change*. New York : Wiley, 3rd ed. pp. 257–310.

Bozarth, J.D. (1998). *The Person-Centered Approach: A Revolutionary Paradigm*. Ross-on-Wye: PCCS Books.

Bozarth, J.D., Zimring, F.M. and Tausch, R. (in press). Client-centered therapy: Evolution of a revolution. In D. Cain and J. Seeman (eds) Handbook of Research and Practice in Humanistic Psychotherapies. Washington D.C.: American Psychological Association

Cramer, D. (1990). Towards Assessing the Therapeutic Value of Rogers' Core Conditions. *Counselling Psychology Quarterly*, 3, pp. 57–66.

Duncan, B. L. and Moynihan, D. (1994). Applying outcome research: Intentional utilization of the client's frame of reference. *Psychotherapy* , 31, pp. 294–301.

Gurman, A. S. (1977). The patient's perception of the therapeutic relationship. In A. S. Gurman and A. M. Razin (Eds.), *Effective Psychotherapy: A handbook of research*. New York: Pergamon, pp. 503–43.

Hart, J.T. and Tomlinson, T.M. (1970). New directions in client-centered therapy. Boston: Houghton Mifflin.

Lambert, M. J., DeJulio, S. J. and Stein, D. M. (1978). Therapist interpersonal skills: Process, outcome, methodological considerations, and recommendations for Future Research. *Psychological Bulletin*, 85, pp. 467–89.

Mitchell, K. M., Bozarth, J. D. and Krauft, C. C. (1977). A reappraisal of the therapeutic effectiveness of accurate empathy, non-possessive warmth, and genuineness. In A. S. Gurman and A. M. Razin (Eds.), *Effective psychotherapy: A handbook of research.*. New York : Pergamon , pp. 482–502.

Parloff, M. B., Waskow, I. E. and Wolfe, B. E. (1978). Research on therapist variables in relation to process and outcome. In S. L. Garfield and A. E. Bergin (Eds.), *Handbook of psychotherapy and Behavior Change: An empirical analysis*. New York: John Wiley and Sons, 2nd ed. pp. 233–82.

Patterson, C. H. (1984). Empathy, warmth, and genuineness in psychotherapy: A review of reviews. *Psychotherapy*, 21(4), pp. 431–38.

Schmid, P. F. (2001). Authenticity: The Person as His or Her Own Author. Dialogical and Ethical Perspectives on Therapy as an Encounter Relationship. And Beyond. In G. Wyatt (Ed.), *Rogers' Therapeutic Conditions. Volume 1: Congruence*. Ross-on-Wye: PCCS Books, pp. 213–22.

Standal, S. (1954). The need for positive regard. A contribution to client-centered therapy. Unpublished doctoral dissertation, University of Chicago.

Raskin, N. (1996). Person-Centred Psychotherapy. In W. Dryden *Twenty Historical Steps in Developments in Psychotherapy*, London: Sage, pp. 1–28.

Rogers, C.R. (1939). The clinical treatment of the problem child. Boston: Houghton Mifflin.

Rogers, C.R. (1946). Significant aspects of Client-Centered Therapy. *American Psychologist*, 1, pp. 415–22.

Rogers, C.R. (1951). *Client-Centered Therapy*. Boston: Houghton-Mifflin.

Rogers, C.R. (1957). The Necessary and Sufficient Conditions of Therapeutic Change. *Journal of Consulting Psychology*, 21, pp. 95–103.

Rogers, C.R. (1959). A Theory of Therapy, Personality, and Interpersonal Relationships, as Developed in the Client-Centered framework in Koch S. (Ed.), *A Theory of Therapy, Personality and Interpersonal Psychotherapy*. New York: McGraw Hill, pp. 184–256.

Rogers, C. R. and Dymond, R. F. (1954). *Psychotherapy and personality change*. Chicago: University of Chicago Press .

Rogers, C. R., Gendlin, G. T., Kiesler, D. V. and Truax, C. B. (1967). *The therapeutic relationship and its impact: A study of psychotherapy with schizophrenics*. Madison: University of Wisconsin Press.

Rogers, C.R. and Sanford, R.C. (1984). Client-Centered Psychotherapy. In Kaplan, H.I. and Sadock, B.J. (Eds.) *Comprehensive Textbook of Psychiatry, IV*. Baltimore: Williams and Wilkins Co, pp. 1374–88.

Stubbs, J. P. and Bozarth, J. D. (1994). The dodo bird revisited: A qualitative study of psychotherapy efficacy research. *Journal of Applied and Preventive Psychology*, 3(2), pp. 109–20.

Truax, C. B. and Carkhuff, R. R. (1967). *Toward effective counseling and psychotherapy: Training and practice*. Chicago: Aldine .

Truax, C. B. and Mitchell, K. M. (1971). Research on certain therapist interpersonal skills in relation to process and outcome. In A. E. Bergin and S. L. Garfield (Eds.), *Handbook of Psychotherapy and Behavior Change*. New York: Wiley, pp. 299–344.

Watson, N. (1984). The empirical status of Rogers' hypothesis of the necessary and sufficient conditions for effective psychotherapy. In R. F. Levant, and J. M. Shlien (Eds.), *Client-Centered Therapy and the Person-Centered Approach: New directions in theory, research, and practice* . New York: Praeger, pp. 17–40.

Wyatt, G. (2000). *Presence: Bringing together the core conditions*. Paper presented at ICCCEP Conference in Chicago, USA.

Introduction to Volume 1: Congruence

Gill Wyatt

Congruence, genuineness, transparency, authenticity, realness — these are all words that are used to convey Rogers' condition of congruence. The concept has been described as an attitude, a state of being, a way of living. Rogers, prior to conceptualising congruence in his 1957/1959 conditions statement, had referred to the therapist's attitudes of acceptance and understanding needing to be genuine (1942). In 1951 Rogers first used the term 'congruent' in describing his theory of personality (p. 513). In 1956 he used the term 'congruence' with regard to a therapist's condition or attitude for the first time. This then became the third condition in his theoretical statements in 1957 and 1959.

During the next thirty years there was little attention given to the concept of congruence apart from developing scales to operationalise it for the prolific research into the conditions in the 1960s and 70s and Seeman's work on personality integration (1983). There was some renewed interest from, among others, Mearns and Thorne (1988), Adomaitis (1992) and Lietaer (1993) but it wasn't until 1997 that person-centred theoreticians brought their attention to this often neglected and misunderstood concept.[1]

My aim has been to bring together in one volume reviews of past writings and research on congruence, and revised versions of previously published papers. I have also sought to stimulate new theoretical developments and the examination of the significance of these in clinical applications by commissioning new work by a wide range of authors. It is deeply important to me that the differing 'schools' of person-centred therapy[2] (Client-centred Therapy, Experiential and Process-directed Psychotherapy) should be represented in this volume. I want to present to the reader the diverse and contrasting ideas that theoreticians and clinicians have about congruence so that the reader is presented with a plurality rather than a definitive statement of what is 'right'. The divergent and perhaps paradoxical views in this volume will hopefully stimulate and motivate readers to find their personal meaning of the concept of congruence and to extend their understanding.

As an editor, my intention has been to be respectful of each author's individual style of writing yet also finding the balance between the individuality of each author and the accessibility of their writing to the reader. I particularly appreciate and wish to thank those authors for whom English is not their first language — for their commitment to learn foreign languages and then after they have created their written paper to struggle with the complicated process of English translation.

Authors were not given specific instructions with regard to gender specific language rather they were asked to be respectful to prevent both overt and more insidious gender biases that can be unconsciously present in our language as a result of these deeply held prejudices within our culture and society.

---

1. This renewed interest included doctoral (Grafanaki) and masters (Haugh) theses, presentations at conferences and published papers by, among others, Brodley, Ellingham and Wyatt (revised versions of each are included in this volume as chapters 5, 7 and 6 respectively
2. I am using therapy to denote psychotherapy and counselling.

CONGRUENCE IN OTHER THEORETICAL APPROACHES

There is insufficient space to more than briefly touch on similar concepts to congruence found in other theoretical approaches within this short introduction. Information about authenticity in existential and encounter philosophy can be found in Chapter 14. The significance of presence and its link with congruence and authenticity are important in Gestalt and Existential psychotherapy. Over the last 30 years the psychodynamic tradition has been influenced by Kohut's self psychology, Gill's re-experiencing therapy, Stolorow's intersubjectivity and social constructionism (cited in Kahn, 1991). These have all strongly challenged the analyst's position of the 'blank screen' and although some classical analysts maintain this position, the therapeutic relationship is now seen as the arena for the resolution of the client's transference. Jacobs acknowledges it is 'essential' for the (psychodynamic) counsellor to be 'genuine, accepting and empathic' (1988 p. 98). While Kohut states the need for therapists to express their humanity (cited in Kahn 1991, p. 99), and Kahn directs the therapist to '. . . aspire to genuiness' (ibid., p. 163). As the therapeutic relationship has gained importance within all theoretical orientations questions concerning the realness and genuiness of the therapist are increasingly asked.

LOCATING THE BOOK'S MAJOR THEMES

The predominant focus of the book is congruence within the therapeutic relationship rather than in the wider context of applications of the person-centred approach. The book divides into three sections: Historical Perspectives, Theory and Practice and The Wider Context and Links with the Other Conditions For those who wish to approach this book looking at specific themes I have listed them below with their main, but perhaps not only, location.

- Congruence as a Cartesian-Newtonian, or an organismic/holistic, concept (Chapters 5, 6, 7, 10 and 12).
- Congruence has been defined in both narrow and broad terms; sometimes this difference is simply that congruence is seen as having two components (experience and awareness) as opposed to three components (experience, awareness and communication). Congruence, as the internal state of the therapist is a narrower conceptualisation (Chapters 3, 4, 7 and 12); whereas congruence referring to the integrity or maturity of the therapist is a broader conceptualisation is included in most chapters.
- Different psychological theories of experiencing and the processes involved in experiences and awareness (Chapters 1, 6, 8 and 10).
- Congruence, incongruence, Rogers' concept of the fully functioning person, and the idea of optimal functioning as the person-centred theory of general and mental health (Chapters 1, 10 and 13).
- The appropriateness for a therapist to communicate their congruence and the guidelines in determining that appropriateness (Chapters 3, 4, 5 and 8).
- The significance of therapist incongruence juxtaposed with their congruence and the resulting professional practice issues (Chapter 3, 4, 5, 8 and 11).

- The related question of how a therapist develops their congruence with regards the training of therapists and their continuing professional development (Chapters 8, 9 and 11).
- Congruence as an inter-relational process between therapist and client rather than simply being an ingredient required for personality change (Chapters 2, 3, 4, 8, 14 and 15).
- How this inter-relational process then extends to groups, communities and the social, political and ecological systems (Chapters 13, 14 and 15).
- How Complexity Theory can subtly yet profoundly effect the conceptualisation of congruence (Chapter 7).
- The link between congruence, 'authenticity' and 'spontaneity', terms used in existential and spiritual philosophies (Chapters 5, 14 and 15).
- The relationship between congruence and the other conditions with regard to whether therapist congruence is preparatory for the therapist to have UPR and empathic understanding and whether there is in effect one meta-condition (Chapters 4, 12, 14 and 15).
- The connection between presence and congruence (Chapters 8, 12, 14 and 15).
- Congruence and the therapist's presence as the manifestations of unconditional positive self-regard (Chapter 12).

REFERENCES

Adomaitis, R. (1992). *On Being Genuine: A Phenomenologically Grounded Study of the Experience of Genuineness and its Place in Client-Centered Psychotherapy.* Unpublished PhD. Dissertation, Northwestern University, USA.

Lietaer, G. (1993). Authenticity, Congruence and Transparency, in D. Brazier (Ed.), *Beyond Carl Rogers.* London: Constable, pp. 17-46.

Jacobs, J. (1988). *Psychodynamic Counselling in Action.* London: Sage.

Kahn, M. (1991). *Between Therapist and Client.* W.H. Freeman and Company (Revised edition 1997).

Mearns, D., and Thorne, B. (1988). *Person-centred Counselling in Action.* London: Sage.

Rogers, C.R., (1942). *Counselling and Psychotherapy.* Boston: Houghton and Mifflin Company.

Rogers, C.R., (1951). *Client-Centered Therapy.* London: Constable and Company 1987.

Rogers, C.R., (1956). Client-Centered Therapy: A Current View. In Fromm-Reichmann, F., and Moreno, J., (Eds.), (1956). *Progress in Psychotherapy.* Vol. 1. New York: Grune and Stratton, pp. 199-209.

Rogers, C.R. (1957). The Necessary and Sufficient Conditions of Therapeutic Change. *Journal of Consulting Psychology*, 21, pp. 95-103.

Rogers, C.R. (1959). A Theory of Therapy, Personality, and Interpersonal Relationships, as Developed in the Client-Centered framework in S. Koch (Ed.), *A Theory of Therapy, Personality and Interpersonal Psychotherapy.* New York: McGraw Hill, pp. 184-256.

Acknowledgements

I want first to thank the authors who have contributed chapters to this volume and their willingness to stay with the editorial process of my quest for ever greater elaboration and coherence. I'm sure at times they may have wished I was less tenacious but they rose to my challenges, for which I am very appreciative.

Pete Sanders and Maggie Taylor-Sanders at PCCS Books have been a continual support to me during the creation of this book and I particularly have enjoyed turning to Pete as a sounding board for my ideas and difficult decisions. He was also a wonderful copy editor for several of the chapters.

I appreciate Jo Cohen as Editor of the *Person-Centered Journal* for generously giving permission for the revised versions of Barbara Brodley's *Congruence and its Relation to Communication in Client-Centered Therapy, The Multifaceted Nature of Congruence in the Therapeutic Relationship* by myself and Ivan Ellingham's *Carl Rogers' 'Congruence' as an Organismic; not a Freudian Concept* to be included in this volume. Thanks also go to David Brazier, editor of *Beyond Carl Rogers* published by Constable 1993, and the publishers, Constable and Robinson Publishing Ltd., for giving their permission to Germain Lietaer to revise his chapter *Authenticity, Congruence and Transparency.*

I want to thank my colleagues and friends in the international person-centred community (Sheila Haugh, Janet Tolan, Maureen O'Hara, Peter Schmid, Allan Turner and Jerold Bozarth) for their friendship, for their support, for their challenge — I've laughed and cried and learnt. Thanks to Barbara Brodley and others too many to mention from the CCT/PCA e-mail network for providing stimulating discussion and often supplying information for which I was searching.

Becoming more whole and congruent, and becoming the author of my life has been, and will continue to be, a lifetime goal of mine. I want to thank the teachers, facilitators and healers who have been the most instrumental in helping me to find my path — Anne Hawkins, Colin Lago, Phil Lapworth and Charlotte Sills. I have loved them all and have felt their love for me. Thanks go particularly to Anne, Colin, Lizzie and Sarah for being there for me so often.

1   A Historical Review of the Development of the Concept of Congruence in Person-Centred Theory

Sheila Haugh

As one of the conditions hypothesised by Rogers (1957, 1959) as being necessary and sufficient for the therapeutic process, and being a definition of psychological health, the concept of congruence is one of the cornerstones of person-centred counselling/psychotherapy. This paper reviews the development of the concept in Rogers' work and the contributions made by other person-centred[1] theorists. Of course, the notion of congruence did not just appear as a completely new concept to Rogers — it had a history and influences from other theorists. In particular, Otto Rank, Jessie Taft and Frederick Allen, all played their part in influencing Rogers' developing theories. For those interested, Nat Raskin (1948) looks at the work of Rank, Taft and Allen (and indeed Freud), and Tony Merry (1998) examines how their work specifically influenced Rogers. In addition, worthy of mention is the work of Karen Horney (1937, 1939) whom Rogers acknowledged as one of the influences on his theories (1942, p. 28).

I begin by reviewing the development of the concept of congruence in Rogers' work including the formulation of the fully functioning person as it relates to congruence. I offer an overview of Rogers' conceptualisation of the concept and the times in the therapeutic interview when he seems to suggest a congruent response may be appropriate. I then consider the developments and refinements suggested by Gendlin and Wexler, following on to consider the work of Mearns and Thorne, Brazier, Lietaer, Tudor and Worrall, Natiello, Barrett-Lennard, Haugh and Bozarth. Finally, I offer some concluding comments on what I see to be the current state of play concerning the concept of congruence and how may it be communicated. It is perhaps worth stating that I have not considered the development of the concept of incongruence in its own right, as I consider that, most often, incongruence can be defined as the opposite of congruence.

THE DEVELOPMENT OF THE CONCEPT OF CONGRUENCE IN ROGERS' WORK

When writing of 'relationship therapy' in 1939, Rogers set out four qualifications necessary for the therapist. They should have: objectivity, respect for the

---

1. The term 'person-centred' is used in its broadest sense, therefore including experiential and process-orientated therapy.

individual, psychological knowledge and an understanding of self (p. 283). Understanding of self included an understanding 'of his [sic] outstanding emotional patterns, and of his own limitations and shortcomings ... the therapist must have some insight into his own personality' (ibid.). This particular qualification was intended to enable the therapist to 'thoroughly…understand and be objective in regard to the [client's] problems' (ibid.) and shows Rogers' early preoccupation with a therapist having knowledge of themselves. By 1942, in *Counselling and Psychotherapy*, he had added four more qualifying characteristics, describing them as 'Basic Aspects of a Therapeutic Relationship' (p. 87). These were, firstly, 'warmth and responsiveness on the part of the counsellor', which expressed itself 'in a genuine interest in the client and an acceptance of him as a person'. The second was 'permissiveness in regard to the therapeutic interview', which meant that anything the client wished to say or feel should be fully accepted by the therapist. Thirdly, Rogers said that there should be limits to the therapeutic interview, by which he meant the relationship should be a clearly defined relationship, for example with a time limit to the therapeutic hour. The last aspect of a therapeutic relationship was 'freedom from coercion', meaning the 'counsellor refrains from intruding his [sic] own wishes, his own reactions or biases, into the therapeutic situations' (pp. 87–90). The overall requirement was that there needed to be a genuinely open acceptance of the client. In 1939, the therapist is non-directive, almost an observer. By 1942, although still non-directive, there is a movement toward a relationship with the client, one characterised by warmth and responsiveness. More especially, Rogers was developing a conceptualisation of the being of the therapist. A part of this conceptualisation was genuineness, which later became known as congruence.

Rogers developed the theme of the genuineness in the therapist when, in *Client-Centered Therapy* (1951), he wrote of the need for the attitudes of the therapist to be genuinely held. He suggested that if the therapist was unable to genuinely hold notions such as the freedom of the client to choose their own direction, be that 'regression rather than growth', 'neuroticism rather than mental health', then 'it seems doubtful that therapy will be a profound experience for the client' (p. 48). This book also saw Rogers describing psychological adjustment in terms that were very clearly antecedents of his later, more precise, descriptions of the concept of congruence. Contained in the 'Nineteen Propositions' (pp. 483–524), psychological adjustment was when 'the concept of the self is at least roughly congruent with all the experiences of the organism' (p. 513). Further, 'that all the sensory and visceral experiences are admissible to awareness through accurate symbolization, and organizable into one system which is internally consistent and which is, or is related to, the structure of self' (pp. 513–4). Rogers also made the point that '[I]t is the fact that all experiences, impulses, sensations are *available* that is important, and not necessarily the fact that they are present in consciousness' (p. 151).

In 1956, continuing the theme of the authenticity and genuineness of the therapist's experience toward the client, Rogers first employed the term 'congruence' itself in relation to the therapist, using it interchangeably with 'wholeness' and 'genuineness'.

It appears essential that the therapist be genuine, or whole, or congruent in the relationship. What this means is that it is important for the therapist to be what he (sic) is in his contact with the client. To the extent that he presents an outward façade of one attitude or feeling, while inwardly or at an unconscious level he experiences another feeling, the likelihood of successful therapy will be diminished (1956, pp. 199–200).

From this general description of the concept, the following three years saw a refinement and greater exposition of the notion of congruence. In 1957 Rogers published *The Necessary and Sufficient Conditions of Therapeutic Personality Change*. This was followed in 1959 by *A Theory of Therapy, Personality and Interpersonal Relationships, As Developed In The Client-Centered Framework*. These two papers detailed Rogers' formulation for therapy in general (1957), and for client-centred therapy in particular (1959). In 1957, congruence, which Rogers also described as being genuine and integrated (p. 97), was defined as meaning 'that within the relationship he [sic] [the therapist] is freely and deeply himself, with his actual experience accurately represented in his awareness of himself' (ibid.). In 1959 congruence was, in part, defined as being 'in this particular moment of this immediate relationship with this specific person he (sic) [the therapist] is completely and fully himself, with his experience of the moment being accurately symbolized and integrated into the picture he holds of himself' (p. 215).

After 1954/56, Rogers continued to hold 'that what the therapist does should be an accurate reflection of his or her thoughts and feelings' (Adomaitis, 1992, p. 19). This was particularly evident from Rogers' writings concerning research with people experiencing schizophrenia (the Wisconsin Study). Rogers (1967) wrote that working with people who had psychotic symptoms had 'deeply reinforced' his view 'that the person who is able *openly* to be himself [sic] at that moment, as he is at the deepest levels he is able to be, is the effective therapist' (p. 186, original emphasis).

This general formulation of congruence was, in its essential character, one Rogers held for the rest of his life. In a much later paper, he stated that genuineness, or congruence, meant,

> ... the therapist is willing to express and to be any persistent feelings that exist in the relationship ... When the therapist is feeling neither empathic or caring, she must discover what the flow of experiencing is and must be willing to express that flow, whether it seems embarrassing, too revealing, or whatever (Rogers and Sanford, 1989, p. 1491).

For Rogers, if the therapist is unaware of their experience, or they do not realise they are not being empathic or caring, then,

> ... my communication contains contradictory messages. My words are giving one message, but I am also in subtle ways communicating [for example] the annoyance I feel and this confuses the other person and makes him [sic] distrustful, though he too may be unaware of what is causing the difficulty (Rogers, 1961, p. 51).

Hence the importance of congruence, defined as being aware of one's experience and expressing it when it is interrupting empathy and caring, lies in the need for clear communication at a verbal and non-verbal level. If there is ambiguous verbal or non-verbal communication from the therapist, the client will become distrustful. A distrustful client will not feel free to explore issues that are threatening, or provoke anxiety. The therapist being aware of his or her own experience is an important aspect of Rogers' hypothesis of congruence. For Rogers, congruence is not simply stating thoughts and ideas that come into the therapist's head. It involves an awareness of a lack of empathy and unconditional positive regard. Whilst Rogers did not deem it necessary to substantially revise the statements concerning congruence that he presented in 1957 and 1959, detailing the notion of the fully functioning person in his work permits his conceptualisation of congruence to become clearer.

The fully functioning person

Rogers' concept of the fully functioning person, 'is synonymous with optimal psychological adjustment, optimal psychological maturity, *complete congruence*, complete openness to experience, complete extensionality' (Rogers, 1959, p. 235, italics added), and, as such, is perhaps his most detailed exposition of the concept of congruence. The fully functioning person exhibits at least ten 'characteristics' (ibid.):

1. He [sic] will be *open to his experience* . . .
2. Hence all *experiences* will *be available to awareness*.
3. All *symbolizations* will be as accurate as the experiential data will permit.
4. His *self-structure* will be congruent with his *experience*.
5. His *self-structure* will be a fluid gestalt, changing flexibly in the process of assimilation of new *experience*.
6. He will experience himself as the *locus of evaluation* . . .
7. He will have no *conditions of worth* . . .
8. He will meet each situation with behavior which is a unique and creative adaptation to the newness of that moment.
9. He will find his *organismic valuing* a trustworthy guide to the most satisfying behavior because . . .
   b. No datum of *experience* will be *distorted* in, or *denied* to, *awareness* . . .
10. He will live with others in the maximum possible harmony, because of the rewarding character of reciprocal positive regard. (pp. 234–5)

Six of the ten characteristics, 1, 2, 3, 4, 8 and 9 respectively, can be described as definitions of congruence. Characteristics 5, 6, 7 and 10 can be summarised as outcomes of congruence. This is of little surprise for, in person-centred theory, the level of congruence defines psychological health (Speierer, 1990, p. 339).

Calvin Hall, Gardner Lindzey and John Campbell (1998, pp. 463–4) draw out three aspects of congruence in Rogers' work related to the fully functioning person.

1. When symbolized experiences of the organism that constitute the self faithfully mirror the experiences of the organism, the person is said to be adjusted, mature, and fully functioning. Such a person accepts the entire range of organismic experience without threat or anxiety.

Rogers defines 'symbolization ' as synonymous with 'awareness' and 'consciousness' (1959, p. 198). His description of symbolisation is somewhat circular. 'When an experience can be symbolized freely, without defensive denial and distortion, then it is available to awareness' (ibid.). However, he clarifies 'awareness' 'as the symbolic representation (not necessarily in verbal symbols) of some portion of our experience' (ibid.). In short, when a person is functioning fully, any internal organismic experience will be fully received in conscious awareness without distortion.

2. Congruence or lack of it between subjective reality (the phenomenal field) and external reality (the world as it is).

An aspect of congruence is 'accurate symbolisation'. This is defined by Rogers to mean 'that the hypothesis implicit in the awareness will be borne out if tested by acting on them' (p. 199). For example, person A feels that person B is suspicious of them. Person A checks this out with person B. Person B, whose organismic experience is available to them without distortion, confirms that they do indeed feel suspicious of person A. Therefore person A was congruent. The symbolisation between his/her subjective reality and external reality (person B's feelings) was accurate.

3. The degree or correspondence between the self and the ideal self.

In describing the change in self through therapy, Rogers states of the client, 'that what he [sic] wished to be has shifted to a point where it is a more achievable goal, and that actually he is himself changed to a degree which brings him much more in accord with his ideal' (1951, p. 142). Therefore, both the self-evaluation and the ideal the client had of themselves has moved to a more harmonious, or more congruent, position.

In summary, the fully functioning person means a 'process of functioning more fully' (Rogers, 1961, p. 191). In functioning more fully, the person increases his/her 'openness to experience', has 'a tendency to live fully in each moment' and develops 'an increasing trust in his [sic] organism' (pp. 187–9). Functioning in this way would mean functioning in total congruence.

A definition of the concept of congruence in Rogers' work

I have highlighted the various aspects of the conceptualisation of congruence throughout Rogers' work, including that of the fully functioning person, and I believe it is possible to present a more concise description of the notion of congruence as hypothesised by Rogers. However, before doing so, it is interesting to consider the development of the concept in Rogers' work as suggested by Ray Adomaitis (1992), who suggests that there is a further aspect of the conceptualisation of congruence intimated in Rogers' work.

   In his review of the development of genuineness[2] in client-centred

---

2. I follow the terminology as used by Adomaitis.

psychotherapy, Adomaitis (1992) identifies two eras in Rogers' thinking, pre-1956 and post 1954–56. In the time leading up to 1956, Adomaitis suggests that 'Rogers believed that the warmth, respect, acceptance, [and] belief in the client's ability to mature, should be real and that the therapist's enactment of beliefs in these should be genuine' (p. 19). An example of this is in a paper written in 1954, *Some Hypotheses Regarding the Facilitation of Personal Growth*, where Rogers (1961) states that genuineness 'means that I need to be aware of my own feelings, in so far as possible, rather than presenting an outward façade of one attitude, while actually holding another attitude at a deeper or unconscious level' (p. 33). From 1956 onwards, Adomaitis (1992) considers that Rogers' continuing conceptualisation of genuineness and congruence was one of integration with the other core conditions of empathy and unconditional regard. Finally, Adomaitis suggests that there is a fourth aspect of congruence that is hinted in Rogers' later work. Adomaitis believes congruence underwent a subtle 'twist' toward a mystical, transpersonal view (p. 43). Although initially believing that no one could ever be fully congruent (Rogers, 1961, p. 61), nearly 20 years later, when describing the notion of presence, Rogers wrote,

> I find that when I am closest to my inner, intuitive self, when I am somehow in touch with the unknown in me, when perhaps I am in a slightly altered state of consciousness, then whatever I do seems to be full of healing. Then, simply my *presence* is releasing and helpful to the other. There is nothing I can do to force this experience, but when I relax and be close to the transcendental core of me, then I may behave in strange and impulsive ways in the relationship, ways which I cannot justify rationally, which have nothing to do with my thought processes. But these strange behaviours turn out to be *right*, in some odd way: it seems that my inner spirit has reached out and touched the inner spirit of the other. Our relationship transcends itself and becomes a part of something larger. Profound growth and healing and energy are present (Rogers, 1980, p. 129).

To Adomaitis, this explanation of presence suggests there can be a deep, spontaneous self, a self whose presence is innately healing. To be in touch with this self intimates a moment of total congruence. As Rogers never made any formal theoretical statement of this fourth facet of congruence, Adomaitis' suggestion can only be speculation.

Drawing together the different elements of Rogers' work, the following is a systemisation of his hypothesis for the concept of congruence and the appropriateness of congruent responses.

The congruent therapist

(a) The therapist will be someone whose internal experience is available to, and accurately symbolised in, their awareness. This means that no part of their inner experience will be denied to awareness, or distorted in awareness.
(b) In addition, and as a consequence, the therapist's experience of the external world will also be accurately symbolised in awareness.
(c) The therapist's self and ideal self will match, thus further ensuring that experience is not distorted or denied.

The practice of the congruent therapist

When it came to the timing of congruent responses in therapy, Rogers described this question as the 'growing edge' of his theory (1959, p. 214). Taking an overview I can find four suggestions offered by Rogers:

(a) When the therapist's feelings are interrupting the core conditions. Rogers writes, 'If you have other feelings, other than empathy, then congruence takes preference over anything else' (Rogers in Hobbs, 1985, cited in Bozarth, 1990, p. 61).

(b) When these feelings are persistent. He says, 'If the therapist finds himself persistently focused on his [sic] own feelings rather than those of the client … or if he finds himself persistently experiencing some other feeling than unconditional positive regard' (Rogers, 1959, p. 214).

(c) When to not do so would result in the therapist not being 'real' in the relationship. For example, Rogers writes, 'It is preferable for the therapist to be real, than to put on a false posture of interest, concern, and liking that the client is likely to perceive as false' (Rogers, 1966, p. 185).

(d) When it is appropriate. Rogers comments that it is important 'To be able to voice it [congruence] if it's appropriate, and to express it in some behavioural way' (Evans, 1975, p. 20). I deduce that when it is 'appropriate' will be assessed on points (a), (b) and (c).

Other theorists have seen Rogers' work on congruence in a different light and/or have attempted a development of his conceptualisations and it is to their work I now turn.

DEVELOPMENTS TO ROGERS' CONCEPTUALISATION OF THE NOTION OF CONGRUENCE

Eugine Gendlin and David Wexler

To many person-centred theorists of the classical mode, Rogers' formulation of the notion of congruence was, and still is, an adequate conceptualisation (for example, Bozarth, 1998). However, for some there were inherent difficulties in Rogers' theory of congruence. One such person was Eugene Gendlin (1962) who felt that Rogers' notion of congruence was problematic insofar as 'the constructs of "experience" and "congruence" [are] not observable' (p. 258). A second person was David Wexler, who by 1974 was lamenting that '[C]ongruence has come to be seen as the equivalent of therapist self-expression' and further, the notion was increasingly regarded as 'something that is primary and an end in itself' (p. 112). Although there had been attempts to systemise the use of congruence in the therapeutic setting (Carkhuff, 1962, cited in Patterson, 1985, pp. 65–7; Kiesler, 1967, pp. 581–2) there were problems. Both scales relied on the outward, behavioural manifestation of congruence. Could congruence, as described by Rogers, really be assessed by outside observation?

For many the answer was no, and Gendlin attempted to clarify the notion of congruence by positing it much more explicitly than Rogers within the context of experiencing. Gendlin described experiencing as referring 'to something directly observable by the individual and observable by others indirectly in his [sic] expression of such observation'. He continued, 'it is something present, although it is chiefly *felt* rather than *known*' (1962, p. 242, original emphasis). Gendlin was interested in a process description rather than a content description of the concept of congruence. Using this more explicitly based process model,[3] Gendlin identifies four aspects of congruence that develop from his theory of experiencing. The first feature he considers is that of 'optimal adjustment'. In contrast to what he believes to be the 'Rogerian definition of adjustment . . . defined, not socially or culturally, but in terms of the individual' (p. 254), Gendlin suggests that by the use of the concept of experiencing, 'that felt meaning is aware and *implicitly* containing meaning' (p. 255), optimal adjustment includes a definition of the individual being aware and affected by other individuals in their social system. For Gendlin, the congruent person would be socially inclined and aware of others rather than selfish and self-seeking, a notion Gendlin felt was implicit rather than explicit in Rogers' work (p. 255).

The second feature Gendlin considers is how the concept of experiencing can aid clarity in respect of the congruence and genuineness of the therapist (p. 257). He describes therapist genuineness as 'analogous to experiencing for the client' (p. 259), which requires not just 'counselor statements of conceptualizations of the client, but also the counselor's *experiencing* of the client' (ibid., original emphasis). He states,

> The question of genuineness is simply: does the counsellor have the present experiencing *as well as* the conceptualisations he [sic] expresses, or only the latter? If he has experiencing as well as the conceptualization, then the counselor genuinely experiences the client (p. 258).

Although this statement implies a one-way process, in that the counsellor experiences the client, it is to be remembered that, for Gendlin, experiencing is an interpersonal process. The experiencing of both participants will be affected by the experiencing of each other. The third feature Gendlin believes follows from this model is the important distinction, as mentioned above, between a process model and a contents model of the concept of congruence. Gendlin describes Rogers as taking genuineness to be 'a comparison between the contents of conceptualizations and the contents posited in the construct of "experience"' (ibid.). Gendlin, on the other hand, conceptualises the notion of congruence by taking the genuineness of the therapist to 'refer to the presence or absence of aware, felt experiencing *expressed* by conceptualizations' (ibid., italics added). In this formulation Gendlin is referring to 'The Newtonian concept' which 'views the human individual as constituted of "things" — defined contents' (p. 12). Whether these contents, be they '"needs", "drives", "motives" . . . "self-concepts" . . . or whatever' (p. 106) are 'in' awareness or 'in' the unconscious, the contents are viewed as already defined, fully formed, and unaffected in their nature by

---

3. Prouty (1994) describes the years between the late 1950s and the early 1970s as Gendlin's 'Person-Centered Phase' (p. 15). It was later that Gendlin developed his 'new therapy' (Gendlin, 1970, p. 73), which became known as focusing orientated therapy (see Gendlin, 1981, 1986, 1996).

'coming into' awareness' (p. 12).

Gendlin finally considers the process of therapy and therapist responses. The process of therapy is one whereby the client becomes increasingly aware of the incongruities between experiencing and self-concepts and, in consequence, becomes more congruent (p. 259). In essence, the client becomes more able to connect with, and symbolise, 'the powerful *felt* dimension of experience that is pre-logical' (p. 1). Congruent responses of a person-centred therapist 'give conceptualizations of what . . . the client is *now* experiencing but perhaps not making explicit' (p. 260), and the therapist's effort is to be 'exactly congruent with the client's unformed emotional experience' (p. 259).

By contrast, Wexler (1974) suggested that the condition of congruence be 'subsumed by the task of responding empathically' (p. 111), using the term 'empathic responding' to 'stress the fact that it [empathy] is not merely an attitude but a consistent style of overt behaviours given as responses to a client' (p. 96). He states that he reinterprets Rogers' notion of congruence as 'pointing to the importance of the therapist's devoting all his [sic] attention and processing capacities to the task of understanding the client and responding empathically' (p. 111).

Unlike Gendlin's process model, Wexler offered his *Cognitive Theory of Experiencing, Self-Actualisation, and Therapeutic Process* (1974) as a 'new theoretical framework' (p. 49) and this model conceptualises experiencing as an outcome of cognitive processing. Briefly described, information is received from the external world through the five senses. Information is also received from the internal world via muscle movement and stored information from the long-term memory. This information enters the short-term memory and, in the process, some information is retained and some of the information is lost because there is too much information to be processed. Between the short- and long-term memory there is a 'central processing unit' (Wexler, 1974, p. 61) that operates on, and organises, information into structures. It is this attending to, and organising of, information 'that enables us to make "sense" out of our world' (ibid.). The long-term memory also contains the rules by which the central processing unit will operate. If there are no rules the information will be lost from the short-term memory. It is important to note the difference between 'lost' and 'forgotten'. The information does not go somewhere it can be accessed later; it no longer exists in any form and is truly lost. In this model, affect is produced for three reasons:
- When information elaborated produces disorganisation.
- When a person is unable to organise the information and is therefore overwhelmed.
- When the information is producing change and restructuring in the person's field.

A person's psychological health rests on the complexity, or lack of it, in their cognitive processing functions. '[T]he implication is that growth can be blocked for many people by the way in which they have learned to process some of their own organismic experience' (Rice and Greenberg, 1990, p. 399).

Wexler reframes Rogers' notions of denial and distortion of material to awareness to be the outcomes of inadequate processing capacities. He describes the phenomena of defence as being,

> . . . the case either where there are no rules present for organising the information and it is lost in short-term memory and not processed further in the system (denial), or the rules available can only organise some of the features of the information contained in short-term store and not others; hence the organisation does not adequately reflect all that can be seen to be contained in the information (distortion) (Wexler, 1974, pp. 62–3).

With this definition of denial and distortion, Wexler posits a theory of congruence based on the processing capabilities of the individual, rather than on their level of awareness of their internal experience. The congruent therapist, having a rich and complex processing ability, will put all these towards responding empathically to a client. In essence, as a surrogate processor, the task of the therapist is to attempt 'to organize and articulate the *meaning* of the information the client is processing' (p. 97). The optimal empathic response is described as being *'a structure or group of structures that more fully captures, and better organizes, the meaning of the information in the field that the client is processing than had the structure(s) the client had generated himself* [sic]' (ibid., original emphasis) If the therapist is able to capture and organise the meaning of the client's information, 'insofar as his [sic] [the therapist] expression fits the information in process in him [the therapist] he will also be what Rogers calls congruent' (p. 111).

More recent developments

Although Rogers (1966) had described congruence as the 'most basic of the three conditions' (p. 184), Dave Mearns and Brian Thorne, writing in 1988, commented that it was a concept 'largely ignored in the literature' (p. 87) and it is difficult to find published papers dealing with the concept of congruence. The major texts over the years (Hart and Tomlinson, 1970; Wexler and Rice, 1974; Levant and Shlien, 1984) do not include specific chapters on congruence, and it is not until the late eighties and the nineties that much more attention is given to the concept (Lietaer et al., 1990; Hutterer et al., 1996). Indeed, six of the 12 papers considered below were published or presented in 1998 and 1999 alone!

Mearns and Thorne (1988a) were the first to attempt some redress at the lack of exploration and development in the notion of congruence seeing authenticity as synonymous with congruence and realness (1998a, p. 76). They defined congruence as a 'state of being' (p. 75), where the manner in which the counsellor 'is behaving is perfectly reflective of what she [sic] is feeling inside — where her response to her client is what she feels and is not a pretence or a defence' (p. 75). An important corollary is that the counsellor will have also 'learnt how to describe her [sic] feelings accurately' (p. 80). They suggest that 'congruence does not imply that the counsellor is open about herself [sic] and her life' (p. 81); rather congruence is the 'genuinely felt response to the client's experience at that time' (ibid.). In short, their conceptualisation of the concept of congruence is that the therapist is able to experience their 'underlying feelings' (1988b, p. 85), have awareness of those feelings and is able to express those feelings. In contrast they identify two types of therapist incongruence. One is where the 'counsellor has underlying feelings in response to the client but is *unaware* of these and hence does not give expression to them' (p. 94). The second is 'where the counsellor is aware of her feelings but *chooses* not to give expression to these' (p. 95).

As to when to be explicitly congruent with a client, they offered three guidelines for judging the appropriateness of congruent responses:
- That congruence refers to 'the counsellor's *response* to the client's experience'.
- That the response 'must be one which is relevant to the immediate concern of the client'.
- That 'the feelings which the counsellor responds to tend to be those which are *persistent* or particularly *striking*' (1988a, pp. 81–2, original emphasis).

In 1994, Mearns widened the concept of congruence, arguing that the core attitudes of empathy and unconditional positive regard must also be genuine — 'wholly congruent' (p. 41). These attitudes 'cannot be "portrayed" towards a client with any degree of effectiveness: clients are not so easily fooled by incongruent portrayal' (p. xi).

Writing in 1993, David Brazier suggested, as far as genuineness and congruence were concerned, 'what matters is that we not deliberately try to conceal' (p. 4), and he distinguished between 'explicit congruence' and 'implicit congruence' (p. 3). As the terms imply, explicit congruence is congruence that is communicated, whilst implicit congruence, or awareness, is not explicitly communicated. For Brazier, inner congruence is deeply connected with secrets, secrets being those parts of us that are 'the things laid up in our hearts' (p. 6). Therapist congruence is 'the therapist's capacity to be true to her [sic] own secret nature' (p. 5). He clarifies this statement by adding that he does not advocate that the therapist should have no secrets, rather it 'is about being true to one's secrets' (p. 6). In this manner, Brazier describes inner congruence as the 'therapist's capacity to be true to her [sic] own secret nature', believing that this 'enables the client to rediscover and cherish his [sic] own mystery again' (ibid.)

Brazier approached the question of appropriateness of outer congruence — the communication of congruence — by making clear that congruence 'does not stand alone' from the other core conditions. He continues that congruence could be shared, '[W]hen all the other core conditions are in place' (p. 10). Here, Brazier seems to be positing a more active expression of congruence than perhaps Rogers. Brazier implies that any response from the therapist will be therapeutic if the other core conditions are present. He also adds that outer congruence may be appropriate, 'when the therapist being explicit about his or her inner feelings will restore the other conditions if they have lapsed' (ibid.). He clarifies that 'congruence is not a matter of saying things at particular times, but is, as Rogers says, a way of being with the client' (p. 11).

In his paper, *Authenticity, Congruence and Transparency*,[4] also published in 1993, Germain Lietaer divided genuineness, or 'authenticity' into two aspects, the inner, which he called congruence, and the outer, which he called transparency. For Lietaer — echoing Gendlin — congruence is 'the degree to which the therapist has conscious access to, or is receptive to, *all* aspects of his

---

4. A revised version of this paper in included in this volume, Chapter 3.

own flow of experiencing' (p. 18) and he details a number of facets of congruence. Firstly, there is the 'personal presence' of the therapist — the therapist's way of being with a client is without 'artificiality and haziness' (p. 19). Secondly, he posits that therapist interventions should be a genuine reflection of their philosophy, a genuine reflection of who they are as a person (p. 20). Thirdly, Lietaer argues that congruence is the 'upper "limit" of the capacity for empathy' (p. 23, quoting from Barrett-Lennard). Lastly, there is the pragmatic facet of congruence. A congruent response 'guarantees a personal flavour to the communication of empathy' (p. 25) thereby ensuring the empathic responses are not experienced as techniques being used by the therapist on the client.

Lietaer locates his exploration of transparency, 'the explicit communication by the therapist of his [sic] conscious perception, attitudes and feelings' (ibid.), within the assertion that between '1955 and 1962 . . . [C]lient-centered therapy evolved from "non-directive" to "experiential"' (p. 32). Thus, he writes of 'interventions where the therapist starts from his [sic] own frame of reference' (ibid.). In communicating congruence, the therapist needs to ask two questions. 'Does our self-revelation serve the client's growth process?' and 'can our client use and integrate this information?' (p. 38). He adds that the therapist can reveal 'his [sic] feelings towards the client in the here-and-now, towards what happens in the session between both of them' (p. 39). He cautions, however, that the therapist should remain sober. 'Only persistent feelings count, and besides, the therapist has to ask himself if the moment is appropriate' (ibid.). Through congruence and transparency the therapist will be, and be experienced as, authentic.

The following year, Keith Tudor and Mike Worrall described their paper, *Congruence Reconsidered* (1994), as extending the schematic interpretations of Brazier and Lietaer (p. 198). They identified four requirements of congruence; self-awareness, self-awareness in action, communication and lastly, appropriateness (ibid.). Self-awareness is described as an awareness 'of the flow of feelings and sensations within us as we work' (ibid.). This requires the ability 'to be and live these feelings and experiencing' (ibid.), which is self-awareness in action. Self-awareness in action also includes the ability to 'think clearly' (p. 199). They see this as necessary because the therapist 'also needs to account for a range of awareness' (ibid.). This implies that the therapist needs their thinking in order to help them discriminate between appropriate and inappropriate congruent responses (communication), for example between self-involving responses and self-disclosing responses.[5] Self-involving responses are 'the appropriate communication of self-awareness', whereas self-disclosing responses are 'the sharing . . . of some part of my recent or distant history' (p. 200). With different aspects of communication possible, it is the thinking of the therapist that enables them to discern the appropriate response. Tudor and Worrall add that the appropriate response of congruence needs to focus 'more on communicating our experiencing than on disclosing our experience' (p. 201).

The same year, Peggy Natiello (1997) developed the theme of authenticity in her paper *Therapist Authenticity and Connectedness: Key to Healing*. She believes

---

5. Tudor and Worrall use the distinction made by Mearns and Thorne (1988a).

that therapist authenticity 'is the context that gives the relationship integrity and builds a foundation of trust' (p. 7). For Natiello, as with Lietaer, this includes the notion that the attitudes the therapist holds should be genuine. Additionally, 'the content of the therapeutic interactions is almost always focused on client experience' (p. 2). Focussing on the notion of authenticity rather than Rogers' conceptualisation of congruence she defined the 'authentic, connected, therapeutic relationship' as being 'characterised by openness, respect, autonomy, empathic understanding and cooperation' (p. 2). For Natiello, such a relationship 'brings about profound healing in therapy' (p. 11).

The following year, in his book *Carl Rogers' Helping System, Journey and Substance*, Godfrey Barrett-Lennard (1998) described congruence as the 'consistency between the three levels of (a) a person's primary experience, (b) their symbolized awareness, and (c) their outward behaviour and communication' (p. 82). He makes the point that the matching of the first two levels is the 'determining condition for congruence between awareness and communication' (ibid.), later adding that 'no expression that is unauthentic or incongruent can be substantially therapeutic' (p.102).

In the same year, building on the work of Rogers, Gendlin (1962), Wexler (1974) and the concept of the 'active intentional person' (Zimring, 1997, p. 4), I (Haugh, 1998a) suggested a definition of the concept of congruence and guidelines for the use of congruent responses. This proposal was based on the subtle but important distinction between experience and experiencing, experiencing being the 'ongoing psychophysical flow' (Rogers, 1980, p. 141). The definition of congruence proposed was;

> (a) The therapist will be someone whose internal experiencing can be symbolised.
> (b) In addition to, and as a consequence, experiencing of the external world can also be symbolised.
> (c) The therapist's experiencing will match their self-concept and their ideal self (Haugh, 1988a, p.100).

The proposal for the use of congruent responses was based on the conceptualisation of the therapist acting with volition toward the client rather than reacting to the client. This demands that the therapist be clear in their intentions with respect to what they are trying to do in the therapeutic encounter. The proposals were;

> (a) In the service of the core conditions of empathy and unconditional positive regard.
> (b) When the therapist's feelings are persistently interrupting the core conditions of empathy and unconditional positive regard.
> (c) When it is appropriate. When it is appropriate will be assessed through consideration of points (a) and (b) (ibid.).

In summary, the difference from Rogers' work was to describe the notion of congruence in terms that were explicitly process based, a notion that was more implicit in Rogers' work. The proposals for the use of congruent responses suggested that the intention of the person-centred therapist be focused solely on the activity of feeling and communicating empathy and unconditional positive regard.

Also in 1998, Jerold Bozarth posited the idea that there is a 'genuineness-empathy loop wherein the two concepts are ultimately one' (p. 80). He argues that congruence must be the most fundamental of the conditions 'because it enables the therapist to hold unconditionality for the client more completely' (p. 82). In this way Bozarth, more explicitly than previous writers, brings together the three conditions of empathy, congruence and unconditional positive regard as 'functionally one condition' (p. 80).

In summary, in explicating Rogers' concept of congruence, both in theory and practice, all writers are in general agreement that congruence demands that the other conditions of empathy and unconditional positive regard should be genuine rather than, to use Mearns' term, a mere portrayal, with Bozarth positing that they are in fact one condition. Gendlin and Lietaer see congruence as the degree of a person's ability for experiencing, an idea echoed by Mearns and Thorne, Tudor and Worrall, Barrett-Lennard and Haugh. On the other hand, Wexler sees congruence as being an outcome of a person's cognitive processing capabilities. All seven writers link an ability to be aware of experiencing/processing to an ability to be able to express this awareness. Lietaer and Natiello postulate that authenticity is a vital aspect of genuineness and, Natiello and Barrett-Lennard in particular, that authenticity is a key concept in successful therapy.

Gendlin describes congruent responses as therapist conceptualisations of the client's experiencing, Wexler, as the ability of the therapist to be able to express the information in process in him or her. Likewise, Mearns and Thorne describe congruent responses as, in essence, coming from the client's frame of reference, except where the feelings of the therapist are persistent or striking, a position Natiello (1997, p. 3) and Haugh would support. Whilst Tudor and Worrall clarify the importance of the differentiation between self-disclosing and self-involving responses, Brazier and Lietaer propose a more active form of congruent responses than the other writers. Lietaer, in particular, suggests that the therapist may start from his or her own frame of reference when it is appropriate.

There are three further papers that deserve consideration. As these papers are reprinted in this current volume, either in their original form or as revised papers, I will only summarise their main points. Barbara Brodley's 1998 paper, *Congruence and its Relation to Communication in Client-Centered Therapy*, examines, in some depth, concepts that are integral aspects of the notion of congruence. Specifically, she explores and re-emphasises Rogers' conceptualisation of congruence and how this conceptualisation relates to the communication of congruence. In *The Multifaceted Nature of Congruence within the Therapeutic Relationship*, Gill Wyatt (1998) also considers what congruence might be and how it may be communicated, seeing, as the title of her paper suggests, the nature of congruence as being multifaceted. She explores these facets, including the 'whole beyond the facets' and explicates the interesting idea that the notion of congruence includes a process whereby the therapist extends their belief in the actualising tendency to themselves. Finally, Ellingham (1999) considers what he describes as the 'critical flaw in person-centred theory', based as it is on a 'Cartesian-Newtonian' worldview. He suggests that 'congruence . . .

need(s) to be defined in exclusively organismic/process terms'. This is a particularly interesting idea, which opens the exploration of the notion of congruence into wider terrain than has previously been considered.

SOME CONCLUDING COMMENTS

Having reviewed the development of the concept of congruence in Rogers' work, I suggested an overview of his work both in terms of what congruence was and when it may be communicated. I then reviewed the work by other theorists and described how their work agreed and disagreed, particularly around the question of when to communicate congruence. In taking an overview of the development of the concept of congruence, one is struck by the apparent level of agreement between theorists concerning the nature of congruence and, at the same time, the level of implicit disagreement concerning the communication of congruence. Theoretically, the concept of congruence is clearly seen to be connected to the degree to which a person can be in touch with their organismic experiences, be that defined as experiencing or information processing capabilities. Further, that the individual be able to symbolise these experiences. The disagreements of when a congruent response is appropriate, for example from the therapist's own frame of reference or only when feelings are interrupting the conditions of empathy and unconditional positive regard, confusingly, also rests upon the apparent agreement of how congruence can be defined. How can this be? Perhaps one answer is the lack of cross fertilisation between the various groups that are under the umbrella of the Person-Centred Approach.

Lietaer (1990) identifies four such groups that developed around particular people. Rogers, based at the Center for the Studies of the Person, who continued to elaborate upon his basic philosophy; Gendlin and his colleagues, who were 'attempting to ground his [Gendlin's] work in the European existential philosophy' (p. 21); Charles Truax and Robert Carkhuff, who took on 'an eclectic model of the helping relationship' (ibid.) and David Wexler and Laura Rice, who chose 'the cognitive learning psychology as a theoretical framework' (ibid). Lietaer comments, '[T]hese four subgroups seemed to go their own way and lost touch with each other's work' (ibid.). In the period since the late fifties, there has been little mutual development of ideas between these four groups within person-centred theory. In consequence, a full understanding of theoretical concepts within each 'group', including conceptualisations of congruence, is not present. This, in turn, leads to lack of clarity between theory and practice; the conceptualisations of congruence, both in theory and in practice, can suffer from that lack of clarity. Perhaps it is time for there to be more communication between these various groups as this may be useful in the development of the concept of congruence.

REFERENCES

Adomaitis, R. (1992). *On Being Genuine: A Phenomenologically Grounded Study of the Experience of Genuineness and its Place in Client-Centered Psychotherapy.* Unpublished PhD. Dissertation, Northwestern University, USA.

Barrett-Lennard, G.T. (1998). *Carl Rogers' Helping System, Journey and Substance.* London: Sage Publications.

Bozarth, J. (1990). 'The Essence of Client-Centered Therapy'. In Lietaer, G., Rombauts, J. and Van Balen, R., (Eds.), (1990) *Client-Centered and Experiential Psychotherapy in the Nineties.* Belgium: Leuven University Press, pp. 59–64.

Bozarth, J. (1998). *Person-Centered Therapy: A Revolutionary Paradigm.* Ross-on-Wye: PCCS Books.

Brazier, D. (1993). *Congruence.* Occasional paper from Eigenwelt Interskill.

Brodley, T. B. (1998). Congruence and its Relation to Communication in Client-Centered Therapy. *The Person-Centered Journal.* 5(2), 83–106.

Ellingham, I. (1999). Carl Rogers' 'Congruence' as an Organismic Not a Freudian Concept. *The Person-Centered Journal.* 6(2), 121–40.

Evans, R.I. (1975). *Carl Rogers. The Man and his Ideas.* New York: E.P.Dutton and Co.

Gendlin, E.T. (1962). *Experiencing and the Creation of Meaning.* Illinois: Northwestern University Press, 1997.

Gendlin, E.T. (1970). Existentialism and Experiential Psychotherapy. In Hart, J.T. and Tomlinson, T.M. (Eds.), (1970) *New Directions in Client-Centered Therapy.* Boston: Houghton Mifflin, pp. 70–94.

Gendlin, E.T. (1981). *Focusing.* Second Edition. New York: Bantam Books, 1988.

Gendlin, E.T. (1986). *Let Your Body Interpret Your Dreams.* Illinois: Chiron Publications.

Gendlin, E.T. (1996). *Focusing Orientated Psychotherapy.* New York: Guilford Press.

Hall, S., Lindzey, G. and Campbell, J.B. (1998). *Theories of Personality: Fourth Edition.* New York: John Wiley and Sons.

Hart, J.T., and Tomlinson. T.M. (Eds.), (1970). *New Directions in Client-Centered Therapy.* Boston: Houghton Mifflin Company.

Haugh, S. (1998). *An Exploration of the Concept of Congruence in Person-Centred Theory.* Unpublished Masters Dissertation, Regent's College. London.

Horney, K. (1937). *The Neurotic Personality of Our Time.* London and New York: W.W.Norton (1964).

Horney, K. (1939). *New Ways in Psychoanalysis.* London and New York: W.W.Norton (1966).

Hutterer, R., Pawlowsky, G., and Stipsits, R. (Eds.), (1996). *Client-Centered and Experiential Psychotherapy.* Frankfurt: Peter Lang.

Kiesler, D.J. (1967). Appendix B.3. A Scale for the Rating of Congruence. In Rogers, C.R., Gendlin, E.T., Kiesler, D.J., and Truax, C.B. (1967) *The Therapeutic Relationship and Its Impact. A Study of Psychotherapy with Schizophrenics.* Madison: University of Wisconsin Press, pp. 581–4.

Kirschenbaum, H. (1979). *On Becoming Carl Rogers.* New York: Delacorte Press.

Levant, R.F., and Shlien, J.M. (Eds.) (1984). *Client Centered Therapy and the Person Centered Approach.* New York: Praeger Publishers.

Lietaer, G. (1990). The Client-Centered Approach After the Wisconsin Project: A Personal View On Its Evolution. In Lietaer, G., Rombauts, J. and Van Balen, R. (Eds.), (1990) *Client-Centered and Experiential Psychotherapy in The Nineties.* Belgium: Leuven University Press, pp. 19–45.

Lietaer,G. (1993). Authenticity, Congruence and Transparency. In Brazier, D. (ed.), (1993) *Beyond Carl Rogers.* London: Constable and Company, pp. 17–46.

Lietaer, G., Rombauts, J. and Van Balen, R. (Eds.), (1990). *Client-Centered and Experiential Psychotherapy in the Nineties.* Belgium: Leuven University Press.

Mearns, D. (1994). *Developing Person-Centred Counselling.* London: Sage Publications.

Mearns, D., and Thorne, B. (1988a). *Person-Centred Counselling in Action.* London: Sage Publication.

Mearns, D., and Thorne, B. (1988b). *Person-Centred Counselling in Action.* London: Sage Publication. Second Edition (1999).

Merry, T. (1998). Client-Centred Therapy: Origins and Influences. *Person-Centred Practice.* 6(2). Reprinted in Merry, T., (Ed.), (2000) *The BAPCA Reader.* Ross-on-Wye: PCCS Books, pp. 17–24.

Natiello, P. (1997). *Therapist Authenticity and Connectedness: Key to Healing.* Paper presented at the Conference 'Ten Years On'. Organised by the Institute for Person-Centred Learning,

Sheffield, September 1997.

Patterson, C.H. (1985). *The Therapeutic Relationship.* Monterey, CA: Brooks/Cole.

Prouty, G. (1994). Theoretical Evolutions in Person-Centered/Experiencial Therapy. Applications to Schizophrenic and Retarded Psychoses. Westport CT: Praeger.

Raskin, N.J. (1948). The Development of Nondirective Therapy. *Journal of Consulting Psychology.* 12, 92–110.

Rice, L.N., and Greenberg, L.S. (1990). Fundamental Dimensions in Experiential Therapy: New Directions in Research. In Lietaer, G., Rombauts, J., and Van Balen, R. (Eds), (1990) *Client-Centered and Experiential Psychotherapy in The Nineties.* Belgium: Leuven University Press, pp. 397–414.

Rogers, C.R. (1939). *The Clinical Treatment of the Problem Child.* Boston: Houghton and Mifflin.

Rogers, C.R. (1942). *Counselling and Psychotherapy.* Boston: Houghton and Mifflin Company.

Rogers, C.R. (1951). *Client-Centered Therapy.* London: Constable and Company (1987).

Rogers, C.R. (1956). 'Client-Centered Therapy: A Current View'. In Fromm-Reichmann, F., and Moreno, J., (Eds.), (1956) *Progress in Psychotherapy.* Vol. 1. New York: Grune and Stratton, pp. 199–209.

Rogers, C.R. (1957). The Necessary and Sufficient Conditions of Therapeutic Personality Change. *Journal of Consulting Psychology*, 21(2), pp. 95–103. Reprinted in Kirschenbaum, H. and Henderson, V.L., (Eds.), (1990) *The Carl Rogers Reader.* London: Constable and Company, 1996, pp. 219–35.

Rogers, C.R. (1959). A Theory of Therapy, Personality, and Interpersonal Relationships as Developed in the Client-Centred Framework. In Koch, S. (Ed.), (1959) *A Psychology: A Study of a Science.* Vol. 3. New York: McGraw-Hill, pp. 184–256.

Rogers, C.R. (1961). *On Becoming a Person.* London: Constable and Company, (1984).

Rogers, C.R. (1966). Client-Centered Therapy. In Avieti, S. (Ed.), (1966) *American Handbook of Psychiatry, Volume 3.* New York: Basic Books, pp. 183–200.

Rogers, C.R. (1967). Some Learnings from a Study of Psychotherapy with Schizophrenics. In Rogers, C.R, and Stevens, B. (1967) *Person to Person.* Worcester: Billing and Sons Ltd., pp. 181–92.

Rogers, C.R. (1980). *A Way of Being.* Boston: Houghton Mifflin Company.

Rogers, C.R., and Sanford, R.C. (1989). Client-Centered Psychotherapy. In Kaplan, H., and Sadock, B. (Eds.), (1989) *The Comprehensive Textbook of Psychiatry.* V. Baltimore: Williams and Williams, pp. 1482–501.

Speierer, G. (1990). Toward a Specific Illness Concept of Client-Centred Therapy. In Lietaer, G., Rombauts, J. and Van Balen, R. (Eds.), (1990) *Client-Centered and Experiential Psychotherapy in the Nineties.* Belgium: Leuven University Press, pp. 337–59.

Tudor, K., and Worrall, M. (1994). Congruence Reconsidered. *British Journal of Guidance and Counselling.* 22(2) 197–206.

Wexler, D.A. (1974). A Cognitive Theory of Experiencing, Self-Actualization, and Therapeutic Process. In Wexler, D.A. and Rice, L.N. (Eds.), (1974) *Innovations in Client-Centered Therapy.* New York: John Wiley, pp. 49–116.

Wexler, D.A. and Rice, L.N. (Eds.), (1974). *Innovations in Client-Centered Therapy.* New York: John Wiley.

Wyatt, G. (1998). *The Multifaceted Nature of Congruence within the Therapeutic Relationship.* Paper presented to the Person-Centred Forum, Johannesburg, S. Africa. Also in *The Person-Centred Journal* 7(1), 52–68.

Zimring, F. (1997). *Looking at our Internal Life and at Empathy in a New Way.* Paper presented at the 4th International Conference on Client-Centred and Experiential Psychotherapy, Lisbon, Portugal, July 1997.

2   What Counselling Research has Taught us About the Concept of Congruence: Main Discoveries and Unresolved Issues

Soti Grafanaki

INTRODUCTION

This chapter offers a brief review of empirical studies into the concept of congruence. It is important to highlight that assumptions and difficulties in defining congruence have led to research investigations that have omitted to examine thoroughly all aspects of congruence: the experience, awareness and communication (Rogers, 1961, 1967).

Even Rogers in his writings did not always pay equal attention to all three components. For example, in his highly influential 1957 paper on the 'necessary and sufficient conditions', Rogers did not clearly mention the importance for the therapist to communicate their congruence. This may have contributed to an over-emphasis on the experience and awareness of congruence, rather than its communication and expression in therapy. Such emphasis may have discouraged researchers from looking into this concept in its own right, because of the difficulties involved in accessing the experiential world of a person and their level of awareness. Nevertheless, a closer look into Rogers' written work clearly indicates that since 1954, the core aspects of this concept have remained largely consistent: openness to internal experience, accurate representation of this experience in awareness and communication of relevant experience to the other person.

In the literature, the concept of congruence has usually been described and operationalised, as either a personality 'trait', or a 'state'. It has been defined more as a 'way of being' rather than a state of 'experiencing'. This has partially contributed to limited direct observation of internal experience during moments of congruence and incongruence, and lack of accurate methods for evaluating and assessing the match between internal experience and awareness.

It is important to mention that, at a personal level, congruence represents a cognitive and affective process, which interpersonally may be expressed and communicated in a number of different ways according to the idiosyncratic characteristics of the person. Therefore, congruence may remain unnoticed in the contact of the counsellor with the client (Mearns and Thorne, 1988) and not be readily visible in the therapist's interventions (Lietaer, 1984). Most research conducted in this area has offered limited access to the internal processes which are taking place in moments of congruence and the way these processes are portrayed in the interpersonal responses of the person during a therapeutic encounter.

The highly subjective nature of congruence and its possible co-occurrence with other phenomena, such as empathy and acceptance, have created additional difficulties in accurately understanding and studying this concept in its own right, with all its richness and complexity. It has been suggested that 'congruence is the most difficult of the therapeutic conditions to develop' (Mearns, 1994, p. 41; Stuart, 1995, personal communication), and 'its verbal explication and analysis is more difficult than, for example, the analysis of empathy' (Bozarth, 1984, p. 75).

The appropriateness and timing of the congruent response in a therapeutic encounter have not been adequately discussed and investigated in the literature. It seems that more emphasis has been put on the idea that whatever one expresses needs to be real and genuine, rather than operationally define and study the characteristics and processes of the therapeutic or facilitative congruence, versus the anti-therapeutic or non-facilitative congruence. This omission mainly lies in the absence of close observations of the client's experience during moments that the counsellor is exhibiting congruence (Greenberg, 1994).

These difficulties have made the concept of congruence one of the most complex within the person-centred approach of psychotherapy and research. This chapter offers a review of empirical studies into congruence in an effort to expand our understanding of both what research has taught us about this concept; and some of the unresolved issues regarding the experience, expression, and impact of this phenomenon in therapy interaction.

The body of literature presented here has been divided into four parts:

A. *Meta-analytic reviews of studies conducted on the 'necessary and sufficient conditions' (Rogers, 1957) and the role of congruence on therapy outcome.* This part of the chapter deals with the functional role/impact of congruence in counselling, as one of the 'necessary and sufficient conditions'.

B. *Studies of displayed or observed congruence, as an interpersonal phenomenon, communicated through verbal and non-verbal messages.* Examining the behavioural portrayal of congruence and reviews the studies which have been conducted on the interpersonal aspect of congruence and its expression through verbal and non-verbal cues of communication i.e., the aspects of congruence that can be objectively observed in therapy interaction.

C. *Studies that have focused on the experiential/subjective aspects of congruence.* This section reviews studies that have been conducted on the subjective experience of 'being congruent', rather than the impact of congruence on therapy process and outcome.

D. *A qualitative study conducted by the author of this chapter on client and counsellor experience of congruence during helpful and hindering moments of on-going person-centred therapy.* This study focused on the personal, interpersonal and relational aspects of congruence as well as the impact of congruence on therapy process and outcome.

Part A

Investigating the role of congruence in therapy outcome: major meta-analytic reviews on congruence as one of the 'necessary and sufficient' conditions
In the research literature, empathy, unconditional positive regard and congruence

have been considered as therapist interpersonal skills or attitudes that facilitate constructive personality change and most of the research on 'necessary and sufficient' conditions (Rogers, 1957) has focused on these three conditions. The impact of these skills and attitudes on therapeutic outcome has been tested in a series of studies which, according to Patterson (1984), constitute 'a body of research that is among the largest for any topic of similar size in the field of psychology' (p. 431).

It is difficult in the space available here to be able to offer a thorough review of all the existing studies on the 'necessary and sufficient conditions'. It was decided instead to present the information collected about the concept of congruence from major meta-analytic reviews conducted the last few decades on this area of research (e.g., Truax and Carkhuff, 1967; Truax and Mitchell, 1971; Mitchell, Bozarth and Krauft, 1977; Lambert, DeJulio and Stein, 1978; Orlinsky and Howard, 1978, 1986; Parloff, Waskaw and Wolfe, 1978; Lockhart, 1984; Patterson, 1984; Watson, 1984; Beutler, Crago and Arizmendi, 1986; Cramer, 1990).

Until the 1970s there was considerable support for Rogers' (1957) hypothesis regarding the sufficiency and necessity of the facilitative conditions (i.e., empathy, congruence and unconditional positive regard) for constructive personality change. Yet by the late 1970s this evidence was increasingly questioned (Watson, 1984).

In particular, in an early review, Truax and Carkhuff (1967) argued that all three therapist-offered conditions were effective with a wide range of clients, and across a wide range of counsellors, regardless of their training or theoretical orientation. They concluded.

> therapists or counsellors who are accurately empathic, non-possessively warm
> in attitude and genuine are indeed effective. The greater the degree to which
> these elements are present in the therapeutic encounter, the greater is the
> resulting constructive personality change in the patient (p. 100).

Truax and Mitchell (1971) also reached similar conclusions. They reported that an effective therapist is non-phoney, non-defensive and authentic or genuine in his/her therapeutic encounters. They also noted that it is the absence of incongruence and phoniness that contributes to good therapy outcome, rather than an abundance of genuineness. In addition, they emphasised that empathy and warmth could not be facilitative unless they were given by a person who was at least minimally 'real'.

In 1977, Mitchell, Bozarth and Krauft came to some different conclusions. They argued that findings from the research on the 'necessary and sufficient' conditions and their impact on therapy outcome were much more complex than earlier studies and reviews had suggested. They noted that the three conditions had to be re-examined and variables such as therapist orientation, type of client, and type of therapy had to be taken into account. Nevertheless, they pointed out that there was some evidence that congruence was moderately related to outcome, although nothing definitive could be said about its effectiveness in creating positive therapeutic outcomes.

In the following year, Parloff, Waskaw and Wolfe (1978) argued that there was no evidence that high levels of accurate empathy, warmth and genuineness were necessary and sufficient conditions for effective therapy.

The same year, Lambert, DeJulio and Stein (1978) also concluded that the:

Rogerian hypothesis has been only modestly supported and the lack of support is due both to the difficulties encountered in sampling and rating therapy sessions, and to the failure of client-centred theory to specify more precisely the times when specific conditions might be most facilitative (p. 467).

According to these reviewers there was a lack of a consistent relationship between facilitative conditions and therapy outcome. They argued that more sophisticated methodologies were needed.

Orlinsky and Howard (1978) found that two-thirds of the studies they reviewed on therapist genuineness or congruence (20 studies in total), showed a significant positive relationship between genuineness and outcome. However, in contrast to their observation they also added that 'therapist genuineness is at least innocuous, is generally predictive of good outcome, and at most may be a causal element in promoting client improvement. Beyond a reasonable minimum, however, it is probably neither a necessary nor a sufficient condition of therapeutic benefit' (p. 307).

In Orlinsky and Howard's later review (1986) they found that 20 of the 53 studies they reviewed showed the same positive relationship between congruence and outcome. They also commented that this positive relationship was present in studies where the researchers had used client's perceptions to assess counsellor's genuineness.

In 1984, Patterson reviewed a number of earlier reviews on the therapeutic conditions. He commented that the reason for not finding significant positive results between facilitative conditions and therapeutic outcome was mainly because of reviewers' biases, and the way that reviewers had chosen specific studies for review, while they had excluded others. He concluded that 'the evidence for the necessity, if not the sufficiency, of the therapist conditions of accurate empathy, respect, or warmth and therapeutic genuineness is incontrovertible' (p. 437) and far greater than recognised by many reviewers.

Watson (1984), by contrast, argued that none of the earlier studies had adequately tested Rogers' hypotheses. Aspects such as client's perception of counsellor's congruence and client's degree of incongruence, which constitute important points in Rogers' theory, had not all been examined in any one study, and consequently research neither supported nor rejected Rogers' theory about the 'necessary and sufficient' conditions.

Lockhart (1984) also reached the conclusion that Rogers' position had not been adequately tested. He also noted that there was a need for much greater specification concerning the times during therapy when high levels of conditions were particularly helpful and appropriate. He pointed out that research findings indicated that the conditions were unlikely to be stable within sessions or across clients. He concluded that therapeutic conditions 'may be helpful, but perhaps not necessary and sufficient' (p. 121) and their relationship with outcome was much more complex.

Beutler, Crago and Arizmendi (1986) also suggested that
'research needed to turn away from simplistic conceptualisations of the therapeutic relationship, as being dependent solely upon therapist's attitudes (such as congruence, empathy and acceptance), as Rogers' originally proposed, and to investigate the interactive processes of the client and counsellor that facilitate the client's view of the therapist as supportive and helpful' (p. 279).

Cramer (1990) derived similar conclusions and stressed the methodological limitations of previous studies that had tested the impact of therapist's facilitative attitudes on therapy process and outcome by using independent judges and quasi-experimental designs, which do not adequately test Rogers' hypothesis. He concluded that 'the importance of empathy, acceptance and congruence for therapeutic outcome remains unknown' (p. 65).

It appears that most research on the 'necessary and sufficient' conditions (and the role of congruence as one of these conditions) is based on brief segments of analogue therapy interactions and ratings from college students serving as external observers. Due to the methodological shortcomings of these studies, it seems that we are far from providing a definite answer about the impact of congruence and other conditions on therapy outcome.

In conclusion, the controversial comments offered by various reviewers seem to suggest that Rogers' conditions have not been properly investigated. Although, some reviewers seem to recognize them as a necessary element of effective therapy, some appear to doubt their effectiveness, where others doubt that any of the research into this area has been properly designed and carried out. Judging from this lack of agreement among reviewers, it appears that the research on the effectiveness of congruence and the other facilitative conditions is open to several interpretations and suggests a need for further investigation that would allow us to understand the *how* or *why* congruence contributes to therapy outcome.

Part B

Investigating the objective portrayal of congruence in therapy: empirical research on the interpersonal aspects of congruence

A large number of empirical studies have considered congruence as a factor which promotes clarity and understanding in human interaction, whereas incongruence is a phenomenon which confuses communication. Direct evidence of lack of congruence (i.e., presence of incongruence) includes inconsistency between what one says and what one implies by expression, gestures, or voice tone (Barrett-Lennard, 1962). In these studies, congruence has been defined as 'the extent to which, the verbal and non-verbal communications of an individual present non-contradictory information' (Haase and Tepper, 1972, p. 423). Most of these studies focus on the behavioural manifestations of the concept of congruence and examine it along with other counselling phenomena, such as empathy, self-disclosure, etc.

The main findings of these studies, and the knowledge generated about the concept of congruence as an interpersonal communication phenomenon, are presented in the following paragraphs. For reasons of brevity, only the actual findings of these studies are summarised here. (For details of method, samples etc., see original studies or Grafanaki, 1997.)

Shapiro, Foster and Powell (1968) found out that congruence could be communicated through the counsellor's non-verbal behaviour and judgements about therapist's genuineness could be reliably made even from still photographs of the therapist's whole person, or of facial expressions alone. Their findings were based on judgements by both experienced and inexperienced raters of photographs of counsellors.

Haase and Tepper (1972) in an analogue, experimental study investigated the relative contributions of verbal and non-verbal cues to the judged level of empathy. This study examined various combinations of counsellor non-verbal behaviours during simulated therapy interactions, which were subsequently rated by external observers. The findings suggested that congruence was an essential underpinning of the communication of empathy, and that inconsistencies between verbal and non-verbal messages undermined even highly empathic messages. The findings of the study supported the definition of congruence which posits that there is 'congruence when verbal and non-verbal cues of communication present non-contradictory information' (p. 424).

Fischer and Apostal (1975) focused on paralinguistic aspects of communication and in an analogue study examined the impact of certain vocal, paralinguistic cues (i.e., 'uh', 'um', 'uh-um' and silent pauses, false starts, response latencies, etc.) on the perception of counsellor genuineness, anxiety and self-disclosure. In this study, counsellor genuineness was considered as a personality characteristic. External observers rated the counsellor's level of genuineness during audio recordings of simulated counselling sessions, using the Truax and Carkhuff (1967) scale. This study failed to produce any statistically significant evidence about the impact of specific paralinguistic cues on the perception of counsellor genuineness.

Graves and Robinson (1976) carried out an analogue study which tested the hypotheses that non-verbal cues play an important role in judgements about congruence, and that inconsistency between non-verbal cues and verbal content would exert a strong influence on such judgements. These hypotheses were confirmed by their findings, which suggested that judged counsellor congruence was significantly less when verbal and non-verbal cues were inconsistent. Moreover, inconsistent counsellor messages were associated with greater interpersonal distance, and with lower ratings of counsellor genuineness, especially when the non-verbal messages were negative and the verbal messages were positive. In addition, when verbal and non-verbal channels conveyed identical messages, the intensity and credibility of the verbal message was enhanced; and on the contrary, when these channels conveyed different information, the intensity and credibility of the verbal message was somewhat weakened. Graves and Robinson (1976) also pinpointed that 'counsellors were frequently capable of manipulating their own non-verbal behaviours in order to induce "desirable" changes in the behaviour of their clients' (p. 333).

The relationship between verbal and non-verbal aspects of the communication process in counselling has also been investigated by Tepper and Haase (1978), with regard to therapist empathy, respect and genuineness. In this study, external judges rated videotaped simulated therapeutic interactions using the Carkhuff scales. The findings suggested that non-verbal cues of communication accounted for twice as much of the variance than verbal cues in judged empathy (2:1), five times as much of the variance in judged respect (5:1), and twenty-three times as much of the variance in judged genuineness (23:1). In the case of genuineness this ratio (23:1) reflected the overwhelming importance of the non-verbal cues for communicating the condition of genuineness. In addition, the counsellor's facial expression was found to be the most influential factor in the communication of all facilitative conditions. Paralinguistic cues, such as vocal intonation, also proved to be significant contributors to the final judgement of facilitative conditions. These results suggest that non-verbal and paralinguistic cues of communication play a dominant role in determining the facilitativeness of a message.

In the study by Tipton and Rymer (1978), congruence was considered as a dimension of counsellor effectiveness along with competence and self-confidence. Ratings of counsellor genuineness, competence and self-confidence were obtained by external observers during brief simulated counselling interactions. The findings of the study suggested that the ratings of genuineness were directly related to amount of eye contact. In addition, the counsellor was judged as more *congruent*, the more they focused on the client's feelings and thoughts, rather than on the client's problems.

In an effort to further investigate the impact of the counsellor's specific non-verbal behaviours on client evaluations, Fretz et al., (1979) conducted three studies. In these studies external observers and clients examined whether high levels of eye contact, direct body orientation, and leaning forward resulted in more favourable ratings of counsellor congruence, empathy and acceptance. The findings suggested that high levels of counsellor eye contact, direct body orientation and forward lean all had an impact on how the counsellor was perceived and described by observers. Regardless of the level of verbal empathy, when the counsellor was exhibiting high levels of these non-verbal behaviours, he was also rated high by external observers on the level of unconditional positive regard and congruence. However, these results could not be replicated when judgements about counsellor facilitativeness were made by clients instead of non-participant observers. These results seem to suggest that there is a profound difference between the impressions of people who *observe* the therapy interaction, and those people who *actually participate in* that interaction, even in cases where the interaction is brief.

Seay and Altekruse (1979) tried to improve previous research by letting counsellors display their non-verbal behaviour naturally and not according to pre-decided experimental conditions. Nevertheless, the counsellors still had to conform to experimental conditions — they were trained to display specific verbal styles (i.e., affective versus behavioural style) and use appropriate verbal responses relevant to the specific style, (i.e., use reflections with the affective style or questions with the behavioural style). Non-verbal behaviours were displayed naturally. In this study, clients shared minor, but real problems for 15 minutes. The main aim of the research was to investigate the counselling process in terms of the effects of counsellor verbal and non-verbal behaviour on client perceptions of counsellor empathy, warmth and genuineness. Counsellor empathy, warmth and genuineness were rated by the clients, whereas counsellor non-verbal behaviour was assessed by trained non-participant observers. The findings of the study, with regard to congruence, indicated that the longer counsellors smiled the higher the clients' rating. In addition, eye contact was predictive of congruence, but not of unconditional positive regard or empathy. Leaning forward was related to congruence and unconditional positive regard. These findings suggested that different counsellor non-verbal behaviours served different purposes during the counselling interview, and verbal and non-verbal behaviours had both separate and interactive effects on the quality of counselling. However, Seay and Altekruse (1979) argued that counsellors' non-verbal behaviours were idiosyncratic in nature, thus, it was probable that non-verbal behaviours did not always communicate what was intended.

Reade and Smouse (1980) suggested that verbal and non-verbal communication could not be studied in isolation from the total communication process and that both verbal and non-verbal channels of communication should be treated as an inseparable unit. However, they failed to let the counselling process unfold naturally. In their study, the counsellor had to practice for six hours how to manipulate his verbal and non-verbal behaviour, in order to correspond to the experimental conditions. In turn, external judges had to rate the level of counsellor effectiveness, as it was portrayed in his verbal and non-verbal behaviour.

The research findings suggested that it was very important for the counsellor to present congruent verbal and non-verbal messages while communicating with a client. Reade and Smouse (1980) also added that when the counsellor is confronting or using responses involving intimate or stressful material, they need to be aware of what is being communicated to the client non-verbally. The findings generally supported the desirability of counsellor congruence.

Sherer and Rogers, R. (1980) tested once more the hypothesis that counsellor non-verbal behaviours have an impact on judgements about counsellor warmth, empathy and genuineness. In their study they employed similar methodology to that of previous research investigations and they came to similar conclusions. In addition, they pointed out that ratings of empathy, warmth and genuineness were highly interrelated, indicating that although the meaning of these concepts could be semantically different, they were quite similar at a non-verbal level.

Hill et al., (1981) examined both counsellor and client non-verbal communication and verbal and non-verbal congruence. The purpose of the study was first to assess and compare counsellor and client perceptions of their own verbal and non-verbal congruence and then to determine if congruence was related to outcome. The study involved real clients and counsellors. However, each counselling dyad only met once and just for 30 minutes. In addition to measures commonly used in earlier research (i.e., BLRI, 1962), Hill et al., (1981) employed one new method, which invited both clients and counsellors to report their affective state during each minute of the recorded counselling interaction, using a 13-category affective adjective list. In this study, congruence was operationalized as the consistency between affective state and one or more of the following aspects of participants' communication: verbal, paralinguistic, kinesic, interpersonal and intrapersonal communication.

The findings suggested that both client and counsellor relied on their perceptions of their own congruence in evaluating outcome. For example, when the counsellor was congruent, she rated herself as more helpful to the client. Moreover, when the counsellor's feelings were accurately communicated to the client, then the client also perceived the counsellor as more helpful. Hill et al., (1981) reported that the methodology employed in this study was particularly helpful and revealing for the participants, and they highly recommended the use of recall methods with single case designs in naturalistic settings in future research conducted in this area.

Despite the suggestions of Hill et al., (1981) more analogue studies were conducted in the 1980s. Tyson and Wall (1983) examined congruence between verbal and non-verbal counsellor behaviour in an analogue study. The counsellor's congruence was again manipulated to fit the experimental conditions, while the client's behaviour remained the same in the different experimental conditions. External judges rated counsellor levels of congruence during brief simulated therapy interactions, which represented the various experimental conditions. The findings of the study suggested that congruent verbal and non-verbal behaviour enhanced the impact of the counsellor's verbal message.

Hermansson, Webster and McFarland (1988), following the same tradition of experimental analogue studies, examined the relationship between counsellor deliberate postural lean and judged levels of congruence and the other facilitative conditions. In this study, counsellor non-verbal behaviour was manipulated during the therapy interaction. There was a light giving signals to the counsellor for how long to stay in this position, and when it was time to change position. It is not surprising that no significant results were reported for congruence, under such strange circumstances.

Finally, Gallagher and Hargie (1992) conducted a quasi-naturalistic study that put emphasis on investigating whether specific counsellor verbal and non-verbal behaviours and skills (such as smiling, leaning forward, touching, listening, reflecting, questioning, etc.) were related to perceived levels of counsellor congruence, empathy and acceptance. Ratings were made by counsellors, clients and non-participant observers. The findings of the study indicated that counsellor ratings of their own congruence were significantly related to counsellor verbal behaviours and skills, such as judgements of reinforcement, open-ended questions, closing and self-disclosure. Client ratings of their counsellor's congruence were significantly correlated with counsellor verbal acknowledgement and questioning. External observers' ratings of counsellor congruence were significantly correlated with counsellor self-disclosure and interruptions. In addition, counsellor perceptions of their own congruence, with regard to specific non-verbal behaviours and skills, were significantly correlated with the use of functional gestures and pauses. Client ratings of counsellor congruence were negatively correlated with head nods. No significant correlation in these areas was reported for the external observer ratings. These findings suggest that perceptions of counsellor attitudes seem to vary according to whether judgements are made by the counsellor, the client or independent judges. Furthermore, Gallagher and Hargie (1992) recommended that:

> . . . future research should attempt to develop methods of assessing counsellor skills, which take the appropriateness and timing of counsellor behaviour into consideration, in addition to examining the contribution of interactive sequence of a number of behaviours (p. 14).

Summary: main findings and unresolved issues

The findings presented in the previous paragraphs support the hypothesis that congruence can be objectively observed and expressed through verbal and non-verbal cues of communication. This research also suggests that non-verbal cues of communication have greater impact than verbal cues in the assessment of congruence, and that failure to take them into consideration may lead to inadequate measurement of congruence. For example, voice tone, body posture, and gestures tend to 'leak' undisclosed information, and people who are attempting to hide their emotional state often portray inconsistent verbal and non-verbal cues (Beutler *et al.*, 1994).

In addition, research findings indicate that non-verbal and verbal communication is complex and can be portrayed in a number of different ways (Bull, 1987). It can also be deliberately manipulated in order to convey a specific message or to conform to specific conditions. The same behaviour could be perceived differently according to the point of view of the person that is assessing the behaviour (i.e., non-participant observer, client, counsellor). Thus, different interpretations may be available for the same kind of behaviour.

The differences across studies suggest that future investigations may need to focus not only on how often congruence or incongruence occurs, but also when it occurs and how it is affected by variations on counsellor's experience, number of therapeutic contacts, client characteristics and design differences (Beutler, 1986).

In conclusion, while verbal and non-verbal cues of communication appear to be the main sources of influence in the creation of perceptions about congruence and incongruence, it still remains quite unclear *how* clients and/or observers come to view therapists as congruent or incongruent (Gurman, 1977a, b). It appears that the *amount* of congruent behaviour may not be as important as its *timing* in therapy interaction (Hill and Stephany, 1990).

Part C

Investigating the subjective and/or relational aspects of congruence: the concept of congruence as an experiential and/or relational phenomenon

Most of the research has been conducted on the impact of congruence on therapy outcome and the relationship of congruence to therapy effectiveness. Research has not paid enough attention to the relational aspects of congruence that involve the dynamic interaction between two people (i.e., client and counsellor). Even in studies where the concept of congruence has been examined as part of the therapy process, the main focus is on how congruence is communicated or portrayed, rather than how it is experienced and processed at an experiential level.

In the literature there are a few studies conducted on the phenomenological and relational aspects of congruence. These studies are reviewed below.

In 1971, Lovejoy investigated whether it was possible to give a relational meaning to the concept of congruence and incongruence. In the study it was suggested that it may be difficult for one person to judge another person's level of congruence, when that judgement involves discriminating the extent to which the other person's awareness matches their experiencing. Using Kelly's theory of Personal Constructs, the study concluded that 'one person will judge another as congruent to the extent they share similar constructs' (p. 91). In this study, congruence was conceptualised as an interactional phenomenon affected by the perceptions each person carries for the other person in the interaction. The findings suggested that the 'manner in which we construe other people does affect our interaction with them and the concepts of incongruence and defensiveness enable us to construe others as malfunctioning' (p. 80). This study used the Barrett-Lennard Relationship Inventory (BLRI, 1962) as the measurement instrument for the concept of congruence and Kelly's Role

Construct Repertory Test (RCRT) to measure similarity of constructs. The results indicated that perceived congruence as measured by the BLRI was significantly and positively correlated with similarity of constructs. Moreover, it was argued that 'the concept of empathy theoretically overlapped with that of congruence' (p. 92). This study was, however, not conducted in a psychotherapeutic setting. The study used volunteers willing to nominate two friends (one as 'congruent' and one as 'incongruent') and to fill the BLRI and the RCRT for each friend. Subsequently, these friends were contacted and they completed an RCRT, thus enabling the evaluation of the extent to which they shared similar constructs.

In sum, the study suggested that perceived congruence could be related to similarity of constructs people share when they interact with each other. It also stressed the difficulty in making judgements about the level of congruence of others. The study highlighted the possibility that a person who is considered not to be congruent or 'open to their experience' construes their experience quite differently from the observer.

In 1992, Adomaitis investigated the concept of congruence from an experiential point of view by retrospectively examining counsellors' experience of being genuine in client-centred psychotherapy. Nine highly experienced client-centred therapists were asked to describe, in qualitative interviews, what the experience of genuineness was like for them. The study focused on both the internal experience of genuineness and its expression in the therapy interaction. The findings indicated that being open to experience, being oneself and being centred, represent major themes in the experience of counsellor genuineness. Moreover, the communication or enactment of genuineness was embedded in the themes of presence, encountering, representing self accurately, disclosing and answering. Additional aspects of genuineness included: trust in self-experience as a reliable referent, being focused in the moment, being one's intentions, empathising and caring, willingness to be known, and recognising choice. The emerging themes stressed that the experience and enactment of congruence is a multi-level, multi-modal phenomenon, which can be examined in relational as well as intrapersonal terms.

Adomaitis (1992) argued that 'phenomenological research is an effective methodology in the study of genuineness, and that the existing literature is far from exhaustive of what can be said on the subject' (p. 179).

Another phenomenological study (Rahilly, 1993), examined in retrospect the experience of being authentic of 14 members of a psychotherapist training group. During qualitative interviews that lasted from 20 to 90 minutes, participants were invited to describe an authentic experience they had had. Participants' authentic experiences covered many different situations and emotions, such as loving, being fearful and separate, becoming a parent, being figuratively buried alive, emerging sexuality, childbirth, and realising one's self-worth. The narrative accounts shared by participants during the interviews were analysed by the researcher and were also reviewed by three independent judges. The analysis indicated that an 'authentic experience' was exhibited by: (a) intensity of emotion, usually expressed using hyperbolic language; (b) a significantly heightened awareness of somatic experience; (c) a sense of being fully present and aware of self; and (d) a heightened awareness of others involved in the particular situation being experienced. Participants reported that their 'authentic experience' arose from 'a precipitating honest and self-disclosing remark made by themselves or the others in their experience' (p. 65). Finally, the findings of this study pointed out that 'authentic experience is not always a positive experience' (p. 67), thus an experience is no less authentic for being negative in its nature. According to Rahilly (1993), negative authentic experiences (i.e., fear, terror, submission) may be 'the first step on the path of living an authentic life' (p. 68). This study supported the idea that phenomena such as authenticity or congruence are embodied experiences that 'come straight from the individual's own sensory and visceral experience' (Rahilly, 1993, p. 70), and they are not necessarily experienced as positive in nature.

Summary: main findings and unresolved issues
The above findings suggested that congruence is a complex, multi-level, multi-modal, 'embodied' experience that is not necessarily positive in nature. This type of research has highlighted the importance of defining, examining and conceptualizing congruence in experiential and relational terms, rather than simply looking only at the behavioural manifestations of congruence. It seems that congruence at times overlaps with empathy and can capture the person's ability to remain open to their experience. Research in this area has highlighted the importance of allowing people to reflect on their experience during moments of congruence and incongruence, instead of making judgements based on external observers.

Some unresolved issues in this type of research come from the fact that some studies (Lovejoy, 1971; Rahilly, 1993) were not conducted in a therapeutic setting, and, while Adomaitis (1992) provided an intensive account on the distinctive aspects of counsellor's experience of congruence, did not offer adequate information on the critical moments of therapy interaction during which congruence seems to be more helpful. It remains unclear *how* congruence develops in the context of an on-going therapy interaction, and *what* the unique contributions of the client to the counsellor's ability to remain congruent are.

Part D

Investigating client and counsellor experiences of congruence during significant moments of on-going person-centred therapy
Taking into consideration some of the main unresolved issues and methodological limitations of previous studies, Grafanaki (1997) conducted an intensive qualitative investigation, which aimed to provide a better understanding of the experiential, interpersonal and relational processes that are taking place during moments of congruence and incongruence in the boundaries of real therapy sessions. In this study, congruence was treated as a process, rather than a product (Barrett-Lennard, 1962, 1986) and was defined as:

> the degree to which one person is functionally integrated in the context of his relationship with another, such that there is absence of conflict or inconsistency between his total experience, his awareness, and overt communication in this relationship (Barrett-Lennard, 1962, p. 4).

Client and counsellor accounts from six person-centred counselling cases (12 sessions each) were collected during Brief Structured Recall interviews after the first, sixth and last therapy session. The recall interviews focused on moments that the client had identified as the most helpful and the most hindering of that particular session. During the interviews, first the client and then the counsellor were invited to share their recollection of feelings, thoughts, verbal and non-verbal behaviour, and what was left unexpressed during the most helpful and the most hindering moment of the session. They also revealed reasons that kept them from sharing their internal experience with the other party in the interaction. In total, 36 interviews were conducted (18 interviews with clients and 18 interviews with counsellors). It is important to mention that during the course of therapy a number of process and outcome measures were also administered to provide important contextual information about therapy process and outcome.

The analysis revealed that participants experienced congruence and incongruence in a variety of ways, suggesting that the construct does not describe a unitary phenomenon. Different types of counsellor and client congruence and incongruence emerged. These types co-existed along with other counselling phenomena such as empathy, self-disclosure, etc. (see table 1 and 2) and varied in intensity, and therapeutic impact.

Table 1: *Counsellor and Client Types of Congruence during Significant Events of Therapy*

Counsellor	*Client*
1. Empathic attunement/ experiential presence	1. Sharing meaningful material about self
2. Process directing/focusing	2. Reporting simple information about self/others
3. Covert use of resolved personal material	3. Momentary heightened awareness/realisation
4. Counsellor disclosure of personal material	4. Process disclosure
	5. Personal contact with the therapist
	6. New ways of being/behaving

Table 2: *Counsellor and Client Types of Incongruence during Significant Events of Therapy*

Counsellor	*Client*
1. Awareness of negative feelings toward the client	1. Unwanted responsibility/ avoidance
2. Disengagement/boredom	2. Deference
3. Fatigue/physical tiredness/ busy extra therapy programme	3. Emerging of warded-off material
4. Covert awareness of unresolved personal material/vulnerability	4. Deconstructing personal image/ new insight
5. Awareness of professional issues/ role boundaries	
6. Professional incompetence/misdirection	

The findings suggested that conceptualising congruence as an individual quality or attribute did not adequately reflect client and counsellor experiences. Participants described their experience in relational terms, and placed particular emphasis on the therapeutic value of achieving a state of 'flow', in which counsellor and client were congruent and co-present with each other. The findings of this study suggested that it is necessary to understand congruence as an intersubjective and relational experience. The different categories or types of congruence and incongruence that emerged supported the idea that being congruent is an active process of working out more creative ways of relating with others and with one's self. Furthermore, moments of incongruence seemed to capture important experiential and process shifts in therapy, including ruptures and repairs in the therapeutic alliance.

The findings of this study supported that there is not a linear relationship between congruence and successful outcome. Both clients and counsellors experienced moments of incongruence even in cases with good therapy outcomes and strong therapeutic alliances. It appeared that even in successful cases where the client experienced a considerable progress and resolution in dealing with his/her concerns, there were moments during therapy that the client perceived as hindering or unhelpful, despite the fact that the counsellor was congruent at that moment. For example: there were times that the counsellor was congruent and was trying to 'direct the therapy process' or 'focus the discussion on an important issue' (see types in Table 1), however these efforts did not always have a positive therapeutic impact. It appeared that the *client's readiness* to work on a particular issue determined the helpfulness of the *counsellor's response* rather than whether the counsellor was congruent or not.

Furthermore, the study revealed that clients played an important role in helping counsellors to be facilitative with them. The counsellor's ability to remain congruent and open during therapy was compromised when the client was not willing to share important material (Gomes-Schwartz, 1978). Most of the counsellors in this study were unable to remain accepting, open and genuine when faced with a client that seemed to focus on superficial issues. In such cases, feelings of boredom, disengagement, resentment or frustration started building up and were accompanied by intense moments of incongruence (see 'types' in Table 2).

The findings of the present study highlighted the importance of taking into consideration both participants' experience and contribution to the interaction in order to assess the therapeutic impact of a particular moment.

Most types of counsellor and client incongruence emerging from this investigation were related to covert processes (i.e., unexpressed thoughts, and feelings) that were usually negative in nature (Hill et al., 1992) or considered as inappropriate material to be disclosed and shared during therapy. For example, one of the counsellors reported:

> he was telling me about his skills as a designer and I was wondering if there was a contrast between how he presents himself to me as a skilled designer and to what extent this might be unreal. I was wondering if his perception matches with reality. Part of what I was thinking was: 'Can I trust you? Do I believe you? Is that true or fantasy?' But when he showed me his design work afterwards, it was really good stuff. I was not transparent, because I was actually questioning his honesty, I was questioning his degree of self-knowledge. (My) transparency was very low and I hope it didn't show (what I was thinking), because it could have been very hurtful, and offensive and destructive thing . . .

The findings also revealed that even when clients enjoyed a good therapeutic relationship with the counsellor, they did not always share everything they were feeling or thinking (Grafanaki and McLeod, 1995).

Counsellors seemed to be more effective than their clients in hiding things that they did not want, or feel comfortable, to discuss, by adopting facilitative non-verbal behaviours, such as relaxed, open posture, head nodding, etc. Both clients and counsellors seemed to be able to control their verbal messages better than their gestures and voice tone. Usually these channels of communication were more reliable witnesses of participants' covert processes.

The findings of this investigation supported the existence of the client's deferential behaviour. In the present study, client's deference was usually activated during moments that the counsellor was congruent, and was either trying to 'direct the therapy process' on a topic that the client was not ready to discuss, or she/he was embarking on a personal or process disclosure that the client did not consider as relevant or appropriate at that point in time. During moments of deference, clients experienced incongruence, and they did not actually share their thoughts and feelings with the counsellor. They usually pretended that things were alright, when in reality they wanted to change the topic or move on.

These findings stressed the importance for the counsellor of encouraging and empowering the client to comment on the therapy process and to participate in the way the therapeutic plan is arranged (Rennie, 1994).

This study promoted congruence as a relational phenomena rather than an attitude offered by the therapist alone. It appeared that clients' and counsellors' degree of congruence was related to the level of awareness of their inner experience, their ability to accept and acknowledge or honour this experience, and their willingness to communicate it to the other person of the interaction. Congruence appeared to be an intrapersonal as well as a relational phenomenon that was able to capture the level of connection within self and with each other. High levels of congruence were usually present during those moments when the therapy process was experienced as 'flowing' and both participants were deeply involved in the therapeutic process.

CONCLUSIONS

Despite the importance of congruence in person-centred and experiential approaches of psychotherapy, the research literature revealed that this concept has not been adequately examined and not sufficiently grounded in the experience and behaviour of therapists and clients. The meaning and significance of this concept remains too general and abstract in theory and research literature, and its impact on therapy interaction and communication is still quite vague.

The review of the literature revealed that there are only a few studies that have examined congruence in its own right. Furthermore, most of the studies have dealt with the impact of congruence on therapeutic outcome, instead of the experience of being congruent. Hence there is more information about 'what congruence does', than 'how it feels'. Appropriateness and timing of congruent responses have been overlooked at the expense of measuring the frequency of congruent responses. Moreover, little research exists (Grafanaki, 1997) on the development of this concept within the boundaries of on-going therapy.

In the research literature, the client's experience of congruence and incongruence has been overlooked and it is the counsellor's congruence that has been the focus for most of studies. In this way it is implied that it is only the quality of therapist congruence or incongruence that has an impact on therapy. However, Grafanaki's study revealed that clients play an important role in helping counsellors to be facilitative with them. It appears that counsellor's ability to remain congruent and open during therapy is compromised when the client is not willing to share important material.

Quite a lot of the unresolved issues and gaps in our understanding, regarding how congruence works in therapy, come from the fact that most of the research has not adequately looked into the client's experience during moments that the counsellor is in a state of congruence or incongruence. It appears that most of the empirical studies on congruence have implicitly subscribed to the paradigm of 'drug metaphor' (Stiles and Shapiro, 1989), which views therapy as consisting of 'active ingredients' offered to the client by the therapist, in the same way that drugs are prescribed to the patient by the doctor. In this paradigm, congruence has been treated as an 'active ingredient', that if it is offered in high levels by the counsellor, it is expected to produce a positive outcome (Stiles and Shapiro, 1989). The findings generated by Adomaitis (1992) and Grafanaki (1997) suggested that congruence instead of being treated as a 'product' or 'active ingredient' needs to be examined as an active 'process' to which *both* participants — counsellor and client — make significant contributions.

More is still to be discovered on the process of 'becoming congruent'. Future studies need to pay more attention to studying congruence in a way that captures the dialectic nature of therapeutic relationship and the unique interactions between the individual client and counsellor. The use of intensive, qualitative research methods with real clients and counsellors will be a useful avenue. There is also a need for greater understanding of the possible influence of culture on the experience, expression and reception of congruence. Such discoveries will significantly contribute to our understanding about how therapy works and what leads to change.

REFERENCES

Adomaitis, R. M. (1992). *On Being Genuine: a Phenomenologically Grounded Study of the Experience of Genuineness and its Place in Client-Centered Psychotherapy*. Unpublished Doctoral thesis. Northwestern University: Evaston, Illinois, USA.

Barrett-Lennard, G. T. (1962). Dimensions of Therapist Response as Causal Factors in Therapeutic Change. *Psychological Monographs*, 76(43), whole 562.

Barrett-Lennard, G. (1986). The Relationship Inventory Now. In L.S. Greenberg & W.M. Pinsoff (Eds.) *The Psychotherapy Process: A research handbook. New York: Guildford Press*, pp. 439–75.

Beutler, L. E., Crago, M., and Arizmendi, T. G. (1986). Therapist Variables in Psychotherapy Process and Outcome, In: A. E. Bergin and S. L. Garfield (Eds.) *Handbook of Psychotherapy and Behavior Change (3rd Edition)*. Chichester: John Wiley and Sons, pp. 257–309.

Beutler, L. E., Machado, P. P. P., and Allstetter Neufeldt, S. (1994). Therapist Variables. In A. E. Bergin and S. L. Garfield (Eds.) *Handbook of Psychotherapy and Behavior Change (4th Edition)*. Chichester: John Wiley and Sons, pp. 229–69.

Bozarth, J. D. (1984). Beyond Reflection: Emergent Modes of Empathy. In R. F. Levant and J. M. Shlien

(Eds.) *Client-Centered Therapy and the Person-Centered Approach*. New York: Praeger, pp. 59–75.

Bozarth, J. D., Mitchell, K. M., and Krauft, C. C. (1976). Empirical Observations on Antecedents to Psychotherapeutic Outcome: Some implications. *Rehabilitation Counseling Bulletin*, 1, 28–36.

Bull, P. (1987). *Body Movement and Interpersonal Communication*. Chichester: John Wiley and Sons.

Cramer, D. (1990). Towards Assessing the Therapeutic Value of Rogers' Core Conditions. *Counselling Psychology Quarterly*, 3, pp. 57–66.

D'Augelli, A. (1974). Nonverbal Behaviour of Helpers in Initial Helping Interactions. *Journal of Counseling Psychology*, 21, pp. 360–3.

Fischer, M. J., and Apostal, R. A. (1975). Selected Vocal Cues and Counselors' Perceptions of Genuineness, Self-disclosure, and Anxiety. *Journal of Counseling Psychology*, 22(2), pp. 92–6.

Fretz, B., Corn, R., Tuemmler, J., and Bellet, W. (1979). Counsellor Nonverbal Behaviours and Client Evaluations. *Journal of Counseling Psychology*, 24, pp. 304–11.

Gallagher, M. S., and Hargie, O. D. (1992). The Relationship Between Counsellor Interpersonal Skills and the Core Conditions of Client-Centred Counselling. *Counselling Psychology Quarterly*, 5(1), pp. 3–16.

Gomes-Schwartz, B. (1978). Effective Ingredients in Psychotherapy: Prediction of outcome from process variables. *Journal of Consulting and Clinical Psychology*, 46, pp. 1023–35.

Grafanaki, S. (1997). Client and Counsellor Experiences of Therapy Interaction During Moments of Congruence and Incongruence: Analysis of significant events in counselling/psychotherapy. Unpublished Doctoral dissertation. Keele University, Staffordshire, UK.

Grafanaki, S., and McLeod, J. (1995). Client and Counsellor Narrative Accounts of Congruence During the Most Helpful and Hindering Events of an Initial Counselling Session. *Counselling Psychology Quarterly*, 8(4), pp. 311–24.

Graves, J., and Robinson, J. (1976). Proxemic Behaviour as a Function of Inconsistent Verbal and Nonverbal Messages. *Journal of Counseling Psychology*, 23(4), pp. 333–8.

Greenberg, L. (1994). What is 'Real' Relationship? Comment on Gelso and Carter (1994). *Journal of Counseling Psychology*, 41(3), pp. 307–9.

Gurman, A. S. (1977a). The Patient's Perception of the Therapeutic Relationship. In A. S. Gurman and A. M. Razin (Eds.) *Effective Psychotherapy: A Handbook of Research*, Oxford: Pergamon Press, pp. 503–43.

Gurman, A. S. (1977b). Therapist and Patient Factors Influencing the Patient's Perceptions of Facilitative Therapeutic Conditions. *Psychiatry*, 40(3), 218–31.

Haase, R., and Tepper, D. (1972). Nonverbal Components of Empathic Communication. *Journal of Counselling Psychology*, 19, pp. 417–24.

Hermansson, G., Webster, A., and McFarland, K. (1988). Counsellor Deliberate Postural Lean and Communication of Facilitative Conditions. *Journal of Counseling Psychology*, 35, pp. 149–53.

Hill, C., Gronsky, B., Sturniolo, F., and Fretz, B. (1981). Nonverbal Communication and Counselling Outcome. *Journal of Counseling Psychology*, 28(2), pp. 203–12.

Hill, C., and Stephany, A. (1990). Relation of Nonverbal Behaviour to Client Reactions. *Journal of Counselling Psychology*, 37, pp. 22–6.

Hill, C., Thompson, B., and Corbett, M. (1992). The impact of therapist ability to perceive displayed and hidden client reactions on immediate outcome in first sessions of brief therapy. *Psychotherapy Research*, 2, pp. 143–55.

Lambert, M. J., DeJulio, S., and Stein, D. (1978). Therapist Interpersonal Skills: Process, Outcome, Methodological Considerations, and Recommendations for Future Research. *Psychological Bulletin*, 85, pp. 467–89.

Lietaer, G. (1984). Unconditional Positive regard: a Controversial basic Attitude in Client-Centered Therapy. In R. F. Levant and J. M. Shlien (Eds.) *Client-Centered Therapy and the Person-Centered Approach: New Directions in Theory, Research, and Practice*. New York: Praeger, pp. 41–58.

Lockhart, W. (1984). Rogers' 'Necessary and Sufficient Conditions' Revisited. *British Journal of Guidance and Counselling*, 12(2), pp. 112–23.

Lovejoy, L. (1971). *Congruence Intrapersonal or Interpersonal*. Unpublished Doctoral thesis. University of Waterloo, Australia.

Mearns, D. (1994). *Developing Person-Centred Counselling*. London: Sage.

Mearns, D., and Thorne, B. (1988). *Person-Centred Counselling in Action*. London: Sage.

Mitchell, K. M., Bozarth, J. D., and Krauft, C. C. (1977). A Reappraisal of the Therapeutic Effectiveness of Accurate Empathy, Non-possessive Warmth, and Genuineness. In A. S. Gurman and A. M. Razin (Eds.) *Effective psychotherapy: A Handbook of Research.* Oxford: Pergamon Press, pp. 482–501.

Orlinsky, D. E., and Howard, K. I. (1978). The Relation of Process to Outcome in Psychotherapy. In S. L. Garfield and A. E. Bergin (Eds.) *Handbook of Psychotherapy and Behaviour Change.* Chichester: John Wiley and Sons, pp. 283–329.

Orlinsky, D. E., and Howard, K. I. (1986). Process and Outcome in Psychotherapy. In S. L. Garfield and A. E. Bergin (Eds.) *Handbook of Psychotherapy and Behavior Change,* (3rd Edition). Chichester: John Wiley and Sons, pp. 331–81.

Parloff, M., Waskaw, I., and Wolfe, B. (1978). Research on Therapist Variables in Relation to Process and Outcome. In S. L. Garfield and A. E. Bergin (Eds.) *Handbook of Psychotherapy and Behavior Change* (2nd Edition). Chichester: John Wiley and Sons, pp. 233–82.

Patterson, C. H. (1984). Empathy, Warmth, and Genuineness in Psychotherapy: a Review of Reviews. *Psychotherapy,* 21(4), pp. 431–8.

Rahilly, D. A. (1993). A Phenomenological Analysis of Authentic Experience. *Journal of Humanistic Psychology,* 33(2), pp. 49–71.

Reade, M., and Smouse, A. (1980). Effect of Inconsistent Nonverbal Communication and Counselor Response Mode on Client Estimate of Counsellor Regard and Effectiveness. *Journal of Counseling Psychology,* 27(4), pp. 546–53.

Rennie, D. (1994). Clients' Deference in Psychotherapy. *Journal of Counseling Psychology,* 41, 427–37.

Rogers, C. (1957). The Necessary and Sufficient Conditions of Therapeutic Personality Change. *Journal of Consulting Psychology,* 21, pp. 95–103.

Rogers, C. (1961). *On Becoming a Person: A therapist's view of psychotherapy.* London: Constable.

Rogers, C. (1967). The therapeutic conditions antecedent to change: a theoretical view. In C. Rogers, E. Gendlin, D. Kiesler, and C. Truax (Eds.) *The Therapeutic Relationship and Its Impact: A Study of Psychotherapy with Schizophrenics.* Madison, Wisconsin: University of Wisconsin Press, pp. pp. 97–108.

Seay, T., and Altekruse, M. (1979). Verbal and Nonverbal Behaviour in Judgements of Facilitative Conditions. *Journal of Counseling Psychology,* 26, pp. 108–19.

Shapiro, J., Foster, C., and Powell, T. (1968). Facial and Bodily Cues of Genuineness, Empathy and Warmth. *Journal of Clinical Psychology,* 24, pp. 233–6.

Sherer, M., and Rogers, R. (1980). Effects of Therapist's Nonverbal Communication on Rated Skill and Effectiveness. *Journal of Clinical Psychology,* 36, pp. 696–700.

Smith-Hanen, S. (1977). Effects of Nonverbal Behaviours on Judged Levels of Counsellor Warmth and Empathy. *Journal of Counseling Psychology,* 24(2), pp. 87–91.

Stiles, W., and Shapiro, D. (1989). Abuse of the Drug Metaphor in Psychotherapy Process Outcome Research. *Psychology Review,* 9(4), pp. 521–43.

Tepper, D., and Haase, R. (1978). Effects of Non-verbal Communication of Facilitative Conditions. *Journal of Counseling Psychology,* 25(1), pp. 35–44.

Tipton, R. M., and Rymer, R. A. (1978). A Laboratory Study of the Effects of Varying Levels of Counselor Eye Contact on Client-Focused and Problem-Focused Counseling Styles. *Journal of Counseling Psychology,* 25(3), pp. 200–4.

Truax, C., and Carkhuff, R. (1967). *Toward Effective Counselling and Psychotherapy.* Chicago: Aldine.

Truax, C., and Mitchell, K. (1971). Research on Certain Therapist Interpersonal Skills in Relation to Process and Outcome. In A. Bergin, and S. Gardfield, (Eds.). *Handbook of Psychotherapy and Behaviour Change.* Chichester: John Wiley and Sons, pp. pp. 299–344.

Truax, C. B., Witmer, J., and Wargo, D. G. (1971). Effects of the Therapeutic Conditions of Accurate Empathy, Non-possesive Warmth, and Genuineness on Hospitalised Mental Patients During Group Therapy. *Journal of Clinical Psychology,* 27, pp. 137–42.

Tyson, J., and Wall, S. (1983). Effect of Inconsistency Between Counsellor Verbal and Non-verbal Behaviour on Perception of Counsellor Atributes. *J. of Counseling Psychology,* 30(4), pp. 433–7.

Watson, N. (1984). The Empirical Status of Rogers' Hypotheses of the Necessary and Sufficient Conditions for Effective Psychotherapy. In R. F. Levant and J. M. Shlien (Eds.) *Client-Centered Therapy and the Person-Centered Approach: New Directions in Theory, Research, and Practice.* New York: Praeger, pp. 17–40.

3

Being Genuine as a Therapist: Congruence and Transparency
Germain Lietaer

AUTHENTICITY: CONGRUENCE AND TRANSPARENCY

Although Rogers had always attached great importance to the therapist's authenticity[1] (see for example Rogers, 1951, p. 19), it was not until his 1957 paper about the 'necessary and sufficient conditions' that he mentioned it explicitly as a separate therapeutic condition, along with empathy and acceptance. From 1962 on, he even called it the more fundamental of all three basic attitudes, and continued doing this in his later works. Here is how Rogers describes it:

> Genuineness in therapy means that the therapist is his actual self during his encounter with his client. Without façade, he openly has the feelings and attitudes that are flowing in him at the moment. This involves self-awareness; that is, the therapist's feelings are available to him — to his awareness — and he is able to live them, to experience them in the relationship, and to communicate them if they persist. The therapist encounters his client directly, meeting him person to person. He is being himself, not denying himself.
>
> Since this concept is liable to misunderstanding, let me state that it does not mean that the therapist burdens his client with overt expression of all his feelings. Nor does it mean that the therapist discloses his total self to his client. It does mean, however, that the therapist denies to himself none of the feelings he is experiencing and that he is willing to experience transparently any *persistent* feelings that exist in the relationship and to let these be known to his client. It means avoiding the temptation to present a façade or hide behind a mask of professionalism, or to assume a confessional-professional attitude.
>
> It is not simple to achieve such reality. Being real involves the difficult task of being acquainted with the flow of experiencing going on within oneself, a flow marked especially by complexity and continuous change (1966, p. 185).

This definition implies clearly that genuineness has two sides: an inner one and an outer one. The inner side refers to the degree to which the therapist has conscious access to, or is receptive to, *all* aspects of his own flow of experiencing. This side of the process will be called 'congruence'; the consistency to which it

A revision of a paper first published in *Beyond Carl Rogers* (1993) Edited by David Brazier, published by Constable., pp.17–46. Reproduced with kind permission of the publisher and editor.
1. Throughout this chapter I will use authenticity and genuineness interchangeably.

refers is the unity of total experience and awareness. The outer side, on the other hand, refers to the communication — through verbal and non-verbal ways — by the therapist of 'himself'; his perceptions, attitudes and feelings. This aspect is called 'transparency'. Although this splitting up of genuineness into two components may be slightly artificial (because it suggests too much of a dichotomy), we find it justified from a didactic point of view as well as clinically meaningful. Indeed, a congruent therapist may be very or minimally transparent, according to his style or orientation; a transparent therapist may be congruent, or he may be incongruent (something which makes him or her a 'dangerous' therapist). To begin with, we will discuss the concept of congruence, which has always been given the most weight in Rogers' definition. Then we will turn to transparency.

1. Congruence

1.1. Congruence as conditio sine qua non of acceptance and empathy
What is the core meaning of the concept of congruence and why is it so important in our therapeutic work?

Congruence requires, first of all, that the therapist be a psychologically well developed and integrated individual, i.e. sufficiently 'whole' (or 'healed') and in touch with himself. This includes daring to acknowledge flaws and vulnerabilities, accepting the positive and negative parts of oneself with a certain leniency, being capable of openness without defensiveness to what lives in oneself and being able to get in touch with it, having a solid identity and a strong enough sense of competence, being able to function efficaciously in personal and intimate relationships without interference of personal problems. Self-knowledge and ego-strength can perhaps be seen as the two cornerstones of this way of being (see among others McConnaughy, 1987).

Congruence and acceptance are correlative, they are the two sides of a same basic variable of openness: there can be no openness to the client's experience if there is no openness to one's own experience. And without openness there can be no empathy either. In this sense, congruence is the 'upper limit' of the capacity for empathy (Barrett-Lennard, 1962, p. 4). To put it differently: the therapist can never bring the client further on with regards a certain issue than where he is himself as a person; this will be illustrated under the next heading.

1.1.1. Incongruence
The importance of congruence becomes especially clear when it is lacking, i.e. when the therapist is defensive and incongruent. Our personal difficulties may sometimes prevent us from letting the client's experience emerge fully, as it is. Life issues with which we have not dealt yet, personal needs which play along during therapy, personal vulnerabilities and blind spots, all may cause us to feel threatened and unable to follow with serenity certain experiences of our client (Lietaer, 1992). To empathize with the experiential world of another person with values vastly different from our own, to let feelings of powerlessness and hopelessness emerge, to empathize with intense happiness, to deal without undue defensiveness with a client's intense negative or positive feelings towards us: all of this is not easy. Because of our own experienced threat

and defensiveness, there is a danger of us being so busy maintaining our own equilibrium that we break the deepening of the client's self-exploratory process (either by keeping too much distance or by losing ourselves in the other). Rogers puts it as follows:

> Can I be strong enough as a person to be separate from the other? Can I be a sturdy respecter of my own feelings, my own needs, as well as his? Can I own and, if need be, express my own feelings as something belonging to me and separate from his feelings? Am I strong enough in my own separateness that I will not be downcast by his depression, frightened by his fear, nor engulfed by his dependency? Is my inner self hardy enough to realize that I am not destroyed by his anger, taken over by his need for dependence, nor enslaved by his love, but that I exist separate from him with feelings and rights of my own? When I can freely feel this strength of being a separate person, then I find that I can let myself go much more deeply in understanding and accepting him because I am not fearful of losing myself (1961, p. 52).

All this means that we, as therapists, need strong ego boundaries. An important part of being a therapist is to have the capacity to be steady as a rock (Leijssen, 1998): we sometimes have to pull the chestnuts out of the fire, deal with stormy emotions without being engulfed, deal constructively with hate and love without resorting to acting-out, deal with the client's praise and criticism of our own person; and we have to be able to tolerate ambivalence. To share empathically the other's world also implies putting our own world in parentheses, for the time being, and 'risking' personal change through contact with someone who is different from ourselves. Venturing in such an 'egoless state' (Vanaerschot, 1990) is easiest when we feel ourselves to be a sufficiently separate person with a well-defined personal structure and nucleus. Finally, we wish to point to a last aspect which demands a certain strength from the therapist: the fact that the client's discourse can be confronting to the therapist in as far as it addresses dormant issues in himself. Rombauts relates this being confronted with oneself to the kinship which exists between client and therapist, in the sense that both 'share a human existence'. He writes:

> Because of this kinship, it is not only me who holds up a mirror to the client (although I find 'mirroring' a poor term), but also the client who holds up a mirror to me, showing me what I am, feel and experience. Dormant aspects of myself, which I have barely or not at all realized in my own life, can be touched upon and stirred up. As a consequence, I am constantly being confronted with myself when doing therapy, and led to question myself. Something happens, not only to the client but also to the therapist. We are companions-in-fate, in life as well as in therapy (1984, p. 172).

1.1.2. Congruence and empathy   As we have seen, a lack of congruence undermines our therapeutic work. We can perhaps even better illustrate the importance of congruence from a positive angle or, at any rate, draw attention to a few aspects which we have not discussed yet, and which have a lot to do with the quality of our empathic interventions. A high level of congruence certainly guarantees a personal flavour to the communication of empathy so it would not be experienced by the client as a stilted application of technique. Indeed, the client finds himself faced with a therapist who is 'rooted' in his own experience, and who is, from there, trying to understand his message. The therapist does not only summarize the client's words, but puts into words 'what strikes him', what the client's discourse evokes in him, 'how it makes him feel', what he does not yet understand perhaps, but would like to understand, etc. Even though the therapist is, in essence, focused on the client's experiential world, the understanding is always a personal one, in the sense that his responses originate in his own experience of what the client tells him. Occasionally (in my opinion very exceptionally) this can result in the therapist briefly mentioning an experience of his own, not in order to talk about himself or draw attention to himself, but as a way of letting the client know that he has been understood. This personalized form of empathy can perhaps best be illustrated by a couple of fragments from a session with 'A silent young man', where Rogers tries to share the feelings of hopelessness and rejection experienced by Jim Brown (see especially the T-responses with an asterisk).

C: I just want to run away and die.

T: M-hm, m-hm, m-hm. It isn't even that you want to get away from here *to* something. You just want to leave here and go away and die in a corner, hm? (Silence of 30 seconds)

*T: I guess as I let that soak in I really do sense how, how deep that feeling sounds, that you — I guess the image that comes to my mind is sort of a, a wounded animal that wants to crawl away and die. It sounds as though that's kind of the way you feel that you just want to get away from here and, and vanish. Perish. Not exist. (Silence of 1 minute)

C: (almost inaudibly) All day yesterday and all morning I wished I were dead.. I even prayed last night that I could die.

*T: I think I caught all of that, that — for a couple of days now you've just *wished* you could be dead and you've even prayed for that — I guess that — One way this strikes me is that to live is such an awful thing to you, you just wish you could die, and not live.

C: I ain't no good to nobody, or I ain't no good for nothin', so what's the use of living?

T: M-hm. You feel, 'I'm not any good to another living person, so — why should I go on living?' (Silence of 21 seconds)

*T: And I guess a part of that — here I'm kind of guessing and you can set me straight, I guess a part of that is that you felt, 'I tried to *be* good for something as far as he was concerned. I really tried. And now — if I'm no good to him, if he feels I'm no good, then that proves I'm just no good to anybody.' Is that, uh — anywhere near it?

C: Oh, well, other people have told me that too.

T: Yeah. M-hm. I see. So you feel if, if you go by what others — what several others have said, then, then you are *no good*. No good to anybody. (Silence of 3 minutes, 40 seconds)

*T: I don't know whether this will help or not, but I would just like to say that — I think I can understand pretty well — what it's like to feel that you're just *no damn good* to anybody, because there was a time when

CONGRUENCE

— I felt that way about *myself.* And I know it can be *really rough.*
(Comment: This is a most unusual kind of response for me to make. I simply
felt that I wanted to share my experience with him — to let him know he was
not alone.) (Rogers, 1967b, pp. 407–9).

Deep empathy always means 'listening with the third ear', in which a regressive
contact with one's own deeper feeling levels and the ability to imagine what one
would feel in a similar situation are important elements. Rogers (1970) describes
how he gradually developed more confidence in his own deeper intuitive levels:

I *trust* the feelings, words, impulses, fantasies, that emerge in me. In this way I
am using more than my conscious self, drawing on some of the capacities of
my whole organism. For example, 'I suddenly had the fantasy that you are a
princess, and that you would love it if we were all your subjects.' Or, 'I sense
that you are the judge as well as the accused, and that you are saying sternly to
yourself, You are *guilty* on every count'.

Or the intuition may be a bit more complex. While a responsible business
executive is speaking, I may suddenly have the fantasy of the small boy he is
carrying around within himself — the small boy that he was, shy, inadequate,
fearful — a child he endeavors to deny, of whom he is ashamed. And I am
wishing that he would love and cherish this youngster. So I may voice this
fantasy — not as something true, but as a fantasy in me. Often this brings a
surprising depth of reaction and profound insights (p. 53).

Gendlin too (1967b) describes how a therapist may empathically guess, on the
basis of his own stream of thoughts and feelings, what the client is going through,
or can try to evoke the felt sense of what the client says:

The patient talks, perhaps gets much value from having a friendly caring
listener, but nothing of therapeutic relevance is said. There is only talk about
hospital food, the events of the week, the behavior of others, a little anger or
sadness, no exploration.

I become the one who expresses the feelings and felt meanings. I say, 'What
a spot to be in!' or, 'Gee, and they don't even *care* what *you* think about it,' or 'I
guess that leaves you feeling helpless, does it?' or, 'Boy, that would make *me* mad,'
or, 'It must be sad that he doesn't care more for you than *that,*' or, 'I don't know, of
course, but I wonder, do you wish you *could* get mad, but maybe you don't dare?'
or, 'I guess you could cry about that, if you let yourself cry' (p. 398).

All this goes to show that congruence and empathy are not opposites. On the
contrary, empathy is always implicitly carried by the therapist's congruence: we
always understand the other via ourselves, through our kinship as fellow human
beings (see Vanaerschot, 1990 and 1997).

So far we have discussed the importance of congruence mainly in the context
of acceptance and empathy for the client's experiential world, disregarding the
interaction here-and-now. However, empathy for what happens *between* client
and therapist, for the kind of relationship pattern which they create in their
influence on each other, is an equally important aspect of the process, and here
too — maybe especially here — the therapist's congruence is crucial. Indeed,

here it functions as an 'interactional barometer' for what happens in the relationship. We will discuss this aspect later, under the heading 'Transparency'.

1.2. Implications for training and professional practice

Personal maturity, together with the basic clinical aptitudes related to it, can thus be considered as the therapist's main instrument in client-centered therapy. In this respect, we share the view of psychoanalysts. It should thus not come as a surprise that, in our training, special attention is paid to the personal development of the therapists-to-be. We are, of course, not talking here about 'direct training' in congruence, but about the slower and indirect ways of personal therapy and personalized supervision, in which the person of the therapist is as much focused on as the client's process. As far as personal 'didactic' therapy goes, I myself am strongly in favour of participation in intensive long-term group therapy. Indeed, therapeutic experience in a group offers, more than individual therapy, the possibility of observing one's own interpersonal functioning, something which is crucial for therapeutic work (see also Mearns, 1997). Individual therapy may then remain highly desirable, along with group therapy, but it may not be essential for every trainee.

The willingness to work on one's own personality development should not be limited to the training period, but should be viewed as a 'life task'. Therefore, regular peer-review, either within one's own team or outside of it, seems highly desirable. A sufficiently safe atmosphere is, however, a must, in order to allow the taking of personal risks and the acceptance of a vulnerable position. In a broader sense, we, as therapists, should take special care of ourselves, and watch out for signs of overburdening, loneliness, alienation, and of getting stuck in personal problems. When our need is too big, we may not have enough energy left to turn towards our client with serenity. What could we then do to avoid such impasses? 'Caring' for one's own personal relationships, re-entering therapy before it is too late, cutting one's workload and making time to be with oneself . . . may, besides supervision, already achieve a great deal. Exceptionally, changing an appointment with a client may be indicated. Besides this, it may help a great deal to 'prepare' oneself before an interview. Rombauts writes about this:

> It seems important that I stop all my other activities, even if only a few minutes before, in immediate preparation for the contact with a client. I try as much as possible to step out of my own world, and let my worries and concerns fade into the background. I also concentrate mentally on my client, for example by recalling our last session, but also more generally by letting him be present, as it were, with everything he evokes in me in terms of memories and feelings. To use Gendlin's terms, I turn towards the 'felt sense' for the client, which lives in me.
>
> In this way, I try to increase my receptivity towards the client, and remove as much as possible any lack of openness I may feel. However, should I not have succeeded, the first few moments of the session are often enough to create more openness, not only towards my client but also towards myself. There exists thus an interaction: the state of fundamental openness in my personal world is the soil on which the contact with the client grows; but also, this contact, this therapeutic involvement, highly enhances the quality of the openness in my personal world (1984, p. 170).

All this leaves us perhaps with the impression that the therapist should be a 'superman'. But this is not what Rogers and others had in mind. It is indeed so that someone who wants to become a therapist has to be prepared to go through life paying sufficient attention to his own inner life and his way of relating to others. He also has to be, generally speaking, quite sturdy. This, however, does not mean that he could not have problems which may at times be quite acute. The important point here is not to avoid these problems, to dare scrutinizing them, to remain open to critical feedback, to learn to see how one's difficulties interfere with one's therapeutic work, and to do what is needed to remedy the situation. It is furthermore important to get to know and accept with leniency our own limits: we do not have to be able to work well with all types of clients. We may try to change our limits, but learning to know and accept them is not an unimportant task during training and beyond.

And, to conclude, I want to mention this: client-centered literature contains little in the way of concrete forms which incongruence can take. As a process-oriented theory of therapy, it emphasizes mainly the formal signals. We can see this, for example, in Barrett-Lennard's definition of incongruence:

> Direct evidence of lack of congruence includes, for example, inconsistency between what the individual says, and what he implies by expression, gestures, or tone of voice. Indications of discomfort, tension, or anxiety are considered to be less direct but equally important evidence of lack of congruence. They imply that the individual is not, at the time, freely open to awareness of some aspects of his experience, that he is lacking in integration and is, in some degree, incongruent (1962, p. 4).

In the psychoanalytic literature, however, a great deal is said about the diversity in content of 'countertransference reactions' and their psychogenic roots; the interested reader may find a great deal in the following publications: Giovacchini, 1989; Strean, 1986; Wolstein, 1988.

2. Transparency

At the beginning of this chapter, I described transparency as the outer layer of authenticity: the communication by the therapist of himself and of personal aspects of his experiential world. The concept, however, has not always been clearly defined in the client-centered literature and hence has been a source of divergent interpretations (Tudor and Worrall, 1994; Wilkins, 1997; Haugh, 1998; Brodley, 1998; Ellingham, 1999; Wyatt, 2000). For a careful historical analysis of the concept of congruence and its relationship to communication in Rogers' writings, I wish to refer to Brodley's publication of 1998. My own endeavour in this chapter is to reflect — within a somewhat broader context of client-centered, experiential, existential and interpersonal psychotherapy — on some theoretical and clinical issues related to the transparency of the therapist. In doing so, I will make a distinction — which should not be taken as too dichotomic — between on the one hand the personal presence of the therapist (which does not — or not necessarily — imply specific responses), and on the other hand explicit self-disclosure (in which the therapist openly and verbally reveals content aspects of his personal life and/or here-and-now feelings and impressions within the on-going interaction with his client). I will then discuss transparency and transference and the therapist's use of self with regard to practice.

2.1. Personal presence

Personal presence (or the lack of it: putting up a facade) can be defined as the 'shining through' of who the therapist is as a person through everything he does and doesn't do, be it verbal or non-verbal. It is more closely and unavoidably connected to the inner side of (in)congruence than is the case for explicit self-disclosing responses. Together with Tudor and Worrall, I like to look at it as 'self-awareness in action':

> As I allow myself awareness of my experience and the freedom potentially to be and to live my feelings and my experiencing, I am, in turn, more likely to be experienced by my client as full, integrated and genuine — and this before I share overtly anything of myself. Just as I may, out of awareness, communicate to my client feelings or sensations which I have only partly acknowledged to myself, I may also, by how I am rather than by anything I do, communicate my genuineness and dependable realness (1994, p. 199).

Rogers has always been opposed to the idea of the therapist as a 'blank screen'. He designed a 'face-to-face' type of therapy, in which the therapist is highly involved with the client's experiential world, yet without hiding his real feelings behind a professional façade. More than psychoanalysts, he believed in the therapeutic value of a 'real' relationship between client and therapist. In such a working relationship, the therapist serves as a *model*: his personal presence encourages the client to risk himself in deeper self-exploration.

> It is not easy for a client, or for any human being, to entrust his most deeply shrouded feelings to another person. It is even more difficult for a disturbed person to share his deepest and most troubling feelings with a therapist. The genuineness of the therapist is one of the elements in the relationship that make the risk of sharing easier and less fraught with dangers (1966, pp. 185–6).

Along with this, Rogers gradually came to consider the therapist's shining through of congruence as a crucial factor in establishing *trust*, and came to emphasize the idea of acceptance and empathy only being effective when they are perceived as genuine:

> Can I *be* in some way which will be perceived by the other person as trustworthy, as dependable or consistent in some deep sense? Both research and experience indicate that this is very important, and over the years I have found what I believe are deeper and better ways of answering this question. I used to feel that if I fulfilled all the outer conditions of trustworthiness — keeping appointments, respecting the confidential nature of the interviews, etc. — and if I acted consistently the same during the interviews, then this condition would be fulfilled. But experience drove home the fact that to act consistently acceptant, for example, if in fact I was feeling annoyed or skeptical or some other non-acceptant feeling, was certain in the long run to be perceived as inconsistent or untrustworthy. I have come to recognize that being trustworthy

does not demand that I be rigidly consistent but that I be dependably real. The term 'congruent' is one I have used to describe the way I would like to be. By this I mean that whatever feeling or attitude I am experiencing would be matched by my awareness of that attitude. When this is true, then I am a unified or integrated person in that moment, and hence I can *be* whatever I deeply *am*. This is a reality which I find others experience as dependable (Rogers, 1961, p. 50).

This also means that the therapist should give priority to discussing his own feelings whenever they persistently stand in the way of the other two basic attitudes. Initially, Rogers considered such moments of self-expression as a 'help in need', as a therapist's last resort in discarding obstacles to his involvement with the client's experiential world. Gendlin, on the other hand, emphasizes more the gain, for therapist and client, resulting from daring to present oneself as 'not perfect':

> 'Congruence' for the therapist means that he need not always appear in a good light, always understanding, wise, or strong. I find that, on occasion, I can be quite visibly stupid, have done the wrong thing, made a fool of myself. I can let these sides of me be visible when they have occurred in the interaction. The therapist's being himself and expressing himself openly frees us of many encumbrances and artificialities, and makes it possible for the schizophrenic (or any client) to come in touch with another human being as directly as possible (Gendlin, 1967a, p. 121–2).

The personal presence of the therapist should also be apparent from his concrete methodology, from the specific responses and procedures used to facilitate and deepen the client's discourse. Important here is that the 'technique' should rest on an underlying attitude, that the therapist should stand behind it with his whole being (Kinget, 1959, p. 27), and that his work method should suit his personality. Rogers notices 'with horror' in some of his pupils how reflecting feelings had deteriorated in aping, in a 'wooden technique', no longer carried by an inner attitude which emanates from an attempt to understand and check this understanding (Rogers, 1962, 1986; Bozarth, 1984). Rogers' view on the therapist's contribution has thus increasingly evolved towards a *meta*theory, in which a number of basic attitudes are emphasized and in which concrete recipes and formulas of intervention have faded into the background. Gendlin writes about this evolution:

> Gone are formulas — even that most characteristic of client-centered modes of responding, which was called 'reflection of feeling'. As the term 'empathy' implies, we strive as always to understand and sense the client's feeling from his own inward frame of reference, but now we have a wider scope of different behaviors with which therapists respond to clients. In fact, I believe that it was in part the undesirable tendency toward formulas and stereotyped ways of responding which perhaps led Rogers to formulate this condition of 'congruence' as essential (Gendlin, 1967a, p. 121).

Because of the prime importance of the therapist's personal presence — but also

44

perhaps because he was no great believer in the power of technique per se —
Rogers thus emphasizes the respect for each therapist's personal style. He does
not want to put him in a methodological straitjacket which would not suit his
nature. That he is very broadminded about this becomes obvious, for instance,
in his comment about the often widely diverging working methods of the
therapists in the study of schizophrenics:

> Perhaps the deepest of these learnings is a confirmation of, and an extension
> of, the concept that therapy has to do with the *relationship*, and has relatively
> little to do with techniques or with theory and ideology. In this respect I believe
> my views have become more, rather than less, extreme. I believe it is the *realness*
> of the therapist in the relationship which is the most important element. It is
> when the therapist is natural and spontaneous that he seems to be most
> effective. Probably this is a 'trained humanness' as one of our therapists
> suggests, but in the moment it is the natural reaction of *this* person. Thus our
> sharply different therapists achieve good results in quite different ways. For
> one, an impatient, no-nonsense, let's put-the-cards-on-the-table approach is
> most effective, because in such an approach he is most *openly* being himself.
> For another it may be a much more gentle, and more obviously warm approach,
> because this is the way *this* therapist is. Our experience has deeply reinforced
> and extended my own view that the person who is able openly to be himself at
> that moment, as he is at the deepest levels he is able to be, is the effective therapist.
> Perhaps nothing else is of any importance. (Rogers, 1967a, pp. 185–6).

As will be discussed further on, this respect for the therapist's own style is no
passport to 'reckless experimenting'. Attention to the client's process and
continuous following of his experiential track remain the ultimate guidelines for
our responses and interventions.

2.2. Self-disclosure: Its place in the evolution of client-centered therapy

As to the therapist's explicit self-expressive responses, it is remarkable how
reluctantly they were introduced and accepted in the evolution of client-centered
therapy. This should not surprise us. Indeed, it belongs to the nuclear identity of
client-centered therapy that the therapist follow his client *within the client's own
frame of reference.* However, between 1955 and 1962 this principle became more
flexible. Client-centered therapy evolved from 'non-directive' to 'experiential/
interpersonal', and this allowed the therapist to bring in something from his own
frame of reference, as long as he kept returning to the client's experiential track
(Gendlin, 1970; Lietaer, 1998). This was thus the context in which self-expressive
responses became accepted. Thus, we deal here with responses where the
therapist starts from his own frame of reference, as is also the case in
interpretations, confrontations and proposals for the use of particular techniques,
for instance. Gradually, the expression of personal feelings became no longer
restricted to being a 'help in need', i.e. used in cases where the therapist could no
longer genuinely accept and empathize, but it became thought of as having
positive potential for deepening the therapeutic process. What the therapist
experiences in contact with his client is now considered as important material
and potentially useful for the client in his exploration of himself and his

relationship patterns (for a thorough analysis of Rogers' evolution in this regard, see Van Balen, 1990).

Three factors seem to have played a role in this evolution. First of all, there was the study with schizophrenics (1958–64). With this very withdrawn group of patients, the 'classical' type of intervention — reflection of feelings — fell short: there was often very little to reflect. In their attempts at establishing contact, the client-centered therapists learned to use an alternative source of help, their own here-and-now feelings:

> When the client offers no self-expression, the therapist's momentary experiencing is not empty. At every moment there occur a great many feelings and events in the therapist. Most of these concern the client and the present moment. The therapist need not wait passively till the client expresses something intimate or therapeutically relevant. Instead, he can draw on his own momentary experiencing and find there an ever-present reservoir from which he can draw, and with which he can initiate, deepen, and carry on therapeutic interaction even with an unmotivated, silent, or externalized person (Gendlin, 1967a, p. 121).

There was, moreover, the contact with a number of existential therapists, such as Rollo May and Carl Whitaker, who criticized them for effacing themselves too much in the therapeutic relationship, for standing too much behind the client as an alter ego and too little as a real other person with an own personal identity. Thus Whitaker gave the following comments on a number of excerpts from client-centered therapies with schizophrenics:

> It is as though the two were existing in some kind of common microcosm or isolation chamber or like twins in utero. These interviews are intensely personal for both of these individuals but only the patient's life is under discussion. This is so distinct that one sometimes feels there is only one self present and that self is the patient. It is as though the therapist makes himself artificially miniature. Sometimes this is so dramatic that I almost feel he disappears. This is in specific contrast to our type of therapy in which both persons are present in a rather specific sense and the therapeutic process involves the overt interaction of the two individuals and the use of the experience of each of them for the patient's growth (Rogers et al. 1967b, p. 517).

This 'willingness to be known' (Barrett-Lennard, 1962, p. 5), which had gradually found its way into their individual therapy praxis, emerged even more forcefully (perhaps at times too forcefully) in the 'encounter movement' of the sixties and seventies (Rogers, 1970, pp. 52–5). Group dynamics, with its emphasis on 'feedback in the here-and-now' was certainly not foreign to this.

All these influences have made client-centered therapy into a more interactional one, with the therapist not only functioning as an alter ego, but also as an independent pole of interaction, who expresses, at times, to the client his own feelings about the situation. On account of this transparency, the process becomes more a dialogue, an I-Thou encounter (Buber and Rogers, 1957, in Kirschenbaum and Henderson, 1989; Van Balen, 1990, pp. 35–8; Schmid, 1998). In such an authentic mutual encounter, there may be moments in which the therapist almost relinquishes his professional role and encounters the client in a very personal and profoundly human way. According to Yalom, such 'critical incidents' often become turning-points in therapy. He believes that they are seldom mentioned in the psychiatric literature out of shame, or out of fear of censorship; they are also seldom discussed with trainees because they do not fit the 'doctrine' or because one is afraid of exaggerations. Here are a couple of Yalom's many examples (1980, pp. 402–3):

– A therapist met with a patient who during the course of therapy developed signs suggesting cancer. While she was awaiting the results of medical laboratory tests (which subsequently proved negative) he held her in his arms like a child while she sobbed and in her terror experienced a brief psychotic state.

– For several sessions a patient had been abusing a therapist by attacking him personally and by questioning his professional skills. Finally the therapist exploded: 'I began pounding the desk with my fist and shouted, Dammit — look, why don't you just quit the verbal diarrhea and let's get down to the business of trying to understand yourself, and stop beating on me? Whatever faults I have, and I do have a lot of them, have nothing to do with your problems. I'm a human being too, and today has been a bad day.'

Although self-disclosure can be seen as the most explicit form of transparency, I want to underline that its link with congruence may be very 'dubious' in some cases. A highly self-expressive therapist is not necessarily a congruent one. It is possible that he is out of touch with important layers of himself; he may be lacking ego-strength or unknowingly being defensive or manipulative. In these instances his so-called self-disclosure is not a communication of his true feelings but rather a form of acting-out, detrimental to the process of the client. That's why we will emphasize — at the end of the chapter — the enormous importance of self-disclosing responses being embedded in a fundamental attitude of openness: openness towards oneself (congruence) and openness towards the experiencing self of the client (unconditional positive regard).

2.3. Transference and transparency

Working through of the transference is not thought of as a nuclear process, as the 'pure gold', in client-centered therapy. The therapeutic relationship is not structured in such a way as to maximize regression; we do not see this 'detour-process' as essential to personality change. We rather follow an orthopedagogic model, in which growth is stimulated right from the start, and the *real* relationship aspects are emphasized rather than the analyst's blank screen. John Shlien even goes as far as to say that transference is 'a fiction, invented and maintained by therapists, in order to protect themselves from the consequences of their own behaviour' (Shlien, 1987, p. 15). This extreme position, however, is not shared by many (Pfeiffer, 1987; Finke, 1994). Or as Gendlin has it:

If the client is a troubled person, he cannot possibly fail to rouse difficulties in another person who relates closely with him. He cannot possibly have his troubles all by himself while interacting closely with the therapist. Necessarily, the therapist will experience his own version of the difficulties, twists, and hang-ups which the interaction must have. And only if these do occur can the interaction move beyond them and be therapeutic for the client' (Gendlin, 1968, p. 222).

In client-centered therapy too, the client repeats his past in his relationship with the therapist. But the way it is dealt with is partly different from the psychoanalytic orientation. Firstly, there is the belief that certain transference reactions — which can be viewed as security measures on the part of the client — will gradually melt away without explicit working through under the beneficial effect of a good working alliance. Secondly, client-centered therapy does not provide a *priority in principle* to working with a problem in the here-and-now relationship with the therapist. The criterion for further exploration is, according to Rice, the vividness with which a certain type of problem is experienced, and not where this experience is located on the triangle here/elsewhere/in the past:

> In a real sense, any member of a class is as worthwhile exploring as any other. Neither the past nor the present has priority, but rather the vividness with which an experience can be recounted by the client. After all, the more vividly an experience is recounted, the more likely it is to be an experience that is emotionally important to the client. More adequate processing of any one experience should lead to more adaptive responses in a whole range of specific situations (1974, p. 303).

In Rice's view, therefore, the working through of transference reactions in the here-and-now of the therapeutic relationship is not a 'must' but a possibility, a sub-process along with other ones. I personally feel that it is nevertheless an important sub-process which comes into prominence especially in the longer therapies.

What is then the role of the therapist's transparency when transference reactions are worked through in client-centered therapy? Here are some thoughts. The emphasis is not on working to achieve insight, which consists of recognizing and psychogenetically understanding why and how the client distorts the therapist and relates to him in a structure-bound way, but on the corrective emotional experience:

> It isn't enough that the patient *repeats* with the therapist his maladjusted feelings and ways of setting up interpersonal situations. After all, the patient is said to repeat these with everyone in his life, and not only with the therapist. Thus, the sheer repeating, even when it is a concrete reliving, doesn't yet resolve anything. Somehow, with the therapist, the patient doesn't *only* repeat; he gets *beyond* the repeating. He doesn't only *re*live; he lives *further*, if he resolves problems experientially (Gendlin, 1968, p. 222).

This 'further living' sometimes requires more than neutral benevolence (Wachtel, 1987). It requires the therapist not to present himself as a blank screen but — apart from, and in addition to, his empathic interventions — to deal in a transparent way, at the right moment, with what lives in the interaction between the two of them, and hereby to express his version of the interaction. Thus, the therapist may question the client's image of him by putting his own experience next to it. He may give the client feedback about his way of dealing with him and about the feelings he evokes in him. Where needed, he makes his own limits explicitly known: indeed the client can 'discuss' anything; he cannot just do anything. In order to perform this interactional work properly, a therapist should pay special attention to what happens *between* him and his client, to the relationship aspect of the communication; and he should keep in touch with what the client 'does to him'. In Yalom's words, the here-and-now feelings are to the experienced therapist 'as useful as a microscope to the microbiologist' (1995, p. 159). We also find this view in the humanistic branch of the psychoanalytic school, where the 'countertransference' is not seen as a 'crack in the mirror', but as an aid in the analytic work (Wachtel, 1987). Obviously we could find here a link with the interactional approach in which metacommunication about the here-and-now relation between client and therapist is the preferential focus as proposed by Kiesler and Van Denburg (1993) as well as by van Kessel and Lietaer (1998).

2.4. The use of self: suggestions for practice

What can a therapist reveal and what not? And at what moment can this best be done? Rogers dismisses this question — perhaps wisely — with the very general answer '... when appropriate' (1962, p. 417). Wachtel too, a psychoanalyst, writes in the same vein: 'I wish there were hard and fast rules about when exactly such self-revelations are helpful. Unfortunately, there are none ... ' (1987, p. 183). We are thus thrown back on our general clinical feeling and our common sense. This does not mean, however, that there are no guidelines. Indeed, there is the basic criterion which always goes back to the following question: does our self-revelation serve the client's growth process? (Yalom, 1980, p. 414.) Can our client use and integrate this information? In other words, we are talking here about a transparency with responsibility, and this includes right away the presence of important restrictions. As therapists, we have to withhold what does not help the client, and this is a lot. Yalom illustrates this basic principle with a touching story about two famous healers, taken from a book by Hermann Hesse.

> Joseph, one of the healers, severely afflicted with feelings of worthlessness and self-doubt, sets off on a long journey to seek help from his rival, Dion. At an oasis Joseph described his plight to a stranger, who turns out to be Dion; whereupon Joseph accepts Dion's invitation to go home with him in the role of patient and servant. In time Joseph regains his former serenity, zest, and effectance and becomes the friend and colleague of his master. Only after many years have passed and Dion lies on his deathbed does he reveal to Joseph that when the latter encountered him at the oasis, he, Dion, had reached a similar impasse in his life and was en route to request Joseph's assistance (Yalom, 1995, p. 214).

From this focus on the client's growth process follows that the therapist will only exceptionally mention facts from his personal life. But 'exceptionally' does not mean 'never'. A therapist can thus, as said earlier, reveal something about himself as a way of showing empathy. Also, when a personal event in his life comes to weigh heavily on his therapeutic work (such as the death of an important person), it may be better to mention it. And what if the client asks us for our personal philosophy of life, our lifestyle or our values? Obviously, we should be very careful here and explore, with the client, the precise meaning of his question. In most cases the client is not really interested in the therapist, but such questions may be situated within the search for a solution to a personal problem, or within a specific relational context. Our attention should thus go in that direction. Client-centered therapists generally refrain from giving 'personal testimony', in my opinion for good reason: indeed, the client has to find his own way. But one thing does not always exclude another. We should not forget that clients often obtain indirect clues as to 'how we live our lives' and that we can never totally escape a modeling role. This is not wrong in itself, at least not if we can bring the client to becoming independent from it. If we succeed in this, the client gradually comes to see his therapist as 'a fellow pilgrim' (Yalom, 1980, p. 407), with whom and against whom he can clarify his own choices. This happens mostly towards the end of therapy, i.e. in the existential phase (Swildens, 1997, p. 69), in which the client has reached the point where he can choose freely.

As will be clear from what I said before, self-revelation has seldom anything to do with the therapist's personal past or present life. But what can the therapist then reveal? The answer is obvious: his feelings towards the client in the here-and-now, towards what happens in the session between both of them. Here, too, the therapist remains sober. Only 'persisting' feelings count, and besides, the therapist has to ask himself if the moment is appropriate. There is thus a problem of 'timing': is there a chance for the client to be sufficiently receptive to my feedback about how I experience the interaction, or should other therapeutic tasks take precedence? Sometimes the relationship has not yet acquired enough security and solidity, and this should be worked on first. In moments of great vulnerability, empathic closeness is perhaps all that is needed. Sometimes, the client may first need a chance to fully express his feelings towards the 'symbolic' figure of the therapist, without immediately being 'stopped' by a confrontation with the 'reality' of how the therapist experiences it himself . . . But occasionally, the therapist's experience of the interaction may be the most fruitful approach to deepening the process.

Besides the question of what can be said and when, we also should address the one about how to communicate our own experiences in the most constructive way. Here are some suggestions from the client-centered/experiential literature: Boukydis, 1979; Brodley, 1999; Carkhuff and Berenson, 1977; Gendlin, 1967b; Gendlin, 1968, pp. 220–5; Kiesler, 1982; Rennie, 1998, pp. 60–70 and 89–101; Rogers, 1970, pp. 53–7). All illustrate how important it is that the therapist's self-expressive interventions be supported by the basic attitudes. The close bond with congruence is obvious: the feeling for what happens in the relationship, the interactional barometer, thus, should function properly! This presupposes among other things a close contact with one's own flow of experiencing and the meanings which it may contain, sufficient awareness of what may be one's personal contribution to the difficulties arising in the relationship, and when needed, sufficient openness to facing the issue in question (so it would not become a battle about who is right), being capable of communicating one's experience in a process-compatible way, i.e. in all its complexity and changingness. As an example of the latter, Rogers describes how a therapist can communicate 'boredom':

> But my feeling exists in the context of a complex and changing flow, which also needs to be communicated. I would like to share with him my distress at feeling

bored and my discomfort in expressing it. As I do, I find that my boredom arises from my sense of remoteness from him and that I would like to be in closer touch with him; and even as I try to express these feelings they change. I am certainly not bored as I await with eagerness, and perhaps a bit of apprehension, for his response. I also feel a new sensitivity to him now that I have shared this feeling which has been a barrier between us. I am far more able to hear the surprise, or perhaps the hurt, in his voice as he now finds himself speaking more genuinely because I have dared to be real with him (1966, p. 185).

Along with this, there is the link with unconditional positive regard. Self-expressive confrontations are most effective when embedded in, and communicated out of, deep involvement with the person of the client. Consequently, it is important for the therapist not to let negative feelings accumulate for too long, so as to remain sufficiently open to the client. He further has to let it be known clearly that his feelings have to do with a specific behaviour of the client's, and not with the client as a person. Therefore, the therapist's feedback should be as explicit and concrete as possible: how the feeling took shape and what precisely in the client's way of interacting has brought it on. Perhaps most importantly, the therapist should remain focused on the positive life-tendencies behind the client's disturbing behaviour and behind his own negative feelings, and communicate these as well. Thus, in our earlier example, Rogers communicates the inside, the reason for his boredom, which is his desire for more contact with the client. When we give a client feedback about a behaviour which irritates us, we try to get in touch with the needs and positive intentions behind it, and include these in our discussion. Gendlin gives the following example of this, pertaining to setting limits:

For example, I might not let a patient touch me or grab me. I will stop the patient, but in the same words and gesture I will try to respond positively to the positive desire for closeness or physical relations. I will make personal touch with my hand as I hold the patient away from me, contact the patient's eyes, and declare that I think the physical reaching out is positive and I welcome it, even though I cannot allow it. (I know at such times that I may be partly creating this positive aspect. Perhaps this reaching is more hostile, right now, than warm. But there is warmth and health in anyone's sexual or physical need, and I can recognize that as such.) (1967b, p. 397).

Finally, we should always take care in maintaining the process sufficiently client-centered and making it a 'self-revelation without imposition'. It should happen in a true spirit of dialogue. This can best be done by letting the influencing occur as openly as possible. Two 'rules of communication' should be remembered here. The first one, to use Rogers' words, is 'owning' or giving I-messages instead of you-messages: the therapist indicates clearly that he is the source of the experience and tries above all to communicate what he himself feels, rather than making evaluative statements about the client. He will, for example, not say 'How intrusive of you' but 'When you called me for the second time this week, I felt put under pressure and as if taken possession of . . . '. The second rule of

51

communication is, in Gendlin's words, 'always checking' or 'openness to what comes next': after each response — and especially after one which originated in our own frame of reference — tuning in anew to the client's experiential track and continuing from there. This implies, as Rennie writes: ' . . . readiness to negotiate, to pull back, to reconsider, or to dismiss the reaction, depending on how it is received by the client' (1998, p. 69).

All these suggestions should make it clear that constructive self-revelation is far removed from acting-out. It is rather a form of 'disciplined spontaneity' which, along and together with empathy, constitutes a second line from which the client can evolve towards a 'further living' inside and outside of therapy, towards new and more satisfactory ways of dealing with himself and others. Mistakes may, of course, occur if self-revelation is used rather carelessly, but to leave out this important reservoir of relationship information could be equally detrimental: an omission which could lead to substantial reduction in quality of the therapeutic process.

REFERENCES

Barrett-Lennard, G. T. (1962). Dimensions of therapist response as causal factors in therapeutic change. *Psychological Monographs, 76* (43, whole No. 562).

Boukydis, K. N. (1979). Caring and confronting. *Voices. The Art and Science of Psychotherapy, 15*, pp. 31–4.

Bozarth, J. D. (1984). Beyond reflection: Emergent modes of empathy. In R. F. Levant and J. M. Shlien (Eds.), *Client-centered therapy and the person-centered approach: New directions in theory, research and practice* (pp. 59–5). New York: Praeger.

Brodley, B. T. (1998). Congruence and its relation to communication in client-centered therapy. *The Person-Centered Journal, 5*(2), pp. 83–106.

Brodley, B. T. (1999). Reasons for responses expressing the therapist's frame of reference in client-centered therapy. *The Person-Centered Journal, 6*(1), pp. 4–27.

Buber, M., and Rogers, C. R. (1957). Dialogue between Martin Buber and Carl Rogers. In H. Kirschenbaum and V. L. Anderson (1989), *Carl Rogers: Dialogues* (pp. 41–63). Boston: Houghton Mifflin.

Carkhuff, R. R., and Berenson, B. G. (1977). In search of an honest experience: Confrontation in counseling and life. In R. R. Carkhuff and B. G. Berenson, *Beyond counseling and therapy* (pp. 198–213). New York: Holt, Rinehart and Winston.

Ellingham, I. H. (1999). Carl Rogers' 'Congruence' as an organismic; not a Freudian concept. *The Person-Centered Journal, 6*(2), pp. 121–40.

Finke, J. (1994). *Empathie und Interaktion. Methodik und Praxis der Gesprächspsychotherapie.* Stuttgart: Thieme.

Gendlin, E. T. (1967a). Subverbal communication and therapist expressivity: Trends in client-centered therapy with schizophrenics. In C. R. Rogers and B. Stevens (Eds.), *Person to person* (pp. 119–28). Lafayette, Ca: Real People Press.

Gendlin, E. T. (1967b). Therapeutic procedures in dealing with schizophrenics. In C. Rogers et al. (Eds.), *The therapeutic relationship and its impact: A study of psychotherapy with schizophrenics* (pp. 369–400). Madison: University of Wisconsin Press.

Gendlin, E. T. (1968). The experiential response. In E. F. Hammer (Ed.), *Use of interpretation in therapy: Technique and art* (pp. 208–27). New York: Grune and Stratton.

Gendlin, E. T. (1970). A short summary and some long predictions. In J. T. Hart and T. M. Tomlinson (Eds.), *New directions in client-centered therapy* (pp. 544–62). Boston: Houghton Mifflin.

Giovacchini, P. L. (1989). *Countertransference, triumphs and catastrophes.* Northvale/New Jersey/London: Jason Aronson.

Haugh, S. (1998). Congruence: A confusion of language. *Person-Centred Practice, 6*(1), pp. 44–

50.

Kiesler, D. J. (1982). Confronting the client-therapist relationship in psychotherapy. In J. C. Anchin and D. J. Kiesler, *Handbook of interpersonal psychotherapy* (pp. 274–95). New York: Pergamon.

Kiesler, D. J., and Van Denburg, T. F. (1993). Therapeutic impact disclosure: a last taboo in psychoanalytic theory and practice. *Clinical Psychology and Psychotherapy, 1,* pp. 3–13.

Kinget, M. (1959). Deel, I. Algemene presentatie. In C. R. Rogers and M. Kinget, *Psychotherapie en menselijke verhoudingen* (pp. 11–171). Utrecht/Antwerpen: Spectrum and Standaard.

Leijssen, M. (1998). De therapeut. In W. Trijsburg, S. Colijn, E. Collumbien, and G. Lietaer, (Eds.), *Handboek Integratieve Psychotherapie. Inventarisatie en perspectief* (pp. I 2. 1–37). Leusden: De Tijdstroom.

Lietaer, G. (1992). Helping and hindering processes in client-centered/experiential psychotherapy. A content analysis of client and therapist postsession perceptions. In S. G. Toukmanian and D. L. Rennie (Eds.), *Psychotherapy process research. Paradigm and narrative approaches* (pp. 134–62). Newbury Park: Sage.

Lietaer, G. (1998). From non-directive to experiential: A paradigm unfolding. In B. Thorne and E. Lambers (Eds.), *Person-centred therapy. A European perspective* (pp. 62–73). London: Sage.

Lietaer, G., Rombauts, J., and Van Balen, R. (Eds.). (1990). *Client-centered and experiential psychotherapy in the nineties.* Leuven: Leuven University Press.

McConnaughy, E. A. (1987). The person of the therapist in psychotherapeutic practice. *Psychotherapy, 24,* pp. 303–14.

Mearns, D. (1997). *Person-centred counselling training.* London: Sage.

Pfeiffer, W. M. (1987). Uebertragung und Realbeziehung in der Sicht klientenzentrierter Psychotherapie. *Zeitschrift für personenzentrierte Psychologie und Psychotherapie, 6,* pp. 347–52.

Rennie, D. L. (1998). *Person-centred counselling: An experiential approach.* London: Sage.

Rice, L. N. (1974). The evocative function of the therapist. In D. A. Wexler, and L. N. Rice (Eds.), *Innovations in client-centered therapy* (pp. 289–311). New York: Wiley.

Rogers, C. R. (1951). *Client-centered therapy.* Boston: Houghton Mifflin.

Rogers, C. R. (1957). The necessary and sufficient conditions of therapeutic personality change. *Journal of Consulting Psychology, 21,* pp. 97–103.

Rogers, C. R. (1961). *On becoming a person.* Boston: Houghton Mifflin.

Rogers, C. R. (1962). The interpersonal relationship: The core of guidance. *Harvard Educational Review, 32,* pp. 416–29.

Rogers, C. R. (1966). Client-centered therapy. In S. Arieti (Ed.), *American Handbook of Psychiatry* (Vol. 3, pp. 183–200). New York: Basic Books.

Rogers, C. R. (1967a). Some learnings from a study of psychotherapy with schizophrenics. In C. R. Rogers and B. Stevens (Eds.), *Person to person* (pp. 181–91). Lafayette, Ca: Real People Press.

Rogers, C. R. (1967b). A silent young man. In C. R. Rogers et al. (Eds.). (1967a), *o.c.* (pp. 401–16).

Rogers, C. R. (1970). *On encounter groups.* New York: Harper and Row.

Rogers, C. R. (1986). Carl Rogers' Column: Reflection of feelings. *Person-Centered Review, 1,* pp. 375–77.

Rogers, C. R., Gendlin, E.T., Kiesler, D.J, and Truax, C.B. (Eds.). (1967a). *The therapeutic relationship and its impact: A study of psychotherapy with schizophrenics.* Madison: University of Wisconsin Press.

Rogers, C. R. et al. (1967b). A dialogue between therapists. In C. R. Rogers et al. (Eds.). (1967a), *o.c.* (pp. 507–20).

Rombauts, J. (1984). Empathie: actieve ontvankelijkheid. In G. Lietaer, Ph. van Praag, and J. C. A. G. Swildens (Eds.), *Client-centered psychotherapie in beweging* (pp. 167–76). Leuven: Acco.

Schmid, P. (1998). Face to face. The art of encounter. In B. Thorne and E. Lambers (Eds.), *Person-centred therapy: A European perspective* (pp. 74–90). London: Sage.

Shlien, J. (1987). A countertheory of transference. *Person-Centered Review, 2,* pp. 15–49. (commentary: 153–202/455–75).

Strean, H. S. (Ed.). (1986). *Countertransference.* New York/London: The Haworth Press.

Swildens, H. (1997). *Procesgerichte gesprekstherapie. Inleiding tot een gedifferentieerde toepassing van de cliëntgerichte beginselen bij de behandeling van psychische stoornissen.* Leusden: De Tijdstroom.

Tudor, K., and Worrall, M. (1994). Congruence reconsidered. *British Journal of Guidance and Counselling, 22*(2), pp. 197–206.

Vanaerschot, G. (1990). The process of empathy: Holding and letting go. In G. Lietaer, J. Rombauts, and R. Van Balen (Eds.). *o.c.* (pp. 269–93).

Vanaerschot, G. (1997). Empathic resonance as a source of experience-enhancing interventions. In A. Bohart and L. S. Greenberg (Eds.), *Empathy reconsidered. New directions in psychotherapy* (pp. 141–65). Washington, D.C.: APA.

Van Balen, R. (1990). The therapeutic relationship according to Carl Rogers: Only a climate? A dialogue? Or both? In G. Lietaer, J. Rombauts, and R. Van Balen (Eds.), *o.c.* (pp. 65–86).

van Kessel, W., and Lietaer, G. (1998). Interpersonal processes. In L. S. Greenberg, J. C. Watson, and G. Lietaer (Eds.), *Handbook of experiential psychotherapy* (pp. 155–77). New York, NY, USA: Guilford.

Wachtel, P. L. (1979). Contingent and non-contingent therapist response. *Psychotherapy: Theory, Research and Practice, 16,* pp. 30–5.

Wachtel, P. L. (1987). You can't go far in neutral: On the limits of therapeutic neutrality. In P. L. Wachtel, *Action and insight* (pp. 176–84). New York: Guilford.

Wilkins, P. (1997). Congruence and countertransference: Similarities and differences. *Counselling, 8*(1), pp. 36–41.

Wolstein, B. (Ed.). (1988). *Essential papers on countertransference.* New York and London: New York University Press.

Wyatt, G. (2000). The multifaceted nature of congruence within the therapeutic relationship. *The Person-Centered Journal, 7*(1), pp. 52–68.

Yalom, I. D. (1980). *Existential Psychotherapy.* New York: Basic Books.

Yalom, I. D. (1995). *Theory and Practice of group psychotherapy.* (Rev. ed.). New York: Basic Books.

4   Congruence and its Relation to Communication in Client-Centered Therapy

Barbara Temaner Brodley

Lack of attention to the theoretical definition of congruence, and the practice of misidentifying congruence as candor, leads to distortions in client-centered therapy and in person-centered group situations. In individual and other forms of client-centered therapy, the distortion shows up when therapists systematically state their own reactions to, or thoughts about, clients and justify the practice as a form of living the therapeutic attitude of congruence in the relationship. In regard to peer groups, the distortion appears when interpretations, accusations and insulting communications are justified as 'being congruent'. It is necessary to grasp the theoretical definition of congruence in order to have an accurate picture of client-centered therapy (Haugh, 1998). In particular, according to Rogers, communications relating to congruence have specific restrictive and therapeutically relevant characteristics.

In this paper I shall attempt a partial exegesis of Rogers' writings on the concepts of congruence and experience. Understanding Rogers' definition of experience is necessary for understanding congruence. I shall also explain a theoretical basis for client-centered therapists (and practitioners of other applications of the person-centered approach) to adopt an attitude that leads to particular forms of communication relating to their congruence.

THE MEANING OF CONGRUENCE

The meaning of congruence in Rogers' writings changed somewhat over the years, and the different versions can provide rationales for different interpretations and applications of the concept. In effect, the precise meaning of congruence remains somewhat ambiguous. Additionally, Rogers' theory of therapy (1957, 1959) and his theory of interpersonal relationships (1959) present different functions of congruence. Thus, Rogers provided the grounds for different interpretations of the concept and for different roles for congruence in psychotherapy and in work with groups within the client-centered framework.

Rogers did not use the terms 'congruence' or 'incongruence' at all in his 1951 book, which introduced client-centered therapy. He did define adjustment and maladjustment in terms that he later used in his definitions of congruence and

First published in *The Person-Centered Journal* 1998, 5(2), pp. 83–116. Reprinted with kind permission of the publisher and editor.

incongruence. Rogers (1951) defines adjustment in his chapter presenting a theory of personality and behavior in his proposition XV:

> Psychological adjustment exists when the concept of the self is such that all the sensory and visceral experiences of the organism are, or may be, assimilated on a symbolic level into a consistent relationship with the concept of self (p. 513).

Proposition XIV expresses Rogers' definition of maladjustment:

> Psychological maladjustment exists when the organism denies to awareness significant sensory and visceral experiences, which consequently are not symbolized and organized into the gestalt of the self-structure. When this situation exists, there is a basic or potential psychological tension (p. 510).

In the definitions of congruence above, Rogers refers to a person's openness to awareness of all organismic valuing experiences occurring at a given moment such that the person can accurately symbolize the experiences. The meaning Rogers gives to experience, in both definitions, involves sensory and visceral events that are amenable to consciousness. Experience does not refer to events that are inevitably and permanently unconscious.

The term 'adjustment' and the term 'congruence', appear to refer to the same phenomena. They refer to the capability for, and the activity of, accurate symbolization of experiences in awareness. In Rogers' theory of therapy (1957, 1959), congruence is defined differently than adjustment only in the sense that it refers to more temporary and situational states. In the theory of therapy, congruence is characterized as one of the three qualities that the therapist experiences in order to contribute to clients' therapeutic change.

In Rogers' generic theory (1957, 1959), the role of congruence is stated in the third of his six necessary and sufficient conditions for therapeutic personality change as follows:

> The second person, whom we shall term the therapist, is congruent or integrated in the relationship (1957, p. 96).

Rogers explains therapeutic congruence as follows:

> ... the therapist should be, within the confines of this relationship, a congruent, genuine, integrated person. It means that within the relationship he is freely and deeply himself, with his actual experience accurately represented by his awareness of himself ... It should be clear that this includes being himself even in ways which are not regarded as ideal for psychotherapy. His experience may be 'I am afraid of this client' or 'My attention is so focused on my own problems that I can scarcely listen to him'. If the therapist is not denying these feelings to awareness, but is able freely to be them (as well as being other feelings), then the condition (congruence) we have stated is met (1957, p. 97).

This explanation of congruence emphasizes the therapist's personal as well as personality *integration*, in the context of the therapy relation. Keeping this emphasis, Rogers (1959) defines congruence:

> ... when self-experiences are accurately symbolized (in awareness), and are included in the self-concept in this accurately symbolized form, then the state

is one of congruence of self and experience ... terms which are synonymous ...
[are] integrated, whole, genuine (1959, p. 206).

Congruence is thus theoretically defined in terms of Rogers' distinction between self and experience, not in terms of the therapist's behavior. In the theory of therapy, in both the first and second published forms, Rogers (1957, 1959) asserts that for successful therapy to take place, only the therapist's conditions of unconditional positive regard and empathic understanding must be perceived by the client. (Thus they must be communicated or expressed by the therapist.) In neither theoretical statement is it posited that the client must perceive the therapist's congruence. This implies it *need not* be communicated, although it is a necessary condition for therapy.

Congruence is a condition for therapy in the sense that it must be a state or condition *within the therapist.* This state permits the therapist to succeed in his intentions to experience unconditional positive regard and empathic understanding in relation to a client. It does so by permitting the therapist to experience an unconflicted and undistracted dedication to acceptant empathy.

The state of congruence also refers to the therapist's subjective, inner condition as one that results in an appearance of authenticity or transparency. The therapist's integrated, authentic appearance facilitates the client's clear and trustworthy perceptions of the therapist's attitudes of unconditional positive regard and empathic understanding.

Congruence refers to wholeness and integration within, or of, oneself. The congruent therapist's openness to accurate awareness and symbolization of experience is the 'ground' or 'field' which underlies and coexists with the salient 'figure' of the attitudes of unconditional positive regard and empathic understanding. Rogers states the connection between congruence and the other two therapeutic attitudes as follows:

... for therapy to occur the wholeness of the therapist in the relationship is primary, but a part of the congruence must be the experience of unconditional positive regard and the experience of empathic understanding (Rogers, 1959, p. 215).

In order to understand how congruence in client-centered therapy functions in real therapy practice, it is important to understand Rogers' general position about the continua of the three therapeutic conditions. Rogers (1957) asserts that the three therapist conditions, which are all subjective states and attitudes, are not absolutes, but occur on continua. His theory predicts that to the extent the therapist experiences these three therapeutic attitudes while with the client, and if the client perceives the unconditional positive regard and the empathic understanding, to that extent the client will experience therapeutic change.

The therapist (or other kind of practitioner) experiences the therapeutic attitudes only to some degree, not absolutely, in a relationship. The totality of all of the therapist conditions occurs more or less frequently, but not constantly, in any given therapy encounter. The conditions must be present to some degree for therapy to be effective, and the specific degree required is probably dependent upon the needs of the individual client.

In practice, the coexistence of congruence, unconditional positive regard and a pure *intention* to empathically understand (with some inaccuracies in specific understanding from time to time), may function as effectively for many clients as does the pure intention fulfilled by perfectly accurate empathic understanding. In any case, Rogers' theory does not require absolute constancy of the therapeutic conditions for effective therapy to take place. In fact, Rogers does not consider constancy of the therapeutic conditions to be a human possibility. He states, for example, in relation to congruence:

> It is not to be expected that the therapist is a completely congruent person at all times. Indeed if this were a necessary condition there would be no therapy. But it is enough if in this particular moment of this immediate relationship with this specific person he is completely and fully himself, with his experience of the moment being accurately symbolized and integrated into the picture he holds of himself. Thus it is that imperfect human beings can be of therapeutic assistance to other imperfect human beings (Rogers, 1959, p. 215).

Given the inevitable imperfections of therapists in providing the therapeutic conditions, a question then arises. If a therapist has a choice about it when functioning imperfectly, which therapeutic condition has priority over the others?

Rogers asserts that the most important therapeutic condition, the one to be given priority, is congruence (1959, p. 215). In practical terms, the therapist should attend to his feelings if he realizes he is functioning imperfectly. If, at moments, the therapist is not unconditionally accepting or not empathically understanding, he should attend to these experiences and allow accurate symbolization of these experiences in his awareness.

For example, a therapist's congruent experience during a therapy session may include experiences of failing to empathically understand. A lapse in empathy might occur because the therapist is distracted from the client's internal frame of reference. Alternatively, such a lapse might occur because the therapist is experiencing a personal agenda for the client. The therapist's experience of congruence during a session might include experiences of feeling judgmental or critical or disapproving instead of feeling unconditional acceptance towards his client. In the instance of judgmental feelings, Rogers' opinion is that the therapist should remain open and attentive to his own experiences. The therapist should accurately symbolize them to self, rather than deny such experiences to awareness or distort them in awareness and, as a consequence, become incongruent. Denial or distortion in awareness of experiences results in the therapist being unintegrated and not whole, not congruent, in the therapy relationship.

In therapy practice, momentary distractions or momentary judgmental thoughts and reactions, if accurately symbolized in awareness, can be recognized and *accepted* by the therapist who gives priority to his own congruence. They are simply moments during which one of the therapeutic attitudinal conditions are not experienced. They are instances of personal fallibility and are material for introspection or consultation.

For example, a therapist is distracted from empathic attention to the client and the client's narrative by preoccupation with a family problem. Consequently, the therapist is not engaging in empathic understanding of the client at those moments. The client, however, may be continuing to perceive the therapist as empathic. The therapist becomes aware of being distracted, accepts the lapse and refocuses attention empathically towards the client. In this scenario, the therapist has temporarily failed to empathically understand, has remained acceptant towards the client, is self-acceptant and is congruent. To the extent that there was a lapse in empathic understanding, the therapist did not experience all of the therapeutic conditions. The therapy is assumed to be less effective for that client during the moments of lapse.

The most important thing to keep in mind concerning congruence is that it is a *relation*, not an entity or a content of experience. Rogers refers to congruence in terms of an integrated state or wholeness of the person. That is a holistic way of referring to how crucial aspects of the person are related to each other. The theoretical definition of congruence as accurate representation of experience by inner symbols is about the *relation* between the contents of experience and the symbols representing the contents. The congruence is the relation, not the contents. Similarly, as congruence is a state, it is a state defined by the relation between parts of the person.

CONGRUENCE IN REGARD TO COMMUNICATION

The issue of congruence in regard to communication arises practically in certain situations. One situation is when the therapist is congruent but not experiencing unconditional positive regard or empathic understanding. For example, the therapist experiences irritation in reaction to something the client has said. This experience is contrary to unconditional positive regard. Under what circumstances and in what way should the therapist tell the client about his nonacceptant feelings? Rogers acknowledges 'the puzzling matter as to the degree to which the therapist overtly communicates this reality in himself to the client' (1957, pp. 97–8). He further remarks:

> Certainly the aim is not for the therapist to express or talk out his own feelings,
> but primarily that he should not be deceiving the client as to himself (p. 98).

The aim is to *not deceive* the client. But the therapist also does not want to interfere with the client's own narrative and self-exploration or become the focus of the interaction if it is not for the client's benefit. There are two practical variables in this issue, particularly if the nontherapeutic experience occurs only briefly. One has to do with the extent to which the particular therapist's inner reactions are telegraphed in facial expressions, in other gestures, or in tone of voice. The second is the extent to which the particular client is attuned to the therapist's nonverbal expressions.

In the case of many therapists, their momentary distractions or preoccupations or momentary unacceptant reactions cannot be perceived or detected by an observer. They remain private. The therapist may be inhibiting expression or not. An inhibited therapist may be perceived as transparent. Obscurity of inner reactions, however, need not result from the therapist trying to inhibit or control his expressiveness. The therapist who does not telegraph momentary inner states may be relaxed and unguarded. Such a person simply does not tend to manifest brief or undramatic vicissitudes of inner life when self-acceptant about them. Even the highly attuned client is unlikely to be able to perceive such passing inner reactions, if the therapist who has private reactions remains self-acceptant and congruent when experiencing counter-therapeutic subjective reactions.

Authenticity does not require the therapist to be free of the variety of evaluative reactions that are characteristic of subjective experience. Nor does it imply the therapist's inner experiences are not inherently private in the therapy context. The contents of subjective awareness are fleeting, evaluative and varied. There could be no personal authenticity if it required a simplicity and constancy of inner reactions. Logically, authenticity must involve a person having acceptance toward, and perspectives on, the inherent variety and the evaluative nature, of subjective life (Bargh, Chaiken, Raymond and Hymes, 1995; Bargh, 1997).

The second variable is the degree of client attunement to therapist expressiveness. For example, the therapist frowns slightly, realizing he does not understand something the client is expressing. The client perceives this and interprets it as disapproval, or at least as a puzzling contrast to the acceptance she is accustomed to and upon which she depends in the therapy relationship. The interaction that occurs subsequent to this situation depends upon the client's ability to question the therapist or upon the therapist's awareness of his own expressive display. Sometimes a client feels able to ask about the therapist's feelings. The therapist, in aiming to be consistent with Rogers' dictum 'that he should not be deceiving the client as to himself', might respond by disclosing his inner experience.

An alternative situation occurs when a client does not ask the question. In this situation, the therapist is aware that the spontaneous, expressive behavior was likely to be perceived and experienced by the client as disturbing to the client. Then, in aiming to be consistent with the general client-centered aim to communicate clearly to clients, as well as with Rogers' dictum to not deceive, the therapist might choose to disclose inner experience. The reason would be one of wanting to be clear and unambiguous to the client. The therapist wants to correct for the ambiguity that may have been created.

A relaxed and congruent therapist is unlikely to telegraph momentary and fleeting, nontherapeutic, subjective feelings or thoughts into his involuntary expressive behavior. The congruent therapist, however, might choose to communicate about such thoughts or feelings if they happen to have been involuntarily expressed and perceived by a client. The aim in communicating about them would be to correct for an appearance of ambiguity that might have confused or disturbed the client. The characteristics of such communications are extremely important and will be discussed later.

Therapists may also have persistent nontherapeutic experiences when interacting with their clients. Rogers (1957) addresses these situations. Referring to the therapist, he states:

> At times he may need to talk out some of his own feelings [either to the client, or to a colleague, or supervisor] if they are standing in the way of . . . [acceptance and empathy] . . .' (p. 98).

60

Much later, in an interview (Baldwin, 1987), Rogers dropped mention of talking first with colleagues or supervisors and stated:

> When I am with a client, I like to be aware of my feelings, and if there are feelings which run contrary to the conditions of therapy and *occur persistently*, then I am sure I want to express them . . . [to the client] (p. 46).

These statements, particularly the latter one, *appear* to imply that Rogers (or any therapist choosing to follow Rogers' theory and guidance) can responsibly say what he is thinking or feeling to his clients (as that is usually understood) when persistently not experiencing unconditional positive regard or empathic understanding. This meaning seems very unlikely, given the fundamental value of respect and acceptance towards clients that underlies client-centered work. Rogers' statement 'I am sure I would want to express them' does not necessarily mean he would simply say what he thinks or feels to his clients under the circumstances of persistent nontherapeutic feelings. The reason for his wanting to express his feelings to his clients must have to do with fostering the therapeutic relationship and benefiting the client under these imperfect therapist conditions. In this light, it would seem that Rogers' statement, 'I want to express them', refers to having an interaction with the client that might correct for or compensate for the lapse in therapeutic conditions.

Rogers is referring to new moments in the relationship that occur after the therapist's counter-therapeutic experiences. For example, in respect to annoyed reactions to a client or after becoming distracted. The new moments include the therapist's accurate symbolization in awareness (i.e., congruence about the counter-therapeutic experiences) and some communication about the contents of that awareness. They also include the therapist's therapeutic intentions to acceptantly and empathically understand. In these new moments of intention to voice feelings, the therapist would aim to be consistent with a fundamental part of the therapeutic theory:

> . . . a part of the congruence of the therapist must be the experience of unconditional positive regard and the experience of empathic understanding (Rogers, 1959, p. 215).

At the moments of addressing the client to disclose his counter-therapeutic feelings he would also be in touch with both the counter-therapeutic subjective reality and his more pervasive attitudes of acceptant empathy. Or at least he would be in touch with his *intentions* to relate to the client with acceptant empathic understanding. The therapist's manner of addressing the client would be influenced by those intentions. Thus, the thoughts and feelings would not be communicated in an undisciplined manner — one that might hurt or threaten the client.

There are several possible beneficial consequences that may result when the therapist chooses to communicate persistent counter-therapeutic feelings to his client. First, the communication process that ensues between therapist and client can, and often does, dispel the therapist's discordant feelings, distraction, etc. For example, imagine the situation when the therapist has been feeling annoyed by a client who has corrected the therapist's empathic responses. Perhaps the therapist is interpreting the client to be critical of the therapist for not having accurately understood. Something in the client's tone of voice seems to the therapist to betray an unspoken irritation or criticism. If the therapist's annoyance is persistent and he consequently chooses, as Rogers would, to acknowledge those feelings, the interaction might lead to clarification of the client's behavior.

The client's ambiguous behavior might reveal the client's own frustration about not communicating more effectively. If this is what the therapist learns from the client, reoccurrence of the client's previously annoying behavior can be given the correct interpretation — the client's discomfort with self. As a consequence of that knowledge, the therapist no longer perceives criticism and is not annoyed. The therapist also has a better general empathic understanding of the client as a result of the interaction.

Therapist disclosure of counter-therapeutic feelings specifically may result also in a deeper empathic understanding of the client's feelings about the therapist. Using the same example, the therapist's disclosure leads to the client's disclosure that she has been feeling irritated at the therapist, but not because of his inaccurate responses. Assuming the therapist's capacity for an acceptant understanding of this fact, it might well lead to an opening up of feelings and thoughts about the therapist and the client's disappointed expectations of the therapist. Or it might lead down another path, towards the client's phenomenology of expectations and disappointments. There are many possibilities, but in any case, the therapist's empathic knowledge of the client may be deepened as the result of his disclosure of annoyance. Additionally, renewed understanding dispels the therapist's annoyance.

Another beneficial result that may be served by a therapist's disclosure of counter-therapeutic feelings, is that the disclosure may contribute to the therapist's transparence. Rogers introduced the term 'transparent' to refer to the therapist's congruent, acceptant and understanding presence that makes possible the client's perceptions of him as whole, authentic and trustworthy (Rogers, 1961, p. 49, p. 339). Lietaer (1993) interprets transparency as referring to the therapist's self-disclosing communications. I differ with Lietaer and interpret the concept of transparence similarly to Haugh (1998), as a characteristic perceived by the client that is likely to result from the therapist's congruent state. It most often does not involve therapist self-disclosures, although it may involve them. Rogers (1980) stated that a therapist is transparent when the therapist:

> . . . is openly being the feelings and attitudes that are flowing within at the moment . . . the client can see right through what the therapist **is** in the relationship; the client experiences *no holding back* on the part of the therapist (p. 115).

The value of the therapist's transparence in clients' perceptions is its contribution to the therapist's perceived trustworthiness and dependability. Transparence contributes to the client's perception of the therapist's authenticity when the therapist appears to be acceptantly empathic. Returning to the earlier example of the client's experience of the therapist's disclosure of annoyance (assuming this is done in an therapeutic manner): because it reveals a negative response, it may reassure the client that the therapist's negative feelings, if and when they come up, will be brought out. Thus the client can trust the authenticity of the therapist's appearance of acceptance.

At about the same time (circa 1961) that Rogers introduces the term 'transparence' as an aspect of congruence, he somewhat shifts the meaning of congruence to a looser definition, to that of matching. Rogers (1961) states:

> . . . [congruence] has been developed to cover a group of phenomena . . . to indicate an accurate matching of experiencing and awareness. It may be still further extended to cover a matching of experience, awareness and communication (p. 339).

His point is clear. Rogers states that the term 'congruence' refers not only to accurate symbolization in awareness of experiences, but it also refers to communication that accurately represents the accurate symbolization of experiences

Rogers has included the idea of matching communication to inner symbolization into the meaning of congruence. This is along with the prior matching of symbolization in awareness with experience that was implied by the idea that inner symbolization accurately represents experience. The term 'matching' could always have been used loosely in respect to the relation between experience and symbolization in awareness. 'Matching' is colloquial for accurate symbolizing of experience.

Previously, Rogers (1959) emphasized the theoretical bases of congruence in his theories of personality development, disintegration and reintegration. Also, in the therapy context, communication springing from congruence was limited to special circumstances of fleeting nontherapeutic experiences and especially to circumstances of persistent feelings counter to acceptance or empathic understanding. The contents of congruent experience were not referred to as congruence.

CONGRUENCE IN THE THEORY OF INTERPERSONAL RELATIONSHIPS

Rogers' shift to the term 'matching' in regard to congruence coincides with his second published discussion of his general law of interpersonal relationships (1961, pp. 338–46). He had not used the term, but his remarks carried the sense of 'matching' in the earlier statement of that theory (1959, pp. 234–40). In the earlier statement of that theory the matching meaning is revealed when Rogers refers to the *congruence* of distorted perceptions with the self-structure by a vulnerable person, in his discussion of a deteriorating relationship (1959, pp. 236–7):

> . . . Since X is vulnerable, he tends to perceive Y's responses as potentially threatening . . . Hence he tends to *perceive them in distorted fashion*, in ways which are *congruent* with his own self-structure (p. 237).

In this matching usage of the word 'congruent', Rogers implies that conditions of worth, affecting the self-structure, may result in distortions of a person's perceptions of external reality. This usage of 'congruent' can appear to be legitimately extrapolated into the idea that whether or not the symbolizations in awareness are distorted (in relation to experience), communication can be viewed as congruent communication when it matches symbolizations. This idea can be extended further to the view that *saying* whatever it is a person symbolizes to self at a given moment is an act of being congruent. It may be that this portion of Rogers' writings is what has led to the distortions in practice mentioned in my introduction.

Rogers also appears to be using the term 'congruent' to mean 'matching' (without using the term) in the first publication of his 'tentative law of interpersonal relationships' (1959, p. 240) a few pages after the last quote above. Rogers states the law, in part, as follows:

> [T]he greater the communicated congruence of experience, awareness, and behavior on the part of one individual, the more the ensuing relationship will involve a tendency toward reciprocal communication with the same qualities, mutually accurate understanding of the communications, improved psychological adjustment and functioning in both parties, and mutual satisfaction in the relationship (p. 240).

Rogers' wording in this statement is slightly ambiguous in so far as it suggests that the contents of experience, of awareness and behavior are congruence. This is not what Rogers must mean. Congruence always refers to a *relation* and careful reading of his wording suggests Rogers meant 'congruence' as the relation between experience, awareness and behavior. In the basic therapeutic meaning of congruence as 'integration' or 'wholeness', the meaning has to do with a harmonious and effective relation between various aspects of the person. In the strict definition, congruence refers to the accurate relation between the contents of experience and the symbols in awareness. In application to behavior, congruent communications refer to communications that accurately represent inner symbols — again a relation.

Note that *communication* of congruent experience is being given a leading role in Rogers' theory of interpersonal relationships. This is a deviation from the role of congruence in psychotherapy. In therapy, congruence is viewed as the most important therapeutic condition, but is meant as a description of the therapist's inner, subjective state or condition while he is acceptant and empathically understanding.

Returning to congruence in the interpersonal law. Rogers' theory predicates the possibility of distortion in a person's interpretation of external reality. Distortions may occur as a consequence of conditions of worth or as a consequence of the experience of threat. Perceptions of external reality, also, may be simply in error from the perspective of consensual validation. Regardless of the consensual validity of perceptions, persons are congruent if their symbols in awareness are accurate to the experienced perceptions. Accurate symbolization in awareness of distorted perceptions of external reality are none the less congruent.

Rogers' view of human nature recognizes the powerful influence of personality and of immediate emotional influences on persons' interpretations of external events. Nevertheless, human nature is adaptive to external reality and consequently needs means to correct for distortive tendencies. In effect, humans have scientific natures according to Rogers (1961). In the extreme of his view, Rogers commented:

> Science is not an impersonal something, but simply a person living subjectively another phase of himself (p. 223).

Persons make inferences or make interpretations of external events and then test their perceptions by taking some action that tends to validate or qualify the original perceptions. Congruent symbolization in awareness, followed by congruent communication, promotes accurate understandings between persons.

Obviously, Rogers cannot be using congruence to mean simple matching in the interpersonal theory. Rogers' general law of interpersonal relations must be employing the strict meaning of congruence between experience and awareness. The theory refers to an unrestricted accuracy of awareness in respect to experience that permits accurate symbolization.

It should be understood that accurate and undistorted perceptions of inner experience say nothing, however, about the accuracy or adequacy of the perceptions and interpretive processes involved in generating experiences in relation to consensual reality. Nor do they require true knowledge of the intentions of another person whose behavior is being perceived. Whatever they are, the interpretive factors in perceptions that lead to subjective experiences determine the qualities and affective valences of experiences.

Consequently, it may be said that experiences and their accurate symbolizations are experientially true whether or not they spring from the realities of situations from a consensual viewpoint or the viewpoint of the intentions of a person whose behavior is being perceived. Regardless of the adequacy status of a person's perceptions in respect to external criteria for truth, if a person's self-concept is flexible and open to experience, that person will be able to accurately symbolize his or her experiences in awareness. Or, if the person's self-concept is restrictive then certain experiences will be denied to awareness or distorted. Respectively, the person is congruent or incongruent. This is quite apart from determinations of consensual reality or reality from another person's perspective.

Another reason for interpreting Rogers' meaning of congruence in his law of interpersonal relationships as strictly within his theory, not as simple matching, has to do with the fact that his interpersonal theory is designed to foster better understanding, improved adjustment and mutual satisfaction among people. How is it possible that in this context Rogers could be advocating the behavior of saying what one thinks and feels in a given moment? Such behavior often includes judgments, criticisms, insults, accusations, interpretations of other people, etc. All of these behaviors are generally recognized as destructive. They are usually destructive to communication, to personal well-being and to satisfaction between people. Could Rogers be naive? No, he most likely means something else by congruent communication.

Understanding Rogers' view of communications in relation to congruence requires clarification of his usage of experience in that context. It also requires understanding of his views about the processes involved in accurate symbolization of experience.

THE COROLLARY CONCERNING CONGRUENT COMMUNICATIONS

Rogers' conception of congruence between experience and awareness, and between these two elements and communication, has a particular and not always recognized meaning. Rogers (1961) states:

> There is an important corollary of the construct of congruence, which is not at all obvious. It may be stated in this way. If an individual is at this moment entirely congruent, his actual physiological experience being accurately represented in his awareness, and his communication being accurately congruent with his awareness, *then his communication could never contain an expression of external fact.* If he were congruent he could not say, 'That rock is hard'; 'He is stupid'; 'You are bad': or 'She is intelligent'. The reason for this is that we never *experience* such 'facts'. Accurate awareness of *experience* would always be expressed as feelings, perceptions, and meanings from an internal frame of reference . . . I never *know* that the rock is hard, even though I may be very sure that I experience it as hard if I fall down on it . . . If the person is thoroughly congruent then it is clear that all of his communication would necessarily be put in a context of personal perception. This has very important implications (p. 341).

Rogers' corollary introduces the idea of an *attitude of personal perceptions* that has direct implications for the nature of congruent communications. To understand the implications specifically for the nature of the communication that might follow from this corollary, we need to understand Rogers' meaning of experience and the meaning of 'always be expressed as feelings, perceptions, meanings from an internal frame of reference'.

THE MEANING OF EXPERIENCE

The concept of experience, as a noun, is complex in Rogers' most precise theoretical writings. He indicates he is referring to something synonymous with the whole phenomenal field (Rogers, 1959, p. 197) which includes all perceptions, thoughts about these perceptions, the person's responses to his perceptions including thoughts, sensations, feelings and personal meanings. He describes experience as 'all that is present in immediate awareness or consciousness' including '. . . memory and past experience . . .' (p. 197). He also includes '. . . events of which the individual is unaware, as well as all the phenomena which are conscious' (p. 197). The many elements that are aspects of experience also include the person's assessment of what is real and judgments about what is good or bad in moral or ethical terms. This plethora of elements that are included in the term experience as phenomenal field, suggests Rogers' definition is similar to the common English definition:

> [A]nything observed or lived through; an actual living through an event; personally undergoing or observing something or things in general as they occur; individual reaction to events, feelings, etc. (Webster, 1979, p. 645).

In Rogers' and in general usage, experience refers to something happening in or to an individual. In addition, it is from the individual's point of view or frame of reference.

Rogers, however, also appears to give experience a second, much stricter and narrower meaning. Rogers writes of an individual being 'entirely congruent' and '. . . his actual *physiological* experience being accurately represented in his awareness' (1961, p. 341). Although experience is influenced by memory and past experiences, Rogers specifies that these influences are '. . . active in the moment . . . restricting or broadening the meaning given to various stimuli' (Rogers, 1959, p. 197). Also, experience 'includes events of which the individual is unaware' (p. 197). But it does not include events such as 'neuron discharges' that are not directly available to awareness through introspection. He further states that he has used phrases such as 'sensory and visceral . . . (and) organic' to convey what is referred to by experience. Experience in Rogers' narrower definition, of events that are amenable to awareness and symbolization, is apparently being differentiated from relatively complex thoughts or cognitions that are part of the wider definition of the term.

The stricter and narrower of Rogers' usages of the term 'experience' seems to refer to physiological events that can be sensed. He uses the words 'sensory' and 'visceral'. He is referring to perceptible physical events occurring in the individual's body that can be felt at moments with immediacy. Also, they are pregnant with implicit meanings, which can be identified and symbolized through a process of introspective attention.

The particular qualities of feeling that appear to be basic in Rogers' stricter usage of experience are those in dimensions of satisfactory/unsatisfactory, safe/threatening, pleasurable/unpleasurable. These are qualities of the inherent human capability to organismically value perceptions in respect to their organismic meanings and as signaling well-being or ill-being for the individual. Recent research by Bargh, et al. (1995) suggests that all perception is evaluatively tinged as pleasing or displeasing. His findings indicate that the simplest perceptions are not neutrally experienced. The research supports Rogers' conception of the organismic valuing process. It appears that this process is the basic object of awareness in the narrower meaning of experience, in respect to congruence.

Experiences, in Rogers' stricter usage, can be more or less complex experiences in the sense that adequate symbolization of their basic qualities can bring about more or less complex awarenesses through the introspection process. Examples of relatively simple verbal symbolizations of basic experiences are: 'I'm scared', 'I'm elated', 'I'm bored', 'I'm disgusted', 'I'm comforted', 'I'm joyful'. Basic or primitive experiences such as 'I'm scared' may be elaborated through introspection into more complex experiences and understandings about the situation that provokes a basic reaction of fear. Through introspection, the statement 'I'm scared', might become: 'When you moved towards me so fast, and seemed so angry, I was afraid you were going to hit me. I felt sick and weak and scared. I still feel afraid of you. I don't want to be near you.'

Translating basic affective experiences into subjective language or speech will use the language and discriminations available to the individual according to their culture, education and level of language development.

Introspection of experiences, still referring to Rogers' strict usage, may depart from the immediate character of the experiences in the process of understanding the circumstances of the experience and its implications. Memory of the stimulating situations, identification of the particular perceptions, discrimination of their evaluative qualities, assumptions and interpretations that were intrinsic to the perceptions, and historic associations may fill out the person's understandings of the basic affective experiences. Similar cognitive and associative processes may be brought into the exploration of the implications, to the individual, of the experiences. Whatever processes are brought into the introspection process while attending to the basic experience or sequence of experiences, the person is plumbing her own phenomenology and using her own criteria for assessing reality.

All experiences and all thoughts about things intrinsically exist from a person's idiosyncratic perceptual framework. Persons make distinctions, however, consciously or unconsciously, about what is 'out there' in contrast to what is due to the variable of oneself. These distinctions are relevant to understanding Rogers' (1961) idea that a communication of accurate awareness of experience never involves a statement of external fact. And that it would always be expressed as 'feelings, perceptions, meanings from an internal frame of reference' (p. 341).

Developments in awareness concerning an experience are likely to occur through introspection. The congruent voicing of the experience, nevertheless, must involve a conscious discrimination of the experience as an *affective event with its personal meanings* as distinguished from the opinions and ideas the person may have about events and persons that are part of the context for the experience.

For example, a person might voice their congruence concerning an experience as follows: 'I feel very angry with you, so angry I feel like hitting you because you told that story about me'. This statement could be a communication that matches the person's accurate symbolization in awareness of the experience. It also includes the circumstances the person perceives as arousing their anger, because the point of the communication is not only to let their feelings be known, but to engage in conversation that might bring about some restitution, for example, an apology. Or result in some kind of more satisfying experience with their friend in the future. The communication notably does not include interpretation of the friend's motives or character. Presumably the element 'told that story . . .' is consensually valid.

Often, however, an experience is evoked by an event that involves a more complex interpretation of the situation. For example, a person sees an acquaintance coming towards them on the street. As they pass, the acquaintance seems to glance at the person and goes on their way. Later, when they meet again, the person says to the acquaintance: 'I was very hurt when you didn't greet me the other day. At first I was afraid you might be angry with me because I haven't called you in a while. But then I got angry because you ignored me. And I've been stewing about it ever since.' The person has interpreted the acquaintance as deliberately ignoring the person. The behavior of passing without greeting, however, might or might not have been that. The statement 'ignored me' is an interpretation of intentions. The attribution of 'ignored' is stated as a fact about the acquaintance, which is not consistent with Rogers' dictum about communications related to congruence. If the last statement were modified to say 'But then I got angry because *it seemed to me* you saw me and ignored me . . .' it could be considered a communication that voices the person's accurate symbolization of the experience. In the modified statement there is only a tentative interpretation of the acquaintance's behavior, and the speaker acknowledges the interpretive factor in the perception.

In the modified statement the person translated the 'ignore' perception into the consensual observation: 'you didn't greet me', and distinguished the consensual observation from the interpretation of it: 'It seemed to me you saw me and ignored me . . . '. Communication that is intended to be about congruent experience often might need to be first processed to discriminate spontaneous interpretive elements (that would result in assertions of fact such as 'you ignored me') from the affective experience and from the consensual elements in the stimulating or contextual perception. An attitude of personal perceptions is not always easy to realize.

THERAPEUTIC CONGRUENT COMMUNICATIONS

The basic context and concern for this discussion of experience and congruent communication is, of course, client-centered psychotherapy and person-centered peer groups. In these situations, the therapist (in the former) and the participants (in the latter) are attempting to create an interpersonal environment that is therapeutic and that may promote growth for themselves and others. Rogers' theory of therapy asserts that congruence, unconditional positive regard and empathic understanding are attitudes that, when experienced often and together, in context of a relationship, create a therapeutic and growth enhancing climate. Recall that Rogers' early statements of his theory did not assert or imply that the contents of congruent experiences are definitely to be communicated in therapy. Congruence was presented as a condition of wholeness and integration, wherein the therapist is able to accurately symbolize experiences in awareness.

Differently, Rogers' theory of interpersonal relationships gives congruence a communication function. This theory applies particularly to situations where both or all parties involved are participating in order to represent themselves as well as to function constructively in relation to other persons. Thus, this theory seems to apply to person-centered peer groups because participants function in such groups to represent themselves as well as to provide therapeutic conditions for others. In so far as participants in a person-centered group are functioning as individuals serving their own purposes (exploring problems, raising issues, expressing reactions to other participants), the general theory of interpersonal relationships can be appropriately applied.

The attitude of personal perceptions cannot influence all communications that serve group participants' momentary personal goals. Communications that act out destructive impulses may occur in therapeutic or group situations although they are errors in respect to the purposes of those situations. Destructive intentions are contrary to the attitude of personal perceptions as a corollary of congruence. Some participants in group settings may communicate with a form of personal perceptions while experiencing destructive intentions. This may be confusing and augment the destructive impact. If, however, participants have constructive intentions and wish to self-disclose or comment from their personal perspectives, then an attitude of personal perceptions implemented by appropriate forms would apply. In any case, constructive or otherwise, communications in therapy, or in groups, cannot accurately be accounted for or be justified on grounds of congruence.

Rogers' corollary about the nature of congruent communication was incorporated by Gordon (1984) and by Guerney (1977) in their interpersonal training programs. Gordon developed techniques for congruent communications in his training of people for constructive family and professional conversations. Guerney (1977) developed techniques for teaching the role of the 'expresser' to family members. Both psychologists probably understood Rogers' corollary in terms of an attitude of personal perceptions, but their approaches focused upon and taught techniques.

Rogers illustrated empathic understanding in many demonstration interviews and discussed empathy in many of his writings. In several demonstration therapy interviews, Rogers communicates from his frame of reference. He self-discloses or makes observations about his client in some interviews in response to their questions and does so, on occasion, spontaneously. Rogers illustrated his theory of therapy by publishing interviews and by filming demonstrations. He did not, however, explain or classify the occasions for, or the form of, communications that would be consistent with his theoretical concept of congruence in the context of psychotherapy or peer groups. More recently, Lietaer (1993) has ventured to put forward some reasons the client-centered therapist might self-disclose, make comments, or give feedback in the context of his discussion of transparence. The writer (Brodley, 1999) has also ventured to clarify reasons for such responses in client-centered therapy.

In some studies of Rogers' therapy behavior (Brodley and Brody, 1990; Brody, 1991; Nelson, 1994; Brodley, 1994; Bradburn, 1996; Diss, 1996), several rating categories have been employed to cover a variety of statements made from the therapist's internal frame of reference. Some responses captured by these categories might be viewed as instances of Rogers communicating congruently.

Although congruence has not been employed as a category of therapist behavior in this writer's studies, in client-centered work there are two categories that may include responses that can be interpreted as congruent communications. The first category contains responses in reaction to certain kinds of clients' questions or requests. The second is a category of responses from the therapist's frame of reference that are unsolicited by the client, that are spontaneous and unsystematic. Some responses within these categories may conform to Rogers' conception of communications that express the therapist's congruence. They may communicate some of the contents of the therapist's accurately symbolized experience.

The first category of responses are ones in reaction to clients' questions or requests when the appropriate response requires the therapist's introspection to determine his immediate feelings. An interaction illustrating this follows:

Client: What do you feel about what I just said?

Therapist: You want to know my personal reaction about what you told me or

about my reaction towards you?
Client: Both, I guess. I'm afraid your feelings about me will be different now you know I do that. I'm afraid you're disgusted by me.
Therapist: I don't feel disgusted at all. My feelings aren't changed. I do feel a deep sadness that you want to hurt yourself.
Client: Don't you feel it's sick?
Therapist: I don't feel that. My thought about it is it's something that has come out of your suffering. Although it hurts you, it also relieves you.
Client: It's really hard to believe you aren't disgusted with me.

Certain statements from this interaction seem to express the attitude of personal perceptions and may be considered congruent communications: 'I don't feel disgusted', 'My feelings aren't changed' and 'I feel a deep sadness'.

The second category of responses, which may express some of the contents the therapist's experiences in a congruent manner, consists of responses unsolicited by the client but which are reactive to something emotionally unusual or intense that has happened to the client. The responses are spontaneous, unsystematic, and emotionally expressive. Examples are as follows:

- The client has arrived at the session and announced her much-loved mother died. The therapist responds, 'Oh, I'm terribly sorry!'
- The client reports she just got the job she was hoping for. The therapist responds, 'I'm so glad! Congratulations!'
- The client vividly describes a horrible accident. The therapist responds, 'Ohhh, my god!'

The responses 'I am terribly sorry' and 'I'm so glad' are communications that match the therapist's accurate symbolizations in awareness of the two experiences. 'Ohhh, my god!' expresses, but does not verbally represent, the inner experience. Presumably at the time the experience is not expressible in articulate language. They all seem to be congruent communications that conform to Rogers' corollary.

A THEORY OF ATTITUDES

Client-centered therapy and the person-centered approach, in its various applications, are based on a theory of attitudes (Brodley, 1997). Understanding the theory, one realizes that the development of practitioners is a development of their character, especially as attitudes express character. Development of the ability to practice in a client-centered way requires students to reflect upon their implementations in the light of Rogers' (1951) philosophy of the person. The student experiments with implementations of the therapeutic attitudes and observes the effects both from the inside and the outside. How does he feel about engaging in the behavior of the experiment? How much does the experiment appear to conform to the concepts of the theory? How does the experiment impact the client (or participant, or student, as the case may be)?

Implementations of the therapeutic attitudes are not the attitudes themselves. They may, however, effectively express the attitudes. It has been an understandable mistake to identify attitudes with behavior. But it should be recalled that *an attitude is always a subjective experience*, either *an intention* or *a state of mind* that shapes communication and other behavior.

In the case of unconditional positive regard, its attitudinal nature is so obvious and salient it seems strange to refer to implementations at all. The expression of unconditional positive regard is rarely in most client/person-centered therapeutic relations communicated by explicit statements such as 'I accept you and care about you regardless of your . . .' (filling in the dots with some behavior about which the client feels self-hatred).

Unconditional positive regard is almost always transmitted indirectly or by nonverbal expression. The trust clients develop, that they are accepted by their therapist, is stimulated by the therapist's empathic understandings that do not shy away from the painful or socially unacceptable material that the client discloses. The client's perception of the therapist's acceptance is also transmitted indirectly by the absence of judgmental statements, and by a tone of voice and manner that are shaped by the acceptant attitude.

Although there may be rare examples of direct communication of unconditional acceptance, it is so infrequent that there is no class of responses that can be pointed to as implementations or techniques to communicate acceptance. Empathic responses, or responses that attempt to address clients' questions can be shown to be imbued or saturated with acceptance. But these are not statements of acceptance and are certainly not, themselves, the attitude.

In respect to the empathic attitude, there are direct communications — implementations or techniques — that express the attitude. These are primarily empathic understanding responses. There are also some comments expressed from the therapist's frame of reference that communicate empathy. These responses are not, however, themselves the empathic attitude.

Client-centered therapists become more able to implement their acceptant, empathic attitudes as they develop. Their implementations become more purely expressive of the therapeutic attitudes. Therapists also become more confident in their ability to respond accurately and naturally. Their clients perceive them as more accurate in their understandings. Clients less often correct the therapist and more often make comments that the therapist understands 'exactly'. In this process of personal therapeutic development, maintaining congruence, and experiencing the attitudes of unconditional positive regard and empathic understanding become highly consistent qualities in therapists' personality make-up, at least in relation to clients.

There are a number of familiar interpretations and misunderstandings that are held about the concept of empathic understanding as an attitude and as a practice. Some such misunderstandings about empathic understanding are that they are: 'saying back what the client is saying'; 'picking up on and responding to feelings'; 'focusing the client to be more attuned to her experiencing'; 'trying to respond to what is just beneath the surface'. These are common misunderstandings of the empathic attitude particularly among teachers who are acquainted with theory but who have not developed themselves as client-centered therapists. It usually takes students quite a lot of trying to implement the concept, then observing effects of the implementations on practice clients, and introspectively reflecting upon their own experiences, to develop a functional understanding of the concept. *Much* more time and practice are needed in order to have the conceptual clarity to teach empathic understanding to others.

Empathic understanding has been given a great deal of attention in the training of therapists. Even so, there remains a significant range of different interpretations or understandings about it. Rogers' concept of congruence is more difficult to understand and difficult to live in relation to clients, students and others. The question even remains as to whether it is accurate to say it is implemented at all in the context of therapy. It certainly is not being *implemented* when the therapist is experiencing acceptant empathic understanding. It is, rather, a state or condition of the therapist underlying those attitudes.

In the context of acceptant empathic understanding, therapist disclosure of personal feelings and thoughts usually would be a distraction to the client's work. When would the therapist appropriately self-disclose? When would one not? For what purpose would the therapist disclose? Frequent self-disclosures would result in the therapists' feelings dominating the conversation and it would no longer be therapy.

CONGRUENT COMMUNICATIONS

Congruence, as Rogers defined it in his theory of psychotherapy, is *an integrated, whole state of the therapist in which he is capable of accurate symbolization in awareness of all experiences*. In respect to communication, the voicing of personal experiences while maintaining an attitude of personal perceptions may be referred to as 'expressing congruent communications' or as 'communicating congruently'. These terms avoid the suggestion that congruence refers to the contents of experience or the contents of communications.

The idea of congruent communications, itself, is a fiction or at least a generous inference. It is very difficult to determine with certainty one's own congruence. Conditions of worth do not promote full and accurate awareness and conditions of worth are ubiquitous. Much less may the congruent state of another be determined with any certainty. In any case, congruence should be distinguished from communication of the contents of experience. Congruent communication may be better thought of as honest communication that also expresses the attitude of personal perceptions. This might avoid confusion of congruence, a relation, with contents.

Congruent communications of self-experiences refer to communications voiced explicitly from the therapist's frame of reference. Also, they refer to personal feelings and personal meanings rather than statements purporting to be statements of facts. Congruent communications usually would also include some description or statement of the perceptions that set the stage for the revealed experiences. These descriptions or statements of perceptions would also explicitly refer to their source in the evaluations or interpretive processes of the speaker.

The following is an example of communication of a therapist's experiences in a therapy session: The therapist is unusually tired and realizes that the client is becoming less articulate. This calls the therapist's attention to the fact that he has been less attentive and has been less closely following the client for a few minutes. In order to be authentic in relation to the client ('not be deceiving the client as to himself'), and to correct for this lapse in his empathic understanding, the therapist undertakes the following conversation:

Therapist: Have I seemed to be less attentive than usual?

Client: Yes, I guess so, but I wasn't so sure about what I was trying to say either.

Therapist: I'm feeling tired and I just realized I've not been tuned in to you as well as I usually am. I've been a bit distracted.

Client: Maybe I was making it harder because I wasn't very coherent.

Therapist: I really don't think I experienced you that way, I just feel kind of tired and vaguely distracted. I am very sorry about that — I am aware of it now, so I think I can listen better, more like I normally do. Would you be willing to go on with what you were telling me?

Client: OK . . .

The client may have been losing her train of thought because she was aware of the therapist's distracted presence. In the example, the client also blames herself for the therapist's unusual behavior, even when he explains it has to do with his tiredness. This phenomenon is very common. Clients often feel at fault when the therapist appears to deviate from acceptance or empathy. One of the reasons the therapist might choose to self-disclose his problem could be to try to prevent misunderstandings.

In the example, the particular parts of the interaction that show congruent communication are the therapist's statements: 'I'm feeling tired', 'I've not been tuned in to you', 'I've been distracted', 'I'm very sorry', 'I am aware of it now'. The other elements of the self-disclosure express the therapist's intentions and wishes and are also important for the therapeutic character of the interaction.

Another example of a communication of the therapist's experiences takes place in a person-centered peer group. One participant has been the focus of criticisms by several persons in the group but has also been defended by some others.

Participant: I'm very confused right now. So many people have been saying things about me. Some of the comments were criticisms and accusations, but I also heard some support. So many things were said so fast, I've been sitting here having a whole lot of different feelings. I know I feel hurt and angry but a bit touched and grateful too. I don't know what all else. I'm confused and upset. More than anything, I guess, I'd like to get out of here.

She communicates her experiences, in terms that appear to express the attitude of personal perceptions, in the following: 'I'm very confused', '. . . having a whole lot of feelings', 'I feel hurt and angry but a bit touched and grateful', 'I'm confused and upset' and 'I'd like to get out of here'.

Congruent communication of experiences requires responses that are explicitly from the speaker's frame of reference. They are largely affective responses, as well. Reference to the stimulating circumstances are often part of the whole statement, but they are expressed carefully to avoid assuming general agreement about the interpretation of events and to avoid interpretation of other persons' motives.

Communication of one's self according to the attitude of personal perceptions also avoids retaliatory remarks. Congruent communication of experiences, according to Rogers' (1961) theory, takes place in the context of an effort to create constructive interactions. This is regardless of the character of previous interactions. Consequently it takes care and discipline and self-control.

Therapists working with clients, and participants in person-centered groups, are free to experiment with forms of self-representation. Self-disclosures are not restricted to communications about the contents of presumed congruence. However, if one truly wants to communicate congruently, then one should be guided by the meaning of the concept of congruence and the attitude of personal perceptions expressed in Rogers' corollary.

The *attitude of personal perceptions*, expressed in Rogers' corollary, does not refer to techniques. It is likely that communications expressing the attitude will be in the first person. Simply making first-person remarks, however, does not guarantee the attitude. First-person statements — 'I statements' — may communicate congruent experiences. Also, 'I statements' may refer to the speaker's frame of reference but include accusations, interpretations or other assertions of fact. Such statements that begin 'I feel' may have a less assertive communicative quality than they would otherwise. They are, nevertheless, assertions of fact, not congruent communications.

In client-centered contexts, many other kinds of statements besides communications of congruence may be appropriate and often are necessary for adequate self-representation or for responding to others. In client-centered therapy, for example, the most frequently observed form of communication (Brodley, 1994) is the broad category of *empathic following responses*. This category includes pure empathic understanding responses, questions for clarification, empathic fragments, 'I-form statements' where the therapist is speaking in the first person representing the client, informational following responses and metaphorical following responses which use the clients' own metaphors. This broad form of empathic understanding is common in other applications of the person-centered approach as well as psychotherapy. All of these kinds of statement attempt to characterize what the therapist has understood as the client's intended communications. They are expressed to find out whether or not the therapist's inner understandings are accurate according to the client (Rogers, 1986; Brodley, 1998).

There are responses that are *comments from the therapist's frame of reference*, in addition, within the therapy context. They are not following responses. Comments from the therapist's frame are often saturated with empathic knowledge or empathic speculation about the client. An example of this is a response from the therapist's frame of reference that is an inference about the client's behavior. The therapist remarks, 'you seem to be sitting on the edge of your seat and ready to go' in response to a client's description of a plan. The therapist's attitude inquires as to the validity of the statement from the client's frame of reference, when making observations about the client. Clients sometimes perceive empathy-laden responses as if they were empathic following responses, although they spring from the therapist's frame of reference.

Other comments from the therapist's frame are self-disclosures such as 'I must be sure to stop on time, so I may be looking at the clock towards the end of the session'. Some self-disclosures may be communications of congruent experiences. They could be spontaneous reactions such as 'Tears are welling up in me' in response to a moving poem the client has quoted. Self-disclosures could be explanatory statements such as 'I was preoccupied for a moment and didn't hear what you were saying' to correct for the therapist appearing to listen when it was not the case. The most common kind of comment from the therapist's frame of reference are introductions or endings of empathic responses which express the therapist's degree of uncertainty or tentativeness about the accuracy of his or her understandings. An example of this is the introduction 'I'm not sure if this is right, but do you mean . . . ?'

In addition to these categories of statements to clients, client-centered therapists may occasionally (albeit only rarely), and unsystematically, volunteer an *interpretation* or an *explanation about the client*, or ask a *leading or probing question*, or assert an *agreement* with a client. All of the mentioned categories of responses occur as therapists' verbal communications in response to clients who are self-expressing and self-representing. They may occur, also, in response to clients' questions or requests.

FOUR REASONS FOR COMMUNICATION OF THE THERAPIST'S FEELINGS

Responses that congruently communicate the therapist's experiences exist in the client-centered therapist's response repertoire. These responses are expressed from the attitude of personal perceptions. They often include therapist self-disclosures that emphasize the therapist is expressing *an opinion, an impression* or *an interpretation*. I shall not discuss all possible reasons for congruent communications or other therapist self-disclosures in this paper. I have presented reasons for responses from the therapist's frame of reference elsewhere (Brodley, 1999). Four situations that constitute reasons for the therapist to make such responses have been mentioned that seem clearly consistent with Rogers' theory.

One is the situation when a client perceives, or the therapist believes the client perceives, inconsistency of meaning among the therapist's behaviors. The reason for the congruent communication in this situation is in order that the therapist can remain clear, unconfused to the client, and be likely to have the quality of transparency.

The second is the situation of the therapist having persistent experiences that are counter to the therapeutic attitudes of unconditional positive regard or empathic understanding. This is the most likely reason for making such a response and the one Rogers mentions.

I feel conservative in respect to this rationale. I recommend considerable introspection and talking feelings out with a colleague or consultant before voicing the therapist's problems to a client. I recommend this conservative approach to congruent communications because I think clients should not be distracted from self-direction by being presented with the therapist's problems unless there is no other way to solve the problem. I have observed, also, that therapists who have counter-therapeutic feelings tend to be unprepared to cope with clients' complex and unexpected reactions to disappointing information from the therapist.

The third situation occurs when the client asks a direct question or makes a request. A self-disclosure or an honest expression of the therapist's opinion is appropriate in order to be respectful towards the client and allow the client to be the architect of the therapy.

The fourth situation is where there are simply spontaneous eruptions of disclosure of the therapist's feelings. These are unsystematic, infrequent and brief responses coming from the therapist's personal presence and responsiveness.

In all of these situations we assume the therapist remains faithful to the aim to function therapeutically. The therapist attempts to communicate his own feelings and personal meanings in ways that do not undermine or confuse the client. In situations where the therapist chooses to communicate his experiences, or his opinion or perspective about something, he is, also, at the same time, attempting to experience unconditional positive regard and empathic understanding. This attempt exists even when the context of congruent communication or the self-disclosure of opinion involves experiences that are counter to the therapeutic attitudes of acceptant empathy. Communications about personal experiences or self-disclosures of opinions in client-centered therapy require discipline.

CONCLUSION

The respectful democratic and egalitarian orientation of client-centered work is intrinsic to the therapist's character and the therapist's attitudes. These qualities influence all behavior with clients. We emphasize that we are speaking from our own perspectives and inner experiences, in contrast to speaking from the authority of our credentials or our status as therapists. We have this emphasis when making empathic responses and whenever we respond to clients from our own frames of reference. We avoid declarations of fact. Instead we emphasize personal perspectives. We convey our tentativeness when we do express statements of fact. We give the client the anatomy of our reasoning, or give our evidence, when we make statements of explanation or interpretation. We invoke our attitude of personal perspectives when we wish to communicate about our congruent experiences. All of these efforts contribute to the client's sense of being respected as a person.

Client-centered behavior may appear spontaneous to an observer and it may feel spontaneous to the therapist. It is, however, very disciplined behavior. It appears spontaneous when the values, attitudes and concepts about the work have become part of the therapist's character and lived attitudes. A therapist's capability to maintain a congruent state is fundamental and essential to all therapeutic qualities and endeavors.

REFERENCES

Baldwin, M. (1987). Interview with Carl Rogers on the use of the self in therapy. In M. Baldwin and V. Satir (Eds.), *The use of the self in therapy* (pp. 45–52). New York: Haworth Press.

Bargh, J. A. (1997). The automaticity of everyday life. In R. S. Wyer (Ed.), *The automaticity of everyday life: Advances in social cognition, Volume X* (pp. 1–61). Mahwah, New Jersey: Erlbaum.

Bargh, J. A., Chaiken, S., Raymond, P., and Hymes, C. (1995, May). *The automatic evaluation effect: Unconditional automatic attitude activation with a pronunciation task.* Paper presented at the annual conference of the American Psychological Association, New York.

Bradburn, W.M. (1996). *Did Carl Rogers' positive view of human nature bias his psychotherapy?: An empirical investigation.* Unpublished doctoral dissertation. Illinois School of Professional Psychology, Chicago, IL.

Brodley, B.T. (1994). Some observations of Carl Rogers' therapy behavior. *Person-Centered Journal*, 1(2), 37–48.

Brodley, B.T. (1997 July). Client-centered: An expressive therapy. Paper presented at the Fourth International Conference on Client-Centered and Experiential Psychotherapy. Lisbon, Portugal.

Brodley, B.T. (1998). Criteria for making empathic responses in client-centered therapy. *Person-Centered Journal*, 5(1), 20–8.

Brodley, B.T. (1999). Reasons for responses expressing the therapist's frame of reference in client-centered therapy. *Person Centered Journal*, 6(1), 4–27.

Brodley, B.T., and Brody, A.F. (1990, August). *Understanding client-centered therapy through interviews conducted by Carl Rogers.* Paper presented at the annual conference of the American Psychological Association, Boston, MA.

Brody, A.F. (1991). *Understanding client-centered therapy through interviews conducted by Carl Rogers.* Unpublished doctoral dissertation, Illinois School of Professional Psychology, Chicago, IL.

Diss, J.W. (1996). *Facilitative responses leading to client process disruption in Carl Rogers' therapy behavior.* Unpublished doctoral dissertation, Illinois School of Professional Psychology, Chicago, IL.

Gendlin, E.T. (1964). A theory of personality change. In J. T. Hart and T. M. Tomlinson (Eds.), *New Directions in Client-Centered Therapy* (pp. 129–73). Boston, MA: Houghton Mifflin.

Gordon, T. (1984). Three decades of democratizing relationships through training. In D. Larson (Ed.), *Teaching psychological skills: Models for giving psychology away* (pp. 151–70). New York: Brooks/Cole.

Guerney, B.G. (1977). Basic skills of relationship enhancement. In *Relationship Enhancement*, San Francisco: Jossey-Bass.

Haugh, S. (1998). Congruence: A confusion of language. *Person-Centred Practice*, 6(1), 44–50.

Lietaer, G. (1993). Authenticity, Congruence and Transparency. In D. Brazier (Ed.), *Beyond Carl Rogers* (pp. 17– 46). London: Constable.

Nelson, J.A. (1994). *Carl Rogers' verbal behavior in therapy: A comparison of theory and therapeutic practice.* Unpublished doctoral dissertation, Illinois School of Professional Psychology, Chicago, IL.

Rogers, C.R. (1951). *Client-Centered Therapy.* Boston, MA: Houghton Mifflin.

Rogers, C.R. (1957). The necessary and sufficient conditions for therapeutic personality change. *Journal of Consulting Psychology*, 21, 95–103.

Rogers, C.R. (1959). A theory of therapy, personality and interpersonal relationships, as developed in the client-centered framework. In S. Koch (Ed.), *A study of a science. Vol. 3. Formulations of the person and the social context* (pp. 184–256). New York: McGraw-Hill.

Rogers, C.R. (1961). A tentative formulation of a general law of interpersonal relationships. In C.R. Rogers, *On Becoming a Person* (pp. 338–47). Boston, MA: Houghton Mifflin.

Rogers, C.R. (1980). The foundations of a person-centered approach. In C.R. Rogers, *A Way of Being* (pp. 113–35). Boston, MA: Houghton Mifflin.

Rogers, C.R. (1986). Client-centered therapy. In J.L. Kutash and A. Wolf (Eds.), *A psychotherapist's casebook: Theory and technique in practice* (pp. 197–208). San Francisco, CA: Jossey-Bass.

Webster, N. (1979). *Webster's New Universal Unabridged Dictionary.* New York: Simon and Schuster.

5 The Multifaceted Nature of Congruence Within the Therapeutic Relationship

Gill Wyatt

Abstract. *The aim of this paper is to highlight the holistic nature of congruence. An overview of previous writers on congruence is offered. The metaphor of a diamond is used to symbolise the complex and multifaceted nature of congruence where the brilliance of the diamond comes from its entirety as well as the integrity of each facet. Each facet is examined individually. The significance of looking at congruence as a whole is emphasised in relation to accessing, via the actualising tendency, a greater healing potential and beyond to something greater — an interconnectedness with the universe.*

Rogers' concept of congruence evolved over time. His descriptions of congruence vary in different publications and confusion can result if they are drawn from writings on congruence in different contexts, i.e. therapeutic relationships, interpersonal relationships, large groups, families, and so forth. I am only addressing congruence within the therapeutic relationship and all quotes used are taken from writings about the therapeutic relationship.

HISTORICAL OVERVIEW OF THE CONCEPT OF CONGRUENCE

Rogers' position

In his early writings, Rogers focused on the therapist developing certain attitudes that related to respecting and valuing the client's ability and right to self-direct. The therapist's task was to lay aside his own frame of reference and step into the internal frame of reference of the client, seeing the world and the client from the subjective view of the client (Rogers, 1951). He talks about the therapist '. . . providing deep understanding and acceptance' (Rogers, 1946, p. 420).

In his 1951 book, *Client-Centered Therapy*, Rogers does not explicitly talk about congruence or genuineness as a necessary attitude. However, he does quote from his 1946 publication where he makes it clear that the type of therapeutic relationship he was describing could only exist '. . . if the counsellor is deeply and genuinely able to adopt these attitudes', and later in the same quote he speaks of being genuine

A revision of a paper (2000) first published in the *Person-Centered Journal, 7* (1). Reproduced with kind permission. Initially presented to the Person-Centred Forum, Johannesburg, S. Africa 1998.

as the third characteristic of non-directive therapy (Rogers, 1946, p. 421).

While Rogers was working at the Chicago Counselling Center in the 1950s he was influenced by Oliver Bown and Eugene Streich. As a result of these associations Rogers further developed his view that therapists need to be real and genuine and enter more fully and personally into the therapeutic relationship (Raskin, 1996). In 1954 Rogers discussed the significance of therapists finding their 'genuine reality'. This meant that therapists needed to be aware of their feelings as much as possible; not present an outward attitude whilst holding a different attitude more deeply, and express their genuine attitudes and feelings. 'It is only by providing the genuine reality which is in me, that the other person can successfully seek for the reality in him' (Rogers, 1954 in Rogers, 1961, p. 33).

Rogers' 1957 paper '*The Necessary and Sufficient Conditions of Therapeutic Personality Change*' is considered to be one of his primary theoretical statements He proposed that the second condition is that ' . . . the client is in a state of incongruence, being vulnerable or anxious' (Rogers, 1957, p. 96). And incongruence refers to 'a discrepancy between the actual experience of the organism and the self-picture of the individual insofar as it represents that experience.' (ibid.). In his 1959 statement Rogers explains that when an experience perceived by the self structure is incongruent with the self-structure, then the organism either distorts the meaning of this experience or denies it into awareness.

Juxtaposed to condition two is Rogers' third condition which proposes that the therapist 'is congruent or integrated in the relationship' (Rogers, 1957, p. 96). Rogers explained this to mean that 'when self-experiences are accurately symbolised, and are included in the self-concept in this accurately symbolised form, then the state is one of congruence of self and experience' (Rogers, 1959, p. 206). To be congruent is for *experiences* to be *accurately symbolised* into *awareness*. The self-concept or self-structure needs to be constructed with enough flexibility to allow this openness to experience to occur.

THE RELATIVE IMPORTANCE OF CONGRUENCE

In 1959 Rogers raises the question of the relative importance of congruence. His (conservative) view is 'that for therapy to occur the wholeness of the therapist in the relationship is primary, but a part of the congruence of the therapist must be the experience of unconditional positive regard and the experience of empathic understanding' (Rogers, 1959, p. 215). Later he makes a clearer statement concerning the primacy of congruence. 'I regard it as highly important, perhaps the most crucial of the conditions' (Rogers and Stevens, 1967, p. 92) and in the 1980s he says 'Genuineness appears to be the most basic: the other two are important but probably less so' (Rogers and Sanford, 1984, p. 1378).

IS CONGRUENCE AN INTERNAL STATE OR DOES IT HAVE AN EXTERNAL ELEMENT?

In both of his 1957 and 1959 theoretical statements, Rogers defines congruence in relation to experience and awareness. Both of these elements are describing the therapist's *internal* state. Elsewhere, Rogers (1954, 1961, 1967, 1980, 1984 and

1986), writes about congruence involving experience, awareness *and* the therapist's behaviour and communication. In 1954 he wrote:

> This means that I need to be aware of my own feelings, insofar as possible, rather than presenting an outward facade of one attitude, while actually holding another attitude at a deeper or unconscious level. Being genuine also involves the willingness to be *and express, in my words and behaviour,* the various feelings and attitudes which exist in me (Rogers, 1954, in Rogers, 1961, p. 33, italics added).

In 1984, Rogers and Sanford present two changes in how congruence is conceptualised. In a *Theory of Therapy,* the second condition is expanded to include the therapist's communications. 'The therapist is congruent (or genuine or real) in the relationship, his picture of himself and the way he communicates matching his immediate experiencing' (p. 1382). The fifth condition is additionally modified so that *all three conditions* should be perceived minimally by the client. 'The client perceives to some minimal degree the realness, the caring and the understanding of the therapist' (p. 1382).

So by researching some of Rogers' writing on congruence we are left with a dilemma. His theoretical statements (Rogers, 1957, 1959) suggest that congruence is defined as an internal state of the therapist involving the congruence of their experiencing with their awareness, but his other writings (Rogers, 1954, 1961, 1967, 1980, 1984, 1986) suggest there is also an external element — the therapist's behaviour.

The significance of the importance of congruence relative to empathic understanding and unconditional positive regard (UPR); and whether congruence is defined either solely as the internal state of the therapist, or by both internal state and the therapist's behaviour and communication, are relevant, as they will inform clinical practice, i.e. how the therapist is going to be with the client and what he is going to do.

Rogers sometimes emphasises that the therapist should only express his feelings when they are appropriate; or persistent; or limiting the therapist's experience of empathic understanding and UPR (Rogers 1959, 1967). At other times he stresses the necessity to express 'negative attitudes' in order to promote the realness of the relationship, 'the therapist is being herself, not denying herself' (Rogers and Sanford, 1984, p. 1381). It is as if sometimes he is suggesting caution to the therapist and at other times he is promoting the therapist being themselves, being whole, being real and spontaneous — 'It is when the therapist is natural and spontaneous that he is most effective' (Rogers and Stevens, 1967, p. 186).

CURRENT PERSPECTIVES ON CONGRUENCE

Since Rogers, various writers have defined congruence in different ways emphasising a different part from Rogers' writings related to their specific theoretical position. This results in them having a different stance with regard to the place of congruence in therapeutic practice.

Lietaer's position

According to Lietaer (1993), genuineness has two parts. The 'inner part' refers to the therapist's awareness of his experiencing. Lietaer calls this congruence. The 'outer part' refers to the therapist's 'explicit communication' which he calls transparency (p. 18). Quoting Gendlin (1970), Lietaer (1993) explains that from 1955 to 1962 a shift occurred in the client-centred understanding of congruence that 'allowed the therapist to bring in something from his own frame of reference, as long as he kept returning to the client's experiential track' (p. 32). Lietaer views this as a significant shift away from the therapist only expressing feelings that interfere with maintaining their attitudes of empathic understanding and unconditional positive regard. This then meant the therapist had freer expression of their experiences of the client and the therapeutic relationship, if the therapist thought doing so would facilitate the client's experiential process.

Brodley's position

For Brodley (1998), congruence is defined 'in terms of Rogers' distinction between self and experience, not in term's of the therapist's behaviour or communication' (p. 85). Brodley defines congruence as 'an integrated whole, authentic state of the therapist in which he is capable of accurate symbolization in awareness of all experiences' (p. 101). Her conclusion that congruence need not be communicated by the therapist follows primarily from Rogers' (1957, 1959) theoretical statements concerning congruence not needing to be perceived by the client. Congruence is a state 'within the therapist' (p. 85), says Brodley, and its significance is in permitting 'the therapist to succeed in his intentions to experience unconditional positive regard and empathic understanding' (p. 85).

She suggests that '[U]ntherapeutic experiences' (p. 87) and 'counter-therapeutic feelings' (p. 89) usually do not have to be expressed to the client. The congruent therapist who acceptantly allows these experiences into awareness will not show discrepancies in their (verbal and non-verbal) behaviour. As long as the client is not aware of the therapist's 'untherapeutic feelings' there is no reason to distract the client from their own exploration. Although the therapist may choose to communicate congruently these untherapeutic feelings or thoughts occasionally, Brodley advocates a conservative approach.

Bozarth's position

Bozarth (1996) asserts that genuineness is 'an attitudinal development that enables the therapist to be more able to achieve the on-going *experiencing* of empathic understanding and unconditional positive regard towards the client. It is, for the therapist, a way to prepare him or herself as a maximally receptive therapist' (p. 48). Bozarth's position is based on Rogers' 1959 statement concerning congruence as a therapist quality rather than a quality in relation to the client, or that the client must perceive, or that the therapist must communicate or express.

In an earlier paper, Bozarth states that when the genuine therapist is '. . . absorbed in the frame of reference of the client' and lets go of a desired direction for his client, the therapist will allow more 'intuitive' or 'idiosyncratic' responses to emerge '. . . and the presence of the therapist takes on progressively more importance' (Bozarth, 1992, p. 18). For Bozarth the significance of congruence is that it enables the therapist to trust the client's process completely and step very deeply into the client's frame of reference not knowing where that will lead him or what his response might be at any time.

THE DIFFERENT CONCEPTUALISATIONS OF CONGRUENCE

The following questions arise from the differences in the literature on congruence.

1. Does congruence include the therapist's behaviour, their expression or communication of their congruence or does it only relate to the internal state of the therapist?
2. Is congruence only to support or deepen or facilitate the therapist development of empathic understanding and unconditional positive regard?
3. What is appropriate verbal expression of congruence?
4. Does the client need to perceive the therapist's congruence?

According to Haugh (1998), one possible reason for confusion regarding the concept is Rogers' linking congruence with authenticity, genuineness, realness and transparency. Haugh suggests that the word congruence be used to define the condition of congruence and that authenticity, genuineness, realness and transparency are seen as the outcomes of congruence (Haugh, 1998).

This brings clarity to what to call what, but whether you call a therapist's communication and behaviour congruent or authentic, real, genuine or transparent does not really matter. What's significant is how the therapist is, their behaviour and what they chose to say, how this is received by the client and the impact this then has on the therapeutic relationship.

The definition that I find closest to my own understanding of congruence is 'the therapist is openly being the feelings and attitudes that are flowing within at the moment. There is a close matching, or congruence, between what is experienced at the gut level, what is present in awareness, and what is expressed to the client' (Rogers, 1986, in Kirschenbaum and Henderson, 1990, p. 135).

Ellingham has suggested the problem resides in the Cartesian-Newtonian language used to define congruence (Ellingham, 1999). Indeed, some of the writings on congruence do seem to use this dualistic/modernistic language (Rogers, 1957,1959; Brodley, 1998,1999 and Lietaer, 1993). Yet, when reading Rogers' experiences in the therapeutic relationship (Rogers, 1961, 1967, 1980, 1986 and 1987), it is apparent that he is endeavouring to capture something hard to express — something inexpressible in dualistic and linear terms. My calling congruence 'multifaceted' and writing about its different facets is an attempt to express its non-dualistic and holistic nature. In a paradoxical way, seeing and understanding its many facets also means we can catch a glimpse of the significance of the whole concept.

When the therapist is whole, real and congruent within the therapeutic relationship and the concept of congruence is seen in a holistic, non-dualistic way, there are two results. The first is that there is an *openness for the actualising tendency not only within the client but within the therapist and in the therapeutic relationship thus giving access to immense healing potential.* The second is that any separation of the therapist's behaviour or communication from their state of being becomes an arbitrary split that serves no useful purpose. The question of whether a therapist should or should not communicate their experience can shift to a more complex proposition: *How a therapist is whole, real and congruent will be determined by who the therapist is, who the client is, the quality of the therapeutic relationship, where they are in the therapy process and what is happening for the therapist and the client at that moment.*

THE MULTIFACETED NATURE OF CONGRUENCE

The concept of congruence is complex. Imagine a diamond. It has many facets. Each facet, carefully and sensitively cut is important in creating the diamond. Yet the integrity of the diamond comes from more than the skill with which each facet has been cut. Similarly, congruence is multifaceted, each facet needs to be honed and developed, all are needed to make up the whole and within the whole is something extra that goes beyond the separate facets.

1) The core

Being myself
This is the core of congruence — all facets stem from this. My being includes who I am at my very core, my soul and spirit, my identity and my personality. This is my uniqueness. My intention is to bring the whole of my unique being into the therapeutic relationship rather than hiding behind a professional mask. People whom we trust, says Rogers '. . . are being what they *are* . . . we are dealing with the person himself, and not with a polite or professional facade' (Rogers, 1967, p. 91). Being congruent in this way means that no two individuals will ever look alike. How much of myself I am able to bring into the therapeutic relationship will depend on my psychological maturity.

Psychological maturity
Psychological maturity is about knowing ourselves, knowing our issues and blind spots, taking responsibility for our own behaviour and experiences, being a separate autonomous person whilst also being interrelational; acknowledging the separateness of the client and their right to be different from the therapist. Our self-structure needs to be flexible enough to allow most of our experiencing to be accurately symbolised into our awareness, i.e. our denial and distortion of experiences is minimal. Rogers emphasises the need for this openness rather than defensiveness so that the therapist's communication conveys no ambiguity (Rogers, 1958 in Kirschenbaum and Henderson, 1990).

We need to be able to recognise when our client's concerns touch our own issues and conflicts; to assess when our issues impinge on the therapeutic relationship, and to contain our conflicts during the therapy hour. Then we need an openness rather than a defensiveness, to reflect on that issue either alone, with a friend, colleague, therapist or supervisor. Developing our psychological maturity I believe is particularly important for the person-centred therapist. Rogers says '. . . the more psychologically mature and integrated the therapist is, the more helpful is the relationship that he or she provides. This puts a heavy demand on the therapist as a person' (1980, p. 148).

Psychological maturity is related to the capacity for unconditional self-regard. Openness to experiencing and accurate symbolisation of experience into awareness occurs only when we have unconditional self-regard for that experiencing (Rogers, 1959).

Personal style of the therapist

As unique individuals, therapists need to allow their personal style to develop. Every person-centred therapist will appear different despite their shared belief in the actualising tendency and their commitment to genuine, empathic understanding and unconditional positive regard. Lietaer points out that 'Rogers thus emphasizes respect for each therapist's personal style. He does not want to put him in a methodological strait-jacket which would not suit his nature' (Lietaer, 1993, p. 21). Rogers explains 'It is when the therapist is natural and spontaneous that he seems to be most effective'. He continues:

> Thus our sharply different therapists achieve good results in quite different ways. For one, an impatient, no-nonsense, let's put-the-cards-on-the--table approach is effective, because in such an approach he is most openly being himself. For another it may be a much more gentle, and more obvious warm approach, because this is the way *this* therapist is. Our experience has deeply reinforced and extended my own view that the person who is able *openly* to be himself at that moment, as he is at the deepest levels he is able to be, is the effective therapist. Perhaps nothing else is of any importance (Rogers, 1967, pp. 185–6).

Congruence also requires a harmonious relationship between the therapist's theoretical orientation and their personal style. A person-centred therapist's way of relating to a client is not based on using interventions, techniques or skills, but arises from her congruent embodiment of the conditions and who she is as a person. Rogers described how focusing on empathic reflection as a technique led to 'complete distortions' of person-centred therapy and a travesty of empathic understanding as an attitude (Rogers, 1975, p. 3). As soon as a therapist tries to *do* the conditions they are stepping out of the person-centred attitudinal way of being into a skill-based way of working. Yet if the therapist is *being* the attitudes then what might normally be considered a technique or intervention incompatible with the Person-Centred Approach, will be experienced as an embodiment of one of the attitudes (Bozarth, 1984; Lago, 1998, personal communication).

2) The facets

Being open to my moment to moment experiencing

When congruent, the structure of my self-concept is fluid (or wide) enough that I accurately symbolise most experiencing into awareness. Some experiences will arise from who I am as a person; others from who the client is; and still others from the interaction occurring between us. Experiences may also result from other aspects of the environment, for instance, the noise of traffic outside, the colours in the room, and so forth. I can access my experience to determine its potential significance for my client. Some of my experiences will reveal empathic understanding and unconditional positive regard for my client. Others will direct me elsewhere — for instance to the discomfort in my arms and shoulders following a heated disagreement with my partner, or the coldness I feel when with a client when previously the room felt warm. These awarenesses may tell me something about how my client is feeling or how I am responding to my client, or about myself separate from my client. Feeling uncomfortable or vulnerable may indicate an incongruence of mine has been touched by the client's exploration.

Natiello refers to this openness of the therapist as being a part of an 'authentic, connected therapeutic relationship' (1997, p. 7) that she believes is linked to the positive outcome of therapy. She refers to an openness to experiencing the client's frame of reference and also the therapist's own experiences in relation to the client or the therapeutic relationship (see also Rogers, 1959 and Brodley, 1998).

A therapist's willingness to talk about their own experiences will mean the therapist is open to the experience of being vulnerable. If a therapist can successfully balance vulnerability, openness to learning, having their issues touched, *and* maintain professional and ethical practices, there are several advantages. A therapist's openness and acceptance of personal vulnerability may facilitate the client's acceptance of their vulnerability. The resultant mutuality between therapist and client and the empowerment of the client appear surprising. By allowing himself to be vulnerable, and by allowing the client to teach him about his incongruence; our humanness, our sameness, the connection between two ordinary people is highlighted. As Rombauts states:

> Because of this kinship, it is not only me that holds a mirror to the client . . . but also the client who holds up a mirror to me, showing me what I am, feel and experience. Dormant aspects of myself, which I have barely or not at all realised in my life, can be touched upon and stirred up (Rombauts, 1984, p. 172).

The following example illustrates the benefits of this level of trust within the therapist, the client and the therapeutic relationship — from this personal opening, therapists become fully available to the actualising tendency and a greater healing potential for both therapist and client.

I had often felt frustrated with John when I could not make contact with him. In the past I had chosen to tell him about my feelings as I thought that I was picking up his unsymbolised experiences of feeling angry and although I expressed them as my own I hoped that he would recognise them and own his anger. I had stepped into the role of being the expert. Recently I realised that some or all of my anger is to do with my need for connection. When John withdraws — I miss that connection — it hurts and often I am unable to accurately symbolise my hurt or fear and only symbolise and communicate my anger. Having understood this, the next time John withdrew and I felt my frustration — I looked at *the edges of my awareness* and found my fear, my disappointment, my yearning for deep connection. The intensity of this was due to my unresolved incongruencies, not to do with John, yet I felt it was important to say to John that when I looked a little closer at my frustration I also found I missed him and felt a little scared. John looked at me and quietly said 'I miss myself.'

How to be with our incongruities
As therapists we will at times be incongruent with our clients. Mearns and Thorne

(1988) describe two types of incongruity: one is the incongruity between feelings and awareness of those feelings; the second is when the therapist is aware of their feelings but resists communicating them even though they are persistent and relevant to the client. Both types of incongruities are related to the therapist's unresolved therapeutic issues associated with their self-structure.

Rogers' theory suggests that, if the therapist who is incongruent within the therapeutic relationship remains unaware of her incongruence, a negative effect on the client and the outcome of therapy will result (Rogers, 1957, 1959). However, therapist awareness through post-session reflections, either alone or with a supervisor, provides an opportunity to increase congruence thus improving the quality of the therapeutic relationship.

In discussion with a colleague, I realised the importance of the therapist communicating her incongruency congruently! This might even be more significant than expressing congruent communication (Haugh, 1998, personal communication). The therapist can choose to gain understanding of her incongruence away from the client and then openly and honestly share her experience and its possible impact on the client. The therapist needs to be sensitive to where the client is in their therapeutic process. Will talking about their incongruity strongly interrupt the client's exploration or deepen it? Will the therapist's exploration of their incongruity be an expression of holding all three conditions at the same time?

I had been seeing Mike weekly for several years. He had been depressed for much of this time and occasionally out of touch with reality. He was highly critical of himself and quickly felt helpless and hopeless. In this session he talked about how different his perception of himself was from that of others. His colleagues saw him as capable and suitable for promotion; yet he felt he knew and did nothing. I initially thought I was staying with him and congruently maintaining my empathic and accepting attitude but as I became aware of my slight discomfort, I began to realise my subtle criticism towards him. My reflections were emphasising how negative he was being about himself and how he had created something with no way out. Though intending to step into his frame of reference, my reflections were contaminated by my judgmental and critical frame of reference.

I believed that my attitude of subtle criticism was at least partly responsible for his 'stuckness' so I decided to tell him about my incongruence. He responded by telling me how he felt as though I thought he should be able to change. I told him I had thought that. I realised my difficulty in staying with his impotence, his helplessness, his vulnerability, was connected to issues that I had been facing in my life recently. I knew that discussing my issues would take him away from his experiencing. I did decide to tell him how I felt I needed to stretch myself in some way in order to learn to be with him and accept him as he was. I felt it was as if he was in some way waiting for me to learn something. As I was talking he nodded a few times but he said he thought he must be a very difficult client. At this I wondered whether he had distorted what I had been saying to fit his negative view of himself. I said that wasn't what I had meant; rather I wanted to own my difficulties arising from inside of me.

After the session I felt good about telling him about how subtly critical I had been, but was (and remain) uncertain about the appropriateness to share my need to stretch myself, even though I know what I said was connected to my understanding and unconditional positive regard for him. Still the session was pivotal, for afterwards he came out of his depression, and began to see himself more positively, realising he was capable of changing how he was in the world. Maybe my honest communication of my incongruence, being open to being vulnerable, acknowledging my mistake with him and not needing anything from him had a significant effect — maybe he felt deeply met by another real, human being.

Genuine empathic understanding and unconditional positive regard

Being congruent, being real, means empathy and unconditional positive regard will be genuine. A client's trust of a therapist's empathy and unconditional positive regard only occurs when the therapist is real and genuinely interested in her and her experiences. As early as 1946, Rogers made the point that without this genuineness, empathy becomes merely a technique and unconditional positive regard can become patronising or arrogant (Rogers, 1946 quoted in Rogers, 1951, p. 30). Brodley believes the therapist's state of congruence allows them 'to succeed in his intentions to experience unconditional positive regard and empathic understanding' (Brodley, 1998, p. 85). Bozarth states strongly that the therapist's congruence must not interfere with the 'client's self-authority and determinations', that it is rather a preparation of the therapist to experience the other two core conditions (Bozarth, 1998). A therapist's congruence sets the upper limits of their ability to hold the attitudes of empathic understanding and unconditional positive regard.

The therapist's behaviour

Behaviour is what is observable, it is the external manifestation of the internal processes of an individual. Many terms have been used when writing about therapist's behaviour — self-expressiveness (Rogers, 1961), transparency (Lietaer, 1993), authenticity, genuineness and realness (Haugh, 1998), congruent communications (Brodley, 1999), self-disclosure, self-involving, immediacy and the therapist's communication.

The significance of the therapist's behaviour, whether it is verbal or non-verbal, is that this is what the client observes and receives. Rogers links trustworthiness with being dependably real and goes on to ask 'Can I be expressive enough as a person that what I am will be communicated unambiguously?' (Rogers, 1961, p. 51).

A therapist's behaviour includes her own style of communicating and interacting based on her way of being and personality. It will speak to others of his realness, his need to defend or need to mask thoughts and feelings. Behaviour is part of our congruence/incongruence and will demonstrate our level of psychological maturity.

There has been considerable debate as to what may be considered appropriate self-expressiveness for a person-centred therapist. Rogers' writings reveal some inconsistencies regarding this. Sometimes he emphasised expressing feelings only when they are appropriate, persistent, or limiting to the therapist's experience of empathic understanding and unconditional positive regard (Rogers, 1959, Rogers and Stevens, 1967). Other times he emphasised the need to express feelings that 'are not regarded as ideal for psychotherapy' (Rogers, 1957, in Kirschenbaum and Henderson, 1990, p. 224). Still other times he stressed the necessity to express 'negative attitudes' (Rogers and Sanford, 1984, p. 1381) in order to promote the realness of the relationship. He suggested caution and yet advocated for spontaneity, realness and being oneself.

Lietaer (1993) believes that Rogers' views on communicating congruence changed significantly in the late 1950s. Both Brodley (1998) and Bozarth (1998) strongly contest this view. Throughout his career, Rogers promotes therapists being whole and real, to include expressing 'difficult' therapist experiences (Rogers, 1957; Rogers and Stevens, 1967; Rogers and Sanford, 1984; Baldwin, 1987). I believe that while he did not alter his basic theoretical statement (Rogers, 1957, 1959), Rogers appeared to become more accepting of himself as he grew older — particularly with regard to some of his feelings. Consequently, he sometimes became more self-expressive when it felt right within the relationship, for instance telling Gloria (see Shostrom, 1965) she 'seemed like a pretty nice daughter' to him.

Various guidelines have been established to help therapists decide whether or not to express their experiencing to the client. For Rogers, the answer resided in the relevance and appropriateness of the experience in the therapeutic context (Rogers, 1959; Rogers and Stevens, 1967). Mearns and Thorne (1988) say 'when it is in response to the client's experience' (p. 81), 'when it is relevant to the immediate concern of the client' and if it is 'persistent or particularly striking' (p. 82). Lietaer (1993) and Brodley (1998, 1999) have also described careful guidelines.

The problem inherent in using these guidelines is that assessing appropriateness and timing moves the therapist into a position of expert, and out of a mutual encountering relationship. Rogers explores how actively thinking about and being directed by theory while with clients is detrimental to the quality of practice. He says 'the particular theory of the therapist is irrelevant, and if it is in the therapist's consciousness at that moment, is probably *detrimental* to therapy. What I am saying is that it is the existential encounter which is important' (Rogers and Stevens, 1967, p. 186). Rogers clearly advocates trusting ourselves to be natural, real, and spontaneous.

In her erudite discussion of congruence, Brodley (1998, 1999) distinguishes between congruent communications, 'persistent nontherapeutic experiences' (1998 p. 88) and 'countertherapeutic feelings' (p. 89). According to Brodley, experiences need to be communicated with an intention to experience empathic understanding and unconditional positive regard. They are expressed from the therapist's frame of reference, and involve feelings and meanings rather than made as a statement of external fact. However, some of what Brodley would call 'countertherapeutic feelings' I do not.

For example if a client speaks about asserting himself in a way in which I am unable, and I start to feel jealous and angry, my awareness of these feelings should lead me towards reflection and exploration of my unresolved issues away from the therapy session. These feelings if expressed are likely to be countertherapeutic feelings and Brodley and I agree. However, consider a different scenario wherein my client has been increasingly imploring for me to tell her what to do. I begin to feel exasperated by her apparent helplessness to self-direct. I express my feelings gently, taking responsibility for them, and at the same time understanding, accepting her, telling her how I have been experiencing her and how I feel as a result. Initially she is defensive; then she starts to cry and says how tired she feels always being busy and being there for other people. She needed to be looked after by somebody. Here, my feelings of exasperation are not countertherapeutic. My realness facilitated or enabled my client to be real as well. She identifies her tiredness and deep need to be looked after. I often observe that when real feelings are discussed openly and sensitively by me — the client takes a significant step in their self-directed exploration.

A student of mine left a person-centred therapist because he sought a more interactive relationship. There are some clients who need a more interactive 'dialogic' communication with their therapist. I believe that without diagnosing our client but by being centred into our own being *and* being able to step into their frame of reference we can respond to their particular or changing need with a *different* style of communicating. This is a similar idea to Bozarth's 'idiosyncratic empathic responses' (Bozarth, 1984) and Raskin's 'unsystematic responses' (Raskin, 1988).

Through one's developing congruence, a therapist is first able to be fully present for themselves. A therapist needs to be aware of and have access to their experiences, their awarenesses, their values, beliefs — their own frame of reference. Then from this authentic position they are able both to step into their client's frame of reference via their attitudes of empathic understanding and unconditional regard, and sometimes choose to express themselves from their own frame of reference. Both their own frame of reference and their client's frame of reference are available to them.

I have a client who, when exploring something about which she feels vulnerable, I gently stay with her, genuinely checking my understanding of her experiencing and the meaning and significance of this to her. When her vulnerability is extreme I stay very close to using her words. Other times I am highly interactive with her, telling her how I see the world, telling her about some of my related experiences. She says 'I hadn't seen it like that' or 'no that wouldn't work for me I'm different from you'. She and I move quite freely from these different ways of being with each other. I am not consciously deciding, hence not diagnosing or becoming the expert, rather following where she is via my empathic understanding and acceptance of her.

This way of working is characterised by the therapist:
• being the whole of themselves in the relationship
• being open to their own frame of reference and their client's via their empathic understanding and unconditional positive regard
• having a belief in the actualising tendency within the therapist, the client and within the relationship
• having a flexibility to respond in different ways that arise from a complex and subtle interplay between who the therapist is, who the client is, the quality of the therapeutic relationship, the stage of this relationship and what is happening for the therapist and client in any particular moment.

The result of this will be a release in the therapist's ability to deepen their empathic understanding and unconditional positive regard. The significance of working in this way is that the actualising tendency works not only through the client but in addition through *the therapist* and *the therapeutic relationship*. This means a *much deeper healing potential* can be accessed.

Sometimes this idiosyncratic, unsystemised therapist behaviour can appear to be unusual, bizarre and even unprofessional.

- In a session with one client, I gave information concerning Building Societies who were trying to keep their existing customers due to the competition between mortgage providers. He could therefore approach them from a position of strength.
- With another client, at the end of a session I sat her down in the kitchen and gave her a bowl of homemade soup to eat.
- With Lana I did grounding exercises so that she could feel her feet on the ground and her behind on the seat before she left.

I have deliberately not given any supporting information to these events with some of my clients to emphasise the point. The therapist behaviour may well seem strange unless you believe that behaviour arose from her full, unique presence and understanding accepting interaction with a specific client arising at that particular time. Natiello writes 'Each therapeutic interaction is an unpredictable result of the spontaneous process between therapist and client' (Natiello, 1997, p. 2).

Limits and concerns regarding therapist's expression
To return to the question, what is appropriate therapist self-expression? Although Brodley (1999) attempts to delineate the limits regarding therapist communication, this complicated question sustains no definitive reply. Some therapist behaviour is inappropriate. There are always limits.

Our ethical codes of practice give us some guidelines to what is appropriate or not. Having a sexual relationship with a client, hitting a client, and stealing from a client I believe would never be appropriate. The person-centred philosophical position also gives the therapist guidelines for what is appropriate therapist behaviour or self expression. The fundamental philosophical position for the person-centred therapist is a belief in the actualising tendency. The client can be trusted to self-direct. This under pins a willingness to give up the common therapeutic position of being the expert for one of mutuality. Our way of being congruent in the therapeutic relationship needs to, at best, facilitate the client's connection with the actualising tendency and, at the very least, not interfere with it. Our way of being congruent needs to promote the mutuality of the therapeutic relationship.

One concern regarding incongruent self-expression or inappropriate therapist behaviour is that the therapist subtly controls the therapeutic process in order to satisfy their own needs, reflecting misuse and, in extreme cases, abuse of therapeutic power. Another concern is that by the therapist keeping access to their own frame of reference and sometimes expressing themselves from their frame of reference they will become an expert and the client's ability to self-direct will be thwarted.

It is the responsibility of each therapist to self-reflect and self-monitor these concerns. In the UK it is a requirement for every therapist, even when qualified, to have on-going supervision. I see this as vitally important for the continuing development of a therapist's congruence and an integral part of their professional development. Most person-centred therapists keep their philosophical position present: emphasising congruence involves stepping into the client's frame of reference via their empathic understanding and their unconditional positive regard. I realise I am suggesting something riskier. To walk this riskier path the therapist needs to be committed to actively developing their psychological maturity by self-reflection, meditation, personal therapy, trainings, supervision, large group experiences, holistic health programmes — cranial osteopathy, shiatsu, Chinese medicine, etc. Then when they are with their clients they can relax, bring their whole, real, congruent self to the existential meeting with their client.

3) The 'whole beyond the facets'

In being aware of our experiencing moment by moment, by having a flexible self-structure to allow the maximum amount of our experiencing into our awareness, by working at the edge of our awareness, by being able to shift from the logical, rational, view of the world to an intuitive, open, yielding view, by opening to allow the actualising tendency to flow through us, we have experiences of ourselves, our client and of the therapeutic relationship which we sometimes do not understand. We do not understand, in the ordinary sense, where the images, feelings, and words we are saying have come from.

There is a potential moment by moment of a meeting between client and therapist that taps into something which transcends the relationship between client and therapist. I think this in part is what Bozarth is drawing on when he writes about the idiosyncratic empathic response (Bozarth, 1984) and also when he emphasises the significance of the therapist 'being' in the relationship rather than 'doing' (Bozarth, 1992). It is only when we are functioning at this 'being' level that we can tap this potential. This is what I am wanting to access by feeling free to be the whole of myself in my relationship with my client: letting my congruent communications arise from the spontaneous interactions between myself and my client whilst being 'held' by something larger.

I believe what I am describing here is also what Rogers has referred to as there being 'something around the edges of these conditions that is really the most important element of therapy' (Baldwin, 1987, p. 45) and by his much quoted statement about presence,

> I find that when I am closest to my inner, intuitive self, when I am somehow in touch with the unknown in me, when perhaps I am in a slightly altered state of consciousness in the relationship, then whatever I do seems to be full of healing. Then simply my *presence* is releasing and helpful . . . when I can relax and be close to the transcendental core of me, then I may behave in strange and impulsive ways in the relationship, ways which I cannot justify rationally, which have nothing to do with my thought processes . . . Our relationship transcends itself and becomes a part of something larger. Profound growth and healing and energy are present (Rogers, 1986, in Kirschenbaum and Henderson, 1990, p. 137).

Rogers' basic philosophical stance based on the formative tendency in general, and the actualising tendency in particular, leads him to believe that if a person is functioning well, there is not a self-conscious awareness, i.e. there is not a disassociation between experience and awareness. When there is this congruence, then there is this openness and trust in some universal principle and then 'man is wiser than his intellect' (Rogers, 1963, p. 18).

In Rogers' (1980) extrapolation of the growth hypothesis he states his belief '. . . to knowing and sensing below the level of consciousness, to a conscious awareness of the organism and the external world, to a transcendent awareness of the harmony and unity of the cosmic system, including humankind' (p. 133) and 'participating in a larger universal formative tendency' (p. 128). It shows a 'greater complexity' (p. 128). Van Belle (1990) adds 'This is now no longer the impulse of life only but of the universe as a whole' (p. 54). At these moments our openness and belief in the actualising tendency (in the universal life force/God/ the infinite — insert your term of choice dependent on your own philosophical stance on life) is so total that we suspend our rational thought. We step into a different dimension. In shamanic practices this is called shifting from the tonal (everyday existence/reality) to the nagual (the spiritual/the other) reality, (Castenada, 1968, 1973; Sanchez, 1995). If we have or can develop this ability then the healing potential that we can access is unlimited.

THERAPIST'S TASKS

What I am promoting is no soft option where the therapist can indiscriminately self-disclose and meet their needs at the expense of their client. To work in this way the therapist needs to be deeply committed to her own self-development — always moving towards greater congruency and psychological maturity by developing her self-acceptance and self-understanding. She needs to know her own needs and fears so she can minimise the impact of these in her meeting with the client. She needs to offer unconditional self-regard to more and more of her experiencing so she is centred in her own experiencing. By being centred in her own experiencing at any moment, she is able to empathically understand and accept her client's experiences and have access to her experiencing that originates in who she is. She needs to develop the flexibility and trust in herself to sensitively respond in different ways arising from who she is and where her client is at that moment. She needs to develop a deep belief in the actualising tendency both in herself and her client.

The therapist's tasks include a *deep commitment to develop her congruence and psychological maturity, a willingness to learn about theoretical considerations and discuss their significance in practice, reflecting with peers, supervisors and therapists about her learning edges. She needs the ability to suspend this dialogue whilst in the moment to moment encountering with the client — to trust that she is being the best she can be at any moment — and to afterwards renew the process of reflection and learning.*

CONCLUSIONS

Congruence is holistic and multifaceted. Each facet of a diamond is significant but its brilliance comes from its whole. Congruence has a core, its facets and the 'whole beyond the facets'. The core is related to being myself, to my level of psychological maturity and my personal style. The facets include an openness to experiencing, an awareness of experiences free of denial and distortions, the therapist's behaviour and an ability to offer genuine empathic understanding and unconditional positive regard. The 'whole beyond the facets' means a healing potential can be accessed through an openness to the actualising tendency within the therapist, the client and the therapeutic relationship and beyond into the interconnectedness within the universe.

Most literature on congruence has addressed the relevant importance of congruence in relation to empathic understanding and unconditional positive regard, whether congruence only refers to the internal state of the therapist and what is appropriate therapist self-expression. Congruence's holistic and non-dualistic nature shifts the focus. Any separation of the therapist's behaviour or self-expression from their internal state becomes meaningless. There is no one 'right' answer to what is appropriate therapist self-expression or when and how to communicate congruence. Focusing on the 'doing' distracts from the 'being'. *The therapist's congruence will arise from the subtle and varied interaction between who the therapist is, who the client is, the quality of the therapeutic relationship, the stage of this relationship and what is happening for the therapist and client in any particular moment.*

This is not advocating the promiscuous expression of so-called 'congruence' where the therapist blurts out her (incongruent) feelings or becomes the focus or the expert. Nor is it when the expression of therapist-needs directs the therapeutic process. I am supporting the *principled* use of congruence where the therapist has an openness to the actualising tendency within herself, the client and the therapeutic relationship. This openness is also for her experiencing. This allows her to be maximally receptive to her client via her empathic understanding and unconditional positive regard. She has a flexibility, a maturity and trust in herself to respond in different ways that arise out of that moment to moment encountering between client and therapist. This flexibility emerges from her own deep experiencing of herself and her client; from her extended belief in the actualising tendency to include herself and the relationship rather than within the client alone; and from her acknowledgement of an interconnectedness within the universe from which to draw and with which to connect. In so doing the therapist will access a wisdom and embrace unlimited healing potential for therapist and client.

REFERENCES

Baldwin, M. (1987). Interview with Carl Rogers on the Use of the Self in Therapy. In M. Baldwin and V. Satir (Eds.) The *Use of Self in Therapy*. New York: The Haworth Press Inc, pp. 45–52.
Bozarth, J.D. (1984). Beyond Reflection: emergent modes of empathy. In R. Levant and J. Shlein (Eds.) *Client-centered therapy and the Person-Centered approach*. New York: Praeger, pp. 59–75.
Bozarth, J.D. (1992). Coterminous Interminglings of Doing and Being in Person-Centered Therapy. *Person-Centered Journal*, 1(1), pp. 12–20. (Reprinted in Bozarth 1998.)
Bozarth, J.D. (1996). A Theoretical Reconception of the Necessary and Sufficient Conditions for Therapeutic Personality Change. *Person-Centered Journal*, 3(1), pp. 44–51. (Reprinted in Bozarth 1998.)
Bozarth, J.D. (1998). *The Person-Centered Approach: A Revolutionary Paradigm*. Ross-on-Wye: PCCS Books.
Brodley, B. (1998). Congruence and its Relation to Communication in Client-Centered Therapy. *Person-Centered Journal*, 5(2), pp. 83–106.
Brodley, B. (1999). Reasons for Responses Expressing the Therapist's Frame of Reference in Client-Centred Therapy. *Person-Centred Journal*, 6(1), pp. 4–17.
Castenada, C. (1968). *The Teachings of Don Juan*. University of California Press.

Castenada, C. (1973). *Journey to Ixtlan*. Bodley Head.

Ellingham, I. (1999). Carl Rogers' 'Congruence' as an Organismic, Not a Freudian Concept. *Person-Centered Journal*, 6(2), pp. 121–40.

Gendlin, E.T. (1970). A Short Summary and Some Long Predictions. In J.T. Hart, and T.M. Tomlinson, (Eds.) *New Directions in Client-Centered Therapy*. Boston: Houghton Mifflin, pp. 544–62.

Haugh, S. (1998). Congruence: A Confusion of Language. *Person-Centered Practice*, 6(1), 44–50.

Kirschenbaum, H. and Henderson, V. (Eds.) (1990) *The Carl Rogers Reader*. London: Constable.

Lietaer, G. (1993). Authenticity, Congruence and Transparency in D. Brazier (Ed.) *Beyond Carl Rogers*. London: Constable, pp. 17–46.

Lietaer, G., Rombauts, J. and Van Balen, R. (Eds.) (1990). *Client-Centered and Experiential Psychotherapy in the Nineties*. Leuven: Leuven University Press.

Natiello, P. (1997). Therapist Authenticity and Connectedness Key to Healing. *Paper presented to 'Ten Years On' Conference Sheffield University*. Sheffield, UK.

Mearns, D. and Thorne, B. (1988). *Person-centered Counselling in Action*. London: Sage.

Raskin, N. (1952). Client-Centered Counselling and Psychotherapy. In E.L. Abt, and D. Brower (Eds) *Progress in Clinical Psychology*. New York: Grune and Stratton.

Raskin, N. (1988). What do we mean by person-centered therapy? *Paper presented at the second annual meeting of the Association for the Development of the Person-Centered Approach*. Hebron, NY.

Raskin, N. (1996). Person-Centred Psychotherapy. In W. Dryden, *Twenty Historical Steps in Developments in Psychotherapy*, London: Sage, pp. 1–28.

Rogers, C.R. (1946). Significant aspects of Client-Centered Therapy. *American Psychologist*, 1, pp. 415–22.

Rogers, C.R. (1951). *Client-Centered Therapy*. Boston: Houghton Mifflin.

Rogers, C.R. (1954). Some Hypotheses Regarding the Facilitation of Personal Growth. *Paper presented at Oberlin College*, Ohio, USA.

Rogers, C.R. (1957). The Necessary and Sufficient Conditions of Therapeutic Personality Change. *Journal of Consulting Psychology*, 21, pp. 95–103.

Rogers, C.R. (1958). The Characteristics of a Helping Relationship. *Personnel and Guidance Journal*, 37, pp. 6–16.

Rogers, C.R. (1959). A Theory of Therapy, Personality, and Interpersonal Relationships, as Developed in the Client-Centered framework. In S. Koch (Ed.) *A Theory of Therapy, Personality and Interpersonal Psychotherapy*. New York: McGraw Hill, pp. 184–256.

Rogers, C.R. (1961). *On Becoming a Person*. London: Constable.

Rogers, C.R. (1963). The Actualising Tendency in Relation to 'Motives' and to Consciousness. In M. R. Jones (ed). *Nebraska Symposium on Motivation*. Lincoln: University of Nebraska Press, pp. 1–24.

Rogers, C.R. (1975). Empathic: An Unappreciated Way of Being. *The Counselling Psychologist*, 5(2), pp. 2–10.

Rogers, C.R. (1978). *Carl Rogers on Personal Power*. London: Constable.

Rogers, C.R. (1980). *A Way of Being*. Boston: Houghton Mifflin.

Rogers, C.R. and Sanford, R.C. (1984). Client-Centered Psychotherapy. In Kaplan, I. and Sadock, B.J. (Eds.) *Comprehensive Textbook of Psychiatry, IV*. Baltimore: Williams and Wilkins, pp. 1374–88.

Rogers, C.R. and Stevens, B. (1967). *Person to Person: The Problem of Being Human*. London: Souvenir Press.

Rogers, C.R. (1986). A Client-Centered/Person-Centered Approach to Therapy. In I. Kutash, and A. Wolfe (Eds.) *Psychotherapist's Casebook*. San Fransisco: Jossey-Bass, pp. 197–208.

Rombauts, J. (1984). Empathie: actieve ontvankelijkheid. In Lietaer, G. Ph van Praag, and J.C.A.G. Swildens, (Eds.) *Client-Centred Psychotherapie in Beweging*. Leuven: Acco, pp. 167–76.

Sanchez, V. (1995). *The Teachings of Don Carlos: Practical Applications of the Works of Carlos Castaneda*. Sante Fe: Bear and Company.

Shostrom, E.L. (1965). *Three approaches to psychotherapy* (Part 1) [Film]. Orange, CA: Psychological Films.

Streich, E.R. (1951). The Self-experience of the Client-Centered Therapist. Paper: *University of Chicago Counselling Center*.

Van Belle, H.A. (1990). Roger's Later Move Towards Mysticism: Implications For Client-Centered Therapy. In G. Lietaer, J. Rombauts, R. Van Balen, (Eds.) *Client-Centered and Experiential Psychotherapy in the Nineties*. Leuven University Press, pp. 47–57.

6

Carl Rogers' 'Congruence' as an Organismic, not a Freudian, Concept

Ivan Ellingham

Abstract. *The principal purpose of this paper is to illumine the extent to which Carl Rogers' characterization of the central person-centred concept of congruence is couched in terms of a Cartesian-Newtonian, paradigmatic world-view mediated by the theoretical formulations of Sigmund Freud. Crucial problems in such a quasi-Freudian characterization of congruence are delineated demonstrative of a critical flaw in person-centred theory as a whole: its being a mix of concepts deriving from the disparate Cartesian-Newtonian and 'organismic' scientific paradigms. The re-formulation of congruence in organismic terms is envisaged as part of a general need to conceptualize all key person-centred concepts in such a fashion.*

> *The sciences . . . are born under quite special conditions — when their key concepts reach a degree of abstraction and precision which makes them adequate to the demands of exact, powerful, and microscopically analytic thinking (Susanne Langer, 1962, p. 13).*

As the matrix of ideas that underpins and guides person-centred counselling/ psychotherapy (c/p), and crafted almost entirely by Carl Rogers, person-centred theory is not merely 'unfinished' (Mearns, 1997, p. 135), but, in my estimation, crucially flawed.

The crucial flaw intrinsic to person-centred theory has to do, I contend (see Ellingham, 1997b), with its being a mix of concepts deriving from two disparate 'paradigms', two fundamentally different guiding visions of the world: on the one hand, the Cartesian-Newtonian ('C-N') paradigm which underlies Newtonian physics and our contemporary common-sense understanding of reality; on the other, a paradigm which is still in the process of emerging from the Cartesian-Newtonian, a paradigm variously labelled *holistic, organismic, process,* and from which has arisen *field theory, general systems theory* and *eco-psychology* (see Capra, 1982; 1996). A simple measure of the contrast between these two paradigms is that the former employs the machine as its root metaphor, the latter the living organism.

On the following grounds, therefore, (a) that Rogers developed person-centred theory in the attempt to generate scientific understanding of the phenomenon

A revision of a paper first published in *The Person-Centered Journal*, Vol. 6, No. 2, 1999. Reproduced with kindpermission of the publishers and editor.

of c/p; (b) that contemporary advance in scientific understanding embodies a shift from a C-N to an organismic view of the world; (c) that person-centred theory is, at its core, organismic not mechanistic in character (see Hall, Lindzey and Campbell, 1998, p. 454; Bozarth, 1998, p. 28), I further contend that in order to remedy the crucial flaw within person-centred theory and so render it a self-consistent vehicle of more advanced scientific understanding (even a paradigm for the field of c/p as a whole), various of the theory's key concepts need to be organismically 'purified'. We should seek to define all person-centred concepts in exclusively organismic rather than C-N terms — an intellectual exercise with which Rogers himself professed agreement (see Rogers, 1963, pp. 19ff.).

Rogers' concept of congruence constitutes a prime candidate for this kind of organismic 'makeover'. Supportive evidence for congruence's candidacy is provided, in my view, by disquieting appraisals recently voiced by a number of person-centred thinkers. Barbara Brodley concludes that 'the precise meaning of congruence [in Rogers' writings] remains somewhat ambiguous' (1998, p. 83); Len Holdstock remarks that 'the concept of congruence ... seems to be in urgent need of attention' (1996, p. 48); Sheila Haugh avows that 'understanding of the concept of congruence within person-centred theory and practice is at best blurred and at worst misinterpreted' (1998, p. 44); and Gill Wyatt charges that 'different practitioners are using different definitions of congruence and, related to their different theoretical position, they have a different stance with regard the place of congruence in therapeutic practice' (1998, p. 6).

In the present paper, I aim to point up how particular problems relating to Rogers' formulation of congruence arise from that formulation being shot through with C-N notions mediated by the theorizing of Sigmund Freud. As such, the article represents a *deconstructive*, stage-setting exercise preparatory to a constructive attempt to characterize congruence in an organismically refined fashion. In what follows, I first highlight the C-N flavour to Freud's classical conception of psychotherapeutic client change. Next, I consider how, in this regard, Rogers' characterization of congruence bears the imprint of Freud's theorizing. Thereafter, I identify crucial problems involved in Rogers' Freudian characterization of congruence and briefly allude to an alternative organismic approach. Finally, I sketch the general context and character of an organismic re-visioning of congruence.

IN THE FOOTSTEPS OF ISAAC AND RENÉ

It is hardly surprising that when Rogers came to theorize about the nature of c/p that his thinking should have been influenced by the views of Sigmund Freud, the founder of the modern discipline of c/p as the 'talking cure'. Indeed, Rogers had no qualms acknowledging that the development of non-directive or client-centered counselling — earlier terms for person-centred c/p — 'would not have been possible without the appreciation of man's unconscious strivings and complex emotional nature which was Freud's contribution to our culture' (1951, p. 4).

But, as we shall shortly see, Rogers' appreciation in this respect was not merely of a general character. It involved explaining specific psychotherapeutic client change — constructive self-change effected by c/p — in decidedly Freudian terms. As such, it expresses a scheme grounded in the intellectual formulations of Isaac Newton and René Descartes, i.e. the C-N paradigm.

Three features of the C-N paradigm to take note of with respect to Freud's theorizing are:

1. a dualistic view of reality wherein the person is considered made up of two fundamentally different, irreducible and unchanging substances: René Descartes' *res cogitans*, physically unextended, conscious *mind*; and *res extensa*, physically extended, unconscious *matter* (the latter being, of course, the body).

2. the notion that at its simplest level the physical realm of matter is comprised of unchanging 'bits of stuff' called atoms which get moved around in the container of absolute space in the cause-effect manner of parts of a clock or of billiard balls on a billiard table. Recall that it was Isaac Newton who specified such movement with mathematical precision.

3. the presumption that mind/consciousness operates according to the principles of thought which are of a different order than those which govern the workings of the physical domain.

Thus it was that when Freud came upon 'patients' who had no conscious idea of what was causing their 'neuroses' (certain disturbances of bodily, behavioural and mental functioning), he at first sought to explain such disturbances neurologically. As a former student of Ernst Brücke, this meant in terms of unconscious matter governed by Newtonian principles, i.e. in tune with Brücke's advocacy of mechanism, the reductionist doctrine that all mental functioning could ultimately be explained in terms of physico-chemical processes operating in a machine-like way (see Appignanesi, 1979). Unsuccessful in this strictly mechanistic enterprise, Freud put to one side the question of the mind's relationship to the body, to matter, and came up instead with an explanatory scheme which departed from strict C-N assumptions by positing the existence of a psychological realm of which consciousness was not an attribute. Freud labelled this realm 'the unconscious', further departing from a purist C-N view by conceiving both it, and the mind as a whole, in quasi-mechanistic terms. Here Freud appears to have been much influenced by the views of Johann Herbart, who posited the existence of an unconscious mind, along with the notion of 'ideas' as entities (see MacIntyre, 1958, chpt. 2). Thus, in his classical topographical or spatial scheme, Freud conceived the mind to consist of the compartments of consciousness, the unconscious and entity-like mental contents — akin to a C-N physical apparatus.

Although Freud later developed a more complex scheme, as Janet Malcolm relates, it was this '*spatial* arrangement of the unconscious and conscious states' (1982, p. 29, original emphasis) that guided Freud when writing the papers elaborating the basic techniques of *psychoanalysis*.

The crucial discovery that Freud explained on such a basis was that of patients' neurotic symptoms becoming alleviated when, aided by the psychoanalyst, they were able to verbally bring to mind a forgotten idea from their childhood, an idea of a particularly repugnant nature. Given that there seemed to be an associative link between the nature of the idea and the nature of the symptoms,

Freud hypothesized that it was the idea itself that was 'pathogenic', in that it had previously been the underlying cause of the neurotic symptoms in the manner of a cancerous cell. What happened in childhood, Freud reasoned, was that when ideas arose expressive of the primitive infantile impulses of sexual lust and intense hate, they could not be countenanced and allowed entry into the compartment of consciousness. Consequently they became repelled from consciousness and confined in the chamber of the unconscious. Freud coined the term *repression* to denote the defence operation by which this took place.

Psychotherapy, for Freud, thus consisted in the reversal of repression, a restorative process involving the excision from the unconscious of pathogenic repressed ideas (conceived as unchanging atomic mental entities, or things) and their concomitant passage into consciousness — their movement from one chamber of a quasi-mechanical system to another.

Insofar as the therapist's task was to facilitate the entry into consciousness of previously repressed ideas, unconscious contents, Freud described the work of the therapist as that of making 'his [the patient's] unconscious conscious to him' (1973, p. 100). So construed, the effectiveness of the therapist depended on her or him being an expert on the unconscious and an expert in diagnosing the nature of the underlying unconscious idea on the basis of its disguised or masked expression in the patient's behavioural symptoms and mental imagery. The therapist thus *interpreted* to the patient the nature of the idea which lay below the surface in the *reservoir* of their unconscious. This enabled the patient to know the repressed idea for what it was and, through its having its place in consciousness, to cease its subversive influence on the patient's mental functioning.

Overall, then, according to this classical, topographical view the psychotherapeutic process was roughly comparable to the hauling up of an anchor from the depths of the sea in order for it to assume its proper place on board ship. There it could be apprehended directly for what it was rather than being known indirectly through its previous undersea anchorage effects. It was in such a fashion, therefore, that Freud developed a scheme in which the mind, and *ipso facto*, the enterprise of c/p, became 'placed among the inhabitants of the "billiard-ball universe" of Newtonian mechanics' (MacIntyre, 1958, p. 17).

IN THE FOOTSTEPS OF SIGMUND

It is Rogers' formulation of congruence as a concept integral to his explanation of psychotherapeutic change that sees this central person-centred notion being defined in a decidedly Freudian manner. Mirroring Freud's dualistic description of psychotherapeutic change as the unconscious becoming conscious, Rogers depicts such change as 'a shift from incongruence to congruence' (1961, p. 157) — where congruence is associated with awareness and constitutes the state of a person who is 'genuine', 'whole', 'integrated', 'without facade', 'adjusted' (1959, p. 206, 1957, p. 224); while 'incongruence', congruence's polar opposite, is linked with 'denial and distortion to awareness' and taken to represent 'the basis of all psychological pathology in man [sic], and the basis of all his social pathology as well' (1959, p. 205, 1963, p. 21).

Furthermore, paralleling Freud's comparison between the analyst, who is conscious of the unconscious, as against the patient, who is not, Rogers construes the effective therapist as an individual who 'is congruent or integrated in the [therapeutic] relationship', in contrast to the client who, by definition, 'is in a state of incongruence' (Rogers, 1957, p. 221). These respective characterizations of congruent counsellor versus incongruent client constitute two of Rogers' 'six . . . necessary and sufficient conditions for the initiation of a process of constructive personality [i.e. psychotherapeutic] change' (ibid., p. 234).

Turning to the detail of Rogers' formal descriptions of congruence and incongruence, not surprisingly we find a tendency to define congruence with reference to the therapist and incongruence with reference to the client — albeit Rogers considers there to be a continuum from a 'maximum of incongruence' to the 'complete congruence' of the 'fully functioning person' (1961, p. 157, 1959, p. 235). The congruent therapist is not, however, expected to be a paragon of congruence outside the therapeutic relationship (Rogers, 1957, p. 224).

Common to all of Rogers' formal definitions of congruence and incongruence is their specification, respectively, of a concordant or discordant relationship between two or more levels of a person's psychological functioning (Rogers, 1961, p. 339). The two-level definition linked with inner psychological change mainly appears with reference to clients. The three- (or more) level version adds on to the two-level definition an extra level (or levels) relating to outward behaviour and verbal communication and mainly appears in connection with characterizing the state of the therapist (or persons in general, including infants).

The total picture is perhaps easiest to grasp if we start by considering a three-level definition. Here, for instance, (inclusive of alternative terms found elsewhere) is one in which the levels are clearly identified as such, and where the concordant relationship between them is characterized as an 'accurate matching' (1959, p. 206, 1957, p. 97):

> Congruence is the term we have used to indicate an accurate matching of experiencing and awareness. It may be still further extended to cover a matching of experience, awareness, and communication . . . He [the congruent individual] is one unified person all the way through, whether we tap his experience at the visceral [gut, organismic, or physiological] level, the level of his awareness [consciousness, or symbolization], or the level of communication (Rogers, 1961, p. 339).

Complementing this three-level characterization of congruence is a three-level depiction of incongruence. So conceptualized, incongruence comes in two forms, 'incongruence A' and 'incongruence B', as Mearns and Thorne (1988, p. 84) dub them: 'incongruence between experience and awareness . . . usually spoken of as defensiveness, or denial [or distortion] to awareness'; and 'between awareness and communication . . . usually thought of as falseness or deceit' (Rogers, 1961, p. 341).

How congruence might conceivably involve more than three levels is suggested by two definitions relating to the therapist, definitions in which, as 'emotionally toned experiences . . . within the envelope of the organism' (Rogers, 1959, pp. 198, 197), 'feelings' have something of an unchanging 'thing-like' character:

> By this [congruence] we mean that the feelings the therapist is experiencing
> are available to him [sic], available to his awareness, and he is able to live these
> feelings, be them, able to communicate them if appropriate (Rogers, 1961, p. 61).
>
> Thus whether he [the therapist] is angry or affectionate or ashamed or
> enthusiastic, we sense that he is the same at all levels — in what he is
> experiencing at an organismic level, in his awareness at the conscious level,
> and in his words and communications (ibid., p. 283).

To complete the portrayal and begin to gain a sense of how, in Rogers' view, a
psychotherapeutic shift from incongruence to congruence entails constructive
self-change, consider Rogers' depiction of both congruence and incongruence
as two-level notions, the relationship between the two levels specified as 'accurate
symbolization' or 'accurate representation'.

Focusing first on incongruence, 'It', according to Rogers, 'refers to a discrepancy
between the actual experience of the organism and the self-picture of the
individual insofar as it represents that experience' (1957, p. 222). By contrast,
'when self-experiences are accurately symbolized [in awareness] and are included
in the self-concept [self-picture] in this accurately symbolized form, then the
state is one of congruence of self and experience' (1959, p. 206).

The following statement by Rogers shows clearly how when psychotherapeutic
increase in congruence is depicted on the basis of a two-level conception of
congruence then the end result is an account which clearly bears the hallmarks
of Freud's notion of 'the unconscious becoming conscious'. 'In client-centered
therapy', declares Rogers,

> . . . our theory is that in the psychological safety of the therapeutic relationship
> the client is able to permit in his awareness feelings and experiences which
> ordinarily would be *repressed*, or denied to awareness. These previously denied
> experiences may be incorporated into the self. For example, a client who has
> repressed all feelings of hostility may come, during therapy, to experience his
> hostility freely. His concept of himself then becomes reorganized to include
> this realization that he has at times hostile feelings to others. His self-picture
> becomes to that degree a more accurate map or representation of the totality
> of his experience (1961, p. 237, emphasis added).

Here, accentuated by Rogers' deployment of the technical Freudian term of
repression and the entity-like nature of feelings and experiences, we appear to
encounter a similarity between Rogers and Freud that is to the point of identity,
a judgement endorsed by Calvin Hall, Gardner Lindzey and John Campbell (1998).
'Explicitly recognized in Rogers' theory', they affirm,

> is the concept of an organism that has many experiences of which the person
> is not aware. Some of these unsymbolized experiences are denied entrance to
> consciousness because they are inconsistent with the self-image. If this is not
> repression, in the psychoanalytic sense, then the distinction between it and
> repression is so slight as to be negligible (p. 488).

Given this apparent concordance between the views of Rogers and Freud, are we
to say, then, that Rogers' formulations relating to congruence are merely the

masked representation of an underlying Freudian scheme? Is Rogers himself being incongruent in failing to symbolize to awareness unconscious Freudian ideas?

A number of other features in Rogers' theorizing would seem to indicate that the correspondence between his views and those of Freud is some way from being an identity. To gauge the closeness of this correspondence, consider the following five points:

(1) Rogers, as revealed already, did not conceptualize congruence and psychotherapeutic change solely in terms of two levels but of three, or more, so that it might be said that whereas Freud's scheme is dualistic Rogers' is not.

Countering this claim, though, are first the arguments of Brodley (1998) and Haugh (1998) that it is Rogers' two-level formulation found in his 1957 and 1959 theory statements which provide us with the authoritative and delimiting definition of congruence. Back to pure Freud is their implied message.

Also, there is the question of the character of the levels in Rogers' three-level version of congruence. Organismic experience, awareness, and communication can hardly be said to be levels in the sense of being relatively higher and lower categories on a single ladder-like scale of psychological functioning. Certainly, insofar as Rogers associates 'organismic experience' with the functioning of animals, and 'symbolization to awareness' with adult humans (1961, p. 105), we can readily see how the latter can be considered to be on a higher level than the former. But what case can be made that communication is indeed a higher mode of functioning than symbolization to awareness? If there is indeed a ladder linking symbolization to awareness to communication (and from a developmental perspective this would seem hardly to be the case), then it would not seem to be the same one as links organismic experience to symbolization to awareness.

Overall, therefore, a strong case can be made in relation to the definition of congruence that we are still dealing with a Freudian-style dualistic system, of organismic experience and symbolization to awareness, in relation to which symbolization to awareness and communication represent different articulations of the same developmental level.

(2) In spite of the fact that 'Rogers seems to assume that feelings have a ' "thing-like" quality' (Wexler, 1974, p. 53), Rogers' account of feelings 'bubbling through into awareness' (see Rogers, 1961, p. 156) is different from Freud's depiction involving billiard ball-type feeling moving from one chamber in the mind to the other. For his part, Rogers appears to posit that denied feelings come to enjoy a presence at the levels of awareness and communication in tandem with their continued presence at an organismic level. Whereas an incongruent individual's feelings are 'denied to awareness', by contrast the congruent person 'is the same at all levels' (Rogers, 1961, p. 61), such that what he or she 'is feeling at an experiential or visceral level is clearly present in awareness, and is available for direct communication' (Rogers and Sanford, 1989, p. 1490). Of interest here is that such a notion of the same feeling being present at different levels in fact tallies with an alternative conception of Freud. In relation to his 'topographical separation of the systems Ucs. [the unconscious] and Cs. [consciousness]', says Freud, there is 'the possibility that an idea may exist simultaneously in two places in the mental apparatus' (1986, p. 150).

This interpretation of the same 'thing' being present at all levels in the congruent person fits with Rogers having adopted the term congruence 'based on the geometric concept of congruent triangles' (Kirschenbaum, 1979, p. 196), i.e. the notion of triangles 'coinciding exactly when superimposed' (Bozarth, 1998, p. 71), of their being identical clones, 'things' which are no different from one another.

Brodley, on the other hand, draws attention to Rogers' writings supporting a somewhat different interpretation of the above circumstance. Writing from her two-level position, she is of the firm opinion that 'the theoretical definition of congruence as accurate representation of experience by inner symbols is about the ['accurate'] relation between the contents of experience and the symbols ['in awareness'] representing the contents' (1998, pp. 87 and 92). This view of matters would seem to have in mind contents, unchanging things, existing at an experiential level with symbolization involving the simultaneous presence at the level of awareness of a representative mark or label, in the way a mark on a map represents a 'thing' or feature of the real territory. Given the point, though, emphasized by Rogers himself, that the map is not the territory (see Rogers, 1951, p. 485), a difficulty which arises for this interpretation is how to square it with the notion of a congruent person being 'the same at all levels'.

In relation to feelings being things, a further scenario somewhat at odds with Freud arises from Rogers' conception of accurate symbolization involving an openness to experience, i.e. the individual is 'openly aware of his [sic] feelings and attitudes as they exist in him at an organic [i.e. 'organismic'] level' (Rogers, 1961, p. 115). It is as if the process of accurate symbolization is equivalent to the cleaning of a glass panel to enable open apprehension of whatever lies beyond it. So envisaged, feelings denied to awareness are like fish swimming beneath a glass bottomed-boat which cannot be apprehended as such due to the dirty glass. Once the glass is cleaned though, the fish can be accurately perceived for what they are. In such a characterization, then, with the development of congruence the individual comes to enjoy 'the gift of a free and undistorted awareness' of previously denied 'thing-like' feelings which all the time continue to reside at the organismic level (Rogers, 1961, p. 105).

(3) Leaving aside the question of the distorted conscious representation of a denied feeling, which is common to both Freud's and Rogers' accounts, Rogers' conception of feelings coming to awareness incorporates a complexity not found in Freud's equivalent formulation. For Rogers, unlike Freud, it is not only a matter of a previously denied feeling suddenly being consciously apprehended in its full glory in a sudden moment of insight, but of such a feeling being capable of becoming apprehended 'with varying degrees of sharpness, from dim awareness of something existing as ground, to a sharp focus of something which is in focus as figure' (Rogers, 1959, p. 198). There is thus a continuum in relation to being conscious of a feeling, from a complete 'denial to awareness' to the condition of 'experiencing a feeling fully', i.e. with optimal 'richness' (Rogers, 1961, p. 151).

Again, though, it is questionable in this instance just how different Rogers' views are from those of Freud's. David Wexler, for example, comments, given that feelings have a 'thing-like' quality for him, 'Rogers must assume that a richness of feelings exists outside awareness prior to symbolization', such that 'outside of awareness there is some kind of reservoir, not unlike the Freudian unconscious, where a richness of feelings resides and exists' (1974, pp. 53, 54).

(4) If, in Rogers' theorizing, there is indeed an implicit reservoir of denied feelings, then we would have to say that it is certainly different from Freud's with regard both its contents and its structure. For a start, we would have to presume that located within it are not only destructive and negative feelings (equivalent to the repressed contents of Freud's unconscious), but also those of both a neutral and a positive nature, with the more positive and constructive to be found at the greatest depth, at the person's essential core. Thus, in relation to the case of his client 'Mrs. Oak', Rogers reports that 'underneath the bitterness and hatred and the desire to get back at the world which has cheated her, is a much less anti-social feeling, a deep experience of having been hurt'; while 'underneath the bitterness, underneath the hurt, is a self that is without hate' (1961, pp. 96 and 101).

A similar picture also emerges with respect to another client of Rogers. Rogers relates that in his therapeutic work with this second client he was 'responsive both to the anger and the pain that was discovered to be underlying it' (1982, p. 253). Directly referring to the client, Rogers reports that in the course of therapy the client's 'armor begins to crack' such that 'we find the upper layer is anger, but further down in the slime are the unspeakable hurts' (in Farber, Brink and Raskin, 1996, p. 308).

According to Rogers' own hypothesis, what we see in these instances is a process wherein 'only when a gut-level experience is fully accepted and accurately labelled in awareness can it be completed. Then the person can move on' (1980, p. 158).

With congruence resulting from gut-level experience becoming accurately labelled in awareness, the client's moving on — of becoming more congruent — appears to entail the symbolization to awareness of increasingly positive feelings, a descending step-wise process that presumably continues until the hypothetical end-point of complete congruence (of being fully functioning) is reached. As we have seen, it is this congruent condition which is epitomized by the effective therapist in the therapeutic relationship, as one who feels and communicates unconditional positive regard towards another (the client). What we have is a scenario in which there appears to be different storage levels for qualitatively different feelings denied to awareness such that as one delves down the layers one passes from negative to positive feelings.

(5) In the face of criticism from Eugene Gendlin (1962, 1964), Rogers' later writings can be said to show a shift away from a C-N, Freudian-style of conceiving psychotherapeutic change towards a more organismic or process-orientated conception. It might be argued that Rogers' final position regarding the definition of congruence shifted away from that of his earlier quasi-Freudian conception. Whatever the truth of such a claim, there nevertheless remains clear evidence that, in his final writings, Rogers still continued to characterize congruence and psychotherapeutic change in a Freudian manner.

We have already seen how, in his later years, Rogers spoke of discovering feelings at layers 'down in the slime'. But note too how he refers to his own personal satisfaction at being able to be congruent, to 'get close to himself', as he idiosyncratically puts it. 'So it is a very satisfying thing', he says, 'when I sense that I have gotten close to me, to the *feelings and hidden aspects that live below the surface*' (1980, p. 16 — my emphasis).

Note how in the same later period, Rogers declares that the role of the therapist is not that of 'trying to uncover totally unconscious feelings' (1980, p. 142). And finally, note how, close to the end of his life, in a work written jointly with Ruth Sanford, Rogers appraises Ben's account of an experience of personal psychotherapeutic change. 'Ben', Rogers and Sanford comment,

> . . . gives a beautiful description of defensiveness — a denial to awareness of his anger — and the dissolving of that defensiveness in the safe and trusting environment initiated by the facilitator of learning. His masked feelings become unmasked. He can accept himself as angry (1989, p. 1487).

GET THEE BEHIND ME SIGMUND!

To this point my primary concern has been to lay bare the extent to which Rogers' concept of congruence and, *ipso facto*, his conception of psychotherapeutic change, correspond to Freud's C-N formulations. I move on now to consider certain basic problems involved in conceiving congruence in such a quasi-Freudian fashion.

Whether or not they are considered to move from one location to another, as I see it, the central problem endemic to Rogers' quasi-Freudian conception of congruence arises from the treatment of mental events (feelings, in particular) as things or contents which explicitly or implicitly are assumed to dwell in some kind of psychological container or envelope. When leading person-centred authorities Dave Mearns and Brian Thorne (1988) inform me that my congruence as a therapist depends on my ability to 'feel the feelings that are within me' (p. 75); and when in explicating congruence they draw a diagram with a square area housing 'the counsellor's underlying feelings in response to a client' of which the counsellor may be '*unaware*' (pp. 84f, original emphasis), there can be no doubt that Cartesian-Newtonian, topographical Freudianism is alive and well within the person-centred approach. It is a situation in relation to which a suitably augmented observation of Eugene Gendlin is entirely apt. 'Whether', says Gendlin, 'they are "in" awareness or "in" the unconscious, [or 'at the organismic level'], the contents ['feelings'] are viewed as already defined, fully formed, and unaffected in their nature by "coming into" awareness' (1962, p. 30).

As it happens though, it doesn't take too much thought apropos this jack-in-the-box scenario to realize that the idea of an unconscious feeling, an underlying feeling of which one is unaware, i.e. an '*unfelt* feeling', is logical nonsense.

'Incongruence A', declare Mearns and Thorne, 'is where the counsellor has underlying feelings in response to the client, but is unaware of these' (1988, p. 85) — a case in point being the counsellor whose 'incongruence was due to a lack of awareness of the anger within her' (p. 84).

Pause for a moment to consider the kind of notion that is being suggested here: that I am experiencing an unfelt feeling of anger of which I would be aware . . . would be feeling, if only I wasn't actually feeling a feeling of anxiety, of depression, or of exhilaration — or, indeed, were feeling no feeling at all.

Just what, at the moment of my not feeling it, is a feeling of which I am unaware? Perhaps, like an unseen sighting, I am to equate it with the emotional hurt I would be feeling if I were not on Prozac?; or to the pain I would be feeling under the dentist's drill were it not for the anaesthetic, or self-hypnosis?

A feeling of pain where I have no feeling of pain? That is something I definitely think I can handle! A feeling is what I feel, not what I do not feel.

Relevant to such reflections, social constructionist Rom Harré (1986) fittingly pours scorn on the notion of an already fully-formed feeling of anger existing 'within the envelope of the organism' prior to our awareness of it. On Harré's testimony,

> there is a relatively new 'anger' language game that is played in T-groups and Rogerian therapy sessions. 'Let's let all that *anger* out!' This kind of talk suggests that there is a buried affective state, a kind of emotional boil, that can be lanced and the poison removed. But even a brief encounter with 'encounter' groups shows that there is almost certainly no such thing as 'buried anger'. The anger displayed by the members seems to be created by the therapy session itself (p. 7)

Feelings of anger or of other emotions, Harré thus points up, are always a social construction, very much a product of our cultural values and language system. Not only, too, are they *about* some societal circumstance, but most importantly they are *created* in the here and now — our feelings being, in Gendlin's phrase, 'newly produced each moment' (1981, p. 97).

Such a conception of the momentary and creative formation of feelings highlights, in particular, Rogers' inevitably passive conception of symbolization. For him, symbolization can only be a simple labelling process, a process of opening up our awareness to what is already present at the level of organismic experience, a shining-the-light-upon a pre-existing, previously hidden thing.

These days there is an increasing awareness that individuals from different cultures live in different worlds. Thanks to the modes and schemes of symbolization passed on as part of their cultural heritage we see that whatever may be going on at an organismic level, the feelings we become aware of are the result of a creative act involving our cultural values. It is for this reason, as Len Holdstock recounts in his specific discussion of 'anger and congruence', that 'very little anger is elicited in some . . . cultures' (1996, p. 50). It is not that there are feelings of anger lodged inside us which some cultures let out while other cultures 'keep them in', or 'repress', but that what actually is felt is a function of the culturally specific way a person interprets certain configurations of the total field of events relevant to their life, events both 'internal' and external.

Such a social constructionist approach to the experiencing of feelings also sheds light, in my view, on a further difficulty intrinsic to Rogers' Freudianesque conception of congruence — a difficulty related to the notion of feelings, of which we are unaware, dwelling at different organismic layers or levels according to how negative or positive they are.

The precise definition of congruence and incongruence becomes more than problematic when we envisage positive feelings of affection and regard, say, underlying more negative ones like anger. For, under such circumstances, a person might be said to become congruent by accurately symbolizing feelings of anger to awareness, but yet remain incongruent in terms of not yet having accurately symbolized feelings of positive regard. To resolve this difficulty, one can decide to characterize congruence solely in terms of accurately symbolizing to awareness the positive feelings at the core of the person. However, this would

106

mean that the conscious awareness and expression of anger, say, would be regarded as an instance of 'incongruence'; that anger itself became interpreted as an incongruent emotion.

Certainly such an approach could prove helpful in combating the psychologically damaging situation of therapists expressing therapeutically destructive negative feelings in the name of congruence. But, even so, it still leaves us with a bizarre picture where 'out of awareness at the organismic level' and 'stacked in order of positivity', there exist different ready-made feelings patiently waiting to step up in turn into surface consciousness. And in any case, aside from the bizarreness, there is still the issue of feelings being conceived as things.

An alternative explanation of such a progressive experiencing of increasingly positive feelings, one influenced by social constructionism, would relate whatever feelings a person experiences to the socio-cultural context in which they occur, with the therapeutic relationship itself constituting such a context. So, for example, with two therapists the same incongruent client might become aware of feeling anger or the less negative feeling of deep hurt. Through the quality of the relationship that she offers, the second therapist may have facilitated expressing feelings arising from the client's core incongruence, whereas the first therapist facilitated experiencing feelings expressing less fundamental incongruence.

One question which arises from such an interpretation, therefore, is whether or not clients, either in individual or group therapy, must necessarily first get in touch with negative feelings before they can experience more positive ones. A related question is whether or not Charles Truax and Robert Carkhuff (1967) were right in the judgement they formed when in a particular study of client-centred therapists it was observed 'that the client-centered process of therapy somehow avoids the expected and usual patient expressions of negative, hostile, or aggressive feelings' (p. 503). Truax and Carkhuff's conclusion was that 'the client-centered therapist for some reason seems less open to receiving negative, hostile, or aggressive feelings' (ibid.). Might it not be possible that such unpleasant feelings only existed for the practitioners of other therapeutic approaches?; that person-centred practitioners did not act in such a way as to create them for the client?

In a lively 'dialogue' with Rogers, we find Rollo May endorsing the same judgement of person-centred therapists as Truax and Carkhuff. May pronounces that 'aspects of evil — anger, hostility against the therapist, destructiveness — need to be brought out in therapy' (1982, p. 246), even as he suggests behaviour by the therapist likely to generate the experiencing and expression of 'evil' by the client. We seem to be back to the same old blaming the victim/transference game to which psychoanalysts are prone. The client's present problem in relating to the therapist has nothing to do with the therapist's behaviour towards the client, but is entirely the result of the nasty unfelt feelings which lie within the client.

When, therefore, person-centred authority Germain Lietaer (1998) makes reference to the preceding statement of Truax and Carkhuff to warn us that 'our training within a certain therapeutic orientation may sharpen or blunt our sensitivity to certain types of experiential content' (p. 70), I, for one, would want to be reassured that such a warning was not being issued from a quasi-Freudian point of view.

In concluding this discussion of problems arising when congruence is defined in a Freudian fashion, a fundamental point to be kept in mind is that Cartesian mind/body *dualism* is inherent in such a definition. That is to say, that in a situation in which mental phenomena — ideas, thoughts, feelings, etc. — are conceived of as 'bits of stuff', the question as to how these form a unity with physical counterparts composed of a fundamentally different kind of stuff/ substance continues to remain unanswered. It is the question, in other words, of how one goes about resolving the notorious mind-body problem.

Instead of speaking of feelings being experienced at an organismic level, Rogers at times refers to such experiencing taking place at a physiological level (1961, p. 340). For instance, an incongruent man is said to be experiencing anger, at a physiological level, when '[c]onsciously he is *not* experiencing anger' (ibid. original emphasis). In this context, Rogers definitely seems to be bringing the physical body into the equation.

However, what needs to be remembered here is that, for Rogers, feelings are a special type of experience (of the 'emotionally toned' variety), where experience itself is defined by Rogers 'as all that is going on in the envelope of the organism at any given moment which is potentially available to awareness'. In Rogers' scheme it is thus 'a psychological, not a physiological definition' (Rogers, 1959, p. 197).

Just like Freud, it seems, Rogers essentially set to one side the question of the relationship of mind and body — although not entirely. For in proposing that we can read from physiological and behavioural activity what a person is feeling — viz. the flushed face, voice tone, shaking finger signifying anger (Rogers, 1961, p. 339) — Rogers seems to be advocating the 'James-Lange' theory of emotions that posits that, for each emotion we feel, there is a specific physiological pattern of skeletal and visceral changes (see Gross, 1996, p. 123). Whether Rogers is advocating such a theory or not, certainly contemporary psychologists are in general sceptical of such a notion (see Ginsburg and Harrison, 1996). In particular, they point to empirical evidence demonstrating that different individuals interpret the same physiological and behavioural events according to their idiosyncratic socio-cultural context, and thereby experience different feelings (see Gross, 1996, pp. 127ff.).

From the preceding discussion of problems that arise from characterizing congruence in a quasi-Freudian, Cartesian-Newtonian manner, it should be clear by now that any adequate formulation of this central person-centred notion will necessarily involve the resolution of certain fundamental issues regarding the nature of human mental functioning and the nature of the human being as a unity of mental and physical happenings. In my final remarks I outline the paradigmatic context by which I believe these fundamental issues can be adequately dealt with, along with some discussion of how congruence might be more precisely defined.

EPILOGUE AND PROLOGUE

According to Susanne Langer,

> Among all the facts with which psychologists deal, the one they seem least able to handle is the fact that we feel our own activity and the impingements of

the world around us. The metaphysical status of 'feelings', 'contents of consciousness', 'subjectivity', or of the private aspects of experience, generally, has been an asses' bridge . . . ever since Descartes treated *res extensa* and *res cogitans* as irreducible and incommensurable substances (1962, p. 11).

In discussing Carl Rogers' concept of congruence, I have sought to convey how his characterization is couched in Cartesian-Newtonian terms derived from Freud. I have endeavoured to make plain how a C-N world-scheme underlies certain crucial problems to do with both Rogers' definition of congruence and his interrelated conception of psychotherapeutic change. Insofar as these formulations of Rogers involve the treatment of feelings as substantive bits of stuff, the Cartesian asses' bridge, to which Langer refers, has definitely lived up to its name. As to how this bridge might be circumvented, I have already postulated that, for this to be achieved, congruence and other key person-centred concepts need to be defined in exclusively organismic/process terms. In the preceding section, I touched upon certain aspects of such an organismic re-visioning of congruence in indicating the relevance of the field theory perspective of social constructionist thought.

Beyond this, through incorporating the conceptual features I have specified elsewhere as the basis for a future person-centred paradigm of c/p (Ellingham, 1996, 1997a, 2000), the whole task, as I see it, will involve giving concrete expression to the radical process-view of the world articulated most profoundly by Alfred North Whitehead, a world-vision which holds that 'the process is the reality' and we best think of ourselves as 'process immersed in process beyond ourselves' (Whitehead, 1925, p. 72, 1938, p. 8). Thereby, with mental and physical 'stuff' construed in terms of differing expressions of patterned activity (process), we humans, as complex rounds of process (organisms), become portrayed in a unitary fashion — with the creative self-actualization of our individual-being caught up in an interrelationship with every other organism courtesy of the all-embracing creative advance and actualization of that organism that constitutes the universe as a whole. So conceived, 'The process of creation is the form of unity of the universe' (Whitehead, 1933, p. 179).

Such a radical process view, I contend, is entirely at one with the core thrust of Rogers' theorizing. In his comprehensive explication of Rogers' thought, Harry Van Belle (1980) attests that 'Rogers thinks principally in terms of process, dynamics, movement and change', the person being defined 'as a tendency, a process, an activity or functioning', not as 'something *other than* this activity, as a substance that is itself to itself regardless of how it functions' (p. 71, original emphasis). '[F]or Rogers', declares Van Belle, 'man [sic] is always and everywhere an organismic actualizing process' (ibid.). Moreover, in that the actualizing tendency powering this personal growth process is part and parcel of a 'formative tendency at work in the universe, which can be observed at every level' (Rogers, 1980, p. 124), Rogers clearly espouses a doctrine in close accord with Whitehead, one wherein 'everything that exists, including human beings, is taken up into this total evolutionary process of becoming' (Van Belle, 1990, p. 49).

To adopt such a radical-process approach in reconceptualizing congruence and psychotherapeutic change is in many ways to proceed along a path already roughly trodden by Eugene Gendlin and others who have developed a form of therapy termed 'experiential psychotherapy', an approach which has its roots in person-centred theory and which many see as falling within the compass of the person-centred approach. Gendlin's own 'focusing-oriented/experiential psychotherapy' originated when Gendlin, 'coming from the philosophical tradition of Dilthey, Dewey, Merleau-Ponty, and McKeon, developed a Philosophy of the "Implicit" and applied it to the work that Rogers was doing' (Hendricks-Gendlin, 1999, p. 2).

Beyond Gendlin, another major development of experiential psychotherapy is that associated with psychologists at York University in Canada, the main principals being Laura North Rice and more recently Leslie Greenberg. Building upon the ideas of Gendlin, this brand of experiential psychotherapy has taken ideas from contemporary cognitive psychology — initially from information processing theory; latterly from neo-Piagetian cognitive developmental theory — in formulating a 'dialectical constructivist model of experiential therapy' (Greenberg and Van Balen, 1998, p. 42). However as part of the present attempt to sketch the general outlines of this organismic reconceptualization of congruence and psychotherapeutic change, I will indicate how my views both accord with and differ from those of Gendlin and Greenberg.

According to Mary Hendricks-Gendlin (1998), during his period of collaboration with Rogers, Gendlin made a 'move to speak in terms of process, using a different underlying philosophical model than Rogers had access to' (p. 1). The point for Gendlin, in Hendricks-Gendlin's words, was that in defining congruence Rogers employed terms which 'use a reductive unit model which has been extremely powerful in the realm of physical science [i.e. in Newtonian physics], but not so good for human process' (ibid.). Gendlin has made clear, she relates, that 'Rogers' formulations imply that experience sits there first outside of awareness waiting to be more or less accurately perceived, as though it were something already separately formed apart from the perceiving' (ibid.). It should be clear, then, that I am in harmony with Gendlin in regarding Rogers' scheme as 'like the "flashlight" model that Freud used with the unconscious id impulses sitting there in the person and the work of therapy [being] to shine the light of awareness or consciousness on them' (ibid.).

I am in agreement with Gendlin, too, insofar as he puts 'activity, or interaction [i.e. process] as the basic, first term [i.e. root concept]' (ibid., p. 2). However, I am at odds with Gendlin, in his apparent inability to completely free himself from Cartesian dualism and think in entirely process terms. Gendlin, for instance, retains *the body* as a base concept, employing it to denote 'the vast number of interactional aspects that we live' (1974, p. 236); 'to mean the total brain-mind environment as we sense it' (Ferguson, in Gendlin, 1981, p. ix). In using the term in this highly idiosyncratic way, Gendlin, on the one hand, appears to concur with Whitehead in affirming that 'the process is the reality' and we are 'process immersed in process beyond ourselves', but, on the other, still wants to retain the notion of a substantive body, as a basic, first term.

Perhaps what motivates Gendlin to retain reference to the body in this fashion (rather than purely construe the person as an organism, i.e. as a system of patterned activity) is his desire to legitimise his concept of experiencing in the

110

guise of a bodily felt sense. For to Gendlin, experiencing, i.e. 'all "experience" viewed in terms of the process framework', is the 'process of concrete bodily feeling which constitutes the basic matter of psychological and personality phenomena' (1964, p. 111).

As summarized by Greet Vanaerschot, '[t]wo levels of interaction can be distinguished in the experiencing process' (1997, p. 142). 'The first level', she says, 'refers to the bodily felt whole concerning a situation and originates in the person and situation or environment' (ibid.). 'This leads us to the second level of interaction, which is the one between bodily sensing and symbols (such as words) through which explicit meanings are formed from preconceptual, implicit, and incomplete meanings' (p. 143). Important for our present discussion is the fact that '[t]he explicit meaning is not a previously hidden or repressed one that now becomes clear, but one that is formed in the interaction between felt sense and symbols' (ibid.). Thus, prior to symbolization, what the counselling client can become aware of through a quasi-meditational technique called focusing is a vague, global, holistic, fuzzy bodily felt sense of a problem situation at 'the edge of awareness' (Gendlin, 1984), a mode of knowing akin to that possessed by animals (Gendlin, 1991). When symbolization occurs in relation to such a mode of knowing, according to Gendlin, an experiential 'felt shift' occurs, a process of 'carrying forward' whereby an implicit meaning becomes explicit. On Hendricks-Gendlin's (1998) testimony, such a felt shift constitutes our becoming congruent (p. 2). It is also this shift from implicit to explicit meaning that explains 'the striking way in which the individual during psychotherapy becomes aware of what (so he now says) he has long felt but has not known that he felt' (Gendlin, 1964, p. 105).

Allied to Gendlin's curious way of conceptualizing *the body* is the peculiar manner in which he characterizes the bodily and physical vis-à-vis what is mental and of the mind. 'A felt sense', he declares, 'is not a mental experience but a physical one', (1981, p. 32); '. . . is body *and* mind before they are split apart' (p. 165). Here my own felt sense of what is at play is a failure on Gendlin's part to appreciate the Whiteheadian insight that, from a process perspective, body, mind, spirit, etc. are discursively symbolized construals of certain facets of process-constituted reality. In my opinion the 'fuzziness' in Gendlin's own theorizing apropos what is body, what is mind, can be overcome by paying heed not only to the formulations of Whitehead, but to those of other organismic theorists, principally of Whitehead's former student Susanne Langer and of her other mentor Ernst Cassirer. Specifically, this involves:

(a) thinking more thoroughly in process terms in the manner of Whitehead.

(b) employing Langer's and Whitehead's notion of *feeling* rather than Gendlin's concept of *experiencing* to denote the fundamental constituent of subjective awareness. Here it is not simply a matter of employing a roughly synonymous term, given that 'in natural language feeling is usually a synonym for "experiencing"' (Bohart, 1993, p. 58), but of adopting Langer's and Whitehead's technical definition of *feeling* as 'felt process'; that is, as analogous to the sound given off by the patterned activity of a vibrating guitar string (see Langer, 1967, pp. 20ff).

(c) joining with Cassirer and Langer in conceiving the human being as '*animal symbolicum*', the symbolizing animal (Cassirer, 1944, p. 28), and so making use of their conceptualization of the process of symbolization to shed light on the psychotherapeutic symbolization process and *ipso facto* on the nature of congruence.

Introduction of the thoughts of Cassirer, Langer and Whitehead in such a fashion also provides a fruitful link with the formulations of Leslie Greenberg. Greenberg's model of experiential therapy is one in which 'a person is seen as a symbolizing, meaning-creating being who acts as a dynamic system constantly synthesizing information from many levels of processing and from both internal and external sources into a conscious experience' (Greenberg and Van Balen, 1998, p. 42). In Greenberg's scheme, principally '[t]hree levels of processing — innate sensory motor, emotional schematic memory, and conceptual level processing — are identified' (ibid.).

Important as I consider Greenberg's model to be — in particular in its incorporation of organismic, neo-Piagetian *schemes* in a multi-level developmental formulation — it suffers, in my view, from being based on an information-processing machine model and thereby on the assumed analogy between hardware/software and body/mind. Thus, though he is at pains not to do so, Greenberg does tend at times to treat feelings and emotions in a substantive sense in accord with Cartesian dualism and so raise the spectre of the existence of unconscious emotion (see Greenberg and Safran, 1987, p. 165; Greenberg and Paivio, 1997, pp. 43 and 48). Further, growing out of Gendlin's theorizing as it does, Greenberg attempts (not particularly successfully, in my view) to integrate into his model Gendlin's notions of *experiencing* and of *a bodily felt sense* (see Greenberg and Paivio, 1997, p. 39; Greenberg, Rice and Elliott, 1993, chpt. 9).

These matters aside, by comparison with Gendlin's two-level scheme, part of the value of Greenberg's model, is his presentation of not just two, but three or more levels of organismic sense-making (information processing) as constitutive of human awareness. Thus, given the importance that Greenberg attaches to the person as 'a symbolizing, meaning-creating being', deserving of special attention, in my opinion, is a developmental scheme of levels of sense-making/symbolization that derives from Cassirer and Langer (see Cassirer, 1955a, 1955b, 1957; Langer, 1967, 1972, 1982). In accord with Greenberg and Gendlin, such a scheme connotes a basic, global affective-cognitive level of sense-making becoming progressively refined from one level to the next. Not too different from Greenberg, the levels identified by Cassirer and Langer are as follows: a bodily, sensori-motor level (exhibited by animals and human infants); an iconic, non-discursive mode of symbolizing (found in mythic consciousness and older infants, i.e. Freud's *primary process*) and the level of conceptual thought, of discursive symbolization .

In such a scheme, an organismically refined formulation of congruence would be couched in multi-level developmental terms, congruence being said to exist where a higher level pattern of process validly symbolizes — has a congruent pattern with — a structural component of the level below. For, as Langer attests,

> . . . formal analogy, or congruence of logical structures, is the prime requisite for
> the relationship between a symbol and whatever it is to mean. The symbol and
> the object symbolized must have the same common logical form (1953, p. 27).

Further, insofar as *feeling*, subjective awareness, is taken to be the felt quality of a particular pattern of process, it becomes possible to explain why there is a before-after *sameness*, as against *identity*, between what the client feels prior to the felt-shift of the psychotherapeutic process and what he or she feels afterwards. For, even though the pattern of process intrinsic to the higher level of sense-making is more complex and qualitatively different from that of the preceding lower level, there is nevertheless a congruence of pattern, and thereby a common feeling, between the two — as say, when different guitar strings play the same note in different octaves.

Both Gendlin and Greenberg, especially Greenberg (see Greenberg and Van Balen, 1998, p. 36), being mindful that Rogers' definition of congruence implies awareness of experience that is outside of awareness, effectively sideline congruence in their own theorizing. Even so, both relate the harmonic functioning of the individual to the condition of being psychologically healthy, with Greenberg proposing a 'principle of *coherence* . . . as supplementing the principle of congruence or consistency in explaining healthy functioning' (p. 43, original emphasis). 'In this view', according to Greenberg, 'aspects of experience as well as levels of processing are coordinated to fit together in an affiliative relationship with each other, integrated into a coherent whole' (p. 43).

Such a conception is, I believe, in accord with my own supposition that in order to adequately define congruence organismically, we will have to characterize it in a multi-level process fashion — in terms, that is, of increasingly complex and differentiated modes of sense-making. So construed, congruence will become defined in the same manner that Bernie Neville (1996) has proposed we define empathy, as a multi-level, developmental affair.

Insofar, therefore, as empathy involves 'an emotional response . . . that is *congruent* with the other's emotional state or situation' (author's emphasis) (Eisenberg and Strayer, 1987, p. 5), this raises the question of whether the road ahead in the organismic refinement of Rogers' concept of congruence is one in which empathy is defined as 'congruence-between-organisms', and congruence is conceived as 'intra-organismic' empathy, possibly as 'self-empathy' (see Barrett-Lennard, 1997). For, for Rogers, deep empathy involved 'resonance'— congruence of patterned activity, between himself and the client 'at all levels' (1980, p. 9). The resonance between himself and the other thus necessitated resonance, congruence, between all levels within himself. The love and unconditional positive regard he radiated was nothing less than being one with himself and the other in this way.

REFERENCES

Appignanesi, R. (1979). *Freud for Beginners.* New York: Pantheon Books.

Barrett-Lennard, G. T. (1997). The recovery of empathy — towards others and self. In A. C. Bohart and L. S. Greenberg (Eds.), *Empathy Reconsidered* (pp. 103–1). Washington, D. C.: APA.

Bohart, A. C. (1993). Experiencing: the basis of psychotherapy. *Journal of Psychotherapy Integration*, 3(1), 51–67.

Bozarth, J. D. (1998). *Person-Centered Therapy: A Revolutionary Paradigm.* Ross-on-Wye: PCCS Books.

Brodley, B. T. (1998). Congruence and its relation to communication in client-centered therapy.

The Person-Centered Journal, 5(2), 83–106.

Capra, F. (1982). *The Turning Point*. New York: Simon and Schuster.

Capra, F. (1996). *The Web of Life*. New York: Harper Collins.

Cassirer, E. (1944). *An Essay on Man*. New York: Bantam Books, 1970.

Cassirer, E. (1955a), (1955b), (1957). *The Philosophy of Symbolic Forms (Vols 1, 2 and 3)*. New Haven: Yale University Press.

Eisenberg, N. and Strayer, J. (1987). Critical issues in the study of empathy. In N. Eisenberg and J. Strayer (Eds.) *Empathy and its Development* (pp. 3–16). Cambridge: Cambridge University Press.

Ellingham, I. H. (1995). Quest for a paradigm: Person-centred counselling/psychotherapy versus psychodynamic counselling and psychotherapy. *Counselling*, 6(4), 288–90.

Ellingham, I. H. (1996). Key strategy for the development of a person-centred paradigm of counselling/psychotherapy. *Person-Centred Practice*, 4(2), 12–18.

Ellingham, I. H. (1997a). On the quest for a person-centred paradigm. *Counselling*, 8(1), 52–5.

Ellingham, I. H. (1997b). Guest editorial. *Person-Centred Practice*, 5(1), 3–5.

Ellingham, I. H. (2000). Foundation for a person-centred, humanistic psychology—and beyond: The nature and logic of Carl Rogers' 'formative tendency'. *Paper presented to the Fifth International Conference on Client-Centered and Experiential Psychotherapy*. Chicago, USA.

Farber, B. A., Brink, D. C. and Raskin, P. M. (Eds.). (1996). *The Psychotherapy of Carl Rogers*. New York: The Guilford Press.

Freud, S. (1973). *New Introductory Lectures on Psychoanalysis*. Harmondsworth: Penguin.

Freud, S. (1986). *The Essentials of Psychoanalysis*. Harmondsworth: Penguin.

Gendlin, E. T. (1962). *Experiencing and the Creation of Meaning*. New York: The Free Press.

Gendlin, E. T. (1964). A theory of personality change. In. P. Worchel and D. Byrne (Eds.), *Personality Change* (pp. 102–48). New York: Wiley.

Gendlin, E. T. (1974). Client-centered and experiential psychotherapy. In D. A. Wexler and L. N. Rice (Eds.), *Innovations in Client-Centered Therapy* (pp. 211–46). New York: Wiley.

Gendlin, E. T. (1981). *Focusing*. New York: Bantam Books.

Gendlin, E. T. (1984). The client's edge: the edge of awareness. In R. F. Levant and J. M. Shlien (Eds.), *Client-Centered Therapy and the Person-Centered Approach* (pp. 76–107). New York: Praeger.

Gendlin, E. T. (1991). On emotion in therapy. In L. S. Greenberg and J. D. Safran (Eds.), *Emotion, Psychotherapy and Change* (pp. 255–79). New York: Guilford Press.

Ginsburg, G. P. and Harrison, M. E. (1996). Bodily states and contexts in situated lines of action. In R. Harré and W. G. Perrot (Eds.) *The Emotions* (pp. 229–58). London: Sage.

Greenberg, L. S. and Paivio, (1997). *Working with Emotions in Psychotherapy*. New York: Guilford Press.

Greenberg, L. S., Rice, L. N. and Elliott, R. (1993). *Facilitating Emotional Change*. New York: Guilford Press.

Greenberg, L. S. and Safran, J. D. (1987). *Emotion in Psychotherapy*. New York: Guilford Press.

Greenberg, L. S. and Van Balen, R. (1998). The theory of experience-centered therapies. In Greenberg, L. S., Watson, J. C. and Lietaer, G. (Eds.) *Handbook of Experiential Psychotherapy* (pp. 28–57). New York: Guilford Press.

Gross, R. (1996). *Psychology: The Science of Mind and Behaviour* (3rd ed.). London: Hodder and Stoughton.

Hall, C. S., Lindzey, G. and Campbell, J. B. (1998). *Theories of Personality* (4th ed.). New York: Wiley.

Harré, R. (1986). An outline of the social constructionist viewpoint. In R. Harré (Ed.), *The Social Construction of Emotions* (pp. 2–14). Oxford: Basil Blackwell.

Haugh, S. (1998). Congruence: A confusion of language. *Person-Centred Practice*, 6(1), 44–50.

Hendricks-Gendlin, M. (1999). Rogers' congruence and Gendlin's carrying forward. CCT/PCA Network, e-mail communication.

Holdstock, L. (1996). Anger and congruence considered from the perspective of an interdependent orientation to the self. In R. Hutterer, G. Pawlowsky, P. F. Schmid and R. Stipsits (Eds.), *Client-Centered and Experiential Psychotherapy: A Paradigm in Motion* (pp. 47-52). Frankfurt am Main: Peter Lang.

Kirschenbaum, H. (1979). *On Becoming Carl Rogers.* New York: Delacorte.

Langer, S. K. (1953). *Feeling and Form.* New York: Scribners.

Langer, S. K. (1962). *Philosophical Sketches.* Baltimore: The Johns Hopkins Press.

Langer, S. K. (1967, 1972, 1982). *Mind: An Essay On Human Feeling, (Vols. 1, 2, and 3).* Baltimore: The Johns Hopkins Press.

Lietaer, G. (1998). From non-directive to experiential: A paradigm unfolding. In B. Thorne and E. Lambers (Eds.), *Person-Centred Therapy: A European Perspective.* London: Sage.

MacIntyre, A. (1958). *The Unconscious.* London: Routledge and Kegan Paul.

Malcolm, J. (1982). *Psychoanalysis: The Impossible Profession.* London: Pan Books.

May, R. (1982). The problem of evil: An open letter to Carl Rogers. In H. Kirschenbaum and V. L. Henderson (Eds.) (1990), *Carl Rogers: Dialogues* (pp. 239–51). London: Constable.

Mearns, D. (1997). *Person-Centred Counselling Training.* London: Sage.

Mearns, D. and Thorne, B. (1988). *Person-Centred Counselling in Action.* London: Sage.

Neville, B. (1996). Five kinds of empathy. In R. Hutterer, G. Pawlowsky, P. F. Schmid and R. Stipsits (Eds.), *Client-Centered and Experiential Psychotherapy: A Paradigm in Motion* (pp. 437–53). New York: Peter Lang.

Rogers, C. R. (1951). *Client-Centered Therapy.* Boston: Houghton Mifflin.

Rogers, C. R. (1957). The necessary and sufficient conditions for therapeutic personality change. In H. Kirschenbaum and V. L. Henderson (Eds.) (1990), *The Carl Rogers Reader* (pp. 219–35). London: Constable.

Rogers, C. R. (1959). A theory of therapy, personality and interpersonal relationships, as developed in the client-centered framework. In S. Koch (Ed.), *A Study of a Science: Vol. 3. Formulations of the person and the social context* (pp. 184–256). New York: McGraw-Hill.

Rogers, C. R. (1961). *On Becoming a Person.* Boston: Houghton Mifflin.

Rogers, C. R. (1963). The actualizing tendency in relation to motives and to consciousness. In M. R. Jones (Ed.), *Nebraska Symposium on Motivation,* Vol. II (pp. 1–24). Lincoln: University of Nebraska Press.

Rogers, C. R. (1980). *A Way of Being.* Boston: Houghton Mifflin.

Rogers, C. R. (1982). Reply to Rollo May's letter. In H. Kirschenbaum and V. L. Henderson (Eds.) (1990), *Carl Rogers: Dialogues* (pp. 251–5). London: Constable.

Rogers, C. R. and Sanford, R. C. (1989). Client-Centered Psychotherapy. In H. I. Kaplan and B. J. Sadock (Eds.), *Comprehensive Textbook of Psychiatry V* (pp. 1482–501). Baltimore: Williams and Wilkins.

Truax, C. B. and Carkhuff, R. R. (1967). The client-centered process as viewed by other therapists. In C. R. Rogers, E. T. Gendlin, D. J. Kiesler, and C. B. Truax (Eds.), *The Therapeutic Relationship and its Impact: A Study of Psychotherapy with Schizophrenics* (pp. 419–505). Madison: University of Wisconsin Press.

Van Belle, H. A. (1980). *Basic Intent and Therapeutic Approach of Carl R. Rogers.* Toronto: Wedge Publishing Foundation.

Van Belle, H. A. (1990). Rogers' later move towards mysticism: Implications for the person-centred approach. In G. Lietaer, J. Rombauts, and R. Van Balen (Eds.), *Client-Centered and Experiential Psychotherapy in the Nineties* (pp. 47–57). Leuven: Leuven University Press.

Vanaerschot, G. (1997). Empathic resonance as a source of experience-enhancing interventions. In A. C. Bohart and L. S. Greenberg (Eds.), *Empathy Reconsidered* (pp. 141–66). Washington, DC: APA.

Wexler, D. A. (1974) A cognitive theory of experiencing, self-actualization and therapeutic process. In D. A. Wexler and L. N. Rice (Eds.), *Innovations in Client-Centered Therapy* (pp. 49–116). New York: Wiley.

Whitehead, A. N. (1925). *Science and the Modern World.* New York: The Free Press, 1967.

Whitehead, A. N. (1933). *Adventures of Ideas.* New York: The Free Press, 1967.

Whitehead, A. N. (1938). *Modes of Thought.* New York: The Free Press, 1968.

Wyatt, G. (1998). The multifaceted nature of congruence within the therapeutic relationship. *Paper presented to the 12th International Forum in the Person-Centred Approach,* Johannesburg, South Africa.

7 The Difficulties in the Conceptualisation of Congruence: A Way Forward with Complexity Theory?

Sheila Haugh

I have long been troubled by what I consider to be the misunderstandings with the concept of congruence in person-centred theory. I have suggested (Haugh, 1998a, p. 64) that before person-centred practitioners can formulate how to offer clients a congruent response they need to be clear what is a congruent response. That is, what are we trying to communicate when we are being congruent? This paper is intended as a very tentative exploration of relatively new concepts and ideas in the domain of physics and how they may relate to the notion of congruence. I am not a scientist in the traditional sense of the word and some of what follows is nearly as new to me as I suspect it will be to many readers. Nevertheless, thanks to the encouragement of many students and colleagues who have heard me struggling with these ideas for some time, I am emboldened to have a go!

Firstly, I consider the difficulties I see with the notion of congruence, as I believe some of the ideas put forward concerning this notion are dubious and I also suggest that there is a fundamental problem with the traditional concept-ualization of congruence. This exploration will set the scene as I then consider the idea of a paradigm shift and explicate some of the ideas that are being presented and explored in the new physics. Finally, I will look at the implications for person-centred theory generally and of the concept of congruence specifically.

DIFFICULTIES WITH THE CONCEPT OF CONGRUENCE

In some ways, it is difficult to understand why the concept of congruence should cause so much difficulty between person-centred practitioners and, in my experience, to be the concept that causes most difficulty for beginning person-centred psychotherapists. The simple idea of being genuine and authentic when working with people (in whatever setting) seems to provide the point of disagreement between many practitioners and/or theorists who, in respect of basic philosophy and intentions, are in total accord. Indeed, it is my contention that in the practice of psychotherapy, the decision to make a congruent response, however that is defined, marks the basic difference between many psychotherapeutic orientations particularly within the Humanistic tradition. In spite of many comments that congruence does not mean 'anything goes' (what I call the 'I felt it so I said it' syndrome) (see Wexler, 1974; Mearns and Thorne, 1988; Rogers and Sanford, 1989; Thorne, 1991; Lietaer, 1993; Spinelli, 1994; Merry,

1995), the concept of congruence has clearly been interpreted that way (Spinelli, 1994, p. 261). In respect of person-centred practice, therapy is often fraught with responses defined as congruent simply because they do not fit into any formulation of empathy or unconditional positive regard. There seem to be a number of reasons why the concept of congruence causes so much difficulty resulting in, what I believe to be, inappropriate therapist behaviour. These reasons fall into three broad areas: the writings of Rogers and his use of language, the suggestion that Rogers changed his own therapeutic practice over the years and a lack of theoretical development of the notion of congruence. I will consider each in turn.

The writings of Rogers and his use of language

Most of Rogers' books (for example 1951, 1961, 1978, 1980) are written in a very personable and accessible manner. I have often heard students describe their reading of Rogers as being an experience of relief. Somehow, he is saying what they had always known about human beings and human relationships and many people gain their understanding of Rogers' theories from these books. Rogers' more academic writings do not gain such a wide readership, in part, because most of these papers were published in journals now unobtainable, or are contained in edited publications now out of print (for example, Rogers, 1959, 1963, 1966; Rogers and Sanford, 1989).

Many person-centred therapists seem to be unfamiliar with Rogers' paper *A Theory of Therapy, Personality and Interpersonal Relationships as Developed in the Client-Centred Framework* (1959). This paper, 'the most disciplined statement of his theory of psychotherapy, personality and interpersonal relationships' (Bozarth, 1996, p. 44), is a piece Rogers worked on for at least three or four years. He considered it 'the most rigorously stated theory of the process of change in personality and behaviour that has yet been produced' (Rogers, 1980, p. 59), and one can surmise that he also felt it to be his most rigorous statement of client-centred theory. Because the understanding of Rogers' theory is taken mainly from his 'popular' writings without due regard to this more demanding statement, I believe this leads to what Ford describes as 'questionable scholarship' (1991, p. 81) and, in consequence, a lack of in-depth understanding of Rogers' theory has suffered as a result.

Although the paper is available in *The Carl Rogers Reader* (Kirschenbaum and Henderson, 1990), it is in an abridged form, lacking the very important 40 definitions of Rogers' theoretical constructs. 'We can only have a genuine theory only with carefully defined terms, and only by using defined terms can we later modify, improve, and extend theory' (Gendlin, 1964, p. 102), and in this paper there are clearly defined terms. However, as this most definitive statement of the theory is not accessible, then perhaps understanding of person-centred theory as a whole is less developed than it could be. In particular, the concept of congruence suffers in that it is often believed that it can be defined as experience being available to awareness, a definition I believe to be overly simplistic. Additionally, for those therapists who do not undertake an in-depth reading of Rogers' work generally, it is easy to miss the greater exposition of congruence found in the hypothesis of the fully functioning person and related concepts.

Thorne believes that, due to their conciseness, Rogers' writings, 'earned [him] the accusation of naivety and oversimplification' (1992, p. 36). On the other hand, I have argued that the misunderstanding is, in part, a result of a confusion of language. I have suggested that Rogers has contributed to this confusion by using alternative words, in particular 'genuineness', interchangeably with 'congruence' (Haugh, 1998a, p. 47). This use of diverse words was clearly an effort to clarify his intention and meaning concerning the congruent attitude of the therapist. Unfortunately, as Mearns and Thorne comment, '[T]his can be confusing to new students since in everyday language the word "genuineness" usually implies some conscious control' (1988, p. 76). Although true that Rogers used terms such as congruence and genuineness interchangeably, in retrospect, I believe we do him a disservice to suggest he confused the understanding of the construct. Like many theorists before him, Rogers uses common-sense words in an uncommon sense and it is clear that what he terms 'genuineness' is *synonymous* with congruence (Rogers, 1959, p. 206). The mistake by many has been to assume the common meaning of the word 'genuineness' and take this common usage as defining the word and construct of congruence. Hence, although a genuine feeling is being expressed (in the common usage of the word), if experience is not available to awareness, or experience is distorted in awareness, the expression of the genuine feeling will not be a congruent statement. Many person-centred practitioners miss this point.

Rogers' changing practice?

In 1998, I (Haugh, 1998b, pp. 48–58) noted the suggestion that Rogers' practice had altered as he got older. This idea seems to come from a number of writers and is used to justify a change, sometimes described as a development, in the practice of person-centred therapy. As person-centred therapy was being increasingly implemented in group therapy, Boy and Pine (1982) observed that,

> The group-centered counselor was utilizing reflections of feelings almost exclusively, clients within counseled groups were instead using a spontaneous, natural, and non-reflective response pattern with peers and were having more therapeutic impact on each other than was the group counselor (p. 169).

They felt:

> ... if the counselor can be more therapeutically helpful in groups by introducing personal meanings, perceptions, observations, and feeling, it follows that the counselor should also be able to engage in the same process in individual counseling (ibid.

Boy and Pine see this link between the counsellor's behaviour in a group and individual therapy as an operational indication of a change in person-centred practice. This change was seemingly sanctioned by a difference Rogers described in his own way of being, particularly in the area of taking risks in expressing his feelings to others (Kirschenbaum, 1979, p. 333).[1] However, although Rogers made

---

1. Footnot on opposite page.

the comment that, 'my behaviour is often quite different in a group from what used [sic] to be in a one-to-one relationship' (1970, p. 45), he did not say that either the change in himself over the years, or his experiences as a group leader/member, altered his behaviour as a therapist in one-to-one therapy. As John K. Wood comments, 'facilitative behavior in groups is somewhat different, and at times may even be contradictory, to therapist behavior in individual therapy' (1995, p. 2).

It is questionable whether it is legitimate to take, in the way of Boy and Pine, the experience of the group therapist and transpose it onto individual therapy, particularly with respect to responses described as congruent. Theoretically, I believe this involves confusing the conceptualisation of congruence and genuineness in the different areas of Rogers' theory (see Brodley, 1998). Diagrammatically presented, the theory of interpersonal relationships is shown at the edges of the person-centred approach, with the theory of therapy holding centre place (see Rogers, 1959, p. 193). Rogers cautions that there is less certainty about what he calls the 'peripheral areas of the client-centered framework' (ibid.). In consequence, there is more theoretical certainty concerning the facilitative environment in one-to-one therapy than there is concerning the facilitative environment in interpersonal relations. I make this point, as I believe care must be taken in mixing Rogers' theory of therapy with his theory of interpersonal relationships — mixing Rogers' behaviour in individual therapy with Rogers' behaviour in groups.

Another suggestion that Rogers' practice changed over the years can be found in various descriptions of, and implications taken from, a study undertaken of psychotherapy with people experiencing schizophrenia (the Wisconsin Study). This was a very large study, the outcome of which was, by and large, somewhat disappointing (Thorne, 1992, p. 17). Nevertheless, one variable associated with constructive social and personality change with this group of clients was 'the extent to which he [sic] [the therapist] is perceived as a real and genuine person by his schizophrenic patient' (Rogers, 1967, p. 92). Gendlin, as one of the therapists involved, commented, '[E]ach therapist finds different behavior to convey *himself [sic]* directly and spontaneously' (Gendlin, 1967, p. 375, original emphasis). In a paper written about three years into the project, Rogers described how the realness and genuineness of the therapist was put into practice with the schizophrenic clients.

> One in particular is moving more and more toward allying himself with the hidden and unrevealed person in the schizophrenic, and openly 'clobbering' the defensive shell ... He is sensitively and obviously committed to the person who is hiding, but he is quite violently and sometimes sarcastically critical of the psychotic symptoms, the fear of relating, the defences and avoidances (Rogers, 1962, p. 11).

Although the Wisconsin Study taught Rogers and his colleagues that they needed to 'use their own feelings more to demonstrate their congruence, understanding

---

1. Notwithstanding the 'development' of Rogers' risk taking, in all probability Rogers would have applauded 'peers having more therapeutic impact'. For him it would not matter who was therapeutic (see Rogers, 1951, 1970, 1980), seeing the group leaders' role to be one of facilitating a therapeutic environment rather than to necessarily be 'actively' therapeutic themselves.

and caring' (Kirschenbaum, 1979, p. 277), it is important to remember that this comment was made in respect of clients who had limited or no verbalisations — the therapist only had their own feelings with which to make contact with the clients and, as therapists, they needed to be more verbally active.[2]

Further evidence cited concerning Rogers' changing practice is his 'change' in personality as he got older. He had apparently lacked 'natural spontaneity', and intimate relationships were rare (Kirschenbaum, 1979, p. 333). He had a tendency to be withdrawn and a number of writers note how he changed over the years (Cain, 1987, pp. 494–5; Thorne, 1991, p. 129). Kirschenbaum states that Rogers' experiences in encounter groups moved him 'toward a greater trust in and openness to his feelings and a greater willingness to risk himself in relationships' (1979, p. 333). Commenting on the impact of his own therapy a number of years earlier, Rogers said that, as a consequence, 'My therapy with my clients has become consistently and increasingly free and spontaneous ever since that time' (p. 193).[3]

The implication of these comments is that Rogers, as a naturally taciturn person, had difficulty in sharing himself with others and therefore also had trouble sharing himself with clients. Further, it is suggested these aspects of his personality became less apparent over the years. In consequence, the assumption is made that Rogers' conceptualisation of the use of congruence in the therapeutic encounter was more a reflection of his personal reluctance to share himself rather than a theoretical construct. That Rogers' formulation reflected characteristics in his personality cannot be denied, for as Shlien comments, 'all personality theory is autobiographical' (1997, p. 75).[4] On the other hand, I believe it is somewhat cavalier to imply that Rogers' notion of genuineness rested entirely on his own personal difficulties. Shlien throws a different light on these comments that characterise Rogers as withdrawn. He describes Rogers as a 'shy' man, who although he found 'intimate and expressive relationships . . . an effort', nevertheless took a 'delight' in them (ibid., p. 70). One can speculate that, as a shy person, Rogers simply found the group experiences personally more challenging than the one-to-one meetings.

From these different views, a picture emerges that Rogers became more active, more expressive of his own thoughts and feelings as a therapist as he got older and more experienced. However, when one considers his therapeutic practice in detail, there is very little difference between the beginning and the end of his career. Merry (1996) undertook an analysis of Rogers' demonstration interviews. He found a high number of empathic responses (eighty-seven percent) (p. 275) with only eight percent of the total responses coming from Rogers' own 'frame of reference' (p. 279). Brodley and Brody (1990) analysed ten of Rogers' therapy sessions spanning a 40-year period from 1946 to 1986. They found that ninety-two percent of Rogers' responses were 'empathic checking responses' (p. 4) and they comment 'only eight percent of Rogers' *responses to clients' explorations and disclosures* could be classified' into other categories[5] (ibid., original emphasis).

---

2. For recent developments in this area, see Prouty (1994).
3. Rogers was in personal therapy for a time, circa 1949, after experiencing profound difficulties with a client.
4. See Atwood and Stolorow (1979) for an in-depth exploration of this phenomenon.
5. The other categories were Rogers' comments, interpretations, agreements or probing questions.

Brodley and Brody state that in client-centred therapy 'empathic following of the client is an optimal and natural realization of the whole gestalt of therapeutic attitudes' (p. 10). In a further piece of research (Brodley, 1994), 31 interviews were examined and analysed. Ninety percent of Rogers' responses were 'nondirective, empathic following responses' (Brodley, 1997, p. 20).

I do not wish to imply that Rogers' practice did not alter in any way at all, for it is clear that over the years there was a change.[6] Nevertheless, I believe this change was a development away from using a technique in therapy and a move toward a 'way of being', a move that would inevitably have been influenced by Rogers' natural personal development. With very few exceptions, Rogers stayed true to his third condition for the therapeutic process, that the therapist be congruent in the relationship, with congruence being an inner state rather than an active and overtly expressed behavioural state.

Theoretical incoherence in the conceptualisation of congruence

Let us take an imaginary therapist in a session with a client. At a particular moment in the session, the therapist has a feeling that is both striking and persistent (Rogers, 1966, p. 185), perhaps it has even lasted over a couple of sessions. The therapist assumes that his/her experience is accurately symbolised in awareness and so shares the feeling with the client. Later, in supervision, the therapist explores this seemingly congruent response to the client and realises that there was another aspect of his/her experiences that had not been (accurately symbolised) in his/her awareness. Clearly, in the initial exchange the therapist had not been as congruent as s/he first thought. The question is posed, 'How can a therapist know at any given moment, whether or not they are being congruent?' — a point made by Adomaitis as long ago as 1991 (pp. 26–9). In consequence, how can the therapist know they are meeting the therapeutic condition of congruence? Rogers was not totally oblivious to this question, stating that a 'lack of congruence is usually unknown to the therapist himself [sic] at the time' (1963, p. 11). However, he does not adequately address this problem and it is not possible to get out of the dead end of Rogers' reasoning. In Rogers' conceptualisation, congruence is the harmony between the actualising tendency and the self-actualising tendency — the expression of the 'unitary actualising tendency' (Rogers, 1963, p. 20). If this harmony is not present, the individual cannot be aware of their incongruence because the incongruent experience is denied or distorted: in the therapeutic relationship the therapist cannot know if they are congruent or incongruent (Rogers' 'dead end' and the incoherence in the conceptualisation of congruence).

I have suggested that lack of in-depth knowledge of Rogers' theoretical writings, including a misunderstanding of his terminology, have played their part in the confusion that surrounds the notion of congruence, as has the erroneous view that Rogers changed his practice. I have also argued that incoherence in the theory of congruence itself poses, what I believe, to be an almost insurmountable problem.

Many minds have put themselves to the task of defining and clarifying the

---

6. For a more in-depth analysis of this, see Haugh (1998b)

concept. However, the most striking aspect of theorists' work from within the person-centred tradition is the almost total lack of any theoretical development of the concept of congruence itself beyond Rogers' own conceptualisations. With the notable exception of Eugene Gendlin (1962) and David Wexler (1974), the content of the work that has been undertaken has tended to be a restatement of Rogers' theory, with an emphasis on an exploration of the communication of congruence. This emphasis means that little has been done to further develop the concept of congruence itself. I do not wish to downplay the concern over the communication of genuineness in the therapeutic relationship, as high levels of explicit genuineness have been found to be unhelpful and 'may even have deleterious effects' (Carkhuff, 1969, p. 90). Nevertheless, a preoccupation with the communication of genuineness has resulted in a paucity of new thoughts concerning the question 'what is congruence?'.

The confusions and disagreements that continue to surround the notion of congruence, and the lack of theoretical development, imply to me that there is a more fundamental problem than those identified. I think this problem can be described as 'being caught between two paradigms' and it is to the idea of shifting paradigms and a new paradigm that I now turn my attention.

A SHIFTING PARADIGM — IS IT RELEVANT TO PSYCHOTHERAPY?

Fritjof Capra (1996) suggests that there was a 'dramatic change of concepts that occurred in physics during the first three decades of the [last] century' and that these changes in concepts 'have brought about a profound change in our worldview, (p. 5). He believes that 'what we are seeing is a shift of paradigms not only within science but also in the larger social arena' (ibid.). A paradigm is described as a set of beliefs that shape the way in which the world and its contents are viewed. A paradigm thus 'acts as a lens through which every observation is filtered, and is maintained as an authoritative bulwark by common convention' (Tarnas, 1991, p. 360). Such is the all-pervasive effect of thinking within a certain paradigm, often theories and hypotheses within that paradigm are considered as facts. For example, one such fact is the concept of the unconscious.

Sigmund Freud (1915) wrote of the 'right to assume the existence of something . . . that is unconscious' (p. 142). The assumption Freud made of the unconscious has become, for many people, a statement of fact (whether it is couched in Freudian or Rogerian terms). This dominant worldview, a worldview influenced by western ideas, can be described as a paradigm. Fred Zimring illustrates how this paradigm affects psychotherapy when he writes of the 'old paradigm'. The old paradigm assumes 'that unaware feelings and impulses cause psychological maladjustment, that there is resistance to becoming aware of these feelings and impulses and that becoming aware frees us of maladjustment and distress' (Zimring, 1995, p. 36). He continues, 'it is hard to believe that these observations about our feelings and behaviours are assumptions and not statements about reality' (p. 37).

Some writers and theorists have considered these changing ideas and have cautiously explored how they may impact on person-centred practice and theory. As early as 1985, Bozarth had considered the implications of Quantum Theory on the Person-Centred Approach commenting that, '[M]ost writers have explained the client-centered conceptual model in a manner consistent with the Cartesian-Newtonian model of science' (1985, p. 179). Ivan Ellingham has made a number of references to the Cartesian-Newtonian model, most recently suggesting that '(T)he critical flaw intrinsic to person centred theory has to do . . . with it being a mix of concepts deriving from two disparate paradigms' (1999, p. 121).[7] The two paradigms he describes are the 'Cartesian-Newtonian paradigm, and the second he describes as being 'labelled *holistic, organismic, process*' (ibid., original emphasis). In 1993, Ruth Sanford reflected on the parallels between chaos theory and the Person-Centred Approach. Her paper, *From Rogers to Gleick and Back Again*, examines how Rogers' work was compatible with the emerging science of chaos. She concluded that the difficulty would be the recognition of the 'intersection [of the parallels between person-centred theory and chaos theory] intellectually *and* acceptance of it in personal experience' (Sanford, 1993, p. 272. italics added). Vlado Hlavenka (1995), concerned that in respect of theory the Person-Centred Approach was stagnating, also considered the parallels between the approach and the theories of chaos and complexity. He made tentative connections between the two theories, for example, when considering the role of the person-centred facilitator and the concept of self-organisation in complexity theory.

Does any of this thinking about the hard sciences and a new paradigm really matter to the individual psychotherapist sitting with a distressed client? I believe it does. I feel that the confusions associated with the concept of congruence may benefit from a consideration of the notion from a different worldview. Further, I agree with Michael Bütz and Linda Chamberlain (1998a) when they write, '[T]he important things for clinicians to understand . . . is that many established psychotherapy orientations have their basis in science — the science that was prevalent at the time they emerged' (p. 17). They go on to warn that '[C]linicians must recognize that if they are working from outdated notions of scientific dynamics, their concepts may be outmoded as well. Not only might the notions be outdated, they may even be dangerous or counterproductive' (ibid.). It seems to me that it is imperative, that as theorists and practitioners, we take heed of these radical developments and consider our theories and practice in light of them. To be able to integrate the dramatic change of concepts suggested by the new paradigm, to understand the fatal flaw suggested by Ellingham, to be able to understand it intellectually and accept it personally, I believe it is necessary to understand, as fully as possible, the emerging paradigm, a paradigm known in the hard sciences as the theory of complexity.

Complexity theory — the emergence of a new paradigm

Complexity theory evolved from the study of chaos, which some might remember as the study of the edge between order and chaos. Chaos theory has been described by Vandervert (1996) as the 'third great scientific revolution of this century' (cited by Bütz and Chamberlain, 1998a, p. 16), the first two being the

7. A revised version of this paper is included in this volume.

theory of relativity and quantum physics. To describe complexity theory as the new paradigm, of course, begs the question what was the old paradigm? The old paradigm, a Newtonian worldview, was based on the model of a machine, in other words, a closed system. The qualities of a machine mean that from the moment it comes off the production line there is 'a progressive downward spiral until the machine finally (breaks) down (a phenomenon known as entropy) ... it can be fixed, but it was never as "good as new"' (ibid., p. 18). This is a worldview that makes sense to us, the terms being 'familiar to us' (Goodwin, 1994, p. 168) and I doubt if many people would have much disagreement with this model. This familiarity, with what are known as linear systems, is born of the fact that they 'have been the mainstay of science for more than three hundred years' (Coveney and Highfield, 1995, p. 9). A linear world is where 'because one plus one equals two, we can predict that the volume of water flowing down a drain is doubled when a tap drips twice as long'. On the other hand, a complex, non-linear, system would be those 'phenomena that regulate the quantity of water in the human body, or the movement of water vapour in the clouds overhead' (ibid.). If we think of the dripping tap, in simplistic terms it seems clear that by doubling the flow rate we would double the volume of water flowing down the drain. But what if the washer on the tap split, or the drain was blocked? The volume of water flowing would be changed. Whilst this may seem fanciful, this is how the world actually works,[8] '[R]eal world complex systems do not behave with clockwork regularity' write Coveney and Highfield (ibid.), adding that 'precise long-term forecasts about them are frequently moonshine'. The term 'real world' is not meant in a trivial manner — it is the very stuff of complexity theory. Ironically, these real world matters were known in linear physics but scientists simply chose to ignore them. In particular, they knew that their measurements of different quantities were not perfect. Gleick (1988) describes it thus; '[S]cientists marching under Newton's banner [of deterministic, predictable outcomes based on unchanging parameters] actually waved another flag that said something like this: given an *approximate* knowledge of a systems initial conditions and an understanding of natural law, one can calculate the *approximate* behaviour of the system' (p. 15, italics in original), and for some systems 'small non-linearities were easy to disregard' (ibid., p. 41). For example, knowing that there is a high possibility of rain in the South East of England is usually approximate enough. The floods in that area towards the end of 2000 show how, in real life, these approximations can be woefully inadequate.

In fact, the study of weather systems is the area that saw the advent of complexity theory. Fascinated by the challenge of predicating the weather, the development of number-crunching computers enabled one Edward Lorenz to analyse vast amounts of data. Towards the end of 1961, wanting to analyse a past sequence of variables associated with a weather system, Lorenz took a short cut and inputted .506 rather than .506127. He assumed that the difference, one part in a thousand, would be of no consequence. He was wrong. The pattern of the new print out showed the hypothetical weather system 'diverging so rapidly from

---

8. This is a very simplistic description. In fact, even in linear physics it was realised that although the dripping tap was constant, elements of turbulence (or noise) were present. However, linear physics chose to ignore this noise.

the pattern of the last run that, within just a few months, all resemblance has disappeared' (Gleick, 1988, p. 16). If it can ever be said that a particular field was born on a particular day this was the birth of complexity theory.

The phenomena that Lorenz identified, overwhelming changes caused by the very slightest change in input, became one of the central ideas of complexity theory. These central ideas are; sensitive dependency on initial conditions, strange attractors, punctuated equilibria, bifurcation, irreversibility and self organisation and it is useful to know a little about these six concepts.

- *Sensitive dependency on initial conditions (SDIC)*. Named by Lorenz and often more poetically known as the butterfly effect — if a butterfly flaps its wings in Hong Kong there will be a Hurricane in New York.[9] 'Sensitivity . . . to the initial input data means that tiny fluctuations could wreak enormous change in . . . patterns' (Coveney and Highfield, 1995, p. 170).

- *Strange attractors,* which exist in phase space, were first recognised by David Ruelle (ibid., p. 170) and Floris Takens (Gleick, 1988, p. 133). Phase space is a mathematical term that allows physicists to visualise many numbers simultaneously (Chamberlain, 1998a, pp. 8–9), giving them the tools to collapse everything known about a system, at a single instant in time, into one point. The following instant everything will have changed and the point moves (Gleick, 1988, p. 134). Strange attractors live in phase space. Whilst a system may be complex, unpredictable and disorderly, when everything known about the system is collapsed into consecutive points, patterns emerge that 'show[s] a system that moves in orbits, that have some order, and stay in a well-defined region even though they are not periodic' (ibid.). The region where the patterns intersect 'is called a strange attractor . . . because of the way the orbits wander in an unpredictable way, while remaining confined to the region' (Goodwin, 1994, p. 52). This means that strange attractors can be described as 'an organising principle' (Chamberlain, 1998b, p. 82).

- *Punctuated equilibria* suggests that, for example, 'the evolution of individual species takes place in well-defined steps (the punctuation marks) separated by long periods of stability (equilibria or stasis)' (Coveney and Highfield, 1995, p. 232). This means that systems change in leaps rather than in measured steps. As Chamberlain (1998a, p. 10) points out, this concept challenges the very firmly held belief in Darwinian evolutionary theory.

- *Bifurcation*, or crisis point, is where chaos and order meet. It is the term in chaos theory to describe the dynamics that initiate a transformation. The bifurcation point 'in effect says "expect novel behavior here"' (ibid., p. 12).

- *Irreversibility* simply means that something cannot start over again. 'Time cannot be reversed' (ibid., p. 13), 'it is a medium that flows' (Coveney and Highfield, 1995, p. 9).

9. Of course, it is more complicated than that — ifa butterfly flaps its wings in Hong Kong and then another butterfly flaps its wings in London, the second butterfly will also have an impact.

• *Self organisation* emerges when systems are in chaos; 'as dynamic systems move further from equilibrium, new structures and new types of organisation in the system can emerge spontaneously' (Chamberlain, 1998a, p. 11). Additionally, '[N]ew orders are established when a system interacts in some new way either with itself or with the environment or with both' (ibid.).

These then are some of the basis concepts associated with complexity theory. What it means is that we are witnessing and experiencing a radical shift away from an evolutionary model of change toward a process model of change. It can be described as recognition that the developmental paradigm is no longer an adequate explanation of the phenomena that surround us, and that a paradigm of emergence (Waldrop, 1992, p. 88) more accurately describes the world we live with. Within this paradigm new possibilities arise; 'at each level of complexity, entirely new properties appear. [And] at each stage, entirely new laws, concepts and generalizations are necessary, requiring inspirations and creativity, to just a degree as in the previous one' (Anderson, 1972 cited in Waldrop, 1992, p. 82).

IMPLICATIONS FOR PERSON-CENTRED THEORY GENERALLY AND THE CONCEPT OF CONGRUENCE SPECIFICALLY

I feel extremely cautious in thinking and writing of the implications of chaos, complexity and the new physics for person-centred theory. I am wary of new theories being taken as blueprints, when there may be little understanding, and even misunderstanding, of those theories. I am particularly wary that my own worldview makes it difficult for me to hold onto this 'new way of seeing' (Gleick, 1988, p. 39). Consequently, there is a danger that the implications of the new physics become mangled in my old linear worldview. As Goodwin (1994) says, '(A)t first glance, the shift of perspective ... doesn't look too significant. However, its consequences become more dramatic the further we follow them' (p. 3). So hoping I can keep my worldview broad enough to be aware of the consequences, I will tentatively begin to consider the implications of this new paradigm, both generally and specifically.

A clear implication of the new paradigm is that it seems to support Rogers' contention of both the formative and actualising tendency. Goodwin states that, in the new physics, 'organisms are not molecular machines. They are functional and structural unities resulting from a self-organizing, self-generating dynamic' (p. 183). Chamberlain (1998b) notes that in Rogers' hypothesis of the actualising tendency, '[T]he importance of becoming, rather than simply being, reflects the dynamic, evolving, self-organising dynamics that are so crucial to chaos and complexity theory' (p. 82). As to whether complexity theory supports the view that the total organism moves in 'a direction' (Rogers, 1961, p. 186), I am unsure. I suspect this is the case but this would necessitate a greater exploration of both concepts than space permits.

As I have alluded to above, perhaps the most fundamental implication is the change in our worldview. This means accepting that our intuition is 'misleading' (Mandelbrot, cited in Gleick, 1988, p. 102), as our thinking and feelings have been learned and developed within a linear, cause and effect (Newtonian), paradigm.

It means we need to fully integrate the meaning of the move from a developmental paradigm to an emergent paradigm into our theory and practice. I think this last point is easier for those people who understand and agree with the Person-Centred Approach. However, I emphasise the point of it being easier — not easy. For example, whilst Rogers' hypothesis of the fully functioning person has an emphasis on a 'person continually changing' (Rogers, 1959, p. 235), which seems to sit quite well with complexity theory, there are echoes of a developmental model when he hypothesises the *process* of becoming more fully functional. Here, Rogers writes of therapy as being 'the discovery by the client that he [sic] is experiencing feelings and attitudes which heretofore he has not been able to be aware of' (Rogers, 1961, p. 187). Although these feelings and attitudes are emergent to the client, they are not emergent in the meaning of the word in complexity theory. In the new physics emergent means something completely new has been created, not that something new (but already existing) has been perceived. This is an example of what Ellingham (1997) describes as person-centred theory having 'its roots and main trunk . . . on the organismic side of the fence' but there being 'bits . . . which still hang over the side of the old paradigm' (p. 4). It may be possible to intellectually mix these two paradigms but the ideas contained in such a synthesis will be incoherent.

It is the problem of incoherence that now leads me to consider the specific implications of complexity theory for the notion of congruence. This is a big undertaking, as in person-centred theory the concept of congruence is one of the pivotal notions. The congruent person is synonymous with the psychologically healthy person. The development of incongruence is synonymous with the development of psychological ill health and incongruence develops due to conditions of worth. To reframe the concept of congruence means re-framing the concept of the fully functioning person; reframing our definitions of psychological ill health; reframing the concept of the development of conditions of worth and, in consequence, reframing our understanding of how therapy is therapeutic. Mindful that complexity theory 'raises more questions than it answers' (Bütz and Chamberlain, 1998b), the following are some initial and hesitant ideas on what complexity theory means for the concept of congruence.

- That congruence does not rest on experience being available to awareness. Rather, it depends on a person's ability, *learnt and developed*, to be open to their experiential field. This means that the development of congruence is not an uncovering of unaware feelings, but a development of the human potential for experiencing.
- That in certain psychologically unsafe conditions, a child does not develop the ability/have the experiencing, for example, to feel loved if s/he cries. This means that conditions of worth are not developed; rather, conditions are not present for worth to develop.
- That psychological health and ill health can be seen as a dynamic interplay between chaos and order. Could psychotic episodes, for example, be seen as a system in chaos?

In the main, these ideas rest on a conceptualisation of the development of human potentialities, the change to higher and higher states of complexity, rather than the uncovering of contents already existing. For example, whilst the need for positive regard may be universal (Rogers, 1959, p. 223), lack of positive regard may not lead to the development of conditions of worth. Instead, lack of positive regard, or conditional positive regard, may inhibit the infant's development of his/her potentialities. This in turn could lead to the inability to be fully open to their experiential field, for his/her experiencing to be less complex.

On a wider note, one thing that is very clear from complexity theory is the importance of the interconnection of the six conditions. No one condition can exist in isolation, as each has an intrinsic and profound effect on the other. At the very least, this means that a congruent response cannot be formulated without reference to empathy, unconditional positive regard and the communication of those particular conditions. It cannot be 'I felt it so I said it' and this statement brings us back to my beginning. To paraphrase T. S. Elliot (1943), we have arrived where we started but maybe we are starting to know the place for the first time. Some of the implications I have suggested are not new ideas (for example see Gendlin, 1962; Wexler, 1974). However, I believe that having an understanding of the changing paradigm not only elucidates these ideas, it also allows us to consider them further and more radically. Indeed, it perhaps allows us to consider concepts, explanations and descriptions that hitherto have been unknown to us.

This paper has been an attempt to explore how the concepts of the new physics may help to enlighten the notion of congruence in person-centred theory and practice. I have looked at some of the reasons for difficulty with the concept of congruence and I concluded that there was a fundamental problem in the conceptualisations of the notion, linked to it having been formulated within the paradigm of linear systems. I have described, from the new physics, the basic principles of chaos and complexity theory and have speculated on the implications for congruence, implications that permeate throughout the whole of person-centred theory. I have deliberately refrained from attempting to pin down and detail these implications for, as I implied above, there is a danger of slipping into old paradigm thinking and problem solving when trying to relate new paradigm ideas to our work and practice. With time, understanding and practice this will change. I believe we need to become friendly towards, and knowing of, this new worldview. Person-centred theory needs to be reframed, step-by-step, within this paradigm, an exercise that I believe could be exciting and stimulating. If nothing else, we owe it to our clients.

REFERENCES

Adomaitis, R., (1991). *On Being Genuine: A Phenomenologically Grounded Study of the Experience of Genuineness and Its Place in Client-Centered Psychotherapy.* Unpublished PhD. Dissertation, Northwestern University, USA.

Atwood, G.A., and Stolorow, R.D., (1979). *Faces in a Cloud.* New Jersey: Jason Aronson, (1993).

Boy, A.V., and Pine, G.J. (1982). *Client-Centered Counseling: A Renewal.* Boston: Allyn and Bacon.

Bozarth, J.D., (1985). Quantum Theory and the Person-Centered Approach. *Journal of Counseling and Development.* November 1985, Vol. 64, pp. 179–82.

Bozarth, J., (1992). Coterminous Intermingling of Doing and Being in Person-Centred Therapy. *The Person-Centered Journal.* 1(1), pp. 33–9.

Bozarth, J., (1996). The Integrative Statement of Carl R. Rogers. In Hutterer, R., Pawlowsky, G., Schmid, P.F. and Stipsits, R., (Eds.), (1996*) Client-Centered and Experiential Psychotherapy.*

Frankfurt: Peter Lang, pp. 25–33

Brodley, B.T., (1994). Some Observations of Carl Rogers's Behavior in Therapy Interviews. *Person-Centered Journal.* 1(2), 37–47.

Brodley, B.T., (1997) The Nondirective Attitude in Client-Centered Therapy. *Person-Centered Journal* 4(1), pp. 18–30.

Brodley, B.T., (1998). Congruence and its Relation to Communication in Client-Centered Therapy and the Person-Centered Approach. *Person Centered Journal.* 5(2), pp. 83–106.

Brodley, B.T., and Brody, A.F., (1990). *Understanding Client-Centered Therapy Through Interviews Conducted by Carl Rogers.* Paper prepared for the panel, *Fifty Years of Client-Centered Therapy: Recent Research,* at the American Psychological Association Convention in Boston, Massachusetts, August 1990.

Bütz, M.R., and Chamberlain, L., (1998a). Chaos and the Clinician: What's so Important About Science in Psychotherapy. In Chamberlain, L., and Bütz, M.R., (Eds.) (1998) Clinical *Chaos. A Therapist's Guide to Nonlinear Dynamics and Therapeutic Change.* USA: Taylor & Francis, pp. 15–25.

Bütz, M.R., and Chamberlain, L., (1998b). Chaos Theory and the Future of Psychotherapy: Conclusions and Questions. In Chamberlain, L., and Bütz, M.R., (Eds.) (1998) Clinical *Chaos. A Therapist's Guide to Nonlinear Dynamics and Therapeutic Change.* USA: Taylor & Francis, pp. 207–12.

Cain, D.J., (1987). Carl Rogers's Life in Review. *Person-Centered Review.* 2(4), 476–506.

Capra, F., (1996). *The Web of Life: A New Synthesis of Mind and Matter.* London: Harper Collins.

Carkhuff, R.R., (1969). *Helping and Human Relations, Volume I. Practice and Research.* New York: Holt, Reinhart and Winston.

Chamberlain, L., (1998a). An Introduction to Chaos and Nonlinear Dynamics. In Chamberlain, L., and Bütz, M.R., (Eds.) (1998) Clinical *Chaos. A Therapist's Guide to Nonlinear Dynamics and Therapeutic Change.* USA: Taylor & Francis, pp. 3–14

Chamberlain, L., (1998b). Humanistic/Existential Perspectives and Chaos. In Chamberlain, L., and Bütz, M.R., (Eds.) (1998) Clinical *Chaos. A Therapist's Guide to Nonlinear Dynamics and Therapeutic Change.* USA: Taylor & Francis, pp. 79–86

Chamberlain, L., and Bütz, M.R., (Eds.) (1998). *Clinical Chaos. A Therapist's Guide to Nonlinear Dynamics and Therapeutic Change.* USA: Taylor & Francis.

Coveney, P., and Highfield, R., (1995). *Frontiers of Complexity. The Search for Order in a Chaotic World.* London: Faber and Faber.

Ellingham, I., (1997). Guest Editorial. *Person-Centred Practice.* 5(1), 1–5.

Ellingham, I., (1999). Carl Rogers' 'Congruence' as an Organismic; Not a Freudian Concept. *Person Centered Journal.* 6(2), 121–140.

Elliot, T.S., (1943). Little Gidding V, *The Four Quartets.*

Ford, J.G., (1991). Inherent Potentialities of Actualization: An Initial Exploration. *Journal of Humanistic Psychology.* 31(3), 65–88.

Freud, S., (1915). The Unconscious. Reprinted in Freud, A., (eds.), (1986) *Sigmund Freud. The Essentials of Psychoanalysis.* England: Penguin Books.

Gendlin, E.T., (1962). *Experiencing and the Creation of Meaning.* Illinois: Northwestern University Press, (1997).

Gendlin, E.T., (1964). A Theory of Personality Change. In Worchel, P., and Byrne, D., (Eds.), (1964), *Personality Change.* New York: John Wiley and Sons, pp. 102–48.

Gendlin, E.T., (1967). The rapeutic Procedures in Dealing with Schizophrenics. In Rogers, C.R., Gendlin, E.T., Kiesler, D.J., and Truax, C.B., (1967) *The Therapeutic Relationship and Its Impact. A Study of Psychotherapy with Schizophrenics.* Madison: University of Wisconsin Press, pp. 369–400.

Gleick, J., (1988). *Chaos: The Amazing Science of the Unpredictable.* Great Britain: Heinemann.

Goodwin, B., (1994). *How the Leopard Changed Its Spots. The Evolution of Complexity.* London: Phoenix.

Greenberg, L.S., and Van Balen, R., (1998). The Theory of Experience-Centered Therapies. In Greenberg, L.S., Watson, J.C., and Lietaer, G., (Eds.) (1998) *Handbook of Experiential Psychotherapy.* New York: Guilford Press, pp. 28–57.

Haugh, S., (1998a). Congruence: A Confusion of Language. In Merry, T., (Ed.) (2000) The *BAPCA Reader.* Ross-on-Wye: PCCS Books, pp. 62–7.

Haugh, S. (1998b). *An Exploration of the Concept of Congruence in Person-Centred Theory.*

129

Unpublished Masters Dissertation, Regent's College, London.

Hlavenka, V., (1995). *Chaos, Order and PCA*. Presentation given at the Person-Centred International Forum, Greece.

Kirschenbaum, H., (1979). *On Becoming Carl Rogers*. New York: Delacorte Press.

Kirschenbaum, H., and Henderson, V.L., (1990). *The Carl Rogers Reader*. London: Constable.

Lietaer, G., (1993). Authenticity, Congruence and Transparency. In Brazier, D., (Ed.), (1993) *Beyond Carl Rogers*. London: Constable and Company, pp. 17–46.

Mearns, D., and Thorne, B., (1988). *Person-Centred Counselling in Action*. London: Sage Pubs.

Merry, T., (1995). *Invitation to Person Centred Psychology*. London: Whurr Publications.

Merry, T., (1996). An Analysis of Ten Demonstration Interviews by Carl Rogers: Implications for the Training of Client-Centred Counsellors. In Hutterer, R., Pawlowsky, G., Schmid, P.F. and Stipsits, R., (Eds.), (1996) *Client-Centered and Experiential Psychotherapy*. Peter Lang, pp. 273–83.

Prouty, G., (1994). *Theoretical Evolutions in Person-Centered/Experiential Therapy. Applications to Schizophrenic and Retarded Psychoses*. Westport CT: Praeger.

Rogers, C.R., (1951). *Client-Centered Therapy*. London: Constable and Company 1987.

Rogers, C.R., (1959). A Theory of Therapy, Personality, and Interpersonal Relationships as Developed in the Client-Centered Framework. In Koch, S., (Ed.), (1959) *A Psychology: A Study of a Science*. Vol. 3. New York: McGraw-Hill. pp. 184–256.

Rogers, C.R., (1961). *On Becoming a Person*. London: Constable and Company, (1984).

Rogers, C.R., (1962). Some Learnings from a Study of Psychotherapy with Schizophrenics. Paper presented at Conference on Psychotherapy of Schizophrenia: Adults and Children, published in *Pennsylvania Psychiatric Quarterly*, Summer.

Rogers, C.R., (1963). The Actualizing Tendency in Relation to 'Motives' and to Consciousness. In Jones, M.R. (1963) *Nebraska Symposium on Motivation. Current Theory and Research in Motivation, Volume XI*. Lincoln: University of Nebraska Press, pp. 1–24.

Rogers, C.R., (1966). Client-Centered Therapy. In Avieti, S., (Ed.), (1966) *American Handbook of Psychiatry, Volume 3*. New York: Basic Books, pp. 183–200.

Rogers, C.R., (1967). The Findings in Brief. In Rogers, C.R., Gendlin, E.T., Kiesler, D.J., and Truax, C.B., (1967) *The Therapeutic Relationship and Its Impact. A Study of Psychotherapy with Schizophrenics*. Madison: University of Wisconsin Press, pp. 73–93.

Rogers, C.R., (1970). *Carl Rogers on Encounter Groups*. New York: Harper and Row.

Rogers, C.R., (1978). *Carl Rogers on Personal Power*. London: Constable and Company, (1996).

Rogers, C.R., (1980). *A Way of Being*. Boston: Houghton Mifflin Company.

Rogers, C.R. and Sanford, R.C., (1989). Client-Centered Psychotherapy. In Kaplan, H. and Sadock, B., (Eds.), (1989) *The Comprehensive Textbook of Psychiatry*. V. Baltimore: Williams and Williams, pp. 1482–501.

Sanford, R., (1993). From Rogers to Gleick and Back Again. In Brazier, D., (Ed.), (1993) *Beyond Carl Rogers*. London: Constable, pp. 253–73.

Shlien, J.M., (1997). Empathy In Psychotherapy: A Vital Mechanism? Yes. Often Therapist's Conceit? All Too Often. By Itself Enough? No. In Bohart, A.C., and Greenberg, L.S., (Eds.) (1997) *Empathy Reconsidered*. Washington: American Psychological Association, pp. 63–80.

Spinelli, E., (1994). *Demystifying Therapy*. London: Constable and Company.

Tarnas, R., (1991). *The Passion of the Western Mind*. London: Pimlico Press, (1996).

Thorne, B., (1991). *Person-Centred Counselling; Therapeutic and Spiritual Dimensions*. London: Whurr.

Thorne, B., (1992). *Carl Rogers*. London: Sage Publications, (1994).

Waldrop, M.M., (1992). *Complexity: The Emerging Science at the Edge of Order and Chaos*. Great Britain: Penguin Books. 1994.

Wexler, D.A., (1974). A Cognitive Theory of Experiencing, Self Actualization, and Therapeutic Process. In Wexler, D.A., and Rice, L.N., (Eds.), (1974) *Innovations in Client-Centered Therapy*. New York: John Wiley, pp. 49–116.

Wood, J.K., (1995). From the Person-Centered Approach to Client-Centered Therapy: What do Some Sixty Years of Experience Suggest. Paper presented at the 3rd International Conference on Client-Centered and Experiential Psychotherapy, Gmunden, Austria, 1995.

Zimring, F., (1995). A New Explanation for the Beneficial Results of Client-Centered Therapy: The Possibility of a New Paradigm. *The Person-Centered Journal*. 2(2), pp. 36–48.

8   Congruence and Therapeutic Presence

Leslie S. Greenberg

and

Shari M. Geller

Congruence is probably the most complex of Rogers' three therapist-offered conditions, yet the least explicated. As Rogers developed his ideas, he came to see genuineness as the most basic of the conditions (Rogers and Sanford, 1984). Possibly because of its later emergence as a central element, it has not received as much attention as the other conditions, particularly empathy. We will discuss the concept of congruence and suggest that to be clearly understood, congruence needs to be seen as being a process embedded in an appropriate network of beliefs and intentions. We will in addition suggest that it is this tacit framework of intentions and beliefs that informs the therapist in how to be skilful in communicating congruently. We will also review the concept of presence and discuss its relation to congruence, suggesting that therapeutic presence be viewed as an encompassing concept that acts as a pre-condition to congruence and possibly as a precondition to therapeutic effectiveness in humanistic therapies in general.

CONGRUENCE

Of the three therapist-offered conditions, congruence often has been the most troublesome to the general disciplines of psychology and psychiatry. It has been misinterpreted either as being a license for the therapist to openly express all of his or her feelings or needs in an undisciplined manner, or has been viewed as condoning what psychodynamic therapists would view as negative counter-transference. In the sixties and seventies, being authentic, self-disclosing and encountering, often was proclaimed as central to good therapy by a number of humanistic therapists — without much further specification of what authentic meant or how it was therapeutic (Schutz, 1967). This rightfully led to the concern among many that unbridled openness could be destructive. These misunderstandings of what is meant by therapeutic congruence require the clarification of this concept and an explication of some of its underlying assumptions.

Lietaer (1993) pointed out that congruence or authenticity can, at an initial level of analysis, be broken into two separate components. These are (1) the ability to be aware of one's own internal experience, and (2) transparency, the willingness to communicate to the other person what is going on within. Rogers (1961), in using the notion of being 'real' with other people, appeared to emphasize both dimensions. By being congruent he meant not only being aware of one's own internal experience but also of sharing it with the other. Thus congruence clearly has two components — an internal component involving awareness of one's own flow of experience and transparency, an outer component, that refers to explicit communication. It is with this latter component of openness and honesty that much of the controversy around congruence has raged.

The claim that being transparent *is* therapeutic requires, in our view, the specification of the set of preconditions and beliefs, intentions and attitudes that are needed for this aspect of congruence *to be* therapeutic. To simply teach young or novice therapists that they should be congruently transparent is not always helpful. This is because being transparent presumes a certain level of personal development and certain intellectual and value commitments. Congruence thus does not stand alone as a therapeutic ingredient. In our view, therapeutic congruence, as well as involving awareness and transparency, also requires that the therapists' internal experience arises out of attitudes, beliefs and intentions related to doing no harm to clients and to facilitate their development. This is the psychotherapeutic equivalent of a Hippocratic Oath.

In person-centered therapy, congruence has always been seen as being a part of a triad of therapeutic attitudes along with empathy and unconditional positive regard. In dialogical Gestalt therapy, the emphasis on therapist's genuineness or authenticity is based on Buber's (1958) I-Thou relationship in which a genuine meeting of client and therapist involves, among other things, the therapist's presence and non-exploitiveness. The Rogerian attitudes of a willingness to understand the client and the prizing of a client's experience, and Gestalt notions of presence and non-exploitiveness, all entail intentions that are necessary for congruence to be therapeutic. To be facilitatively congruent, therapists thus need to be committed to understanding and respecting their clients. They need to operate both with a genuine desire not to have power over their clients and with a belief in the therapeutic importance of accepting their clients' experience as valid. Finally they need to be fully present and in contact with their clients as well as themselves. These intentions both precede being facilitatively congruent and are themselves important aspects of therapeutic congruence.

Varieties of congruence

One of the major purposes of congruence in psychotherapy is to help establish trust. As Rogers said, when we are 'real' with each other, this facilitates trust and communication (Rogers, 1961). But, of course, being real is in and of itself very complex and needs further clarification. In a post-modern era, in which constructivist notions highlight how much is either psychologically or socially constructed (Neimeyer and Mahoney, 1995), notions of what is real become fuzzy. Being one's real self, for example, has always been a problematic idea because it implies there is such an entity as a real self, rather than seeing that the self is a process of construction (Greenberg and van Balen, 1998; Whelton and Greenberg, 2000). Being congruent, however, when seen as a process of awareness and openness in the moment, escapes the problem of claiming some greater ontological validity for certain aspects of self. Being real in facilitative relationship thus implies that the therapist does not hide relevant feelings and thoughts and, at particular times communicates certain present and persistent feelings or thoughts in certain ways to help build trust and openness in the dyad. This, however, is not done manipulatively or strategically. Rather it is done from the therapist's experience in the moment of a genuine desire to help. It is important to emphasize that the *doing* aspect of congruence involves an expressive intention rather than a goal-oriented one.

Congruence, like empathy, (see Bohart and Greenberg, 1997) is not a unitary phenomenon. Rather it includes a variety of intentions, beliefs and attitudes and manifests in a variety of experiences and behaviours that differ at different times. We need to recognize that although congruence is a holistic concept, it refers, in therapy, to a complex, multifaceted, phenomenon that is embedded in a network of attitudes, beliefs and intentions that results in doing different things at different times.

When I am being congruent, as well as being open to my experience, I am also *doing* different things at different times depending on the person I am with, the situation and the specific in-therapy context in which I am being congruent (see Wyatt, 2000). Being present or fully attuned to the moment is a necessary guide, both to being open to my own experience and to knowing how to respond to the unique interplay of person, situation and context. Different situations call forth different congruent actions. These can, and need to be, specified further if we are to clearly understand what is meant by therapeutic congruence.

For example, being congruent may involve the therapist saying what she is feeling in her body at the time. It may involve speaking of a feeling that has been persisting over time, and actually is not being felt at the moment, in any visceral way. Or being congruent may involve the therapist saying something that spontaneously captures her sense of the moment. Also, the current or general feelings being expressed congruently may range from compassion to anger, from threat to joy, and depending on which feeling is being felt, it will be expressed in a very specific way with its own expressive intentions. Anger, for example, may be expressed in order to set boundaries and to assist in resolving the feeling of being wronged; compassion may be expressed in order to share it and to comfort; fear is probably often expressed in order to inform the other of one's reaction to him or her.

In addition to disclosing what one is feeling, being congruent may involve saying what one is thinking, disclosing an image, sharing a past experience of one's own, or commenting on the interaction between persons. The intentions here may be to convey one's understanding or deal with a relational difficulty. A highly integrated and/or well-trained therapist, dedicated to helping, will produce congruent responses of a different kind and quality than will an undifferentiated or egocentric therapist or a novice. Being therapeutically congruent thus can be seen to involve a complex set of interpersonal skills as well as the intrapersonal skill of awareness.

We suggest that the communicative aspects of congruence involve the ability to translate intrapersonal experience into certain types of interpersonal responses, such that these responses will be consistent with certain implicit intentions. The deeper level intentions include, in addition to valuing and understanding the other, the intentions to facilitate the other's development, to be accepting and non-critical of the other, to confirm the other's experience, to focus on their strengths and, above all, to do the other no harm. These intentions, and more, are what determine whether congruence is therapeutic. If one had a genuine desire to harm, being congruent would not be therapeutic.

To acknowledge the tacit intentions underlying congruence does not mean that congruence is not a spontaneous emergent experience in which one feels whole. Feeling whole when being congruent results from the therapist's intentions and actions being integrated and forming a coherent whole. In a congruent state, intentions are not in opposition and do not conflict with each other — neither does one intention or experience obscure or suppress another, opposing one.

Being congruent — the internal awareness component

Being aware of one's own flow of internal experience and connecting with the essence of one's feeling, is a central component of congruence (Rogers, 1980). The internal awareness component is the easiest aspect of the concept to endorse as universally therapeutic. In our view it is always therapeutic for the therapist to be aware of her own feelings and reactions as this awareness orients her, and helps her be interpersonally clear and trustworthy. This inner awareness and contact naturally flows from the experience of therapeutic presence. Therapeutic presence is important in the practice of experiential therapies. As we will elaborate later, therapeutic presence involves, among other qualities, being receptively open and sensitive to one's own moment by moment, changing experience; being fully immersed in the moment; feeling a sense of expansion and spaciousness; and being with and for the client. These and other aspects of presence will be discussed more explicitly in the next section. Throughout this paper we assert that therapeutic presence is thus essential to congruence.

With awareness there is less likelihood of a discrepancy between verbal and non-verbal behavior and clients come to know that what they see is what they get — they learn that there are no hidden agendas. This helps the client feel safe and reduces interpersonal anxiety. This reduction in interpersonal anxiety allows clients to tolerate more intrapersonal anxiety and thereby to explore more deeply. If the therapist is not aware of her feelings in interaction with her client she is unlikely to be an effective helper because she will not have access to vital information being generated in her therapy relationships — it would be like operating in the dark. We know that we are most effective in helping others when we are clear and aware of our own flow of internal experience, especially experience that is generated out of our moment by moment interactions with our clients.

Types of incongruence

Looking now at incongruence in the dimension of self-awareness, it is important to note some of the different ways in which therapists can be incongruent. Different types of incongruence for example occur:
 (1) when therapists are aware of their experiencing but deliberately not
     communicating. (Sometimes this is appropriate and sometimes not.)
 (2) When therapists are not clearly aware of what they are fundamentally
     experiencing because of being anxiously unclear.

(3) When therapists are completely unaware of their basic experience.

The first occurs when the therapist is clearly aware of feeling or thinking something and is deliberately not saying this. Here the therapist can be dissembling, trying to convey something he is not feeling. Then he is being phony or fake, trying either to be nice or supportive or appear interested when he is not. Another form of deliberate non-transparency is when he deliberately chooses not to say something of what he feels or thinks, because it seems like it would be distracting, or when what he is feeling seems to be more of his own 'stuff', or the timing seems wrong.

The second type of incongruence is being anxiously unclear. Here a therapist's anxiety blocks his ability to have a flow of experience. When this occurs he is usually unable to put this experience into words, especially at first. He may become aware of being threatened but is unable to process this, and his awareness becomes fused with a bodily sensed quality of tension and tingly-ness. Consciousness becomes prickly, breathing is altered and shoulders and arms tense up. He is then unable to listen clearly to his clients' words or to be in touch with his own flow of experience. The anxious body sense interferes both with attending to his client and with putting his experience into words and may dominate the therapist's awareness.

In the above examples, the therapist is clearly aware of a feeling of threat. However, there are other states in which so much is happening or everything is occurring so quickly, that the therapist is not aware. It is only later that he can notice that he was threatened. Trainers can see that trainees often are not able to be aware of feeling threatened when it is occurring. In this third type of incongruence there is no awareness at the time of feeling threatened, nor of what is occurring internally. At such times the first step for therapists in becoming congruent, is to be able to recognize that they are feeling threatened. Yet other forms of this type of lack of awareness in congruence can occur. For example, a therapist can express something, in the belief that it is truly what he means, but he is unaware that certain currently unrecognized needs are influencing his expression. Another form of being incongruently unaware occurs when the therapist expresses what we have called a secondary emotion rather than a primary emotion (Greenberg et al. ,1993). Thus the therapist may experience and express anger without, at that moment, being able to recognize his underlying hurt. Here, the therapist expresses a secondary reaction to what was said and is not in touch with essential or core self-experience.

These three forms of incongruence — conscious non-disclosure, anxiety that prevents clear awareness and lack of awareness — all differ from one another. Each type of incongruence involves a different process of becoming congruent, even though it involves the common elements of being aware, and the ability to articulate one's own internal experience. One process involves attending to that which is known, another focusing on the not yet articulate, and another entails getting to what is core and acknowledging the previously unacknowledged.

Therapists generally are neither fully congruent nor incongruent, but are congruent to differing degrees. Thus congruence itself is a process. Another problem with the concept of congruence/incongruence is that the concept has a realist flavor to it, suggesting that the therapist feels something explicit and is either aware or not aware of it. The situation, however, is much more complex. The second form of incongruence above, for example, involves the therapist being unable to articulate in the moment what he or she is experiencing. Here the therapist is unable to construct meaning from what is going on rather than denying to awareness something already formed — it is not that he has a feeling, for example of feeling 'diminished' sitting inside fully formed, and is unaware of it. Rather he is unable, at the moment, to create a coherent description or narrative of himself in the situation (Greenberg and van Balen, 1998). Thus he is unable to articulate or configure his experience into a conscious description; he cannot symbolize his tacit experience and is not able to make sense of his experience as, perhaps, that of feeling diminished. The anxiety or threat is often a symptom of being stuck and unable to carry-forward one's experience in one's body with words. This, of course, is what Gendlin (1964) was pointing out in his concept of experiencing. We (Greenberg and Pascual-Leone, 1995, 1997, 2001; Greenberg and van Balen, 1999) have moved to the use of the word 'coherence' to replace congruence in an attempt to capture the constructive element of being genuine and to deal with the difficulty mentioned above with the concept of being real.

In being congruent, I *form* the moments of my experience, as much as I purely *discover* them. This is a creative process, and when I'm being incongruent it is this process that is blocked. In asserting this, I am not saying there is not something there in me to which I can attend. There really is some bodily felt experience there, but, until I put words to it to create coherent meaning, I am stuck. This process of becoming congruent by coherence is more like the 'seeing' of a rabbit in a cloud formation than seeing a rabbit behind a tree. In seeing a rabbit in the clouds I configure what I see from what is there. So too do I configure myself in each moment from the elements of my experience. One form of incongruence, therefore, is not being able to find the words, symbols or referents to an experience, so as not to be able to make sense of and experience meaning.

Being congruent — an interpersonal skill

The case of transparency, or the communication component of congruence, is much more complicated than the self-awareness component. It seems that being facilitatively transparent involves many interpersonal skills. This component involves not only the ability to express what I'm truly feeling but to express it *in a way that* is facilitative. Transparency thus is a global concept for a complex set of interpersonal skills embedded within a set of therapeutic attitudes. We argue that the skills depend on three factors. First on therapist attitudes, second on certain processes such as facilitativeness, discipline and comprehensiveness, and third on the interpersonal stance of the therapist.

First, and probably most important, congruent responses, as we have seen, need always to be embedded within the therapist conditions and need to be communicated non-judgmentally. In life, clearly one can be congruently destructive. Thus one can congruently attack or even murder. We all know this is not what we mean by the term 'congruence' in therapy, because the term 'congruence' is really qualified, tacitly, by a number of other beliefs and views.

We thus find it helpful to use the word 'facilitative' to qualify the word congruent.

When person-centered therapists say they are expressing themselves genuinely, they mean they are being transparent in a disciplined manner. In order to do this, therapists need first to be aware of their deepest level of experience — and this may take time and reflection. Next, they need to be clear in their intention for sharing their experience — that this is for the client or the relationship and not for themselves. It is also always important for therapists to be sensitive to the timing of disclosure — sensing whether clients are open to, or too vulnerable to receive what one has to offer. Discipline thus involves not blurting out whatever the therapist is feeling and making sure that what is expressed is a core or primary feeling rather than a secondary. Another qualifying concept that helps to clarify the transparency aspect of congruence is comprehensiveness — that congruence needs to mean 'saying all of it'. The therapist not only expresses the central or focal aspect that is being felt, but also the meta-experience — what is felt about what is being felt and communicated. Thus saying that one feels irritated or bored is not saying all of it. Therapists need also to communicate their concern about this potentially hurting their clients and express that they are communicating this out of a wish to clarify and improve a connection, not destroy it. This is what we mean by 'saying all of it'.

Figure 1: *Structural Analysis of Structural Behavior* — (Adapted from Benjamin, 1996)

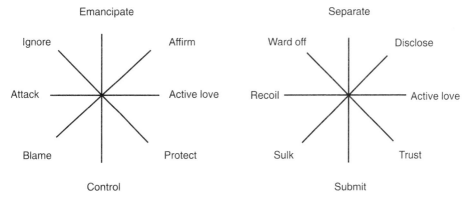

SASB simplified cluster model of focus on other   SASB simplified cluster model of focus on self

Interpersonal stance — the third factor

The set of skills involved in facilitative congruent communication can be explicated further, by looking at congruent interaction in terms of the interactional stance as described by a circumplex grid of interpersonal interaction. This grid is based on the two major dimensions of dominance/control and closeness/affiliation. Lorna Benjamin (1996) has devised a coding system called the Structural Analysis of Social Behavior (SASB) that can be used to describe interpersonal interaction along these dimensions (see Figure 1). Consistent with interpersonal theory, this grid outlines a set of complementary responses that fit each other and that interactionally 'pull' for each other. Thus, attack 'pulls' for defend or recoil, and affirm 'pulls' for disclose or reveal. The skill of congruent responding involves not reacting in a complementary fashion to a negative interpersonal 'pull' of the client — like recoiling when attacked — but rather to act in such a way as to 'pull' for a more therapeutically productive response from one's client, such as 'clearly express'. This would be achieved, for example, by an empathic understanding response to an attack.

The eight clusters of complementary positions are attack-recoil, blame-sulk, control-submit, protect-trust, active love-reactive love, affirm-disclose, emancipate-separate and ignore-wall off. Each cluster in turn is broken into more specific behaviors. The cluster Affirm, for example, includes friendly listen, show empathic understanding and confirm, and responses such as these pull respectively for the complementary responses of openly disclose and reveal, clearly express and enthusiastic show. The blame cluster includes punish, accuse/blame, put down/act superior which respectively pull for complementary responses of whine/defend, justify/appease, sulk/act put upon.

In addition to specifying complementary interactions, this system can be used to understand the type of response that is the antithesis to a certain behavior, and will act as an antidote to entering into an undesirable repetitive circular interaction. The antithesis is *the complement of what one would like the other to do*. Therapists who do not react to the negative pull of the client's response — but instead respond in a new way — will pull for a more constructive response from their clients. Thus, to overcome a blame-sulk cycle, a response from a therapist to a client's blame, of affirm rather than sulk, would pull for disclose rather than continued blame. The affirming response has a high probability of leading to a change in the interaction, as it will more likely pull for disclosure or exploration from the client.

Facilitative congruent responses are most likely to fall in the high-affiliation, low-dominance portion of the grid, or what Benjamin terms the friendly differentiation quadrant. These responses include those in the affirming and emancipate clusters mentioned above. Some of the specific behaviors included in the emancipate cluster are entitled 'encourage separate identity', 'you can do it fine' and 'carefully consider'. Responses by a therapist in the high-dominance, low-affiliation portion of the grid — what is called the hostile differentiation quadrant — are generally not facilitative. These include the clusters of attack and ignore, with behaviors such as attack, angrily dismiss, abandon and neglect. These behaviors pull for desperate protest, withdraw, detach and wall off, respectively. The other two quadrants in this grid are friendly and hostile enmeshed. They include clusters of responses such as protect, in the friendly enmeshed quadrant, and blame, in the hostile enmeshed quadrant, with a cluster of controlling responses at a mid-point between friendly and hostile.

The issue of whether hostile responses in therapy are ever therapeutically congruent, remains to be explored. These types of hostile, disaffiliative interactions certainly generally would not promote trust, but at times, however, for example if a client is testing a therapist's limits to the extreme, a congruent response of anger at violation in particular circumstances might be a trust building response.

138

Dealing with difficult feelings

The skills of congruent responding in dealing with difficult feelings, then, involve the following: first, identifying one's own internal feeling response — this is the general skill of awareness. Next is the skill of responding. As we have explicated elsewhere (Rice and Greenberg 1984), in order to best describe both client and therapist responses it is useful to look at the context in which they occur. With respect to congruence, the context is where on the interactional grid the person's action, to which one is responding, falls. For example, in the context of being attacked, the first step involves the therapist becoming aware of what he feels when being attacked — which often is feeling threatened. This feeling then needs to be symbolized in awareness. The next step in being facilitatively congruent is being able to communicate feeling threatened in a non-blaming, non-escalatory manner. Here, according to the SASB model, therapist's responses perceived by clients as openly disclosing and revealing are likely to facilitate friendly listening, while empathic understanding will facilitate clear expression from the client. It is the interpersonal stance, particularly that of disclosing, that is crucial in making transparency facilitative. For example, in the context of feeling angry, a therapist's facilitative congruent process involves first checking if her anger is her most core feeling, if it is, then she needs to disclose this in a non-blaming, non-escalatory fashion. If the therapist is feeling more hurt or diminished or threatened, rather than angry, then congruence involves being aware of this and disclosing this in an effective manner.

There are recognizable classes of difficult experiences that are often discussed when addressing congruence in training or teaching counsellors, for example, trainees often ask: What do you do if you feel angry? What do you say if you feel bored? What do you say if you feel sexual? What do you say if the client doesn't leave, or if you feel rejecting? Situations such as these represent interpersonal interactions, which can be well understood and described on the interpersonal dimensions of affiliation and control or dominance. As we have seen, the facilitativeness or destructiveness of expression is dependent on the quadrant in which the expression falls. Anger expressed as attack from the hostile dominant quadrant, or feeling sexual expressed as love in the close quadrant without sensitivity to power and boundary violation issues, will not be facilitative. Similarly, expressions of boredom or expressions of rejection (e.g. of somebody's dependence) that occupy an interactional position of being distant or ignoring, will not be facilitative. These responses respectively will pull for recoil, erotic love or walling off. The issue becomes one of how does a therapist helpfully interact when feeling one of these feelings or when this type of issue arises in a relationship in which the therapist is trying to be facilitative?

As we have already said, if the therapist responds from an affirming stance this is likely to be facilitative. This is the baseline response in person-centered and other supportive therapies. But what to do when the therapist is not feeling affirming but is feeling angry, critical and rejecting and can't get past this feeling, to something more core? Each interactional response, in order to be facilitatively congruent, involves first connecting with the fundamental attitudes or intentions of trying to be helpful, understanding, valuing, respecting and non-intrusive or non-dominant. This will lead to these feelings being expressed as *disclosures*. If the interpersonal stance of disclosing is adopted, rather than the complementary stances of attack, expressing erotic desire, or rejection, then this congruent response is more likely to be facilitative. It is not the content of the disclosure that is the central issue in being facilitative, rather it is *the interpersonal stance of disclosure in a facilitative way* that is important. What is congruent is the feeling of wanting to disclose in the service of facilitating, and the action of disclosing.

The different ways of being facilitatively congruent in dealing with different classes of difficult feeling are, then, to some degree specifiable — they all involve adopting a position of disclosing. Thus, expressing a feeling that could be perceived of as negative in a stance that is disclosing, rather than expressing it in the stance that usually accompanies that feeling, will help make it facilitative. Disclosure implicitly or explicitly, involves willingness to, or an interest in, exploring with the other *what* one is disclosing. For example, when attacked or feeling angry, a therapist does not attack the other but rather *discloses* that he is feeling angry. He does not use blaming, 'you' language. Rather he takes responsibility for his feelings and uses 'I' language that helps disclose what he is feeling. Above all, he does not go into a one up, escalatory, position in this communication but rather openly discloses feelings of fear, anger or hurt. When the problem is one of the therapist experiencing non-affiliative, rejecting feelings or loss of interest in the client's experience, the interactional skill involves being able to disclose this in the context of communicating congruently that the therapist does not wish to feel this. Or, the therapist discloses these feelings as a problem getting in the way and that she is trying to repair the distance so that she will be able to feel more understanding and closer. The key is communicating what could be perceived as negative feelings in a congruently facilitative way, generally occupying an interactional position of disclosure in the non-dominant affiliative quadrant.

For example, a very fragile and explosive client once told me in an intense encounter that she feared me and hated me because I was so phony and that I acted so presumptuously in assuming that I understood what she felt. She said she saw me as a leech trying to suck her emotional life out of her and that, although I professed good intentions, I was really out to destroy her. Under the mounting, relentless attack I told her I felt afraid of her anger, and tears came to my eyes as I told her how I hurt. This was disclosed without blame or recrimination or without an explicit power or control related intention to get her to stop. Just a disclosure of what it felt like inside for me in that moment. This disclosure did have her stop and drew from her some of her concern for me.

Can genuineness be specified?

Some readers may feel that specifying what it is to be genuine is a contradiction in terms, because if congruence involves internal awareness and revealing it, then trying to specify what the therapist should do, defeats the purpose of revealing what is real. If genuineness means only spontaneity, it cannot be viewed as a skill. Being genuine involves, first and foremost, feeling whatever one is experiencing. Therefore anything employed as a skill has to be felt or used genuinely. Genuineness, as the experience of a unique agent, cannot be specified beforehand. It is what it is. But what one does with it, provided it is done genuinely, can be seen as a skill.

The discussion of whether the Rogerian attitudes can be translated into behavioral principles and skills has a long and extensive history (Barrett-Lennard, 1998). Fundamentally, the conditions, including congruence, are attitudes not behaviors, but if the appropriate attitudes are there, they will translate into behaviors that have noticeable characteristics. We are suggesting that laying out some of the principles that govern facilitative congruent communication will help make congruence more specifiable. The SASB grid, or some such system of describing interpersonal behavior, will help greatly to do so. The principles being specified here for therapeutic congruent communication are that the therapist responses be embedded in helping attitudes and be affirming or disclosing responses, and that it is the interpersonal stance, not the content of the transparent response, that is important in making it therapeutic.

It is significant to recognize that this is not a proposal that a therapist's genuine responses be determined by some pre-existing system, or that therapeutic responses be deliberate or strategic position taking. Rather, congruent responses have to be a genuine reflection of what the therapist feels and thinks. People are extremely perceptive and sensitive to the genuineness of any response and so it is only when the response genuinely fits the correct stance and has facilitative intentions, that we will have a congruent response that is facilitative.

As in learning any complex performance, like playing a piano concerto, or playing soccer, having both the requisite skill and developing a higher level of integration is necessary. It is the tacit synthesis of skills and other elements that produces masterful performances. The dilemma in training therapists is that some people naturally seem to have the ability to be facilitatively congruent without specifying what this involves, but some don't. I have trained many students who do not perform well initially in how they are genuine or congruent. It often can be quite confusing for them. To people outside of a humanistic tradition the prescription to be genuine often seems incomprehensible. This is because the concept has not been fully explicated. Some grasp it intuitively but others don't. If we are to train people to be better therapists and not just select those with natural abilities we need to train them in both the attitudes *and* skills of congruence.

While the practice of specific skills can be helpful to the development of therapeutic abilities, letting go of these skills and any planned intent on how to be congruent, when entering the therapy session, is extremely important and the basis of therapeutic presence. This letting go of preconceptions and skills is a part of a preparation that occurs with therapeutic presence, as can be seen in the model of therapeutic presence in the next section. The learning of skills becomes integrated on a tacit level and the appropriate response arises out of the in-the-moment interaction of person, situation and experiencing. Being empty, open, and receptive to this in the moment, and experiencing and responding from the therapists' authentic center involves trust, in the process, in the therapist's own emerging experience, and in the client's experience, and is the foundation of therapeutic presence as we will see below.

THERAPEUTIC PRESENCE

Presence involves being fully in the moment and directly encountering all aspects of experience with one's whole being on a multitude of levels — including physical, emotional, mental and visceral — from a grounded and centered position within oneself. Presence is a quality that can be experienced in many life situations such as art, watching a sunset, teaching, or in quiet meditation with one's self. This discussion and the subsequent research is focused on the therapist's presence in the psychotherapeutic encounter, which we term *therapeutic presence*. The experience of presence in art, or other life situations, and therapeutic presence share similar qualities. Therapeutic presence, however, is distinguished by focusing on the therapist's presence in an encounter, intended as healing, in which the therapist intention is to be with and for the other. Even though the focus here is on therapeutic presence, we will use the terms 'presence' and 'therapeutic presence' interchangeably as has been done in the literature.

The concept of congruence, then, needs to be qualified in order for its therapeutic nature to be understood. We propose that in addition to the importance of the above-mentioned intentions, beliefs and skills, the therapist needs to be fully *present* in the therapeutic encounter in order for congruence to be therapeutic. Therapists cannot bring extraneous personal baggage, needs, or even agendas for therapy into the encounter. Being able to be fully present to the other is a highly developed skill that requires a letting go of preconceptions and full attention in the moment. In order to be fully present, the therapist needs to have developed a level of psychological maturity or level of functioning that is rather high, or at least be able to attain this while in session.

A number of humanistic theorists suggest that therapist presence is a necessary condition for creating a positive and supportive therapeutic environment. It also has been seen as a key means to help clients to become more present with their own experience and hence move in a direction of inner growth and understanding (Buber, 1958; Bugental, 1983, 1987; Hycner, 1993; Hycner and Jacobs, 1995; Schneider and May, 1995).

Rogers (1980) in his later writings claimed presence as important:

> When I am at my best, as a group facilitator or as a therapist, I discover another characteristic. I find that when I am closest to my inner, intuitive self, when I am somehow in touch with the unknown in me, when perhaps I am in a slightly altered state of consciousness, then whatever I do seems to be full of healing. Then, simply my presence is releasing and helpful to the other. There is nothing I can do to force this experience, but when I can relax and be close to the transcendental core of me, then I may behave in strange and impulsive ways in the relationship, ways in which I cannot justify rationally, which have nothing to do with my thought processes. But these strange behaviors turn out to be right, in some odd way: it seems that my inner spirit has reached out and touched the inner spirit of the other. Our relationship transcends itself and becomes a part of something larger. Profound growth and healing and energy are present (p. 129).

May (1958) uses Rogers' general comments on the nature of what it means to be a therapist to show what he means by presence:

I let myself go into the immediacy of the relationship where it is my total organism which takes over and is sensitive to the relationship, not simply my consciousness. I am not consciously responding in a planful or analytic way, but simply in an unreflective way to the other individual, my reaction being based (but not consciously) on my total organismic sensitivity to this other person. I live the relationship on this basis (p. 82).

Few theoretical writings exist on therapist presence and most of what is written is qualified by the ineffability of this important quality.

Hycner and Jacobs (1995) describe presence as a turning of the whole self to the other — not just attending to the other but turning away from preoccupation with self and offering one's whole being to the other. This involves viewing the other in his/her uniqueness and acceptance that this is a different and unique person, where 'no other concern is paramount'.

Bugental (1987) writes that presence is 'A name for the quality of being in a situation or relationship in which one intends, at a deep level, to participate as fully as she is able. Presence is expressed through mobilization of one's sensitivity — both inner (to the subjective) and outer (to the situation and the other person(s) in it) — and through, bringing into action one's capacity for response.' And that 'full presence means being truly accessible and appropriately expressive' (p. 222).

Schneider and May (1995) posit that 'presence holds and illuminates that which is palpably (immediately, kinaesthetically, affectively, and profoundly) relevant between therapists and clients and within clients. It is the ground and eventual goal of experiential work' (p. 174). The goal of presence, in their view, is to illuminate the client's experiential world, provide a safe container for immersion to occur, and to deepen the client's ability to constructively use her discoveries.

Therapeutic presence can be viewed as an essential therapeutic stance to open the way for other therapist stances, such as Rogers' therapist-offered conditions of congruence, empathy, and positive regard, to be used and lived as part of the therapy process. A greater specification of therapeutic presence, then, seems important. In order to further understand and describe therapeutic presence, a number of therapists were therefore interviewed on their experience of presence in therapy.

Figure 2: *Therapeutic Presence*

Preparing the ground	Process of presence	Experiencing presence
		(a) Immerson
	(a) Receptivity	
(a) Arriving and clearing a space immediately before the session		
		(b) Expansion
	(b) Inwardly acting	
(b) Practicing presence in life		(c) Grounding
	(c) Extending and contact	
		(d) Being with and for the client

Understanding therapeutic presence

The authors (Geller, 2000; Geller and Greenberg, 2000) conducted a qualitative study whereby seven experienced therapists from four different theoretical orientations, who were familiar with, and knowledgeable about, the qualities of therapeutic presence, were interviewed on their experience of presence in therapy. A form of qualitative analysis combining condensation and categorization of meaning was used to extract meaning units from the interviews (Kvale, 1996).

The analysis resulted in the model shown in Figure. 2. Three overarching categories of therapeutic presence were formed from the respondents' reports. One category was labeled *preparing the ground for presence*, referring to the pre-session and general life preparation for therapeutic presence. Another category described the *process of presence*, the processes or activities the person is engaged in when being therapeutically present, or what the therapist *does* when in presence. The third category reflected the actual in-session *experience of presence*.

Expanded description of presence

Preparation
Therapists described the importance of preparing the ground for therapeutic presence to emerge, both prior to the session and through practice in their daily life. The therapist arrives at the session holding the intention to be fully there with the client and to let go of his own and daily concerns. The therapist brackets or suspends his own beliefs, assumptions, needs and concerns in order to fully attend to what is occurring in the moment and to respond to the other based on the experience of the moment. The therapist clears a space inside where he can receive whatever experience emerges in the client, in the self, or in the relationship between the two, with a sense of openness, acceptance and non-judgment.

Therapists also discussed a sense of commitment in their daily lives to the practice of presence. Some of the therapists interviewed referred to their meditation practice as an essential aid in being in the moment. On-going care for self-needs, relationships and personal growth were also viewed as support to the practice of presence in session with the client. Being present in one's own life and in personal relationships appear to be a part of the growth and development essential for developing presence in session.

The process
Preparation appears to be an essential part of moving into presence, however, once in session the therapist responds to whatever presents itself in the moment. This involves a shifting awareness of the many different elements that go into a moment of encounter with the client, including the professional and personal being of the therapist, the being of the client, and the relationship between them. The interaction of all these aspects in a given moment guides the therapist in his/her understanding and response.

There is a quality of movement in the process of presence that demands the therapist be fully immersed in each moment as it arrives. This movement involves shifting from taking in the fullness of the client's experience in one moment

144

(receptivity), to being in contact with how that experience resonates in the therapist's own body (inwardly attending), to expressing that inner resonance or directly connecting with the client (extending and contact). Put another way, the therapist is touched by the essence of the other, is in contact with her own experience of how she is touched by the other, and offers this inner experience in a way that touches the other's essence. The therapist's movement of attention and contact is guided by what is most poignant in the moment.

The experience
The experience of presence involves a sense of total absorption, inner expansion, grounding in one's self, and being with and for the client. Therapeutic presence involves feeling intimately engaged in the experience of each moment with the client, with an expanded sense of awareness of the subtleties and depth of the experience of each moment. The therapist experiences a melding with the client and a loss of spatial boundaries, while maintaining a sense of center and grounding within himself in that shared space. A sense of love and respect is felt towards the other as the therapist meets the client in a way that is with, and for, the client's healing.

Therapeutic presence thus involves having a heightened awareness and sensitivity to the many dimensions of experience on a moment to moment basis. There is an absence of awareness of time, a lack of a sense of past or future. With therapeutic presence, the therapist is highly absorbed and engaged in the encounter with this other human being and with the person's suffering. The therapist does not turn away from the suffering of the other by labeling, categorizing, or objectifying. Nor is the therapist engaged in focusing on her own burdens or sufferings or worrying about how she should act or intervene. Rather, the therapist meets the other's suffering and pain with care, openness, awareness, and acceptance. The therapist engages with the other as a human being and allows herself to get as close as possible to the client's experience while maintaining a sense of center and grounding within her own existence. With presence, the therapist experiences a deep sense of trust within self, with the process, and with the experience of the client. The therapist trusts that whatever emerges is important and necessary for healing to occur. This openness to and allowing of experience is accompanied by an energized and flowing experience in the body and in the interaction between the therapist and client.

In summary, therapeutic presence involves therapists being open and sensitive to their own and their clients' moment by moment, changing, awareness and experience. This is a process of being receptive, being fully there with oneself, and extending and making genuine contact with the client. The experience is one in which the therapist feels fully immersed in the moment while feeling a sense of expansion and spaciousness, and feeling grounded and centered. It involves a 'being with' the client rather than a 'doing to' the client. It is a state of being open to all aspects of being with the client and receiving the client's experience in a gentle, non-judgmental and compassionate way, rather than observing and looking at or even into the client. This inner receptive state of the therapist is the ultimate tool in understanding the client. Therapeutic presence involves meeting the other in the moment where the person is, rather than trying to change her or him in some way.

Presence involves an absence of judgment and instead allows for a deeper understanding and acceptance of the client's world. This promotes moments of genuine meeting and this in turn invites clients to safely express and explore their conflicts and issues. Therapeutic presence is therefore an essential stance in humanistic therapies, where the therapist provides a safe and supportive container for the client's natural growth tendency to emerge.

THERAPEUTIC PRESENCE AND CONGRUENCE

Despite presence having been posited by some as the groundwork for therapy, the relationship between presence and congruence has not been discussed very extensively and little empirical literature on therapeutic presence has been generated to date. Some authors have written about presence in a way that equates presence with congruence (Kempler, 1970; Webster, 1998). Based on this study, it is our view that the concept of congruence does not incorporate all the subtle aspects of presence, yet therapeutic presence includes therapist authenticity in feeling and expression. Therapeutic presence thus prepares the ground for congruence, is a precondition of congruence, and also goes beyond it.

Beyond internal awareness and expression

Congruence as we defined it involves *awareness* and *transparency*. Therapeutic presence as determined from this investigation involves the process of *receptivity, inwardly attending* and *extending* and *contact,* and the experience of *immersion, expansion, grounding* and *being with and for the client.* It appears that the process of *inwardly attending* and *extending* and *contact,* to some degree, parallel *awareness* and *transparency.* What therapeutic presence appears to add to congruence is first the preliminary necessity of receptively being empty and open to receive the totality of the client's and one's own experience. Receptivity comes prior to Inwardly Attending to one's experience of being with the other (*awareness*) and Extending and sharing one's genuine experience (*transparency*). Therapeutic presence in addition adds to congruence a specification that the therapists be fully Immersed in the moment with the client, experience a sense of Expansion while maintaining a Grounding in themselves. Further, although Being With and For the Client is implied by congruence it is not explicitly in the definition. The *awareness* and *transparency* components of congruence, therefore, do not capture the state of receptivity and intimacy with the moment involved in presence, nor do they capture the experience of intense focus, and the combination of expansiveness and grounding in the self.

In our view congruence therefore is an aspect of, and flows from, therapeutic presence, but is not fully encompassing of the total experience of presence. However, the more presence there is for the therapist, the more she will be congruent in experience and responses.

Receptive and open: a prerequisite

Therapeutic presence precedes congruence in that the therapist must first be present to be receptive to, and make contact with, the fullness of the client's and her own immediate experience in order to understand what is being experienced and how to respond. The experience that is received, and experienced, resonates in the therapist's body and is experienced as a bodily sense in the form of feelings, words, or images. Being congruent at this point involves a moment of attending inwardly to that which is being presently experienced. As we discussed, a key aspect of congruence is being open to, and aware of, one's on-going flow of inner experiencing. Here the therapist uses her bodily sense as a navigational tool in responding to the client. If the therapist was not present and hence not fully open and involved, she would not be accessing the rich source of experience to which to attend that allows her to make a split-second choice as to whether, or how, to respond from this experience.

Immersion, expansion, and grounding: going beyond congruence

In order to be acutely aware within his experience and to genuinely share his experience with the client, the therapist needs to be immersed in the experience of the moment with the client. Congruence is thus experienced and held in the larger space of presence. With therapeutic presence, the therapist experiences a sense of expansion and openness. There is a sense of deep trust and a sense of spaciousness containing the intensity of what is being felt and expressed.

Therapeutic presence also adds to congruence a sense of grounding which includes the therapist trusting his own felt and expressed experience. For example, even though the therapist may be feeling intense shame, there is a calm and trust with what is being experienced and expressed. With congruence (and therapeutic presence) there is a match between the intensity that the therapist feels and the behavior that is shown. With therapeutic presence, the therapist feels that intensity while feeling a sense of grounding in self. He feels trust in his experience and in the process itself.

Being with and for the client: facilitative congruence and therapeutic presence

A key aspect of the experience of therapeutic presence also involves the intention of being with and for the client in a healing encounter. Holding the intent to not harm the other, but instead being with the other in a way that is helpful is key in therapeutic presence. This helping motivation is also central to being congruent in a way that is facilitative, as mentioned previously in this paper. If the therapist is present with his own experience, and with the client, then the decision to share his genuine experiencing is going to be guided by this intention. The therapist needs to be present with, and aware of, his own experience and be able to assess whether it is his own issues that are emerging — and need to be put aside temporarily — or if what is emerging could be of benefit to the client's healing process. The therapist thus needs to be open and aware of his own internal experience and genuinely sharing, while being in contact with the intention of being there with, and for, the client.

This aspect of therapeutic presence also allows the therapist to be aware and sensitive to his experience (and of course the client's experience) so that he can be congruent in expression in a way that is sensitive to timing. What is being felt does not just leak out in a way that is impulsive or driven by the need to release — hence the need for discipline. This quality also takes a level of development and maturity and even skill in being present with what is true in each moment. It could mean being able to withstand some discomfort (for example, in the case of shame) and to show that potentially vulnerable feeling to the client in a way that does not ask anything more than for the client to also be present. What makes the therapist therapeutically present is his willingness to be with that experience of shame and to express it to the client while holding the intention of helping the client or bettering the therapeutic relationship.

CONCLUSION

We have argued that, for congruence to be therapeutic, the concept requires further specification. We have suggested that, first, congruence needs to be seen as being embedded within a network of intentions and attitudes, among which the intention to do no harm is primary. Second, we have suggested that the skill of communicating congruently in a facilitative and disciplined manner appears to be characterized by the adoption of a non-dominant, affiliative, stance. Congruent communication of this type conveys a therapeutic intent to either disclose the therapist's internal experience, or to affirm the client's experience and further, these pull for listening or disclosure from the client. Finally we have suggested that therapeutic presence is a necessary precondition of congruence and at the same time is a larger experience that contains congruence as an aspect. More particularly, it allows the type of receptivity and intimacy with the moment that will promote both a true meeting of client and therapist, and the healing that occurs through this type of meeting.

The self of the therapist is brought to the encounter with the client with a willingness to experience all that the encounter entails. She is receptive and sensitive to the fullness of the client's experience. This direct and immediate encounter with the depth of the client's experience and with a deep trust that what is emerging is important and helpful in the process, is the very essence of therapeutic presence. It is the sensitivity to the moment and grounding in oneself that allows the therapist to know how to be with the other in the therapeutic encounter — when to be transparent with experience or when to purely resonate with the client's pain.

Therapeutic presence is an essential precondition for congruence, particularly to allow the type of receptivity and intimacy with the moment that will promote a true meeting of client and therapist and the healing that occurs through this type of meeting. Therapeutic presence is also a larger experience that contains congruence and allows it to be more completely facilitative and genuine.

REFERENCES

Barrett-Lennard, G. T. (1981). The empathy cycle: Refinement of a nuclear concept. *Journal of Counselling Psychology, 28,* pp. 91–100.

Barrett-Lennard, G. T. (1998). *Carl Rogers' Helping System: Journey and Substance*. London: Sage.

Benjamin, L. (1996). *Interpersonal diagnosis and treatment of personality disorders*. New York: Guilford.

Bohart, A. and Greenberg, L. (Eds.) (1997). *Empathy Reconsidered: New Directions in Theory Research and Practice*. Washington, D.C. : APA Press.

Buber, M. (1958). *I and Thou: Second edition*. New York: Charles Scribner's Sons.

Bugental, J. F. T. (1983). The one absolute necessity in psychotherapy. *The Scrip*, 1–2.

Bugental, J. F. T. (1987). *The Art of the psychotherapist*. New York: W.W. Norton and Company.

Geller, S. M. (2000). Being in the here and now: Therapist's experience of presence and the development of a measure of presence. Unpublished doctoral dissertation, York University, Toronto, Canada.

Geller, S. M., and Greenberg, L. (2000). *Presence: A working definition and a measure*. Paper presented to the Society for Psychotherapy Research, Chicago, Ill.

Gendlin, E. T. (1964). A theory of personality change. In P. Worchel and D. Byrne (Eds.). *Personality change*. New York: John Wiley.

Greenberg, L., Rice, L. and Elliott, R. (1993). *The Moment by Moment Process: Facilitating Emotional Change*. New York Guilford Press.

Greenberg, L.S., and Pascual-Leone, J. (1995). A dialectical constructivist approach to experiential change. In R. Neimeyer and M. Mahoney (Eds.), *Constructivism in psychotherapy*. Washington, DC: American Psychological Association. pp. 169–94.

Greenberg, L.S., and Pascual-Leone, J. (1997). Emotion in the creation of personal meaning. In M. Power and C. Brewin. *Transformation of meaning*. London: John Wiley. pp. 157–74.

Greenberg, L.S., and Pascual-Leone, J. (2001). Dialectical constructivism and the creation of meaning. *Journal of Constructivist Psychology*.

Greenberg, L.S., and Van Balen, (1998). Theory of Experience Centered Therapy. In L. Greenberg, J. Watson and G. Lietaer, (Eds.). *Handbook of Experiential Psychotherapy: Foundations and Differential Treatment*. (pp. 28–57) New York: Guilford Press.

Hycner, R. (1993). *Between Person and Person: Toward a dialogical psychotherapy*. New York: The Gestalt Journal Press, Inc.

Hycner, R., and Jacobs, L. (1995). *The Healing Relationship in Gestalt Therapy: A dialogical/self psychology approach*. New York: The Gestalt Journal Press.

Kempler, W. (1970). The therapist's merchandise. *Voices*, 5, 57–60.

Kvale, S. (1996). *InterViews: An introduction to qualitative research interviewing*. London: Sage.

Lietaer, G. (1993). Authenticity, congruence and transparency. In D. Brazier (Ed.). *Beyond Carl Rogers*. London: Constable. pp. 17–46.

May, R. (1958). Contributions to existential therapy, In R. May, E. Angel, and H. Ellenberger (Eds.), *Existence: A new dimension in psychiatry and psychology*. New York: Basic Books. pp. 37–91.

Neimeyer, R. and Mahoney, M. (1995). *Constructivism in Psychotherapy*. Washington D.C.:APA.

Rice, L., and Greenberg, L. (Eds.) (1984). *Patterns of change: An intensive analysis of psycho-therapeutic process*. New York: Guilford Press.

Rogers, C. R. (1951). *Client-centered therapy: Its current practice, implications, and theory*. Boston: Houghton Mifflin.

Rogers, C. R. (1957). The necessary and sufficient conditions of therapeutic personality change. *Journal of Consulting Psychology*, 21, pp. 97–103.

Rogers, C. R. (1961). *On becoming a person*. London: Constable.

Rogers, C. R. (1980). *A way of being*. Boston: Houghton Mifflin.

Rogers, C. R.,and Sanford, R. C. (1984). Client-centered psychotherapy. In H. I. Kaplan and B. J. Sadock (Eds.), *Comprehensive textbook of psychiatry, IV*. Baltimore: Williams and Wilkins. pp. 1374–88.

Schneider, K. J., and May, R. (1995). *The Psychology of Existence: An integrative, clinical perspective*. New York: McGraw-Hill, Inc.

Schutz, W. (1967). *Joy*. New York: Grove Press.

Webster, M. (1998). Blue suede shoes: The therapist's presence. *Australian and New Zealand Journal of Family Therapy*, 19, pp. 184–9.

Whelton, W., and Greenberg, L. (2000). The self as a singular multiplicity: A Process Experiential perspective. In J. Muran, *The self in psychotherapy*. Washington, DC. APA Press. pp. 87–106.

Wyatt, G. (2000). The multifaceted nature of congruence within the therapeutic relationship. *The Person-Centered Journal*, 7(1), pp. 52–68.

149

9   Authenticity Training:
an Exercise for Therapists
Mia Leijssen

Abstract. *The exercise offers several possibilities for training in various aspects of authenticity. In the first stage, participants are invited to focus on their internal state — assessing what physical sensations, events, feelings, issues, etc. are effecting them at this moment. They learn how to consciously set their personal concerns aside. In this way they heighten their chances of being more alert and functioning effectively in the therapeutic encounter without being burdened by the interference of their own problems. In the second stage, they are asked to focus on their felt senses to another person's nonverbal communication. What is their awareness of this other person and are they congruent with the state of this person or has their awareness been distorted by their own projections? In the third stage they are communicating their 'congruent' and 'incongruent' or 'projected' awarenesses to the particular participant. This gives them an opportunity to develop transparency. In the final stage, participants disclose what this was like, how they received the other's transparency and ascertain how accurate their feedback was.*

INTRODUCTION

The fundamental importance of the therapist's authenticity has been addressed in no uncertain terms in client-centred, experiential and existential literature (Rogers, 1951, 1961,1962, 1966, 1986; Gendlin, 1967, 1968; Bugental, 1981; Yalom, 1980). In other therapy orientations it is also recognised that the actual presence of the therapist and the manner in which he or she expresses his or her own personality has a profound effect on the therapeutic work (Kottler, 1986; Lazarus, 1996). Attention within the context of training, therefore, needs to be given to the personal development of the therapist-to-be. Lietaer (1993) remarked 'We are not talking here about direct training in congruence, but about the slower and indirect ways of personal therapy and personalized supervision, in which the person of the therapist is as much focused on as the client's process' (p. 29).

I believe it is important that therapists are experientially confronted with the consequences, whether advantageous or disadvantageous, of their personality as revealed in their fundamental attitudes. I have, therefore, long sought means other than simply those of personal therapy and supervision, which can result in the development of the therapist's authenticity. This exercise is one of these 'other means'.

150

In line with the literature on this complex basic attitude, I shall use the terms 'authenticity' and 'genuineness' as synonyms denoting the therapist's global attitude (Lietaer, 1993). Genuineness has two sides: an inner one (congruence) and on outer one (transparency). Congruence, the inner side, refers to the degree to which the therapist has conscious access to, or is receptive to, all aspects of his or her own flow of experiencing. Transparency, the outer side, refers to the explicit communication by the therapist of his or her conscious perceptions, attitudes and feelings.

In this paper I shall present an exercise to be carried out in stages; I will demonstrate how each stage of the exercise relates to the therapist's authenticity. Then I shall discuss what impact the exercise has on the participants. In conclusion, I shall formulate various considerations regarding the possibilities and limits of the exercise.

THE EXERCISE

Clearing space

The most important 'instrument' for therapists is their own person. The awareness of this instrument and its 'tuning' is then the first preoccupation for therapists before they can begin their work. If this instrument is not correctly tuned it will produce false tones. Rogers (1966, p. 185) has strongly emphasised that 'being genuine' is first and foremost the difficult task of being acquainted with the flow of experiencing going on within oneself. Self-awareness here means that the therapist's feelings are available to his or her consciousness. Rombauts (1984, p. 170) explains how he prepares himself for a conversation by maintaining a fundamental openness for his own life-world. In paying attention to his own world, he can allow his own concerns to fade into the background thus preparing himself to make contact with his clients.

The first stage of the exercise enables the therapist to put these principles into practice. A reader familiar with focusing (Gendlin, 1978), will recognise here the first step in that procedure, 'clearing space'. I have previously described the therapist's side of this microprocess as 'mental hygiene for the therapist' (Leijssen, 1998, pp. 134–5). The process supposes that people notice whatever concerns come up, at that moment, and that subsequently they can choose which problem or point of attention to set aside, even if only for a moment. In this exercise I introduce the step of 'creating space' as a first stage in developing congruence, thus addressing the therapist's awareness of their inner process.

Participants normally sit on a chair, or perhaps on the ground if they so choose; the facilitator discourages lying on the ground because an 'alert attitude' rather than a very 'relaxed' disposition is required for this exercise. Everyone needs a blank sheet of paper and a pen or pencil which is near to hand; these are momentarily laid down at some distance on the ground or table. If participants wish to close their eyes, this may help to focus more attention inward and literally shut out the outside world. With their gaze directed inwardly, group members first systematically direct awareness around their body, giving attention to the sensations they may encounter. Where the group is less experienced, it is recommended that the facilitator call out the various parts of the body (feet, legs, seat, lower body, middle torso, upper torso, shoulders, arms, hands, neck, face, head) and invite the participants to register carefully what they notice in their perceptions of the different parts of the body. Whoever wishes may, after this body 'screening', quietly write some of their awareness down on their paper.

The following questions are posed: 'What are you up to in life at this moment?' 'What preoccupations do you carry around with you?' 'Are there things which genuinely interest you at the moment or cause you to worry?' It should be explained at this point that these may be large or small matters, pleasant or unpleasant experiences, recent or long-past events. Participants are asked to notice, uncensored, whatever they become aware of. In order to facilitate this process it is helpful to explain that participants will not be required to share any of these matters with the group in subsequent activities; the private life of each is respected. Then each participant is invited to write down a 'key word' on the sheet of paper. Finding a 'key word' and the action of giving it its place on the paper acknowledges the significance of this in their life. When the facilitator observes that someone has difficulty in expressing something, the person is invited to record this. The facilitator encourages the group member to consider when they might give full attention to this matter, explaining that the participant's commitment to self is an important aspect of the work of a therapist.

This phase comes to an end when participants realise their most important concerns have been acknowledged and each has now been allocated their own 'place' so the participant doesn't forget it, and at the same time doesn't need to pay attention to it any more at this time. This usually results in a sense of relief that is physically felt. This part of the exercise requires 10 to 15 minutes. Participants should now have the sense of having explored and 'tidied up' their inner space, ready for focusing attention upon something more specific. Continuing with the metaphor of the instrument, an individual might decide that the instrument is now 'tuned' and is ready, along with others if so desired, to begin work on a 'piece of music'.

This first stage of the exercise can stand alone when used as preparation for receiving clients. In that context the therapist might choose to tune in to the client who is about to arrive, reading through notes of previous sessions and so forth.

Identifying nonverbal communication

Researchers estimate that from 65 to 85 percent of the communication in groups takes place through nonverbal communication and may play an especially important role in communicating reactions that are not consciously controlled or monitored. Voice tone, body posture, and proxemic presentations tend to 'leak' the undisclosed information (Beutler, Machado and Allstetter Neufeldt, 1994). In a survey of research results, Heppner and Claiborn (1989) conclude that nonverbal therapist responses exert a more powerful and consistent effect on clients' perceptions of therapist skills than verbal behaviour or therapy content. For therapists, it is important to be aware of their nonverbal communication. Their nonverbal expressions may be congruent with their inner experience or they may reveal some incongruence.

152

The next phase of the exercise represents an attempt to sharpen the participants' awareness and perception of nonverbal communication, and to learn to perceive the incongruence in themselves as therapists. In order to do this, participants form groups of four or five (less than four allows for too little variety while more than five requires too much time). These subgroups all remain in the same room so that the facilitator can continue verbally to guide the whole process. The participants are directed to not speak to each other. Each has several sheets of paper at his or her disposal and writes the names of all the participants in the subgroup on separate sheets. The participants take turns in being the 'centre' of the group. The facilitator asks for a volunteer 'A' to go first.

Each member of the group now takes his or her sheet of paper bearing the name of 'A'. 'A' says nothing while the other members of the subgroup attune themselves to 'A'. Participants are invited to identify their perceptions, ideas, impressions, sensations, associations, and so on, that occur when they carefully attune themselves to 'A'. After a few minutes the facilitator asks them to look for some key words, expressing their felt sense and writing these down on the sheet marked 'A'. They are then invited to take a second look at everything they have written and to ask themselves whether each expression tells them something about 'A', or whether what they have written down actually reflects one of their *own* themes or an important personal sensitivity. When a participant suspects that his or her own projection overshadows the impressions given by a felt sense of 'A', a question mark is placed next to the expression. After five minutes the phase with 'A' being the focus may be brought to an end. The participants set their papers on 'A' aside. The group is instructed to allow the focus on 'A' to dissipate by moving around or 'shaking oneself loose from "A"' and prepare for the next participant.

The next person 'B' volunteers to be the focus, the other participants in the subgroup prepare a sheet marked with 'B's name; without speaking, they attune themselves to 'B', repeating the above process. After another five minutes 'C' takes the centre of the group, then 'D' and so on. With four participants per subgroup this phase takes a little more than 20 minutes; for five participants one should add five minutes. The facilitator takes responsibility for the timing and delivering the various instructions.

Exchange of experiences

In the previous stage of this exercise, participants began the process of learning to identify their own stream of thoughts, feelings and interactional felt meanings. By making conscious their internal experience, and expressing this in the form of writing down key words, participants can become more congruent. Group members now proceed a step further in learning to exchange this information. By making their perceptions explicit and communicating the inside information with other participants, all group members have an opportunity to experiment with some transparency and to feel the effect of receiving feedback.

In this stage each member of the subgroup receives the sheets of paper pertaining to themselves (i.e., 'A' receives and reads what 'B', 'C' and 'D' have written about him or her; 'B' reads what 'A', 'C' and 'D' have noted, and so on). To

153

allay their curiosity, they are given a short while to read their co-participants expressions. Following this activity there is some space for participants to talk freely within the subgroup; this allows them to share some of their tensions and make general remarks regarding the exercise. This stage takes 10 to 15 minutes. The exercise can be concluded when this exchange is completed. Participants have had an opportunity to be transparent by expressing their insights of the other participants and hearing these insights may have facilitated the development of their own.

When the goal or need of the training group is to focus on and develop their skills of giving and receiving feedback — going more deeply into examining their transparency, their congruency and the relational nature of these concepts — participants can continue with the next stage.

Deepening the experiences

This stage offers participants a chance of deepening their learning. A pause is suggested to allow the participants to 'recharge their batteries' and put a little distance between themselves and the information they received in the previous stage.

Work in the same subgroups continues so each person receives adequate time to benefit from the exercise. 'A' summarises the feedback she or he has received. 'A' differentiates between elements of the feedback which are familiar and those elements which are surprising — even unpleasant or difficult to accept. If the same feedback has been provided by several of the group members, yet is still unacceptable to the person concerned, other participants allow some space for the person to identify which elements of the feedback are not felt to be appropriate, or those for which the person does not wish to take responsibility. If a participant has given feedback which is not shared by anyone else in the group, that participant is invited to explore any aspects of his or her own history which might be having an impact.

It is especially here that the exercise provides an opportunity for group members to discover incongruence in themselves and to develop congruence as they are asked to look deeply within themselves to find the motivation and sensitivities behind their feedback. Transparency is encouraged by making explicit exactly what it is that they sense and to which particular aspect of the other they react. Participants also describe in more detail exactly how they perceive and react to such feedback.

Care should be taken that all feelings are heard and recognised — the facilitator needs to make sure that first there is accurate understanding of what is expressed by one group member, before another member adds their own comment.

In this exercise, participants learn on a personal level how to deal with the 'give and take' of feedback; it is, nonetheless, neither a 'group therapy' session nor an 'individual therapy' for one or another participant. The facilitator ensures this distinction is respected by saying that if strong emotions are raised or if intriguing feedback is given that cannot be adequately placed (in the context of the exercise), such aspects will not be explored in depth. Participants can be directed to the relevant group therapy session within the training programme, or to their personal therapy. The facilitator may need to be available for participants for those circumstances where there remains something unfinished from the subgroup, but in practice this is seldom necessary.

Approximately 20 minutes per participant in a subgroup will be required for this deepening stage of the exercise.

THE IMPACT OF THE EXERCISE

The impact of 'clearing space'

Participants often report differing effects from the stage of 'clearing space'. After this step, the majority often have an experience of 'being more clearly present', alongside gaining a sense of having achieved a greater measure of 'at ease with oneself'. One participant explained: 'I began the day with the well-known feeling that "this is not my day". After the exercise I felt more clear-headed and had greater interest in being here.' Another participant declared: 'I left the house in chaos this morning and became even more stressed in the rush-hour traffic. Taking time to stand still did me much good.' Regarding the recognition of one's own interests, most participants are surprised by how much they bring with them. In this context, people often discover that certain bodily sensations (a sensitive throat area, a tight stomach, or faster heart rate, for example), point to problematic areas of which they were not immediately aware, or they detect that some topics provoke deeper emotions than they would have suspected. For some, such 'confrontations' have a liberating effect, in the sense that they find it relieving to recognise their concerns. The invitation to give a place to every concern that arises, by writing on a sheet of paper, has a clarifying effect and fulfils a 'containment' function. People who in the course of the exercise have been touched by something or have difficulties in putting a specific topic down on paper usually decide here to take up these issues in the context of therapy. For some, this is a warning that they are carrying with them 'explosive material' and that it is high time to do something about it.

Nonverbal communication

Some participants initially find it uncomfortable to be involved in a process based on the perception of solely the nonverbal aspects of another. This is usually expressed in some giggling at the start of the exercise. But once they have overcome an initial feeling of uneasiness they are all amazed at how much is brought to the surface. Later they state that they have become aware that, without this assignment, they have been able to perceive this sort of thing — a sensation of someone having a 'sexy aura' or a 'tired facial expression', for example — but in the past they had seldom paused to reflect or consciously act on that awareness.

When they are asked to assess which of their associations say more about themselves than about the other, most discover that it is precisely the themes identified earlier in the first stage 'clearing space' that enables them to gain clarity with regards whether their awareness comes from the person observed or their own projection. An example of this is someone receiving an image of a 'lonely boy' when tuning into a colleague; on further reflection the person doubts that this was a pure perception; later she recalls one of her concerns, identified in the phase 'clearing space', and the feeling of a lump in her throat confronting her with how she had dropped her young son off at the before-school care when no other children had yet arrived.

Exchange

Participants find it especially exciting to hear from others what they perceive about themselves. What is remarkable is that there are always several perceptions that correspond; often the group member recognises this correspondence him or herself, but the confirmation remains just as interesting and can be perceived as challenging. That one communicates nonverbal 'sadness' or 'uncertainty', for example, is normally not strange to someone who receives this sort of feedback, yet the fact that others can 'see' it is somehow confronting.

In this part of the exercise, participants learn that their fellows, without verbal explanation, take in information and thus often allow these felt senses to guide their reactions without really being conscious that the nonverbal communication serves to orientate them. An example is a participant sensing 'aggression' in a group member; she decides not to confront him, because she is afraid of his reaction.

Participants are also often surprised that they can know so much about another without there having been any verbal communication. Most participants usually do not trust their intuition or their sensitivity to nonverbal signals, however, they now discover that these felt senses can convey a lot of truth. In one particular subgroup, one participant was scared of the diagnosis of a possible illness; she didn't mention it to the other participants, yet they all felt a sort of cramp in their belly while focusing on her. It was remarkable that she 'perceived' possible physical problems in other participants. All participants experienced having previously drawn up a list of their 'concerns' as helpful, and they also were surprised to find that this step helped clarify issues when they reflected on whether they had perhaps 'projected'.

Deepening

For the aspiring therapist, the deepening phase is an opportunity to discover in a real-life situation how self-knowledge and congruence can be increased with an exchange of feedback. Participants not only receive new information about themselves but also receive direct evidence of their transparency through interaction with others; they also learn how to select and clarify information and to communicate this information in a way that makes it useful for the other.

In this process, each participant discovers in an experiential way that, on the one hand, people are vulnerable when giving and receiving feedback, but also that, on the other hand, they learn so much from this experience that intimacy is increased and that each person therefore participates with a more energetic presence. After the exercise, everyone is convinced that transparency is exceptionally effective in enhancing the interest of the participants and the liveliness of the interaction. An example of this is the participant whose nonverbal presence is perceived as 'overpowering' and 'dominant'. Other group members may be inclined to make themselves 'small' in his presence and to retreat from any interaction. During this exercise, they discover that being transparent about their perception not only helps the person to be aware of the effect of his presence, it is also the start of an interesting exploration about their coping styles and the way it influences the interaction in the 'here and now' as well as the 'there and then'.

CONCLUSION

This exercise offers many possibilities for therapists to focus on various aspects of the fundamental attitude of authenticity. Typically, those undertaking the exercise have an enthusiasm which beneficially influences their work with their clients. As a result, participants are more prepared to take the initiative with their clients based on their own felt sense. This is possibly because they have found that there is a considerable amount of meaningful information hidden in their felt sense, having gained some confidence in their ability to separate this from their own projections or current issues, and be able to communicate this feedback effectively.

They also understand the need for caution in expressing their subjective impressions — having themselves been in a vulnerable position in receiving feedback within the exercise. For many, this is above all an enhancement of the liveliness, intensity and intimacy of the interaction and facilitates a deepened self-knowledge — reason enough to allow more 'risky' interventions to take place in therapy. Thus Rogers' experience (1970, p. 53) in his later life — that he gradually learned to trust more in a deeper layer of intuitive feelings — can be discovered and developed by beginning therapists at an ever earlier stage.

This sort of exercise also has its limits. It will be most effective in diverse educational and training contexts, when certain conditions are fulfilled:

1. There needs to be sufficient trust in the group for participants to feel secure enough to be vulnerable or to risk themselves personally.
2. Many unspoken conflicts lurking within the group will hinder this process.
3. Each participant needs a certain measure of interpersonal security.

This exercise, however, can never serve as a substitute for the necessary learning process that therapists undergo in their personal therapy and supervision. The deeper layers of the personality are reached in the exercise, but in this context alone, they do not receive enough attention. The exercise reveals both strong and weak aspects of the personality, thus pointing out where further work is necessary or 'lays bare' particular problematic points.

Therapists report that they use the experience of the exercise in their work in different ways. The step 'clearing space' used before receiving clients can help therapists to touch the various experiences that live in them at the beginning of their work. Having gained awareness of their current issues and concerns, the chances of mixing up their own problems with those of the client are thus decreased and, not being so preoccupied, will enable them to give their full attention to the client. This discipline of acknowledging their own flow of experiencing and making space is a form of 'mental hygiene' for the therapist. It

157

guarantees the presence of a more congruent therapist, whose transparency is not mixed up with their own worries or sensitivities.

As a result, therapists will not only have more self-knowledge, they also are more trustworthy in their 'interactional barometer'. The feeling for what happens in the relationship with the client functions more properly and the sensitivity for the nonverbal communication of the client is enhanced. Therapists report that they express more often how a feeling in them took shape and what precisely in the client's way of expression has led to this. With such explicit and concrete feedback, and an openness to acknowledge the possible contribution of the therapist's projections, the therapist can develop the instrument of their 'self' and a true dialogue can take place during therapy.

REFERENCES

Beutler, L.E., Machado P.P., and Allstetter Neufeldt, S. (1994). Therapist variables. In A.E. Bergin and S.L. Garfield (Eds.), *Handbook of psychotherapy and behavior change,* (pp. 229–69). New York: Wiley.

Bugental, J. (1981). *The search for authenticity: An existential-analytic approach to psychotherapy* (enlarged ed.). New York: Irvington.

Gendlin, E. T. (1967). Subverbal Communication and Therapist Expressivity: Trends in Client-Centered Therapy with Schizophrenics. In C. R. Rogers and B. Stevens, *Person to Person* (pp. 119–28). Lafayette, Ca.: Real People Press.

Gendlin, E. T. (1968). The Experiential Response. In E. F. Hammer (Ed.), *Use of Interpretation in Therapy: Technique and Art* (pp. 208–27). New York: Grune and Stratton.

Gendlin, E.T (1978). *Focusing.* New York: Everest House.

Heppner, P. P., and Claiborn, C. D. (1989). Social Influence Research in Counseling: A Review and Critique. *Journal of Counseling Psychology, 36,* pp. 365–87.

Kottler, J.A. (1986). *On being a therapist.* San Francisco: Jossey-Bass.

Lazarus, A.A. (1996). Some reflections after 40 years of trying to be an effective psychotherapist. *Psychotherapy, 33,* pp. 142–5.

Leijssen, M. (1992). Experiential focusing through drawing. *The Focusing Folio, 11*(2), pp. 35–40.

Leijssen, M. (1998). Focusing Microprocesses. In L.S. Greenberg, J.C. Watson and G. Lietaer (Eds.), *Handbook of Experiential Psychotherapy* (pp.121–54). New York: Guilford Press.

Lietaer, G. (1993). Authenticity, Congruence and Transparency. In D. Brazier (Ed.), *Beyond Carl Rogers* (pp. 17–46). *London*: Constable.

Rogers, C. R. (1951). *Client-Centered Therapy.* Boston: Houghton Mifflin.

Rogers, C. R. (1961). *On Becoming a Person.* Boston: Houghton Mifflin.

Rogers, C. R. (1962). The Interpersonal Relationship: The Core of Guidance. *Harvard Educational Review, 32,* pp. 416–29.

Rogers, C. R. (1966). Client-Centered Therapy. In S. Arieti (Ed.), *American Handbook of Psychiatry, 3,* pp. 183–200. New York: Basic Books.

Rogers, C. R. (1970). *On Encounter Groups.* New York: Harper and Row.

Rogers, C. R. (1986). Carl Rogers' Column: Reflection of Feelings. *Person-Centered Review,* 1, pp. 375–77.

Rombauts, J. (1984). Empathie: actieve ontvankelijkheid. In G. Lietaer, Ph. van Praag, and J. C. A. G. Swildens (Red.), *Client-centered psychotherapie in beweging* (pp. 167–76). Leuven: Acco.

Yalom, I.D. (1980). *Existential psychotherapy.* New York: Basic Books.

10   A Conceptual Exploration of Incongruence and Mental Health

Per-Anders Tengland

INTRODUCTION

Recently, as part of a growing interest in the theoretical basis for person-centered therapy, there has been much debate over the terms congruence, authenticity, genuineness and transparency (Lietaer, 1993; Haugh, 1998a, 1998b; Bozarth, 1998; Wyatt, 1998; Brodley, 1998, 1999; Ellingham, 1999). The concept of 'incongruence', however, has so far met with less interest.[1] Incongruence is an important concept in person-centered theory since it is the only theoretical concept referring to the underlying 'pathology', or inner problems, of the troubled individual.[2]

In Rogers' 1957 statement of the six necessary and sufficient conditions for therapeutic personality change, the second condition states that 'the client, is in a state of incongruence, being vulnerable or anxious'. The therapist, on the other hand, is supposed to be congruent or integrated (Rogers, 1957, p. 96).

In this chapter I will first discuss various interpretations of the important concepts involved in Rogers' theory. I will then place Rogers' theory in the wider context of a general theory of health and try to show why this is important.

INCONGRUENCE

In this section I will present one interpretation of Rogers' theory, and I will later present a slightly different one. I will mainly be focusing on Rogers' papers from 1957 and 1959.

Incongruence,[3] according to Rogers, 'refers to a discrepancy between the actual experience of the organism and the self-picture of the individual insofar as it represents that experience' (1957, p. 96). In the 1959 paper, Rogers similarly states

---

1. Some exceptions are Biermann-Ratjen, 1998; Speierer, 1990; Lambers 1994a–d.
2. Using the term 'pathology' is perhaps risky in this context. However, in using this term I am taking nothing for granted concerning etiology, or on what level the 'pathology' lies (physiological, structural, functional), neither am I taking any therapy for granted. I only use this concept as an abbreviation for complex mental states that are problematic for the individual. The concept is not, here, part of any kind of 'medical model'.
3. In *Client-Centered Therapy* (1951), Rogers uses the term 'psychological maladjustment' instead of 'incongruence'. In his 1959 paper he makes clear that these terms are synonymous (p. 206). I will therefore not discuss or use the term 'psychological maladjustment'.

that incongruence means that there is a 'discrepancy . . . between the self as perceived, and the actual experience of the organism' (Rogers, 1959, p. 203). Further on in this paper, Rogers also states that 'the state is one of incongruence between self and experience' (ibid.). This discrepancy creates tension and confusion within the individual, sometimes experienced as anxiety. This confusion in turn leads to 'discordant and incomprehensible behaviors', sometimes labeled 'neurotic behavior' (ibid.), but also to other types of mental 'pathology', like psychosis and personality disorders (Lambers, 1994a–d). The individual does not always experience the incongruence: 'then he is merely vulnerable to the possibility of anxiety and disorganization', says Rogers (1957, p. 97).

First there appears, then, to be two important components involved in incongruence, the self-concept and the organismic experiencing. Second, the incongruence gives rise to anxiety and other 'negative' feelings, or vulnerability to such feelings, which can result in maladaptive behaviour.

I would first like to focus upon the two components used to describe incongruence, the experiencing of the organism and the self-concept.

Experiencing of the organism

Rogers speaks about 'organismic experiencing'. The 'organism' is a biological notion which refers to more than the mind, or consciousness (Schmid, 1998, p. 47). The 'experience' refers to everything that is potentially there for this biological organism to be aware of.[4] In Rogers' words, experiencing 'includes all that is going on within the envelope of the organism at any given moment which is potentially available to awareness' (1959, p. 197). It would, then, refer to sensations, like pain and hunger; to moods, like anguish and calmness; to emotions, like fear and love; to perceptions, like smell and touch; to cognitive processes, like remembering, fantasizing and reasoning.[5] Also value judgments of various sorts are included in the concept. It is, thus, a very broad notion.

The self-concept

The self-concept refers to the 'organized, consistent conceptual gestalt composed of perceptions of the characteristics of the "I" or "me" and the perceptions of the relationships of the "I" or "me" to others and to various aspects of life, together with the values attached to these perceptions' (ibid., p. 200). The self-concept is also referred to as the 'self', 'self-picture', 'self-structure' and 'the self as perceived' (ibid., pp. 200–3).[6] In other words, the self-concept is a notion consisting of beliefs and values having to do with the self and its relation to the world.

---

4. The concept of 'experience' is not always used in this way. Often it is used as 'that of which the person is aware'. Thus, in this sense, speaking about an experience of which the person is not aware would be a contradiction.

5. Note that some of these experiences can be the result of incongruence. An incongruence between a feeling and the self-concept can create a tension. This tension is in itself potentially an experience, for example anxiety. This experience might furthermore lead to a 'secondary' incongruence, since it might be 'denied' (kept from awareness) too. Theoretically, at least, this in turn can create a tension and might lead to more anxiety, also an experience, etc.

6. Footnote on next page.

The self-concept, thus, consists of a number of components: (1) beliefs about the self, (2) beliefs about the relation of the self to others and to various aspects of life, and (3) values concerning self and these aspects of life.

With all these aspects included in the self-concept we get a rather broad notion. This broad notion is also indicated by Rogers' claim that experiences, accurately symbolized, should (in order to be congruent) be included in the self-concept (Rogers, 1959, p. 206). Experience is also a very broad concept. For example, ordinary perception of the world is a kind of experience, and the only way this kind of experience can be included in the self-concept is as beliefs about the world.

However, it is not self-evident that the term 'self-concept' should be used in this broad sense. It seems that the terms 'self-concept', 'self', 'self-picture', etc., are partly misleading, since they, by their name, suggest a more narrow interpretation. They indicate self-esteem (which has to do with *valuing* different aspects of the self), and perhaps self-confidence (having various *beliefs* about one's capacity).

Furthermore, at times the self-concept is used in a much more narrow sense, even by Rogers himself. Rogers writes, for instance, that the self-concept is to be used when talking of the 'person's view of himself' (ibid., p. 200). Other writers sometimes also seem to use a narrow concept. For example, Biermann-Ratjen, when she talks about 'the threat to one's self-concept and self-esteem', implies a close connection between the two (1998, p. 121). Also the conception of the 'ideal self', as defined in Rogers' 1959 paper, indicates a more narrow view of the self-concept. The ideal self, according to Rogers, denotes the self-concept 'which the individual would most like to possess' (p. 200). It has even been suggested that the person is congruent when the real self and the ideal self are the same (see Haugh, 1998b, p. 17). This suggestion also indicates a narrow notion of the self-concept, since this statement does not make sense if a broad conception of the self-concept is used. Something as 'trivial' as wanting to own a Porsche would then be part of the ideal self, since this want is no doubt a relationship 'of the "I" or "me" . . . to various aspects of life, together with the values attached to these perceptions' (Rogers, 1959, p. 200). Furthermore, were the ideal self to be taken in the broad sense it should be synonymous with 'world view', and it is clearly not. It is more likely that 'ideal self' refers to what kind of individual one wants to be, the narrow conception.[7] At most, then, the ideal self (relating to the individual's self-picture) should be a part of the general self-concept.

Having two definitions of the self-concept, a broad one and a narrow one, is not acceptable. I suggest that the self-concept is best used in the broad sense (maybe even more broadly than Rogers himself suggests), and it could be called 'the individual's belief and value system', or even 'world view'.[8] I will present two examples that support this version of the self-concept. Since incongruence is the only general 'pathology' in person-centered theory it should be able to explain

---

6. Rogers speaks of 'perceptions' of the 'I' or 'self'. Since 'perception' often refers to various types of experiencing (seeing, hearing, touching, etc.), I prefer not to use this term, since it risks leading to confusion. I will be speaking about *beliefs* about the 'I' and the world. Other good synonyms might be 'apprehension', 'conception', or 'understanding' of the self and the world.
7. This conclusion is supported by Rogers' discussion of how the concept of the 'self' evolved in his thinking (Rogers, 1959, pp. 200–3).
8. A similar idea is presented by Janet Tolan (2000), but for different reasons. She calls this very broad view the 'self-structure'.

every specific kind of mental 'pathology'. Given the narrow definition of self-concept this appears to pose a problem. Take a relatively healthy person whose life is suddenly threatened, say by an accident. The individual, physically uninjured, nevertheless falls into a state of shock. The shock can be seen as a state of distorted awareness, for instance, lack of memory of the event. If there is incongruence, it is between awareness and experiencing,[9] but the self-concept, narrowly construed, does not appear to be involved in this specific state of 'pathology'. There is, no doubt, the threat of the annihilation of the person, and thus of the self, but there seems to be no threat to the self-concept narrowly construed.

Let me give another example that does not appear to involve the self-concept in this sense. A parent might expel from awareness, or distort, all the signs that his/her son is using drugs. This could, but need not, involve the self-concept (in the narrow sense). The parent might just 'want to' protect the conception of the son as well-adjusted. Thus, there is no incongruence involving the self-concept in the narrow sense. This means that there are more kinds of 'pathology' than the theory can explain.

The problem is this: if the self-concept is not involved in creating the incongruence, which it is not necessarily if the narrow conception is used, something is missing, namely that which causes or creates the incongruence between experience and awareness.[10]

The solution to these problems is using the broad conception of the self-concept, one that might even be broader than the one Rogers had intended. There seems to be no natural distinction between apprehension of oneself, one's relationships to other persons and one's relationship to the world (and the values connected to all these beliefs), and the rest of one's beliefs and other values. Thus, the 'self-concept' could include all the individual's beliefs and values. Using this broader conception of the 'self-concept' solves the problem identified above, since even if the self-concept in the narrow sense is not involved in the incongruence, the self-concept in the broad sense still can be.

There is further work to be done here. If the broader conception, i.e. a 'world view', is used, it could perhaps be divided into parts: self-esteem, beliefs about the self, beliefs about the world, value system, etc. I do not here have the space to develop such a framework.

The emergence of the self-concept

Since the self-concept is important in the theory of incongruence, it is of interest to see how it evolves in the individual, and what it consists of (Rogers, 1959, pp. 223 ff.). Rogers claims that the individual has a psychological need to experience positive regard from significant others. The experience that receives positive regard is internalized, as beliefs and values, and constitutes the 'self-regard' of the person (ibid., p. 224). This positive regard of the other is *unconditional* when

---

9. This is the second version of incongruence to which I will return.
10. The term 'causal' should not be interpreted 'mechanistically'. It stands for influences on a functional level where parts of the mental realm can be seen as having effects on other parts, as, for instance, when the self-concept blocks out certain experiences from awareness.

the experiences of the individual are accepted and valued by the other whatever they are about. The positive regard is *conditional* if the individual has to conform to various norms in order to receive this positive regard. This is termed 'conditions of worth' by Rogers (ibid.). The person who is met with conditions of this kind, due to the need for positive regard, internalizes these (initially alien) norms (conditions of worth) and they become part of the self-regard. Thus, the individual rejects those experiences that are at odds with these norms. Hence, the internalized experiences that were met with unconditional positive regard constitute the 'healthy' side of the self, since there will arise no conflict between similar new experiences and the self-concept. Experiences influenced by conditions of worth constitute the unhealthy side, since there will appear conflicts between the internalized conditions of worth and certain kinds of experience.

Incongruence between experience and awareness

In the beginning of the chapter I presented Rogers' definition of incongruence as a discrepancy between the actual experience and the self-concept. Now that the terms 'experience' and 'self-concept' have been discussed, I would like to turn to another, slightly different, definition of incongruence (and congruence) found in the person-centered literature, and actually also in Rogers' own writings. In the 1957 paper he claims that a congruent person (here, therapist) 'is freely and deeply himself, with his actual experience accurately represented by his awareness of himself' (p. 97), and in *On becoming a Person* Rogers writes that '[C]ongruence is the term we have used to indicate an accurate matching of experiencing and awareness' (1961, p. 339).[11] There is no mentioning of self-concept in these characterizations.

Other writers use incongruence in the same way. Haugh, for example, makes two statements about congruence: one is that a congruent person's 'internal processes can be accessed at any given moment', and the other that the person's 'symbolization in awareness should be accurate' (1998a, p. 44).[12] The second statement can be seen as a clarification of the first. It adds that the symbolization of the internal processes (experiences) has to be accurate, in order to qualify as congruent.[13]

Barbara Brodley has a similar view of congruence. She claims that '[i]n the strict definition, congruence refers to the accurate relation between the contents of experience and the symbols in awareness', and slightly differently expressed, '[p]ersons are congruent if their symbols in awareness are accurate to the experienced perceptions' (Brodley, 1998, p. 92). Again there is no mentioning of self-concept.

Having two different definitions of incongruence constitutes a problem. The theory becomes incoherent as a result. How is this problem to be solved? In the 1959 paper by Rogers there is another suggestion which appears to solve this

---

11. I have so far not discussed congruence, but I will assume that congruence and incongruence are contrary terms.
12. I take it that 'internal processes' means 'experiencing'.
13. I assume here that 'accessing internal processes' already implies a correct symbolization. If not, the second statement is more than a clarification, it is a necessary addition.

problem. The suggestion actually constitutes a third definition of incongruence. Rogers here states that 'when self-experiences are accurately symbolized [in awareness] *and are included in the self-concept in this accurately symbolized form*, then the state is one of congruence of self and experience' (Rogers, 1959, p. 206, italics added). Thus, the individual is congruent if the experiences are correctly symbolized (in awareness) *and* are included in the self-concept. *Incongruence*, then, is when experiences are inaccurately symbolized and are, in this distorted way, included in the self-concept.

It appears that the self-concept can be included in the definition of congruence, and thus incongruence. However, it seems to me that this is not the best way to view the matter. It is important to be able to say either that incongruence is caused (or influenced) by something, for instance the self-concept, or that incongruence causes or influences something, for example awareness. But if the terms 'experience', 'awareness' and 'self-concept' are all included in the definition of 'incongruence', it is impossible to say these things, and the question arises, what is the cause of incongruence, or what does it influence negatively? Given this third definition I cannot see a plausible answer to these questions.

So, either the 'self-concept' or the 'awareness' should be left out of the definition, and I suggest that a choice is made between two slightly different ways to define congruence and incongruence. The first states that incongruence is a discrepancy between the organismic experiences and the self-concept of a person. In this case the distorted awareness is the result, or *effect*, of the incongruence. The distorted awareness in turn guides the person's choices and actions, and they will therefore be less than optimal.

In the second case the definition of incongruence is that the symbolization in awareness is inaccurate with respect to the experiences. In this case the self-concept negatively influences, or *causes*, this inaccuracy. The effects on health are the same, choices and actions will be made on distorted grounds. Either definition is possible but they lead to slightly different conclusions as to where the inner 'pathology' lies. This is an important theoretical question, so a choice has to be made.

Experiencing and incongruence

Let me return to the experiencing of the individual. According to Rogers it refers to everything that is possible for the individual to become aware of; perceptions, sensations, moods, emotions, and various kinds of thoughts, like beliefs and value judgments. Theoretically, all of these sorts of experiences might be part of incongruence, and thus distorted. However, the examples presented are most often emotions (or feelings) being at variance with the self-concept, as when a person has to deny being envious, angry or disappointed, because these emotions are not acceptable to the self-concept.

Person-centered theory, in order to cover all sorts of mental problems, has to show how all kinds of experience, not only emotions, can be distorted. In the following sections I will investigate if the different kinds of experience can be incongruent, and, if so, try to illustrate in what ways they can be incongruent.

Perception

To perceive is to gain information about the outer world through the five senses, and I will assume here that this is all that is meant by perceiving. Many times, if not always, there is quite a lot of interpretation going on in perception. For instance, seeing a house involves knowing what a house is and how to use the word 'house'. There are, however, instances where there is even more interpretation involved, that is when we 'perceive' social facts or events. Seeing a person rob someone involves knowing what ownership is, what laws are, and so on. As regards seeing physical objects or events, where there is less interpretation involved, it seems that there should be less incongruence. It is likely that a person will accept (in awareness) most of what he/she perceives, since very little of what he/she perceives (of this kind of perceiving) is a threat to the person's self-concept, narrowly or broadly conceived. A tree is usually seen as a tree, a bird heard as a bird.

It is, thus, more likely that we misinterpret social events, thus allowing for more possibility of incongruence. Secondly, it is far more likely that social events threaten the person's self-concept than ordinary physical events, even if this is not always true.

For example, John's next-door neighbour has bought a new car. Since he cannot himself afford a new one, this might pose a threat to John. He might risk seeing himself as failing in life. A distortion in perceiving this car might be that it is really an ugly car and that it looks older than it is (he would never want a car like that). Or John might even fail to see 'it' at all, believing that it is the old one.

When it comes to social facts, the possibility of distortion increases, since they involve actions, and perceiving actions always involves a high degree of interpretation. Say that a mother sees her teenage child take money out of her purse. There is quite a bit of interpretation involved in 'seeing' this action, and here the incongruence might lie in interpreting the theft as 'a loan'. The reason for the misinterpretation, in this case interpreting what is seen as a loan, might be that the action is experienced as a threat to the mother perceiving herself as a good parent.

Sensations

Sensations are often defined as bodily located feelings. Pain is the paradigmatic example. Can pain be an organismic experience denied from awareness because it is not compatible with the self-concept, thus resulting in incongruence? No doubt it can. A very 'macho' man, for instance, might expel from awareness the feeling of pain since it might not be part of the self-concept to feel pain. Other sensations that might be incongruent with the self-concept might have to do with sexuality. Take a young man who is raised in a family where homosexuality is seen as something totally unacceptable. This young man might deny that he has a (potentially) lustful (or sensual) sensation when a male friend puts his arm around his shoulder, and instead conceive it as uncomfortable, or even painful.

Cognitive capacities

Can cognitive capacities like thinking, fantasizing, reasoning and memory be part of incongruence? Not remembering correctly is probably the most common example. Now, in general, people do not remember events very well (Baddeley,

165

1994). However, it seems that some events are more misconstrued than others, and some, significant ones, can be totally forgotten. For example, sometimes adults who have been abused as children do not remember these events, or if they 'remember' them they are distorted in various ways.

It is harder to explain how thoughts can be distorted, since it is assumed, then, that the thought exists before it is represented in awareness. One way to conceive this is to claim that thoughts initially are non-verbal, and that in the process of becoming conscious they become verbal. If, then, the non-verbal thought is in conflict with the self-concept it will be distorted when it comes into awareness in its verbal form. Let me try to exemplify. Say that a person has a 'potential' thought which has to do with hating the parents who neglected him/her during childhood. If the person, due to conditions of worth, has misconstrued his/her childhood as being happy, the thought might turn up in other forms, for instance, as one of self-hatred.

As to reasoning, it is possible to imagine a person notoriously failing in the theoretical exams, reasoning incorrectly, because influenced by a self-concept involving beliefs of the type 'I am not the intellectual type', or 'I never could think abstractly'.

Emotions
In exemplifying incongruence, Rogers and others most often refer to 'feelings'. Feeling is a broad notion which is often divided into sensations, moods and emotions (Nordenfelt, 1995, pp. 82–4). Sensations, as I have already mentioned, have to do with bodily located feelings. Moods and emotions are not bodily located. They are holistic, i.e. they are felt, more or less, in the whole organism. The difference between them are that emotions have a direction, or, as it is sometimes stated, an 'object'. This means that they are about something. Moods do not have objects.

Since I believe that the feelings most often referred to are emotions, I will go a little deeper into this discussion. Often the term 'feeling' is treated as a 'simple' notion, in the same sense in which a 'sensation' is a simple notion, just referring to a feeling and nothing else. However, 'emotion' is a much more complex notion and failing to realize this might lead to confusion in the discussion. For example according to Ellingham (1999, reprinted as chapter 6 this volume), Thorne and Mearns, in discussing person-centered theory, refer to feelings that the person is unaware of. Ellingham points to the absurdness of this claim, the idea being inconsistent, saying '[A]n *unfelt* feeling, is logical nonsense', Ellingham (ibid., p. 130).[14] Given a more complex view of emotion the problem might be solved. In criticizing Rogers, and others, for envisaging emotions as 'thing-like' entities, Ellingham furthermore claims, following Harré and others, that emotions are cultural or social constructions (ibid., p. 131). That something is a social construction can mean a lot of things. I will later show one way to interpret this.

---

14. Ellingham argues that the concept of 'congruence' belongs to a quasi-Freudian conception of mind. Part of this has to do, he argues, with the fact that Rogers is claiming this is still part of the old Cartesian-Newtonian paradigm. Except for the ideas brought up in the text, I will not here discuss Ellingham's interesting, and I believe fruitful, thoughts further.

Let me here present a more complex theory of what emotions are.[15] Emotions are not just feelings, they also have a cognitive side to them.[16] The meaning of the emotional concepts also involve, by necessity, beliefs and wishes. They are, as mentioned, *about* something. To illustrate: it is not, for logical reasons, possible to be angry without, on the one hand, *believing* certain things about reality (for instance, that someone has wronged us), and, on the other, *wishing* certain things (for example, that we do not *wish* to be hurt in this way). All other emotions similarly involve various beliefs and wishes.

Now, saying that someone has a feeling that is not 'felt' does not necessarily mean that there is a contradiction. Let us say that a person is sad, but does not feel the sadness. Saying this is saying several things. It is saying that the individual holds certain beliefs and wishes about something, and that the individual, because of this, is disposed to feel in a certain way. It is also to say that at the present moment these beliefs and wishes, and the accompanying feeling, are not in awareness. If the relevant beliefs are brought to awareness, and the relevant wishes are still held by the person, the felt part of the emotion is likely to appear. And there is nothing strange about saying that someone believes and wishes things that he/she is not presently aware of. There is nothing 'thing-like' about holding beliefs that are not conscious. It would be a strange position to claim that when I am not thinking at all, I don't have any beliefs at all. It would, for instance, be hard to explain why we hold the same beliefs when waking up after having slept. It is important to realize, though, that beliefs as well as wishes change over time. If this happens, it means, by definition, that the emotions change (since the beliefs and wishes are part of the emotion), and, of course, the feelings accompanying them change too.

This sounds as if a person has to be aware of the cognitive aspects before he/she feels something. This is not true, it seems. It is possible to experience incredibly strong feelings (sadness, for instance), only to become aware of what they are about afterwards. It seems, then, that beliefs and wishes can be 'effective' (on a non-conscious level) despite not being present in awareness.

In what sense, then, are the emotions constructions? As I have claimed, the emotions involve beliefs and wishes, and they are framed in the concepts of a culture. If there is no concept 'insult' in a society, there will not be an emotion 'feeling insulted'. An emotion cannot then exist where a relevant belief or wish is absent. If the concept of 'ownership' is absent in a society no one can feel angry when something is taken from them. It has been claimed that there are some fundamental emotions that are common to all societies, for instance anger and sadness. This is probably true, but it does not necessarily mean that these feelings are evoked by the same kinds of events. Death might in one culture lead to sadness and in another not, since beliefs and wishes about death are different.

This, at least, is one way to understand social constructions and I hope this discussion deepens the understanding of the complexity of the emotions and

---

15. Green (1992) represents such a theory.
16. Rogers clearly has a complex view of what feelings (or emotions) are (Rogers, 1959, p. 198). He acknowledges the cognitive side to the emotions. He does not, however, state what the cognitive content consists of.

how they are (partly) created by the culture in which they appear.

I have presented a view of emotions that makes them more complex than is sometimes assumed. What does this mean for the discussion of incongruence? For one thing it means that if someone claims, say, that there is an incongruent emotion, one has to ask which part of the emotion is meant, the beliefs involved, the wishes, or the feeling. First take the beliefs; they might be mistaken or irrational (unjustified), thus changing or distorting the emotion. It is impossible for a mother to be angry at her son if she interprets the theft as a loan. The incongruence, here, is that she distorts the experience, the interpretation of what she perceives. The wish might also be part of the incongruence. Say that a husband suggests a divorce. The wife reacts as if this is terrible. However, her 'real' wish is actually also to get a divorce. The reason for the incongruence is that it is not coherent with the self-concept to end the marriage — 'what will people think?' No doubt the feelings connected with these distortions of beliefs and wishes are not accurate either. The 'shock' after hearing the husband propose a divorce cannot be a real shock. But neither is the potential feeling of relief for being able to get out of a stale marriage possible. Most likely the feelings are instead confused.

Finally there might be a possibility that the *feeling* that goes with the beliefs and wishes is incongruent, as when the correctly represented beliefs and wishes are present but the expected feeling is absent.

In this section I have shown that organismic experiencing involves much more than the emotions, and I have tried to show how these different kinds of experiencing might be distorted, and thus part of incongruence. The theoretical importance in this lies in the fact that when one discusses incongruence and emotions one has to make clear what aspect of the emotions one is speaking about, the wishes involved, the beliefs, or the subjective feeling. It also explains how one can speak of an unexperienced feeling without contradicting oneself.

INCONGRUENCE AND MENTAL HEALTH

Incongruence is, according to the definitions discussed, a theoretical concept and, thus, it is unobservable. It therefore has to be related to the higher mental abilities (or functions) of the individual, and also to actions and behaviour. If a theory is to help us determine who is in need of help, and who has 'progressed in therapy', a theoretical explanation of underlying processes is of no use. It is necessary to know why congruence is of value to the individual. Thus, the theoretical explanation needs to be complemented with a theory of health based on, more or less, observable criteria.

How, then, is the concept of 'incongruence', and its opposite 'congruence', related to concepts like 'health' and 'mental health'? These concepts are seldom, if ever, mentioned by Rogers. Instead he speaks of 'the fully functioning person', and of 'maturity' (Rogers, 1961b, 1959, p. 207). It appears as if these conceptions have to do with what people normally call, and many theories take as, health and mental health.

I wish to place this discussion in the broader context of a contemporary discussion of health and illness. In doing so I will also present a theory of health which I believe is useful as a complement to Rogers' theory.

Health and mental health

There are several kinds of theories of general health. Some use 'well-being' as the key term (WHO), others 'normality of function' (Boorse, 1975, 1976, 1977; Wakefield, 1992, 2000), 'ability' (Whitbeck, 1981; Fulford, 1989; Nordenfelt, 1995) and 'balance' (Pörn, 1984).

I have chosen to work with the holistic theory of Lennart Nordenfelt. This theory, I believe, fits particularly well with person-centered theory. This theory states that health is the individual's general ability to reach his/her vital goals, given acceptable circumstances. A vital goal is a goal, usually chosen by the individual (but often partly determined by the society the individual lives in), which if reached makes the person happy or satisfied. There is then no other standard to evaluate health but by comparing the individual's ability in relation to his/her goals. This means that health is not an absolute state, but something relative. Ill health (not being able to reach vital goals), not 'disease', is the opposite of health. The term 'malady' (which covers disease, impairment, injury, defect) is used to denote mental or physical conditions which tend to reduce health. Incongruence would probably qualify as a malady, since it often reduces the person's ability to reach vital goals.

According to this theory, then, mental health is constituted by the mental part of the individual's general ability. This abstract notion needs to be complemented by what might be called a material definition, in which the concrete mental abilities needed are stated. I have elsewhere tried to do so (Tengland, 1998/2001) and let me here summarize my conclusions.

Since the goals of the individuals differ it is impossible, in the strict sense, to state what mental health in general means. It is, however, likely that, at a fundamental level, people need to have the same basic abilities, despite their different goals. I have postulated that to have 'acceptable (or minimal) health' one has to have the ability to hold some kind of job, to have the ability to take care of oneself and one's home, and to have the ability to have some social relations.[17] I suggest that the following mental abilities are necessary for reaching these basic goals: memory (in various senses), correct perception, rationality (in various senses), flexibility, the ability to experience feelings in general, the ability to feel empathy, self-knowledge, self-confidence, self-esteem, communicative capacity, and co-operative capacity.[18]

The fully functioning person, maturity and mental health

Anyone familiar with Rogers' work will recognize many of the mental characteristics just mentioned as being the same or similar to those used by Rogers in characterizing maturity. Rogers defines 'maturity' as 'the capacity to perceive realistically, to accept responsibility for one's own behaviour, to evaluate experience in terms of the evidence coming from one's own senses, to change

---

17. This, of course, does not mean that everyone actually wants to have a job, a home, or even social contact. It is the *ability* have these things that is of interest.
18. For a more detailed discussion, including definitions of these terms, see Tengland, 1998/ 2001, pp. 149–209.

the evaluation of experience only on the basis of new evidence, to accept others as unique individuals different from oneself, to prize oneself and to prize others' (Thorne, 1992, p. 34). There are several themes here: correct perception of reality, taking responsibility (which implies autonomy), being rational in the sense of critically evaluating one's experience, being tolerant to others, and having a positive attitude toward oneself and others. This implies the ability to experience empathy, sympathy and self-esteem.[19]

Rogers explicitly relates congruence to maturity when he states that '[m]aturity is a broader term describing the personality characteristics and behavior of a person who is, in general, congruent' (Rogers, 1959, p. 207). This gives us reason to believe that maturity comes close to what people normally call mental health.

The concept of the 'fully functioning person' is a theoretical construction which is partly synonymous with congruence. Thus, it is part of a theoretical definition of health. Rogers lists ten features of this concept (Rogers, 1959, pp. 234–5). The list consists of statements like 'being open to experience', 'being able to symbolize experience correctly', 'experiencing oneself as the locus of evaluation', 'having a self-structure that is congruent with experience', 'having no conditions of worth'. All of these features are related to, or defining characteristics of, what Rogers calls congruence.[20] As Haugh notes (Haugh, 1998b, p. 17), the list contains a few features that are not part of the conception of congruence, but which are effects, or outcomes, of it. These effects are: to be able to 'meet each situation with behavior which is a unique and creative adaptation to the newness of that moment', finding 'organismic valuing a trustworthy guide to the most satisfying behavior', living 'with others in the maximum possible harmony...' (Rogers, 1959, p. 235). It is not correct, then, to claim, as Rogers does, that the concept of the 'fully functioning person' is *synonymous* with optimal psychological maturity and complete congruence (ibid., p. 235). These concepts are interconnected but have different roles in the theory. Congruence describes what goes on within the individual and maturity describes what positive mental abilities congruence leads to. The concept of the 'fully functioning person' includes congruence and combines it with some features of general health, 'creative adaptation', 'satisfying behaviors', 'living with others in maximum possible harmony'.

Furthermore, as a characterization of health or mental health, this list of effects of congruence is not satisfying since a lot of the terms used are vague and imprecise. It is important to know why each situation should be met with unique and creative adaptation. We need a specification of what is the 'most satisfying behavior' (ibid.). Finally, the meaning of 'to live with others in the maximum possible harmony' (ibid.) has to be spelt out. A general theory of health is needed in order to determine this.

Maturity, as I have tried to show, describes what is expected of the fully functioning person. It comes close to an (incomplete) ordinary language definition of mental health. Such a definition is important since it is important to know why it is good to be congruent. The explication of maturity gives us one

---

19. For a fuller discussion of the criteria used by Rogers, see Tengland, 1998/2001, pp. 75–80.
20. However, strictly, they are not all part of the definition of congruence. What 'experiencing oneself as being the locus of evaluation', one feature listed, means, has to be explained.

possible answer. But Rogers also gives us a more general explanation as to why it is important to be congruent. In order to live 'optimally'[21] the person needs to have access to his/her undistorted experiences, i.e. perceptions, sensations, beliefs, wishes, emotions, etc. Rogers writes: 'The person who is fully open to his experience would have access to all of the available data in the situation, on which to base his behavior' (Rogers, 1961, p. 190). The assumption is that the more information, about him/herself and the world, the person has access to, the better. If some of the experiences are distorted or kept from awareness, the person is less likely to make the best possible decisions for acting in the situation he or she is in. Openness to (undistorted) experiences is, thus, a requirement for maturity, i.e. mental health.

As said before, in terms of the holistic theory, incongruence is a 'malady' (an inner state) that causally reduces general health (being able to live 'optimally'), i.e. the individual's ability to reach important goals in life. It does so by reducing various specific mental abilities (which for Rogers constitute maturity) like perceiving correctly, being rational, remembering, being able to experience emotions, having self-esteem, and being able to co-operate and communicate effectively with other people.

With this in mind it is now possible to interpret what it could mean to 'meet each situation with unique and creative adaptation' (Rogers, 1959, p. 235). Creativity or uniqueness might be necessary in order to reach important goals in life. The 'most satisfying behavior' (ibid.) could be interpreted as the behaviour that leads to the attainment of important goals in life. Given that 'to live with others in the maximum possible harmony' (ibid.) is a vital goal, or is a requirement for reaching other vital goals, it is self-evident that a person needs the general ability to do this.

I believe that it is important that a theory of mental health does not specify too closely how people should be and behave. I call this 'the principle of tolerance'. This principle is, I believe, very much in line with Rogers' thinking, and the person-centered approach in general. The theory of health presented has two aspects both of which take this into account. First, the general theory of health presented does not state which goals are vital or important to people — they themselves choose.[22] Second, in specifying the specific mental abilities needed to reach vital goals, care is taken not to assume too much — therefore the discussion of *basic* vital goals. It is assumed that the abilities needed to reach basic vital goals form a basic repertoire that is needed for anyone despite the difference in other goals.

CONCLUSION

I have tried to do several things in this chapter. First I have discussed one of the fundamental concepts of person-centered theory, incongruence. In doing so, I have tried to show that there are several ways to define this concept, and I have argued that a choice has to be made between them. In relation to this I have also discussed various possible interpretations of the self-concept, and I have tried

21. The term, 'optimally', seems to be either a general health term or a quality of life term. But a definition of the term is needed in order to know which.
22. Sometimes, of course, (possibly due to conditions of worth) people make mistakes.

to show the complexity of the term 'experiencing'.

In the second part of the chapter I have placed Rogers' theory in a context of a general theory of health, a holistic theory, and in doing so shown how Rogers' theory implicitly relies on an undeveloped theory of general health, using terms like 'the fully functioning person' and 'maturity'.

Terms like 'health', 'mental health', 'disease', 'mental illness' have been absent in much of the discussion in humanistic theory, as they appear to either stigmatize people, or to imply 'the medical model'. However, even though some theories have had this effect, this does not mean that we are better off not defining these terms. The risk of denying that we need to define them usually results in an implicit theory of health that is never fully elaborated. What we need instead are better theories, theories which are not stigmatizing, and do not imply the medical model.

In developing his theory of therapy and personality, Rogers explicitly describes 'ill health' on a theoretical level, when he describes what incongruence is. He also partly develops a theory of mental health (maturity) when he describes what mental features the mentally healthy person has. But he only implicitly addresses the question of what general health is (to be able to live optimally, or, being able to live with others in maximum possible harmony). If person-centered theory is to be complete it has to further develop concepts of this kind. Every psychological theory needs to be related to a general theory of health, and I have argued that a holistic theory is a good place to start.

REFERENCES

Baddeley, A. (1994). Memory, in A.M. Colman (Ed.) *Companion Encyclopedia of Psychology.* London: Routeledge.

Biermann-Ratjen, E.-M. (1998). Incongruence and Psychopathology. In Thorne, B. and Lambers, E. (Eds.), *Person-centered therapy. A European perspective.* London: Sage, pp. 119–30.

Boorse, C. (1975). On the Distinction Between Deisease and Illness. *Philosophy and Public Affairs, 5,* pp.49–68.

Boorse, C. (1976). What a theory of Mental Health Should Be. *Journal for the Theory of Social Behaviour, 6,* pp.61–84.

Boorse, C. (1977) Health as a Thepretical Concept. *Philosophy of Science, 44,* pp. 542–73.

Bozarth, J. (1998). *Person-Centered Therapy: A Revolutionary Paradigm.* Ross-on-Wye: PCCS Books.

Brodley, B. (1998). Congruence and its Relation to Communication in Client-Centered Therapy. *The Person-Centered Journal,* 5(2), pp. 83–106 .

Brodley, B. (1999). Reasons for Responses Expressing the Therapist's Frame of Reference in Client-Centered Therapy. *The Person-Centered Journal,* 6(1), pp. 4–27.

Ellingham, I. (1999). Carl Rogers' 'Congruence' as an Organismic Not a Freudian Concept. *The Person-Centered Journal,* 6(2), pp. 121–40. Reprinted as chapter 6 in this volume.

Fulford, K. W. M. (1989). *Moral Theory and Medical Practice.* Cambridge: Cambridge University Press.

Green, O. H. (1992). *The Emotions: A Philosophical Theory.* Dordrecht: Kluwer.

Haugh, S. (1998a). Congruence: A Confusion of Language. *The Person-Centered Journal,* 6(1), pp. 44–50.

Haugh, S. (1998b). *An Exploration of the Concept of Congruence in Person-Centred Theory.* Unpublished MA thesis, Regent's College School of Psychotherapy and Counselling, London.

Lambers, E. (1994a). The person-centred perspective on psychopathology: the neurotic client. In Mearns, D., *Developing Person-Centred Counselling*. London; Sage. pp. 105–9.

Lambers, E. (1994b). Borderline personality disorder. In Mearns D., *Developing Person-Centred Counselling*. London: Sage, pp. 110–3.

Lambers, E. (1994c). Psychosis. In Mearns D., *Developing Person-Centred Counselling*. London: Sage, pp. 113–6.

Lambers, E. (1994d). Personality disorder. In Mearns D., *Developing Person-Centred Counselling*. London: Sage, pp. 116–20.

Lietaer, G. (1993). Authenticity, Congruence and Transparency. In Brazier (Ed.) *Beyond Carl Rogers*. London: Constable, pp. 17–46.

Nordenfelt, L. (1995, 2nd ed.) *On the Nature of Health*. Dordrecht: Reidel.

Pörn, I. (1984). An Equilibrium Model of Health. In Lindahl, I. and Nordenfelt, L. (Eds.), *Health, Disease and Causal Explanations in Medicine*. Dordrecht Reidel, pp. 3–9.

Rogers, C. R. (1951). *Client-Centered Therapy*, Houghton Mifflin Company, Boston.

Rogers, C. R. (1957). The Necessary and Sufficient Conditions of Therapeutic Personality Change. *Journal of Consulting Psychology*, 21(2), pp. 95–103.

Rogers, C. R. (1959). A theory of therapy, personality and interpersonal relationships, as developed in the client-centered framework. In Koch, S. (Ed.), *Psychology: A Study of a Science* (vol. 3). New York: McGraw-Hill, pp. 184–256.

Rogers, C. R. (1961a). *On Becoming a Person*. Boston: Houghton Mifflin.

Rogers, C. R (1961b) A therapist's view of the good life: The fully functioning person. In C.R. Rogers (1961a) *On Becoming a Person*, Boston: Houghton Mifflin, pp 183–96.

Rogers, C. R. (1963). The Concept of the Fully Functioning Person. *Psychotherapy: Theory, Research and Practice*, 1, pp. 17–26.

Schmid P. (1998). A Person-Centered Understanding of the Person. In Thorne B. and Lambers E. (Eds.), *Person-Centred Therapy: A European Perspective*. London: Sage, pp. 38–52.

Speierer, G.-W. (1990). Towards a specific illness concept of CCT. In Lietaer, G., Rombauts, J. and Van Balen, R. (Eds.), *Client-Centered and Experiential Psychotherapy in the Nineties*. Leuven: Leuven University Press, pp. 337–59.

Tengland, P.-A. (1998/2001). *Mental Health. A Philosophical Analysis*, Linköping Studies in Arts and Science, 177. Accepted for publication, Kluwer Academic Publishers, 2001.

Thorne, B. (1992). *Carl Rogers*. London: Sage.

Tolan, J. (2000). The Fallacy of the 'Real' Self — In Praise of the Self-Structure. Paper presented at the Fifth International Conference on Client-Centred and Experiential Psychotherapy, Chicago.

Wakefield, J. (1992). Disorder as Harmful Dysfunction: A Conceptual Critique of *DSM-III-R*'s Definition of Mental Disorder, *Psychological Review*, 99(2), pp. 232–47.

Wakefield, J. (2000). Aristotle as Sociobiologist: The 'Function of a Human Being' Argument, Black Box Essentialism, and the Concept of Mental Disorder. *Philosophy, Psychiatry and Psychology*, March 2000, 7(1), pp. 17–44.

Whitbeck, C. (1981). A Theory of Health. In Caplan, S. L., Engelhardt, H. T., and McCartney, J. J. (Eds.), *Concepts of Health and Disease: Interdisciplinary Perspectives*. Reading Massachusetts: Addison-Wesley, pp. 611–26.

WHO (1948). Official Records of the World Health Organization, 2, 100.

Wyatt, G. (1998). The Multifaceted Nature of Congruence within the Therapeutic Relationship: Paper presented to the Person-Centered Forum, Johannesburg, S. Africa.

11 Congruence and the Supervision of Client-Centred Therapists

Tony Merry

This chapter suggests that, in order to remain consistent with the theory and principles of the Person-Centred Approach, the emphasis in client-centred supervision should be on therapist congruence in the context of Rogers' 'necessary and sufficient conditions' (Rogers, 1957). This stands in contrast to supervision practice in many other approaches to therapy (and sometimes in client-centred therapy) where client material forms the basis of supervision sessions, and discussion is limited to technical questions concerning the communication of empathic understanding, or the development of treatment plans and goals for therapy.

Supervision is the process through which therapists explore their work with clients in a non-managerial environment with a supportive and experienced colleague. Regular supervision is a requirement for accreditation with most accrediting bodies in the UK, for example, the British Association for Counselling and Psychotherapy (BACP). Most approaches to supervision stress that material for supervision sessions should include such things as the nature of the therapeutic alliance, diagnosing or assessing client problems, techniques used by the therapist, ethical and professional matters, and in the psychodynamic tradition, transference and counter-transference issues. Client-centred supervision shifts the emphasis of supervision away from the individual concerns of clients to the self-structure of the therapist. In this regard, Mearns (1994), referring to therapy rather than supervision, remarks:

> One of the distinguishing features of the person-centred approach is the emphasis it places on the counsellor's use of self. It is this area which brings the approach into its sharpest contrast with those other approaches to counselling where anything beyond the counsellor's use of her intellect is generally regarded to be evidence of over-involvement (p. 17).

Elsewhere (Merry, 1999), with regard specifically to supervision, I suggested that:

> Supervision . . . provides opportunities for supervisees (counsellors) to experience a relationship that is free of threat, and is supportive and understanding so that they can explore non-defensively what the counselling process means to them, *and how they experience themselves in relationship with their clients* (p. 140, emphasis added).

174

What follows is an argument for supervision as a process based in a relationship that conforms to Rogers' six necessary and sufficient conditions (Rogers, 1957). The relationship is organised around a particular approach to developing meaning from experience, and, as a consequence, promotes congruence and an internal locus of evaluation in the supervisee. Finally, it is proposed that such an approach to supervision is entirely consistent with Rogers' phenomenological theory of personality.

SUPERVISION AS A COLLABORATIVE INQUIRY

In a previous publication (Merry, 1999), I proposed that client-centred supervision can usefully be conceptualised as a form of collaborative inquiry. This form of inquiry is in the new paradigm tradition of qualitative research which Heron (1981) and Reason (1988) characterise as democratic and egalitarian, treating all participants as having an equally valid contribution to make in the research undertaking. It is concerned to dissolve artificial barriers between the researcher and his or her research subjects, and to focus on the subjective experience of the participants rather than exclusively on more objective data.

In the supervision context, the research or inquiry consists of attempts to help counsellors describe and make sense of their subjective experience of forming and maintaining therapeutic relationships with clients. The inquiry is conducted as a collaborative process between supervisor and supervisee, and this makes the quality of the relationship between the two people involved a major factor.

Qualitative research is concerned with the description and interpretation of the meanings derived from experiences rather than with statistical analysis of variables. It acknowledges that meaning can be, and usually is, different for the various people involved in an experience, and that all meaning has validity, though often in different ways, to each of the participants. Since qualitative research is concerned with description and interpretation, researchers need to enter relationships with co-participants in ways that differ radically from the distant and objective stance traditionally taken by researchers engaged in quantitative methodology. The notion of supervisor as co-researcher seems more in keeping with general person-centred philosophy than models of supervision that incorporate an overt (or covert) policing role, or are primarily concerned to act as a quality control mechanism.

The Person-Centred Approach (PCA) lends itself particularly well to treating the supervision process as a form of collaborative inquiry because, in all its manifestations (including in client-centred psychotherapy), the PCA adopts a phenomenological approach to the discovery of meaning derived from experience. I have previously offered five general principles of collaborative inquiry in a client-centred supervisory context (Merry, 1999), summarised here as:

- Humans are self-directing (or potentially so). Collaborative inquiry respects and exploits the capacity, underpinned by the actualising tendency, for responsible, self-directed other and self-enhancing behaviour.
- Collaborative inquiry acknowledges that both supervisor and supervisee can

contribute equally to the discovery of meaning within relationships that adopt a democratic, power-sharing stance.

- The process enables deep engagement with therapy (and other) issues because it respects all forms of knowledge (including, for example, intuition) as equally legitimate, to be understood and its personal meanings discovered.
- Collaborative inquiry progressively dissolves the perceived (or subceived) need for defensiveness since the threat of personal evaluations of negative worth is minimised.
- Both parties (supervisor and supervisee) can perceive each other as co-workers in a co-operative endeavour.

These five statements are expressions of underlying philosophy and values inherent in the PCA. Mirroring client-centred psychotherapy, taken together they skew the supervision process away from a diagnostic or quality control process. Instead, emphasis is on recognising that a counsellor's behaviour with clients is derived more from experience and the attribution of personal meaning to that experience, than from understanding theory or mastering skills. At the centre of the process is the therapist/supervisee as a *person* whose self-concept and level of self-awareness is on the line with every therapeutic relationship he or she enters. The attribution of personal meaning to experience (accompanied by its concomitant behaviour) is, in person-centred terms, affected by a person's self-concept with its internalised conditions of worth, and the position on an internal-external axis of their locus of evaluation. It is in these two respects that the concept of 'congruence' is particularly relevant.

CONGRUENCE

Congruence, sometimes referred to as authenticity, or realness, has been defined and discussed many times in the literature, but for present purposes the following definition offered by Barrett-Lennard (1998) is more than sufficient:

> . . . it implies consistency between the three levels of (a) a person's primary experience, (b) their symbolized awareness, and (c) their outward behaviour and communication . . . Thus, congruence first of all is an intrapersonal process state and quality of functioning (p. 82).

Barrett-Lennard places congruence, primarily, as an internal state in which experiences are accurately admitted into awareness because the need for denial or distortion of experience is minimised or, ideally, absent entirely. In the counselling/therapy context, congruence also refers to the extent that a therapist's communication (both verbal and non-verbal) matches his or her inner subjective state. The ideal situation is one where the therapist is accurately admitting into awareness all experience relevant to the therapy relationship, and is living that experience in such a way that all behaviour exactly reflects it. Like most ideals, this situation is probably only theoretically possible, since it is unlikely that any therapist has achieved an internal state of perfect congruence where all conditions of worth have been totally resolved.

THE COLLABORATIVE INQUIRY PROCESS IN SUPERVISION

The collaborative inquiry process in supervision is an attitude of mind or 'a way of being', and cannot be represented by a series of steps or strategies. Supervisor and supervisee are co-operating and equal partners in an endeavour to unravel the complex meanings of therapeutic relationships. The subjective experience of the supervisee is the primary data and the inquiry process is facilitated by the supervisor's dedication to understanding this subjective experience. The supervisor, consistent with general person-centred theory and philosophy, adopts a non-directive approach to the process. In other words, the agenda is derived from the current concerns of the supervisee, but it needs to be understood from the outset that the major concern is with the supervisee's self-exploration, stimulated and informed by experiences with clients. Client material is obviously relevant, but extended theorising about clients and their psychological histories are likely to distract from supervisees' self-exploration.

Tape-recordings of therapist/client interactions can be of considerable benefit provided attention remains focused on the therapist's behaviour, thoughts and feelings. The emphasis is not on diagnosing, assessing or labelling clients or their behaviour. As Patterson has remarked, 'Such an approach views the client as an object to be analyzed and evaluated rather than as a person to be accepted and understood' (1997 in Patterson, 2000, p. 195). Instead, the emphasis is on the evidence present on the tape that the supervisee is creating and maintaining a relationship based on Rogers' necessary and sufficient conditions. The implication here is that effort is given to an exploration of the therapist's underlying attitudes and values, in addition to considering how effectively the therapist is communicating empathic understanding and experiencing positive regard. Most usefully, tape-recordings can help supervisor and supervisee explore the extent to which therapists' outward behaviour and communication is consistent (i.e. is congruent) with their experiences with clients and their awareness of that experience.

In the supervision context, the collaborative inquiry process is predictable only in very general terms. Both participants are dedicated to an exploration of the supervisee's relationships with clients, and how those relationships impinge on the supervisee's sense of self. The supervisor, taking a non-directive stance, empathically enters the subjective frame of reference of the supervisee and offers that understanding for consideration by the supervisee. The exploration can consider technical questions about, for example, effective communication of empathic understanding, issues concerning self-disclosure by the therapist, and ethical, professional and organisational questions. The general aim, however, is to assist the supervisee in the process of internalising and communicating the core conditions, and this inevitably involves issues concerning the supervisee's experience of personal congruence.

SUPERVISION AS A POTENTIALLY THERAPEUTIC EXPERIENCE

Patterson (1997) believes that supervision should not focus 'on the supervisee's personality or problems, but upon his or her relationship with his or her clients.

The supervisee's personality becomes of concern only if it detrimentally affects the therapy. Then it is dealt with only in terms of this situation, that is, the supervisor responds to the difficulty in the supervisee's relationships with his or her clients' (ibid., p. 196).

Whilst agreeing in general with Patterson that supervision is not the place to focus extensively on a supervisee's personal problems, I suggest that a supervision process that does not include therapist's self-experiences misses a crucial area of client-centred theory and practice. Where a supervisee's personal problems interfere with his or her capacity to build client-centred relationships, some exploration of them is inevitable in supervision. The outcome of such an exploration is most likely to be a decision that the supervisee enter personal therapy if the problems are severe or persist. On the other hand, personal problems, stimulated by experiences with clients, are legitimate material for supervision because their resolution (or partial resolution) can contribute to a therapist's sense of control over his or her life and, hence, his or her work with clients. The exploration of personal problems, leading possibly to their full or partial resolution, results, to some extent, in a reorganisation of the self-concept, increasing congruence between the self-concept and experience, and an enhancement of therapeutic relationships with clients.

SUPERVISION AND THERAPIST CONGRUENCE

It is invidious to single out one or other of the core conditions of empathic understanding, unconditional positive regard and congruence as somehow more 'necessary' or more 'core' than the other two, and no such implication should be drawn from the discussion presented here. Moreover, the core conditions are present within the context of Rogers' six 'necessary and sufficient' conditions (Rogers, 1957). Congruence needs to be seen within its total context — it refers to a part of the therapist's experiencing process. He or she experiences some degree of empathic understanding of the client's subjective world, and a non-judgemental acceptance of that world, while remaining open to his or her own subjective experiencing. In Rogers' own words:

> It means that within the relationship he is freely and deeply himself, with his actual experience accurately represented by his awareness of himself. It is the opposite of presenting a facade, either knowingly or unknowingly (1957, p. 97).

The therapist's intention is to dedicate him or herself to deepening the experience of empathic understanding and to communicate the extent of that understanding with as little distortion as possible. Therapists, ideally, are open to the flow of experiencing taking place within themselves that springs from the moment-by-moment interaction with their clients.

It is not often well understood outside of the client-centred world (and sometimes within it) how demanding the concept of congruence is. It requires full engagement with the client's experiencing and openness to the therapist's self-experiencing. At first, this seems to be a mental juggling act that novice therapists find difficult to master, and few therapists, no matter how experienced, do not struggle with this issue. How can I be attentive to another's experiencing while simultaneously being aware of my own? How do I balance self-awareness with awareness of my client?

In my experience, supervisees often bring questions of congruence to supervision, perhaps more so than any other issue. Difficulties with empathic understanding and positive regard are often traceable back to the therapist struggling with some inner experience that distracts from the process of entering the client's subjective world. Working at 'relational depth' as Mearns and Thorne put it (e.g. Mearns and Thorne, 2000) implies that therapists have deep enough self-knowledge and awareness to maintain themselves as separate individuals whilst engaging empathically, congruently and non-judgementally with the lived experience of another.

Client-centred psychotherapy leads to the discovery of aspects of self that have hitherto remained denied to awareness or distorted in awareness. The close engagement with another person that is required of the client-centred therapist can mean that denied or distorted aspects of the therapist's self begin to enter the therapist's awareness. When this happens, the therapist is likely to experience some tension and anxiety. Again, in Rogers' words:

> If the individual dimly perceives such an incongruence in himself, then a tension state occurs which is known as anxiety. The incongruence need not be sharply perceived. It is enough that it is subceived — that is, discriminated as threatening to the self without any awareness of the content of that threat (1957, p. 97).

Incongruence refers to, 'a discrepancy between the actual experience of the organism and the self-picture of the individual insofar as it represents that experience' (Rogers, 1957, p. 96). For example, a therapist whose self-picture incorporates the notion that he or she is entirely free of prejudice, would experience some level of anxiety when confronted by a client of a different ethnic group, if that self-picture were distorted in this regard. In this case, the therapist would find difficulty in allowing prejudiced feelings into awareness because to do so would constitute a threat to the therapist's self-concept, a state of incongruence would now exist, and to this extent the necessary and sufficient conditions would be compromised.

One possibility would be for the therapist to distort this experience into something more admissible, i.e. more congruent with the self-concept, a difficulty with empathic understanding, for example. In supervision this may be how the therapist presents her experience with this client. In this case, the collaborative inquiry is likely to begin with an exploration of empathic understanding, and is more likely to bear fruit if the available 'data' includes audiotape recordings of the interactions between the client and the therapist. In the absence of tape-recordings, the inquiry is limited to the therapist's recall of the interactions and recall of the accompanying feelings.

It should be clear, however, that, whatever form the inquiry takes, its effectiveness will largely be determined by the extent to which the supervisee experiences the relationship with the supervisor as free of threat. In the example given, the issue at stake is the supervisee's self-concept with its internalised conditions of worth, and to admit to prejudice of the type described may prove extremely threatening. As the supervisee gets closer to admitting the prejudice into awareness, she may experience extremes of anxiety, without being aware of the specific content of the threat.

The supervisory relationship shares some common characteristics with the therapy relationship, more so in the person-centred approach than most other approaches. Both relationships are established to explore aspects of the experience of one participant, and both relationships are fertile ground for personal growth and development. I view personal growth and development as effectively synonymous with the development of personal congruence, and an explicitly client-centred therapy relationship is by no means the only relationship where the development of congruence can occur.

It is useful to be reminded of Rogers' remark, in the 1957 paper, that:

> It is not stated that these six conditions are the essential conditions for client-centred therapy, and that other conditions are essential for other types of psychotherapy... my aim in stating this theory is to state the conditions which apply *to any situation in which constructive personality change occurs* . . . (emphasis added).

The term 'constructive personality change' is, in my view, closely allied to (if not synonymous with) congruence, and in this regard the general aims of client-centred therapy and client-centred supervision overlap. In other words, client-centred supervision is less concerned with skills and theory and more concerned with the psychological development of the supervisee as a person. This is not to say that other issues are not also important in supervision. Developing ethical practice and the enhancement of communication skills, for example, are also of on-going concern. However, even these two areas are inextricably bound up with the continuing actualisation of the supervisee, and his or her process of on-going constructive personality change.

In the example given above, while there are almost certainly factors concerning the communication of empathic understanding and the supervisee's unconditional positive regard, the underlying issue is one of personal congruence. Because the collaborative inquiry process is based on a relationship that conforms to Rogers' necessary and sufficient conditions, the psychological history and present experiencing process of the supervisee can be explored in an environment in which the threat to the supervisee's self-concept (manifested in experiences of anxiety) is contained within a congruent, empathic and non-judgemental relationship.

THE LOCUS OF EVALUATION

Closely allied to the question of congruence, is that of the supervisee's locus of evaluation. Theoretically, the degree of a person's incongruence, defined by the extent to which the person distorts or denies certain experiences in awareness, is reflected in the position of that person's locus of evaluation on an (imaginary) internal-external axis. In other words, the more a person is incongruent, the more he or she will rely on the judgements of others (or judgements introjected from others) for what is and is not 'of value', and the more that person will reject the information available from his or her organismic valuing process.

The supervisory relationship has as much potential for reinforcing an external locus of evaluation as for enhancing an internal locus. Where the supervisor takes an authoritative stance, and directs her attention at questioning the supervisee's *performance*, at the expense of exploring the supervisee's attitudes and values through empathic understanding of the supervisee's *experience*, she runs the risk of arousing anxiety and defensiveness in the supervisee. The likely outcome is the strengthening of the supervisee's external locus of evaluation as he becomes dependent on the external authority and expertise of the supervisor.

By contrast, collaborative inquiry involves supervisor and supervisee in a mutual process of discovery in which different areas of expertise can be shared. For example, the supervisor (it is assumed) is expert at contributing her empathic understanding of the supervisee's experience. Her 'unspoken questions' are, 'Am I understanding this person's experience, including his thoughts, feelings, fears, etc. accurately? Am I communicating my understanding with sensitivity, openness and non-judgemental respect? Am I able to hear feedback from the supervisee and adjust my understanding accordingly?' Further, 'Where I experience some disagreement or unease, am I able to communicate it in a way that contributes to a process of open inquiry, rather than as a judgement of my supervisee's worth?'

The development of an internal locus of evaluation is a feature of deeper levels of personal congruence. Rogers (1959) suggested that a person whose locus of evaluation had shifted from the external towards the internal would be, for example, more able to experience positive self-regard, less liable to tension and anxiety, more acceptant of self and others and more confident, self-directing and trusting of his or her own values. All these are qualities of effective client-centred therapists, and a supervisory relationship provides rich opportunities for their development. A strong internal locus of evaluation enables therapists to be more trusting of their own judgement in relation to clients and less liable to defensiveness when considering the inevitable mistakes and misunderstandings in therapy relationships.

Of course, the supervisor's personal congruence is a significant factor in the collaborative inquiry process. In exactly the same way as Rogers' theory requires counsellors to be congruent or integrated in the relationship, supervisors need also to be aware of their own experiencing process, and have the capacity to communicate in ways that are in harmony with that experiencing. Not only is this good 'modelling', feelings and thoughts that arise in the supervisor about the supervisory relationship or about the supervisee are potentially useful material for consideration by both supervisor and supervisee.

PERSONALITY THEORY AND SUPERVISION

The approach to supervision outlined above maximises the potential of the supervisory relationship to promote the congruence of the supervisee. This approach assumes that 'congruence', 'constructive personality change' and 'personal growth and development' are, if not actually synonymous, then very closely allied concepts in Rogers' system since they all refer to the organisation and structure of the self. In broad terms, Rogers' personality theory describes the processes by which an individual becomes subject to the internalisation of conditions of worth which impact on the development of congruence through the denial to awareness of certain experiences. Following this, the theory describes the conditions which are likely to dissolve conditions of worth and enable the person to admit experiences into awareness, assimilate them and revise the self-structure accordingly.

If the supervisee's experience in supervision includes significant and consistent congruent, empathic, acceptant understanding, then any potential threat to the current self-concept arising from experiences with clients can be met with non-defensive consideration. It is important here to realise that any admission into awareness of previously denied or distorted experience has the potential to arouse anxiety and be felt as threatening. Normally, the experience of threat results in a further ossification of the current self-concept. According to Proposition XVI of Rogers' theory of personality (Rogers, 1951):

> Any experience which is inconsistent with the organization or structure of the self may be perceived as a threat, and the more of these perceptions there are, the more rigidly the self-structure is organized to maintain itself (p. 515).

However, the following Proposition (Proposition XVII) provides for the possibility that under some circumstances (which theoretically would include a relationship that conformed to the six necessary and sufficient conditions) something else can happen:

> Under certain conditions, involving primarily complete absence of any threat to the self-structure, experiences which are inconsistent with it may be perceived, and examined, and the structure of self revised to assimilate and include such experiences (ibid., p. 517).

The importance of providing a person-centred relationship in the supervisory context becomes clear when the next Proposition (XVIII) is considered:

> When the individual perceives and accepts into one consistent and integrated system all his sensory and visceral experiences, then he is *necessarily more understanding of others and is more accepting of others as separate individuals* (ibid., p. 520, emphasis added).

The concern to develop an internal locus of evaluation, rather than reinforcing a reliance on the supervisor for determining what constitutes effective client-centred practice, is addressed by Proposition XIX:

> As the individual perceives and accepts into his self-structure more of his organic experiences, he finds that he is replacing his present value *system* — based so largely upon introjections which have been distortedly symbolized — with a continuing organismic valuing *process* (ibid., p. 522, original emphasis).

The implication for supervision of Rogers' 'necessary and sufficient' hypothesis, and his theory of personality, is that some degree of personal growth is inevitable through supervision because the environment is conducive for it and the relationship promotes it. Indeed, any person-centred approach to supervision must incorporate the personal growth opportunities available from reflecting on experiences with clients if it is successfully to enhance a therapist's capacity to internalise the core conditions. Whilst supervision is also concerned with issues other than therapist self-experience, the major concern must remain with the therapist's ability to create and maintain authentic, empathic and non-judgemental relationships with clients. A state of congruence, where the therapist is 'freely and deeply himself' is the necessary condition for the therapist to experience empathic understanding and unconditional positive regard. The process of collaborative inquiry, described above, explicitly sets out to create an open, empathic and non-judgemental environment that is simultaneously questioning and supportive. Perceived or subceived threat to the therapist's self-concept can be explored in ways that are likely to promote congruence and an internal locus of evaluation because the supervisee's self-resources are utilised in ways that match the use of client self-resources in therapy.

REFERENCES

Barrett-Lennard, G. T. (1998). *Carl Rogers Helping System: Journey and Substance.* London: Sage.

Heron, J. (1981). Philosophical Basis for a New Paradigm. In P. Reason and J. Rowan (Eds). *Human Inquiry: a sourcebook of new paradigm research.* Chichester: Wiley, pp. 19–35.

Mearns, D. (1994). *Developing Person-Centred Counselling.* London: Sage.

Mearns, D. And Thorne, B. (2000). *Person-Centred Therapy Today.* London: Sage.

Merry, T (1999). *Learning and Being in Person-Centred Counselling.* Ross-on-Wye: PCCS Books.

Patterson, C. H. (1997). Client-Centred Supervision. In Patterson, C.H. (2000). *Understanding Psychotherapy* . Ross-on-Wye: PCCS Books, pp. 192–207.

Reason, P. (1988). (Ed) *Human Inquiry in Action.* London: Sage.

Rogers, C. R. (1951). *Client-Centred Therapy: Its Current Practice, Implications and Theory.* Boston: Houghton Mifflin.

Rogers, C. R. (1957). The necessary and sufficient conditions of therapeutic personality change. *Journal of Consulting Psychology*, 21(2), pp. 95–103.

Rogers, C. R. (1959). A Theory of Therapy, Personality and Interpersonal Relationships as Developed in the Client-Centred Framework. In Koch, S. (Ed) *Psychology: A Study of a Science, Vol 3. Formulations of the Person and the Social Context.* New York: McGraw Hill, pp. 184–256.

12   Congruence: A Special Way of Being

Jerold D. Bozarth

The intent of this chapter is to examine congruence in relation to client-centered theory and practice. Rogers' theory identifies congruence (C), unconditional positive regard (UPR), and empathic understanding (EU) as the necessary and sufficient *therapist* conditions for client personality change (Rogers, 1959, 1980, pp. 114–7,1986). These conditions are considered integrally related in his major theory statements (Rogers, 1957, 1959). However, Rogers identified congruence as ' the most basic of the attitudinal conditions that foster therapeutic growth ...' (Rogers and Sanford, 1984, p. 1379). He also identified congruence (or genuineness) as an important condition in and of itself:

> It is only by providing the genuine reality, which is in me, that the other person can successfully seek for the reality in him. I have found this to be true even when the attitudes I feel are not attitudes with which I am pleased, or attitudes which seem conducive to a good relationship. It seems extremely important to be real. (Rogers, 1961, p. 33)

Rogers later stated:

> The more the therapist is herself in the relationship, putting up no professional front or personal facade, the greater is the likelihood that the client will change and grow in a constructive manner. (Rogers, 1977, p. 9).

These comments have been interpreted to mean that congruence is the most important condition and are periodically the justification for revitalizing the therapist's views as a central aspect of client-centered therapy (Lietaer, 1993, p. 32).

Rogers, perhaps, went beyond congruence in the 1980s when he identified the therapist's 'presence' as the most important condition (Baldwin, 1987; Rogers, 1980). He identified an altered state in therapy wherein ' ... my presence is releasing and helpful ...' (Rogers, 1986, p. 198). It was in this altered state that he claimed his presence to be full of healing, ' ... a relationship [which] transcends itself and becomes a part of something larger' (ibid.). These statements concerning presence have been interpreted within a spiritual context but also presented from a 'naturalistic' perspective (Brodley, 2001). Although Rogers did not identify presence as congruence, I contend that presence is an extension of congruence rather than a separate dimension. Further, several of Rogers' ambiguous comments about the importance of therapist congruence are out of

184

context with his own theory. As such, these comments are misleading and misinterpreted by others (Bozarth, 1998a). *Congruence cannot be the basic condition unless the conditions of UPR and EU are integrally intertwined. If the other two conditions are not intertwined, client-centered therapy is threatened as a viable theory.* It is congruence that becomes the way of being that blends with the self-directive forces of the client as the therapist experiences unconditional positive regard and empathic understanding. Thus, I propose this definition:

> *Congruence is the manifestation of unconditional positive self-regard (UPSR) and can be identified as the therapist's presence in client-centered therapy. Unconditional positive regard towards and empathic understanding of the client's frame of reference characterize this presence.*

Similarly, Wyatt (2000a) refers to 'therapeutic presence' as arising out of the personal presence (authenticity) of the individual of the therapist and their therapeutic intent (holding the therapist conditions to support the self-directed forces of the client). It is argued that congruence must be integrally related to the conditions of unconditional positive regard and empathic understanding of the client's frame of reference. Moreover, congruence is a complicated concept that is a therapeutic condition for the therapist, a representation of self-actualization of the client and therapist, and is fostered by and fosters unconditional positive self-regard.

The relationship among the conditions results in a 'conditions loop' that manifests unconditional positive self-regard (UPSR) of the therapist (Bozarth, 1998a, pp. 80–1). It is the therapist's UPSR that fosters congruence, unconditional positive regard and empathic understanding. These therapeutic conditions as manifestations of the therapist's UPSR in turn increase the therapist's congruence and UPSR. Moreover, congruence is a mark of the increased realization of the client and the client's capacities, and a primary condition for the identification of a potent therapist.

The focus of this paper is to point out that congruence is an integral part of Rogers' theory of psychotherapy. As such, congruence must be considered in relation to the central axiom of client-centered therapy; namely, the therapist conditions of unconditional positive regard and empathic understanding (and necessarily the ensuing nondirective attitude). The implications of therapist congruence are, however, more profound in that the effective therapist's congruence must be represented by high unconditional positive self-regard (UPSR). It is this UPSR during the therapy sessions that begets the conditions of unconditional positive regard (UPR) and empathic understanding of the client's frame of reference (EU). It is then that the therapist's presence can be identified as a healing presence.

CLIENT-CENTERED THERAPY

The central axiom of client-centered therapy is that there are certain therapeutic conditions that facilitate a natural constructive force in individuals. Carl Rogers proposed that these conditions are the central therapeutic ingredients in all psychotherapies and in all helping relationships that intend to achieve constructive personality change (Bozarth, 1998a; Rogers, 1957). The existence of

185

these conditions are the only therapeutic efforts of the client-centered therapist (Rogers, 1959). In Rogers' most formal statements, these conditions are integrally related and inseparable in their relationship to each other (Rogers, 1957, 1959). These conditions are stated explicitly elsewhere.[1] The crux of the therapist conditions is that a congruent therapist experiences unconditional positive regard towards and empathic understanding of the client's frame of reference. When these conditions are perceived by the client, the conditions come into play with the foundation block of client-centered theory; that is, the actualizing tendency. Actualization is an innate constructive direction in each and every human organism that seeks to maintain and enhance itself in order to 'become our potentialities' (Bozarth and Brodley, 1991; Brodley, 2000; Rogers, 1963; Rogers, 1986). It is this assumption that beckons therapists to trust in the self-authority, self-determination and self-direction of human beings. Congruence must be examined within the context of this central axiom of client-centered theory and as the crux of client-centered therapy as an organismic theory.

HISTORY OF CONGRUENCE

In his early work, Rogers considered congruence as the only way the therapeutic relationship could have reality (Rogers, 1954, pp. 17–46). In Rogers' words: 'It is only by providing the genuine reality which is in me, that the other person can successfully seek for the reality in him' (p. 33). His later comments continue to emphasize the reality of the therapist albeit in more complex ways (Rogers, 1980).

One historical review delineates the first remnants of congruence as starting with Rogers' reference to the therapist's 'understanding of self' (Bozarth, 1998a; Rogers, 1939). Later, Rogers referred to the necessity for the counselor to have ' . . . genuine interest in the individual . . .' (Rogers, 1940, p. 162). The early essence of genuineness was the ' . . . embodiment of the attitudes of warmth and understanding towards the client in order to be effective' (Bozarth, 1998a, p. 70). Neither the term 'congruence' nor 'genuineness' appears in the index of Rogers' book, *Client-Centered Therapy*. He did, however, discuss the importance of the therapist's response to the question: 'Is he genuinely willing for the client to organize and direct his life?' (Rogers, 1951, p. 48).

In 1954, the concept of congruence germinated in client-centered theory (Barrett-Lennard, 1998). Congruence was referred to as the consistency between the perceived actual self, and the ideal self. Barrett-Lennard concludes that the term evolved to a core quality of counselor presence in the therapy relationship (p. 65). The development of this quality of presence was related to the emphasis of the concept of self-regard (Standal, 1954). It is my contention that with this shift of emphasis *the theory of client-centered therapy shifted from a self-theory to an organismic theory.*

Congruence was referred to in two of the six necessary and sufficient conditions (Rogers, 1957). The focus was upon the 'incongruence' of the client (condition 2) and upon the 'congruence' of the therapist (condition 3) (p. 96). Rogers described congruence of the therapist in the following way:

---

1. See 'Introduction to the Series' page iii.

It means that within the relationship he is freely and deeply himself, with his actual experience accurately represented by his awareness of himself . . . His experience may be 'I am afraid of this client' or 'My attention is so focused on my own problems that I can scarcely listen to him'. If the therapist is not denying these feelings to awareness, but is able freely to be them (as well as being his other feelings) then the condition we have stated [that the therapist be congruent in the relationship] is met (1957, p. 97).

Although the importance of congruence was expanded after 1956 (Adomaitis, 1991, p. 23), Rogers continued to view the conditions as integrally related. He was explicit about this in his statement that: ' . . . a part of the congruence of the therapist must be the experience of unconditional positive regard and the experience of empathic understanding' (Rogers, 1959, p. 215). The condition of congruence was part of the client-centered axiom of the necessary and sufficient conditions in Rogers' formal theory of 1959. Historically, this is an important point because congruence was no longer considered to be assessed only by the discrepancy between the self and ideal self. Congruence became a central condition related to the therapist's unconditional positive regard; particularly to unconditional positive self-regard. To repeat, *the theory of client-centered therapy shifted from a self-theory to an organismic theory*. The shift accentuated the importance of congruence in that the UPSR of the therapist became a critical variable. Standal's theoretical doctoral dissertation at the University of Chicago influenced the evolving direction of the theory (Standal, 1954). His dissertation was a major contribution to the language, definition and theoretical explanation for the theories of personality and therapy from a client-centered frame of reference (Barrett-Lennard, 1998, p. 65). The most renowned term introduced by Standal and incorporated by Rogers was the term, 'unconditional positive regard' (Moon, Rice, and Schneider, 2001). These authors also reveal that other phrases intrinsic to Rogers' theory, and introduced by Standal, include the need for positive regard, the need for self-regard, conditions of worth, regard complex and unconditional self-regard. Others contributed to the change of the theory but Standal formulated the formal conceptualizations adapted by Rogers (1959).

Rogers' 1951 theory stating that distortions and denials of self-experience defend the consistency of the self-structure was changed to focus upon self-regard as the distinguishing feature of the theory (Standal, 1954). The curative factor became unconditional positive regard rather than the clarifying 'mirror' of the therapist that allowed the client to rectify the distortions and denials of self-experience. In Standal's words:

[T]he psychologically adjusted individual must have received unconditional positive regard for all experiences comprising his self-structure. The positive regard of a significant social other can be said to be unconditional whenever the individual is unable to discriminate any self-experience in the regard-complex associated with that other as being more or less worthy of positive regard than any other self-experience (Standal, 1954, p. 64).

Although the self continued to be an essential part of the theory, Rogers rarely discussed this concept in future writings. It is in the context of an organismic theory that Rogers' theory of pathology concentrates upon the change of the client's conditions of regard. The client changes from conditional to unconditional self-regard in relation to the therapist's experience of unconditional positive regard towards her (Rogers, 1959).

The concept of 'experiencing' also fits into Rogers' shift to an organismic theory (Gendlin, 1970). The organismic experience of client and therapist could be considered as an experiencing process. Just being present became the essence of Gendlin's developing experiential theory (Gendlin, 1990, pp. 205–24). To Rogers, 'being present' must include the presence of the conditions of UPR and EU to be consistent with his theory of therapy. The experiencing process of the client was not to be facilitated by just the presence of the therapist. Rather, the therapist's presence was to embody certain conditions; the therapist is to be a certain way.

Different attitudes and several factors have contributed to interpretations of congruence. Rogers' theory is reviewed with different emphasis (Bozarth, 1998a; Brodley, 1998; Lietaer, 1993). Lietaer's work demonstrates several of these differences. Lietaer focuses on the empirical definitions of congruence (genuineness). He views congruence as 'the inner side' that refers to the degree to which the therapist is receptive to all aspects of the flow of self-experiences. He views transparency as the 'outer side' of the therapist's communication of conscious perceptions, attitudes and experiences to the client. The transparent therapist expresses more of herself to her clients. This expression includes the therapist's clinical interventions and role as process expert. Lietaer suggests that this change of emphasis is an evolution of nondirective to experiential therapy. Several authors disagree with this assertion (Bozarth, 1998a, 2000; Brodley, 1995 [see chapter 5 this volume], 1997, 1998; Haugh, 1998). These authors contend that nondirectivity is an integral part of client-centered theory and practice. It is a developed attitude and behavioral result of adhering to the central axiom of client-centered therapy (Bozarth, 2000; Brodley, 1997, 1998; Patterson, 1969; Raskin, 1948). *Only deviation from the central axiom of client-centered therapy can account for a change from nondirective to experiential therapies.* Rogers did not make this deviation in his theory or his practice (Bozarth, 1990,1998; Brodley, 1990, 1993, 1994, 1995; Brody, 1991; Merry, 1996). Rogers did not deviate from his trust in the client's way, pace and direction. He did, however, add to the confusion of congruence by (1) interchanging congruence, genuineness, authenticity and transparency in his writings, and (2) referring to congruence as a condition which can stand on its own as previously identified. Several authors have noted this problem (Bozarth, 2000; Brodley, 1995; Haugh, 1998). Haugh advances the idea that such terms as transparency and genuineness are outcomes of congruence rather than interchangeable terminology. My view is that congruence is a process that starts with self-awareness and acceptance of organismic experiences, but which may extend to the therapist's experiential state in a way that intertwines with the client's frame of reference. Wyatt touches on a similar position when she concludes that the therapist trusts her own as well as the client's actualizing tendency in the therapeutic relationship (Wyatt, 2000b).

The use of multiple terminology and varied interpretations has created confusion about therapist congruence in client-centered therapy. Rogers' assertion of congruence as the most important condition, and his periodic reference to congruence as the only necessary and sufficient condition, results in a theoretical crisis for the theory of client-centered therapy.

CONGRUENCE AS A THEORETICAL CRISIS

Client-centered theory is in a theoretical crisis is the thesis of one article (Ellingham, 1999). Ellingham contends that there is a critical flaw in person-centered theory in terms of a quasi-Freudian characterization that is illustrated by congruence. He suggests that it is necessary to reformulate congruence in order to identify person-centered concepts in organismic terms. I believe that client-centered theory is in a theoretical crisis simply because of Rogers' remarks about congruence and the interpretations of his remarks. This appears to provide a window of opportunity to alter the concept of the client as her own best expert of her life. When Rogers states that the conditions may be separate and that congruence is the most important, client-centered therapy no longer exists. If Rogers' statement is true, Lietaer's assertion that the nondirective approach has evolved (actually deviated) to an experiential approach is logically supported. The central axiom, the necessary and sufficient conditions, is then altered to include the clinical impositions of the therapist. The 'instruction' to the client-centered therapist to experience unconditional positive regard and empathic understanding is no longer the central axiom. The therapist's views, values, clinical knowledge become mainstays in the therapy. Re-examination of congruence in relation to the central axiom of the theory is essential.

RE-EXAMINATION OF CONGRUENCE

In a theoretical reconsideration of the necessary and sufficient conditions for therapeutic personality change, I postulate that genuineness (or C) is the state of therapeutic readiness. It is this readiness that enables the therapist to better experience empathic understanding (EU) of the client's frame of reference and unconditional positive regard (UPR) towards the client (Bozarth, 1996, 1998a). This conclusion is reached from examination of Rogers' formal theoretical statements (Rogers, 1957, 1959). Congruence is clearly presented by Rogers in a different way than EU and UPR. These latter two concepts are identified as related directly to the *therapist's experience* towards the client and these are the *two* conditions to be perceived by the client. Empathic understanding is viewed ' . . . as the action state of the therapist in which the client's world is accepted as he or she is experiencing it at any given moment' (Bozarth, 1998a, p. 47). I contend that UPR is ' . . . the primary change agent in which the client's needs for positive regard and unconditional positive self-regard are met, resulting in congruence between his or her experience and self-concept and promotion of the actualizing tendency' (p. 47). UPR must be the curative factor since conditional regard is the bedrock of Rogers' pathological theory (Bozarth, 1998a, p. 83). Paradoxically, the conditions expressed in Rogers' theoretical statements are inseparable. This leaves the perplexing question: How can congruence, as considered by Rogers, be the most important condition when the conditions are inseparable? Such importance can only be true if congruence is an essential therapist trait preliminary to the other attitudinal experiences; or if congruence is comprised of the other two attitudes. As stated earlier, my reconceptualization identifies congruence as a state of therapist's readiness enabling the therapist to experience the conditions of UPR and EU. The relationship of the conditions is further considered in my speculation of a 'conditions loop' (Bozarth, 1998a, p. 80).

CONDITIONS LOOP

The speculation of a conditions loop is related to my argument that empathy and unconditional positive regard are 'part and parcel of one condition', and upon the idea that unconditional positive regard and empathy '. . .are ultimately one' (Bozarth, 1997, 1998a, pp. 51–67). Congruence and unconditionality have also been related to a more basic attitude of 'openness' (Lietaer, 1984). In Lietaer's words:

> The more I accept myself and am able to be present in a comfortable way with everything that bubbles up in me, without fear or defense, the more I can be receptive to everything that lives in my client (p. 44).

Others also contend that openness towards self and openness towards others reflects one basic attitude (Truax and Carkhuff, 1967, p. 504).

I also hypothesize that Rogers' references to congruence as the most important condition are ' . . . because the condition affords the therapist the capacity to experience empathy towards the client' (Bozarth, 1998a, p. 81). My conclusion of the 'conditions loop' phenomenon is a major consideration in the re-examination of the conditions. I propose that the conditions:

> become ultimately one in the service of the client's natural growth motivation. Rogers' designation of congruence as the most important condition may be due to the idea that the therapist is just trying to be a certain way. There may even be the implicit assumption consistent with the theory that when one is congruent that there is an element of unconditionality that exists for the client to perceive . . . Theoretically, the therapist is trying to experience her own unconditionality towards a particular person (the client), and to experience to some extent what it is like to be in the world of that other person (p. 82).

Rogers' theory requires that the therapist 'be a certain way' towards the client. The therapist must experience unconditional positive regard and empathic understanding in order that the client might perceive these conditions.

The substance of congruence includes what the therapist should *not do* as well as what the therapist *must be*. The therapist should not put up a ' . . . professional front or personal facade' (Rogers, 1986, p. 196). The therapist ' . . . is openly being the feelings and attitudes that are flowing within at the moment' (p. 135). Being the feelings and attitudes that are flowing has implications for the therapist's experience of empathy in relationship to congruence. One of the implications is the response format of 'empathic reactions' (Bozarth, 1998a, pp. 63–6). Rogers referred to the meaning of his own experiences with such comments as his actions being ' . . . full of healing' when he was in touch with the unknown in himself; and that when he was ' . . . intensely focused on a client, just my presence seems to be healing . . .' (Baldwin, 1987; Rogers, 1980). In the classic

1966 training film, 'Gloria', Rogers refers to the relationship of his experience in the following manner:

> I find myself bringing out my own inner experience statements which seem to have no connection with what is going on but usually prove to have a significant relationship to what the client is experiencing . . . (Rogers, post-session transcription, in Shostrom, 1964).

Rogers' comments suggest that there may be an integral link between congruence and empathy. Speculation about Rogers' comments induced me to conclude that the basic premise:

> of the person-centered therapist is that of being transparent enough to perceive the world nonjudgmentally, as if the therapist were the other person, in order to accelerate the formative tendency of the other person toward becoming all that he or she can become (Bozarth, 1984, p. 69).

In a more extended statement, I concluded:

> Hence, the therapist must continuously be aware of his/her own feelings as though they were the feelings of the client, perhaps 'as is' rather than 'as if'. The therapist's congruence is viewed as being integrally intertwined with empathy. That is, the more congruent, the more transparent the therapist in the relationship, the higher will be the empathy. I have argued before that if the therapist is authentically and deeply attuned to the client, then most of the therapist's experiences, even bizarre fantasies, will have therapeutic relevance to the client and/or the client-therapist relationship (Bozarth, 1998a, p. 65).

It is postulated in the following discussion that congruence refers to a special way of being of the therapist; that this way of being is the experiencing of UPR and EU towards the client and the client's frame of reference. Moreover, this way of experiencing is directly related to and is a manifestation of the therapist's unconditional positive self-regard (UPSR).

CONGRUENCE: A SPECIAL WAY OF BEING

The therapist ' . . . should be, within the confines of this relationship, a congruent, genuine, integrated person' (Rogers, 1959, p. 224). This meant to Rogers that the therapist within the relationship is able to freely be her feelings and experiences, representing her actual experience and her experience of self. Rogers considered it important that the therapist is aware of and is free to experience all organismic experiences, negative as well as positive. The therapist should be herself in the therapeutic relationship. Congruence is not a static state, it is a process ranging from therapist acceptance of her organismic experiences (e.g., not being phony, not denying or not having a personal or professional facade) to transparency (willingness to be seen through).

Congruence must be associated with the other conditions (which I refer to as Rogers' 'instructions' of how the therapist should be) or, possibly, comprised of the other conditions. That is, congruence represents to varying degrees the therapist's UPSR but is also a manifestation of UPSR. From a clinical perspective,

191

the therapist who does not deny or distort her feelings (who is not phony) is open to increased levels of 'open' interaction with her client. These more 'open' levels are referred to as transparency, authenticity, and genuineness. The increased freedom of self in relationship fosters higher degrees of UPSR, which is then manifested by greater congruence, matching and accepting of organismic experiences. Hence, congruence becomes represented by UPSR. Congruence, UPR and empathic understanding are then manifestations of UPSR.

Rogers explicitly states the central role of UPSR in his theory of family life. This is a succinct and astounding statement. He postulates that the parent experiences therapeutic ' ... *unconditional positive regard only* to the extent that he experiences *unconditional positive self-regard*' (1959, quoted in Kirschenbaum and Henderson, 1989, p. 88). Further, it is ' ... to the extent that he *experiences unconditional self-regard,* the parent will be congruent in the relationship' (p. 88). It is to the extent that unconditional positive regard, unconditional positive self-regard and congruence exist that ' . . . the parent will realistically and *empathically* understand the child's *internal frame of reference and experience an unconditional positive regard for him*' (ibid., p. 88). Rogers identifies this theoretical statement as representing the theory of therapy process and outcome as well as the theory of interpersonal relationships (ibid.).

In essence, it is the therapist's way of being (UPSR) that begets the conditions. In reciprocation, the therapist's experience of empathic understanding and unconditional positive regard increases the unconditional self-regard of the therapist. There is, then, a viable conditions loop among these conditions.

CLINICAL CONSIDERATIONS

Does the way of therapist 'being' (that is, the embodiment of reasonable UPSR) mean that the therapist must be a paragon of perfection? Lietaer, for example, considers 'unconditionality' by therapists to be 'improbable' and asserts that there is a conflict between congruence and unconditionality. He contends that 'unconditionality calls upon the therapist for a devoted self-effacing that often leads to a compensatory reaction in which confrontation becomes a form of self-assertion' (Lietaer, 1984, p. 41). Such statements are simply untrue when congruence is viewed as a manifestation of UPSR. The therapist is not considered to be a perfect individual operating with UPSR at all times. The therapist simply holds a reasonable degree of UPSR during the therapy session.

Does being congruent mean that the therapist confronts, interprets, or offers her own views with intentions to help the client? Such an interpretation of congruence questions the viability of the attitudinal conditions and its fundamental nondirective quality. The remarkable resiliency of the individual's innate constructive force is propelled by UPR. A concrete example of a therapist's struggle with her UPSR is offered.

A THERAPIST'S STRUGGLE

A therapist who is considered quite effective by her clients discusses her personal struggle for UPSR. She reveals that she realizes her *conditional* positive regard for herself. She considers herself brilliant only when she accomplishes something specific. An older brilliant brother always overshadowed her. She cannot consider herself beautiful because a younger sister was more beautiful. Hence, it is often difficult for her to accept *unconditional* positive regard from others. In the therapy hour, she is able to experience UPR towards her clients. She is able to do this through (1) empathic understanding of the client's frame of reference, and (2) ability to set herself aside in the relationship as she accepts her organismic experiences. She is not distorting nor denying her feelings of conditional regard towards herself (in not feeling beautiful and brilliant). Ironically, her awareness and acceptance of her feelings of conditional regard increases her congruence. She is, in effect, experiencing UPSR in relation to her feelings of conditional positive self-regard. In addition, her intent to focus on the client's frame of reference helps her to experience varying degrees of empathic understanding of the client. In her words:

> Being unconditional to my clients helped me to be unconditional towards me . . . since when I was aware and accepted my feelings of conditionality towards me it changed my conditionality . . . I was able to be less conditional. Also being empathic with my clients helps me to be empathic with me (anonymous therapist, confidential communication, October, 2000).

Allowing herself to experience the client's frame of reference helps her to become more accepting of her own conditional attitudes, increasing her C and UPSR in the relationship.

Client scenarios

The following examples are selected in order to depict congruence in relationship. I offer my recall and interpretations on my congruence as the therapist. As such, they are extreme examples of therapeutic interactions. My congruence of the moment is often viewed as UPSR.

Eleanor

Eleanor was a hospitalized 'schizophrenic' whom I worked with in the late 1950s (Bozarth, 1998b). Here, the focus will be on my congruence and UPSR (albeit shaky) in the relationship.

Eleanor was on a locked ward sitting on the floor playing with her feces when I first met her. I still recall my trepidation about how I might help her in my role as a Psychiatric Rehabilitation Counselor. I was a psychotherapist for many of the 'patients' but was also expected to help them obtain training, find employment and eventually to function outside of the hospital. The initial session included an explanation of my job role including some of the training and employment resources. I did this sporadically as we sat on the floor in silence. I asked some basic questions like, 'How long have you been here?' and, 'Do you think you might like to explore possibilities of getting out of the hospital?' There was no response to any question. I was acutely aware of my words being attempts to dissipate some of my anxiety; aware of my tendency to want to 'get out of there' and aware of my discomfort with the odors of the ward. She did stop playing with her feces shortly after I introduced myself. I was also aware of my increasing desperation. I felt that she was aware of me but I could not be sure. I asked myself, 'Why am I asking these questions?' My only goal was to experience some sense of her frame of reference but I did not feel that I was accomplishing this with Eleanor. Near the end of the session, I made the 'spontaneous' statement: 'Do you think that you might want to go to Beauty School?' Immediately, I thought: 'Oh, no, why did I say that?' She did not respond. Shortly, I asked her if she would like for me to return in a few days. She nodded affirmatively. When I returned the next week, Eleanor was washed and neatly dressed. She was patiently waiting in a chair. We started to meet once a week. After a few sessions, she stated her desire to transfer to an unlocked ward. Eleanor was working on a job assignment in the hospital within a month. I do not think that she was ever dismissed from the hospital but her quality of life was significantly improved. I have always thought that my question about beauty school was a stimulant for her change; that is, that from this statement she felt validated as a worthwhile person. The statement reflected my congruence of the moment. My congruence was such that I was able to trust my spontaneous responses in the relationship. I could hold my trust of this severely dysfunctional individual by accepting my own considerable anxiety. My trust in Eleanor through unconditional acceptance increased my UPSR and congruence of the moment. I felt free to spontaneously be with Eleanor in murkiness and uncertainty.

Rose

Rose was a graduate student and client in a university counseling center. She entered therapy with the complaint that working, attending school and being a housewife was causing stress. She wanted to find a way to manage her life. She was very rational and expressed herself with little emotion. I interacted with primarily empathic understanding responses for over a half-dozen sessions. She went through details of her daily life including each activity in her housework, and with some pride, the detailed work on repairing her automobile. I noticed that I was not interested in some of her discussions and continuously had to re-establish my attention to her discourse. I was offering more empathic understanding responses than usual, perhaps as a way to keep myself connected with her. While I was pondering our interactions after one session, I became aware that I had been staring at her breasts during part of the session. I felt clear that I was not sexually attracted to her but was curious about this self-observation. The next session, I observed myself staring at her breasts and being distracted from listening to her. It was somewhat strange to me in that I was not aware of experiencing anything. I was observing my head turning to stare at her breasts. I was embarrassed and concerned about what was going on within me. I did talk with a colleague and felt clear that I was not reacting to Rose with sexual desire. My behavior continued the next session leading me to think that I might have to discuss the matter with her. I remember a couple of sessions where this aberrant behavior did not occur, and I continued to be curious but satisfied that it was over. Several sessions later, Rose discussed in detail her household budget. As she presented her detailed budget in a steady monotone, I was suddenly aware that I was again staring at her breasts. I rather abruptly interrupted her budget

194

delineation to tell her about my behavior. I still remember my fear that she would be insulted and might huff out of the session. As I finished telling her and was contemplating what else to say, Rose continued by switching from the discussion of her budget to a discussion of her bisexual feelings. She did this as though she were just continuing the budget discussion. She continued the following therapy sessions with meaningful discussion about her sexual identification. My gazing behavior was totally dissolved and my attention to her greatly increased. I believe that this was a subtle empathic experience of Rose's struggle with her sexual identity. I became aware of my incongruence when my body behaved in an unexpected way. My body, in a sense, was incongruent with my intention to focus on Rose's verbal messages. It was when I expressed this 'persistent feeling' (really persistent self-observation) to Rose that we were both free to pursue her open struggle of sexual identity. I believe that I held reasonable UPSR during this time, contrary to my conditional self-regard of thinking that I might be behaving in a nontherapeutic way. I accepted my organismic experience and behavior without distortion or denial. My awareness in this instance was expressed to Rose.

Florence
This example is that of a demonstration in a European person-centered training program. I agreed to do a demonstration through an interpreter. The night preceding the demonstration, I had a dream that a particular participant would volunteer, and even dreamed the sequence of the session. The dream sequence was that I responded to great emotional intensity and we ended the session on the floor, embraced and in tears. This dream was strange, in part, because I did not know any of the participants. Florence was the person who volunteered the next morning. She was the person who was in my dream. The demonstration was also strange in that the translations, which were literally accurate, did not fit with my 'gut level' (organismic?) experience of Florence. She was clearly 'stuck'. My varied responses were to my experience of her 'being stuck'. I periodically heard the other participants becoming restless, I assume at the lack of seeing any progress. When I saw tears in Florence's eyes, I felt reasonably certain that mentioning them would lead to the scenario of my dream. The session would be viewed as an intense and powerful success. However, my strongest inner experience was that of her 'stuckness' which was also her more literal communication. I focused on my image of a circle where she was going around and around without being able to break out of it. I stayed with this image, even told her my image, until the group finally got so restless that Florence decided to stop. The session appeared to be a dismal failure. Our post-session discussion with the group confirmed their restlessness. Florence said that she would not want to continue with me as therapist. I imagined Rogers and other therapists saying that they noticed the tears in her eyes and wondered why I followed this dogged determination to stay with her 'stuckness'. Surprisingly, Florence said that she would like to see me for a private session. She acknowledged her initial disappointment that I had not responded to her tears but that she was confirmed in my trust of her. She viewed herself as the person in the group who was the most emotional student in the training program. She was usually the person who volunteered for demonstrations. She always ended up emotional, felt some catharsis but was never

satisfied. She always felt worse later because of being viewed as unstable. She could never get through her struggle of being stuck. Her metaphor was that she would always end as the tearful person on the floor with everyone looking at her.

I do not know if this is the kind of experience that Rogers referred identified as transcendent. I felt that I did not succumb to a conditional self-regard generated by wishing to please the participants. I held my UPSR of the moment, and subsequently, was congruent in a way that freed me to go with the subtle inner struggle of Florence.

REFLECTIONS ON CLINICAL EXPERIENCES

My role as a therapist in the above therapeutic interactions might be summarized as 'naive' and 'noninterfering'. My conscious intentions were to have no pre-conceptions about what the person might do, be or become. My only intent for action is to experience the person's frame of reference. This means that I am open to the person's immediate view of the world including her feelings and ideas. This includes acceptance of murkiness as in Eleanor's world, or struggle with my own aberrant behaviors as in the relationship with Rose. It includes the extreme trust of the client's constructive inner motivation. I also do not want to impose anything including my empathic understanding on the client. I think that these intentions are shown in the above interactions. It seems to me that my unwavering trust in the other individual results in greater trust in myself. It is as though the more I trust the individual, the more I trust my own experiences in the relationship. The more I trust myself, the more I trust and experience the client. My trust in the client helps me to hold UPR towards him. In turn, it helps me to experience UPSR towards myself during the session. I am congruent to the extent that I accepted my observations of my own behavior as with Rose. I do not have any intention to share my experiences with the client but I am willing to share them when they are 'persistent', a term which Rogers used periodically when discussing congruence. I am also open to sharing my experiences if they are spontaneous with high intensity in myself. I never think about my UPSR or about congruence during sessions. My focus is upon the client's world with the intention of setting my self aside, or, perhaps, blending my self with the client's self. My only intention is to be with the client in her world, to be present to the client. Ideally, all of my specific behaviors and responses will emanate from this facet of our interaction. I am free to be a certain way in the relationship. This way is that of experiencing unconditional positive regard towards the client. Being this way, I feel free to 'do' many specific things out of my experience of the client's frame of reference. My clinical experience is that the conditions are one as I affirm the client's experiential world of the moment with UPR. My way of doing this is primarily by my dedication to the client's frame of reference. By knowing as far as possible the client's frame of reference, I enhance my UPR for the client and my own UPSR. My goal is to be myself at any given moment within the context of my experience of the other person. I am, at that moment, being a special way. It is a way of experiencing UPR and EU towards another person. *I want my very presence to embody the attitudes of UPR and EU.* It is, thus, that I am congruent in the embodiment of unconditional positive regard and empathic understanding.

196

TRAINING IMPLICATIONS

Training of client-centered therapists is remarkably simple and thoroughly demanding. The client-centered therapist must be a certain way. This way is propagated through UPSR. UPSR is promoted through the reception of UPR primarily through Empathic Understanding (EU). The goal of the client-centered trainer is to provide a training atmosphere that promotes the student's UPSR. This atmosphere is accomplished by empathic understanding of the therapist and assistance to help the student experience UPSR in therapy sessions. This goal is not different from the therapist's goal to create the necessary and sufficient conditions for the client. Other activities and goals of the trainer may be important but the sine qua non for the training of client-centered therapists is the trainers' UPSR manifested by the congruence and presence of the trainer who is dedicated to UPR and EU for their students. Learning to be empathic helps promote the UPSR of the student. More specifically, the conditions loop is replete in ideal client-centered training. The trainer experiencing UPSR begets the conditions of congruence, unconditional positive regard, and empathic understanding. This 'atmosphere' fosters UPSR in the student therapists that are manifested by the necessary and sufficient conditions toward their clients. These conditions in turn promote the UPSR in the students. In short, the client-centered trainer must also be a special way, a way propagated by her UPSR.

SUMMARY

Congruence can not exist without the integral relationship with unconditional positive regard and empathic understanding or client-centered therapy is threatened as a viable theory. The lack of clarity of Rogers' comments about congruence as the sole and most basic therapeutic condition has created a theoretical crisis for client-centered therapy. Rogers' comments and interpretations of his comments ignore the central axiom of client-centered therapy that the therapist must experience unconditional positive regard towards and empathic understanding of the client. It is the client's perception of these two conditions that fosters the client's actualization process.

Congruence is the manifestation of unconditional positive self-regard (UPSR) and can be identified as the therapist's presence in client-centered therapy. Unconditional positive regard towards and empathic understanding of the client's frame of reference characterize this presence. The only goal of the client-centered therapist is to be a certain way. This way of being entails being congruent in the relationship *in order* to experience unconditional positive regard towards, and empathic understanding of, the client's frame of reference. In order to embody these experiences, the therapist must hold a sufficient level of unconditional positive self-regard in the relationship. The conditions of unconditional positive regard and empathic understanding are manifestations of such self-regard. As such, they are also manifestations of the therapist's congruence.

It is speculated that there is a 'conditions loop' wherein congruence is a manifestation of unconditional positive self-regard but also that congruence is the stimulant for unconditional positive regard. Moreover, congruence as the acceptance of all of oneself at the moment fosters acceptance of all of the other person at the moment. As the therapist accepts the totality of the other person including the momentary frame of reference, the therapist accepts her own organismic experiences in the relationship. The therapist is 'open' to 'all' aspects of self and to 'all' aspects of the other person. The therapist is congruent. The therapist's higher level of UPSR allows the therapist's self to disappear in the unconditional acceptance of the client. The therapist is free to be herself in order to experience the client in a special way.

REFERENCES

Adomaitis, R. (1991). *On being genuine: a phenomenologically grounded study of the experience of genuineness and its place in client-centered therapy.* Unpublished Doctoral Dissertation, Northwestern University, USA.

Baldwin, M. (1987). Interview with Carl Rogers on the use of the self in therapy. In M. Baldwin and V. Satir (Eds.) *The Use of Self in Therapy.* New York: The Haworth Press. pp. 45–52.

Barrett-Lennard, G. T. (1998). *Carl Rogers' helping system: Journey and substance.* London: Sage.

Bozarth, J. D. (1984). Beyond reflection: emergent modes of empathy. In R. Levant, and J. Shlien (Eds.) *Client-centered therapy and the person-centered approach: new directions in theory, research, and practice.* New York: Praeger, pp. 59–75.

Bozarth, J. D. (1990) The evolution of Carl Rogers as a therapist. *Person-Centered Review,* 2(1), pp. 11–3.

Bozarth, J. D. (1996). A theoretical reconsideration of the necessary and sufficient conditions for therapeutic personality change. *The Person-Centered Journal,* 3(1), pp. 44–51.

Bozarth, J. D., (1997). Empathy from the framework of Client-Centered Theory and the Rogerian hypothesis. In A. Bohart, and L. Greenberg (Eds.) *Empathy Reconsidered: new directions in psychotherapy.* Washington D.C.: American Psychological Association, pp. 81–102,

Bozarth, J. D. (1998a). *Person-centered therapy: A revolutionary paradigm.* Ross on Wye: PCCS.

Bozarth, J. D. (1998b). Remembering Eleanor: A way of contact. *Person-Centered Journal,* 5(1), 36–8.

Bozarth, J. D. (2000). Non-directiveness in client-centered therapy: A vexed concept. Presentation at the *Eastern Psychological Association,* Baltimore, Md.

Bozarth, J. D., and Brodley, B. T. (1991). Actualization: A functional concept in client-centered psychotherapy: A statement. *Journal of Social Behavior and Personality,* 6(5), 45–59.

Brodley, B. T. (1990). Client-centered and experiential: two different therapies. In G. Lietaer, J. Rombauts, and R. Van Balen (Eds.) *Client-Centered and Experiential Therapies in the Nineties.* Leuven: Leuven University Press, pp. 87–107.

Brodley, B. T. (1993) Some observations of Carl Rogers' behavior in therapy interviews. *Person-Centered Journal,* 1(1), pp. 37-47.

Brodley, B. T. (1994). Some observations of Carl Rogers' behavior in therapy interviews. *Person-Centered Journal,* 1(2), pp. 37–48.

Brodley, B. T. (1995) Congruence and its relation to communication in Client-Centered Therapy and the Person-Centered Approach. *Unpublished paper, Illinois School of Professional Psychology/Chicago Counseling and Psychotherapy Center.* Reprinted in this volume.

Brodley, B. T. (1997). The nondirective attitude in client-centered therapy. *Person-Centered Journal,* 4(1), pp. 18–30.

Brodley, B. T. (1998). Congruence and its relation to communication in client-centered therapy. *Person-Centered Journal,* 5(2), pp. 83–116.

Brodley, B. T. (1999). About the nondirective attitude. *Person-Centered Practice,* 7(2), pp. 79–92.

Brodley, B. T. (2000). The actualizing tendency concept in client-centered theory. In D. Bower (Ed.) *The Person-Centered Approach: Applications for Living.* New York: Writers Club Press, pp. 81–103.

Brodley, B. T. (2001) Personal presence in client-centered therapy. *Person-Centered Journal,* 7(2), 139–49.

Brody, A. F. (1991). *Understanding client-centered therapy through interviews conducted by Carl Rogers.* Clinical Research Paper in partial fulfilment of requirements for the Doctor of

Psychology Degree in Clinical Psychology, Illinois School of Professional Psychology.

Ellingham, I. (1999). Carl Rogers' 'Congruence' as organismic; not a Freudian Concept. *Person-Centered Journal*, 6(2), pp. 121–40.

Gendlin, E. T. (1970). *Experiencing and the creation of meaning (2nd ed.)*. New York: Free Press.

Gendlin, E. T. (1990) The small steps of the therapy process. How they come and how to help them come. In G. Lietaer, J. Rombauts, and R. Van Balen (Eds.) *Client-centered and experiential psychotherapy in the nineties*. Leuven: Leuven University Press pp. 205–24.

Haugh, S. (1998) Congruence: A Confusion of Language. *Person-Centred Practice*, 6(1), pp. 44–50.

Kirschenbaum, H., and Henderson, V. (Eds.) (1989). *The Carl Rogers Reader*. Boston: Houghton Mifflin.

Lietaer, G. (1984). Unconditional positive regard: A controversial basic attitude in Client-Centered Therapy. In R. Levant, and J. Shlien (Eds.) *Client-centered therapy and the person-centered approach: new directions in theory; research, and practice*. New York: Praeger, pp. 41–58.

Lietaer, G. (1993). Authenticity, congruence and transparency. In D. Brazier (ed.) *Beyond Carl Rogers* London: Constable, pp. 17–46.

Merry, T. (1996). An analysis of ten demonstration interviews by Carl Rogers: implications for the training of client-centered counselors. In R. Hutterer, G. Pawlowsky, P.F.Schmid, and R. Stipsits (Eds). *Client-Centered and Experiential Therapy: A Paradigm in Motion*. Frankfurt am Main: Peter Lang, pp. 273–84.

Moon, K., Rice, B., and Schneider, C. (2001). Stanley W. Standal and the need for positive regard. In P. Wilkins, and J. D. Bozarth (Eds.) *Unconditional Positive Regard*. Ross-On-Wye: PCCS Books.

Patterson, C. H. (1969). Necessary and sufficient conditions for psychotherapy. *The Counseling Psychologist* 1(2), pp. 8–26.

Raskin, N. (1948). The development of nondirective therapy. *Journal of Consulting Psychology*, 12(94), pp. 92–110.

Rogers, C. R. (1939). *The clinical treatment of the problem child*. Boston: Houghton Mifflin.

Rogers, C. R. (1940). The process of therapy. *Journal of Consulting Psychology*, 4(5), pp. 161–4.

Rogers, C. R. (1951). *Client-centered therapy*. Boston: Houghton-Mifflin.

Rogers, C. R. (1954). The case of Mrs. Oak. In C. R. Rogers, and R. F. Dymond (Eds.) *Psychotherapy and personality change*. Chicago: University of Chicago Press.

Rogers, C. R. (1957). The necessary and sufficient conditions of therapeutic personality change. *Journal of Consulting Psychology*, 21, pp. 95–103.

Rogers, C. R. (1959). A theory of therapy, personality, and interpersonal relationships as developed in the client-centered framework. In S. Koch (Ed.) *Psychology: A study of science: Vol. 3 Formulation of the person and the social context*. New York: McGraw Hill, pp. 184–256.

Rogers, C. R. (1961). *On becoming a person*. Boston: Houghton Mifflin.

Rogers, C. R. (1963). The actualizing tendency in relation to 'motives' and to consciousness. In M. Jones (Ed.) *Nebraska Symposium on Motivation*. Lincoln: University of Nebraska Press.

Rogers, C. R. (1977). On personal power. New York: Delta.

Rogers, C. R. (1980). *A way of being*. Boston: MA: Houghton Mifflin.

Rogers, C. R. (1986). A client-centered/person-centered approach to therapy. In I. Kutash, and A. Wolfe (Eds.) *Psychotherapists' Casebook*. Jossey-Bass, pp. 197–208.

Rogers, C. R., Gendlin, G. T., Keisler, D. V., and Truax, C. B. (1967). *The Therapeutic Relationship and Its impact: A Study of Psychotherapy With Schizophrenics*. Madison: University of Wisconsin Press.

Rogers, C. R., and Sanford, R., (1984). Client-centered psychotherapy. In H. I. Kaplan, and B. J. Sadock (Eds.) *Comprehensive textbook of psychiatry IV.* Baltimore: Williams and Wilkins, pp.1374–88.

Shostrom, E. L. (Producer) (1964). Santa Ana, CA: Psychological films. (Film).

Standal, S. W. (1954). *The need for positive regard: A contribution to client-centered theory*. Unpublished doctoral dissertation, University of Chicago.

Truax, C. B., and Carkhuff, R. R. (1967). *Toward Effective Counseling and Psychotherapy: training and Practice*. Chicago: Aldine.

Wyatt, G. (2000a). The multifaceted nature of congruence. *Person-Centered Journal*, 7(1), pp. 52–68.

Wyatt, G. (2000b). Presence: Bringing together the core conditions. Paper presented at ICCCEP Conference in Chicago, USA.

199

13

On Congruence:
A Human System Paradigm
Jules Seeman

Recent essays on congruence have taken a turn toward greater breadth and inclusiveness. In my own thinking, I have linked the concept increasingly with an encompassing whole-person view. That development, together with my own increasing interest in human system models of personhood, leads me to explore in this chapter the meaning of congruence from a human system perspective.

Having staked out a theme for this paper, I wish to preface the paper with reflections on some of the early precursors of the idea of congruence. It is one of the older ideas in person-centered theory, and so it has a long history. Like many ideas in history, this idea emerged slowly, molded by time and honed by discussion.

EARLY STIRRINGS

Though the year 1956 marked the formal birthday of congruence as part of Rogers' paper on the necessary and sufficient conditions for psychotherapy, 1956 was in fact a year of synthesis rather than a year of beginnings. Ideas germinate in many ways, and their origins are often not clearly marked or even perceived. So it was with the idea of congruence. My own recollections about precursors to this concept constitute a mixture of oral history and early writings.

The year 1948 is a useful time to mark the beginnings of discussions concerning congruence in client-centered therapy. Up to that time this new therapy, variously called 'non-directive' and 'client-centered', was the object of basic exploration through the study of therapy process. Process studies of non-directive therapy were made possible because, in 1940, Rogers had introduced the use of verbatim phonographic recordings of therapy. That invention opened psychotherapy to a whole new level of research, a level that was avidly utilized by Rogers and his student-colleagues. That exploration addressed such basic questions as 'What is this new therapy like? What does the therapist do? What is the process of therapy like for clients?'

By 1948, new and more personal questions had begun to emerge. 'What really matters in psychotherapy? Who are we as therapists? What do we need to bring to the therapy hour?' Such questions suggested provocative issues that were beginning to emerge, issues concerning the internal processes of therapists themselves. Staff members spent many hours in informal discussions exploring these personal/professional issues. Ideas of personal integrity were explored, along with ideas of relational integrity. Soon the idea of an 'integrated relationship' was voiced, and its necessary dimensions explored at some length. These were heady days for the predominantly young staff members, as we recognized increasingly the personal demands required of us as therapists.

In 1948 a significant development took place. The Chicago Counseling Center had received funding to move in a new direction for therapy research. Virtually all of the research up to that time had dealt with therapy process issues. The staff and students were productive in this dimension, generating at least two dozen studies on therapy process. Interestingly enough, though there was a searching interest in therapy process, there had been no organized research in outcomes of therapy. Yet we knew that such a direction was a necessary part of a comprehensive program of therapy research, and so the funding was allotted for planning a program in therapy outcome.

As Coordinator of Research for this new program I felt a clear responsibility to define the way in which I conceptualized the outcomes of psychotherapy. The result was an unpublished in-house paper on therapist-client interaction and therapy outcomes (Seeman, 1951). The paper was published many years later (Seeman, 1994). In this paper I was concerned with the role of the therapist, and while we had not yet conceptualized the idea of congruence the paper did in fact deal with an early version of that phenomenon. One section of the paper was entitled *The Function of the Therapist*. Five activities were listed. The fifth item on the list turned out to be a version of congruence, as follows:[1]

> 5. The counselor acts in terms of his degree of integration as a person.

The paper went into some detail concerning the implications of this aspect of the counselor's function. It said that:

> We must then raise the question of the harmony between counselor personality and therapeutic method. For it is most likely that therapy will be more effective for any given counselor when his own ways of functioning are in accord with his inner organization — that is, when the methods he uses are congruent with his own beliefs, attitudes, and values. This is simply another way of saying that the therapist will function most effectively when he is integrated in his behavior as a therapist. What this means is that with regard to the formulation of the therapist's function and behavior we can assume some degree of variability which can best be understood in terms of the uniquely individual personality organization of the therapist, regardless of the theory and method he uses (Seeman, 1951, 1994).

ROGERS ON CONGRUENCE

As I have indicated, the concept of congruence did not spring full-blown into person-centered theory at any one time, but found its way into the theory gradually and in multiple contexts. Thus it is the case that if we are to understand the present theory-related place of congruence we need to keep in mind its multiple contexts.

The first context in which Rogers introduced the concept of congruence was

---

[1] The early papers I quote here used the masculine pronoun form as the norm.

in connection with his systematic presentation of personality theory in his 1951 book *Client-Centered Therapy* (Rogers, 1951*)*. In one section of the theory he was describing and depicting the changes in personality that occurred as a consequence of therapy. Because his presentation was so central to the theory and to his use of *congruent* I have chosen here to describe and depict the process in some detail.

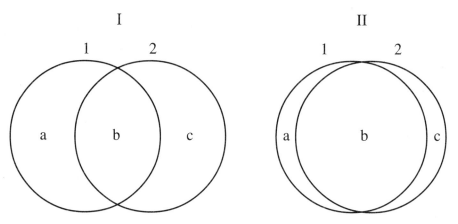

Figure 1. *Depicting two levels of congruence according to the theory — i.e., the circle pair Roman I depicts low self-congruence and the circle pair Roman II depicts high self-congruence. In a sense we can consider the figure Roman I a pre-therapy self and Roman II a post-therapy self.*

In the theory statement Rogers proposed, there were essentially two aspects of self. There was on the one hand the total of all experiences that the person had, or what I shall call the Experiential Self (the Arabic number *1* in each set of circles). There was also a matrix of self-definition, a Self-Concept, that the person evolved over time from these experiences (the Arabic number *2* in each set of circles). A relatively low degree of congruence existed when the person developed a self-concept that denied or distorted aspects of experience (circle set Roman *I*). A high degree of congruence between the two aspects of self existed when the person was able to accept all or most of her/his experiences as aspects of the self- concept (circle set Roman *II*).

Further components of the diagram are as follows: segment *a* of the circles represents those aspects of the Experiential Self that the person cannot admit into awareness; segment *b* represents those aspects of experience that are admitted to awareness. Rogers' own description of segment *b* is as follows: 'Within this portion of the phenomenal field the concept of self and self-in-relationship is in accord with, or is *congruent* with, the evidence supplied by sensory and visceral experiences' (1951, p. 525; italics supplied). Segment *c* represents those aspects of the Self-Concept that do not come from the person's experience but come from attributes and values that are introjected from the influence of significant others.

We find a second mention of congruence later on (p. 530), where Rogers was describing the post-therapy self (Roman II circles). He said, 'The definitions of the circles and areas remain unchanged, but it is evident that they have a different relationship to each other, the structure of the self now being much more *congruent* with the sensory and visceral experience of the individual' (italics supplied).

THE NECESSARY AND SUFFICIENT CONDITIONS

The initial statement on this topic came five years later through the production of a paper by Carl Rogers in the year 1956. The paper first appeared in pre-publication form as a Counseling Center Discussion Paper (Rogers, 1956). Counseling Center Discussion papers constituted a valuable forum for in-house communication of significant ideas among the staff of the University of Chicago Counseling Center. Often the papers were subsequently published in national journals. This was the case for Rogers' paper. The paper was published formally the next year in one of the APA journals (Rogers, 1957). In this paper the concept of congruence was presented as one of the necessary and sufficient conditions of therapeutic personality change.

The 1957 publication by Rogers of the paper on necessary and sufficient conditions generated a surprising degree of national interest. The idea that there might be specific conditions available in the service of effective therapy was a most intriguing and attractive idea for psychologists in these relatively early days of therapy research. As a result, the paper generated hundreds of research studies and much discussion.

One of the consequences of Rogers' paper was to focus such strong attention upon a specific application of the concept of congruence — i.e., its application to a condition for personality change in psychotherapy — that in many ways the broader meaning and significance of the concept was, for a time, lost. Eventually, however, this fact was discerned, and a number of writers in the person-centered community have more recently begun to go beyond the concept of congruence as one of the conditions of positive personality change, and move to emphasize the broader context of congruence. For example, Bozarth (1998) has written an extensive and illuminating chapter presenting multiple perspectives in which congruence has been examined. Wyatt (2000) also has pointed out the multifaceted nature of the concept.

Ellingham (1999) has put forth a fundamental critique of the concept itself as it has been defined by Rogers. His argument is based on an examination of broad historic movements in the development of scientific paradigms. Specifically, Ellingham argued that Rogers' definition of congruence was based on an obsolescent Cartesian-Newtonian paradigm that is mechanistic in character rather than a holistic organismic paradigm that has more recently arisen from field theory, general systems theory, and eco-psychology.

AN ALTERNATIVE DEFINITIONAL BASE: THE HUMAN SYSTEM MODEL

What I wish to do in this section is to put forth a human system model that I have evolved in my own work, and that may offer an alternative view of congruence.

In order to relate the concept of congruence to the human system model, I will need first to trace the development of the human system model itself as it evolved for me in my own work. Consequently, what follows next may seem like a detour away from congruence but will provide an explanatory link to this concept.

The development of the human system model was, for me, a long slow process. It began with my 1951 paper. In that paper I defined the potential outcome of psychotherapy as 'the return to organic order or integration'. I later changed the term 'organic order' to 'organismic integration', which I define as 'the adaptive and self-enhancing interaction among the behavioral subsystems of the person' (Seeman, 1983, p. 42). These behavioral subsystems are depicted in Figure 2 below. As you may note, this definition encompasses a whole-person idea together with an allusion to personal integration. I could not know at the time that this simple statement, and in particular the term 'organic order', would be, for the next 25 years or more, the most important guide to my own research and the research of students who worked with me.

The amplification of the concept of organismic integration required the development of two related concepts: first, it was necessary to evolve a framework that encompassed the whole person; second, it was necessary at the same time to devise a means by which it was possible to study the more detailed characteristics of the integrated person. At first I worked piecemeal on this task of joining the whole and the parts, but something kept seeming incomplete. Soon I began seeing more clearly the relationships that held the various studies together. What I ultimately evolved was a human system model. The model has turned out to be a uniquely useful choice. It not only fulfilled the foregoing two requirements, but also supplied a useful structure for added understanding of psychotherapy.

It is time now to get to the heart of the human system structure and see how it serves to hold and guide our understanding of the person. Figure 2 depicts the human system model (from Seeman, 1989). It is important to note that the model satisfies the twin objectives of having both a whole-person encompassing model and one that attends to subsystems or part processes. The vertical structure in the model details the major subsystems of the person. The arrows between the subsystems depict the transactional interlocking and interdependence of the subsystems. The horizontal dimension indicates the timebound processes that characterize our development.

An elegant two-word definition of such a system has been offered by Angyal (1941). He used the term *unitas multiplex*. The human system is on the one hand an incredibly complex and multifaceted entity. There are many levels of system structure, ranging from individual cells to interpersonal functioning and indeed to the person in an ecological context, and all levels in between. At the same time, the system is also a unitary entity. What is it that makes it possible for a system to be both multiplex and unitary? The answer to this question consists of two concepts that hold the key to the nature of a system. The concepts are *connection* and *communication*. These two concepts are so central to the understanding of system functioning that I hope to explain and illustrate them in enough detail to make clear how they define us as human beings.

I will start with the concept of connection. No matter how complex the system is, or how many components it contains, not one component stands alone as an independent entity. A human system has untold billions of cells, yet not a single one of these cells is independent. Bohm (1981) has described this interconnectedness thus: 'Each part grows in the context of the whole, so that it does not exist independently, nor can it be said that it merely "interacts" with the other, without itself being essentially affected in this relationship'. Bohm makes an important point here when he tells us that the components are so closely linked that the influence of one component can change the way that another component might function.

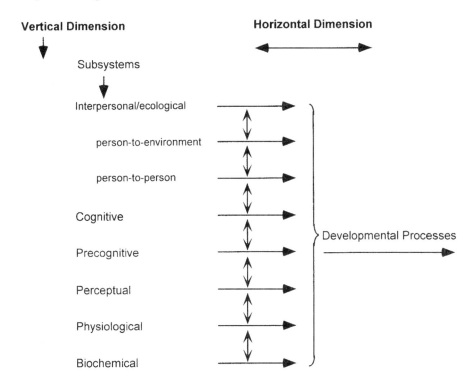

Figure 2. *The Human-System Health Structure*

There is another illustration of system connectedness that I have found particularly intriguing. We know that thoughts can lead to action on the part of a person. How does our organismic structure make that process possible? The structural basis for the process is located in our hypothalamus. In that organ there is a unique conjunction of two kinds of molecular structures, neurons governing thought and endocrine cells governing actions. These two processes can be activated jointly because in the hypothalamus there is a unique combination of these two types of cells. The cells are referred to as *neuroendocrine* cells. These cells combine the two properties that jointly support both thought and action, helping us see concrete ways in which connectedness serves vital functions.

The foregoing description illustrates a way in which communication comes into play and also how the twin concepts of connection and communication serve each other. What we see is that the connectedness of the neuroendocrine cells permits the flow of communication between thought and action. In this illustration we can define the cell connectedness as *structure* and the resulting flow of information through these cells — i.e., the communication process — as *function.* Thus we see the way in which structure and function serve each other.

The description of hypothalamus structure and function serves as but one of many possible illustrations of characteristic organismic functioning in which connection and communication serve as reciprocal interlocking processes. Other illustrations are readily evident. Several years ago, Nobel Prize winner Edmund H. Fischer presented a paper entitled 'How cells "talk"' (Scanlan, 1997). Fischer discussed the nature of intercellular communication and emphasized the way in which cell structure was designed to facilitate transport of information between cells. There are multiple built-in linkages in cells that foster passage of electrochemically coded information in the form of neurotransmitters that make such communication possible. We may tend to think of communication in terms of verbal processes but, in fact, communication pervades our entire human system at every subsystem level. Ruesch and Bateson (1951) have emphasized this point in their statement that 'A person's organism as a whole can be conceived of as an instrument of communication' (p. 29).

A striking illustration of this process, this time in more molar terms, is evident through the work of Bowlby (1980). He points out that the neonate, very early in life, displays biologically given communicative behaviors like crying and smiling. These behaviors communicate the baby's needs to caregivers and thus enhance the baby's attachment to its caregivers, with its consequent adaptive value.

OPTIMAL FUNCTIONING IN THE HUMAN SYSTEM

Having provided a description of the way in which the human system functions, we are in a position now to apply these concepts to a view of optimal organismic functioning, or to what Rogers has called the 'fully functioning person'. As I develop this view I will call upon both conceptual and empirical information to provide us with a pathway in thinking about congruence.

A number of writers have ventured descriptions of optimal functioning. Brody (1973) and Schwartz (1983) both described the attributes of healthy human systems. Brody suggested that for optimal functioning of the system, 'Each of the component systems on each hierarchical level must be intact and functioning. All feedback loops must be intact and free from excessive noise or impedance to signal flow' (p. 76). If we translate the technical language, we can say that Brody is describing a person who has an effective organismic communication system, free from dysfunction. Schwartz made a similar argument, and added an emphasis on the idea that internal feedback loops provide self-regulation and resources for self-correction. He added that when adequate information and self-regulation are in place, a state of health may be said to exist.

At this point I would like to supplement the foregoing conceptual discussions concerning organismic integration with empirical studies that support and confirm the thrust of these conceptual statements. Since the empirical work was done within the human system model we may expect to see in these studies the following guiding principles of the model:

1. The underlying unity of a complex system. This principle is illustrated by the fact that the phenomenon of effective functioning is evident at all levels of organismic functioning, from biochemical to interpersonal.
2. The twin phenomena of connection and communication are evident at all levels of organismic functioning, from the single cell to international discourse.

The first study to be described here is a study that engages the physiological and cognitive subsystems (Cooley and Seeman, 1982). The study concerns effective use of feedback information. The major hypothesis of the study was that highly effective persons would utilize biofeedback information more effectively than less effective persons. Two groups of students were selected, one group designated as highly effective in personality integration and the other group designated as average. The selection measure was a well-validated self-concept scale (the Tennessee Self-Concept Scale) that could differentiate levels of positive functioning. The task requested of the participants was to increase their body temperature as measured by a thermometer attached to their index fingers. Feedback as to their temperature changes was provided to the research participants by an auditory tone that beeped with a higher tone as temperature increased and a lower tone when temperature decreased. We thus have here a task that called for integration of information from two different behavioral subsystems: the physiological subsystem dealing with body temperature and the perceptual/cognitive subsystems dealing with auditory feedback information. Human system theory proposes that the higher functioning persons would be more able to integrate the different levels of information flow to raise their temperatures. The results of the study indicated that the high group was in fact significantly more able to raise their temperatures than was the case for the average group, thus supporting the human system premise of the linkage between high information flow and high organismic integration.

The next study emphasizes both cognitive and interpersonal processes. The human system model proposes that, with respect to cognitive processes, high functioning persons can utilize their intellective resources in effective ways as, for example, in planning and problem solving. In the interpersonal domain the twin processes of connection and communication are generally quite directly evident.

The study that I report here is a study of play behavior of high and low functioning seven- and eight-year-old children (Seeman, 1983). The purpose of the study was to assess cognitive and interpersonal aspects of the child's behavior. The sample consisted of eight high-functioning children and eight low-functioning children. Each child had ten sessions of individual play; a therapist was in the room with the child. An observer in the adjoining room filled out a rating scale eight times during the session. Thus we had a total of 80 ratings for each child, or 640 ratings on each scale item for each group of eight children.

The assessment of cognitive processes was done with an item that we called 'theme development'. The item assessed the degree to which the child engaged in sequential activity that involved spontaneous and meaningful narrative or theme development. There was a five-point scale continuum that went from 'fragmentary unorganized play', through the midpoint 'clear sequence and structure of theme', to 'perseverative repetitive organization'. The high-functioning children, as a group, scored right at the point showing a high degree of theme development. There was very little variability in the ratings for the high group. Each of the children in the high-functioning group showed a freedom and flexibility in their play behavior, along with an enjoyment of the session's activities.

The ratings of the low-functioning group stood out in sharp contrast. The variability in range of theme development among these children was ten times as great as the composite ratings in the high group. Thirty per cent of the low group's ratings were in the category 'perseverative'. These children seemed mired in a repetitive activity that they could not leave.

The measurement of interpersonal behavior between the two groups also showed sharp contrasts. Our observations indicated that virtually all of the children in the low group related to the adult in conflictual ways. They tested limits and behaved with recurrent hostility. The high-functioning children were expressive in their behavior and in their communication with the adult in the room. They displayed virtually no need to test limits or to act in oppositional ways, yet they were also not obeisant or deferential. One of the strongest contrasts was in the quality of the child-adult relationships. The low group acted in a vertical hierarchical style while the high group acted in a horizontal equalitarian style.

I will mention only briefly here that the orientation toward a horizontal equalitarian style in contrast to a vertical status-oriented style of interpersonal behavior appears to characterize high-functioning persons. The horizontal style showed itself also in a very different study, this time with college students. We found that, in a group of high-functioning college students, eighty per cent of the group displayed an exclusively horizontal mode of functioning while in a contrasting average group of college students less than half of the group showed exclusively horizontal functioning (Seeman, 1983).

The final study that I will report here is a study of congruence done by Andrew Swan (1970). He proposed that persons who display a self-concept in which they accept, trust, and value themselves would also behave interpersonally in ways that would be seen as highly accepting and effective. More specifically, Swan proposed that in an intensive encounter group where persons came to know each other well, the higher functioning participants would be recognizable by others in the group as behaving more fully in terms of Rogers' necessary and sufficient conditions of therapeutic personality change. In human system terms, Swan's hypothesis was that within-person functioning and interpersonal functioning are connected aspects of a larger unity of functioning, and that such connectedness would be revealed in communication processes. There is also another fascinating implication embedded in Swan's hypothesis, namely, the proposition that the behaviors of empathy, unconditional positive regard, and congruence are not limited to psychotherapy, but extend in a much broader way to human relationships in general.

With respect to Swan's procedures, he assessed personal functioning through the use of the Tennessee Self Concept Scale. This is a simple 100-item self-description measure. Given its simplicity, it has turned out to be a remarkably accurate instrument for measuring all levels of personal functioning. For the assessment of the participants' extent to which they met the three 'necessary and sufficient' conditions, Swan composed the following three-item peer rating scale which he administered to the 16 group members:

On a blank sheet, list your nominations of persons in the group as follows:

1. The three persons who are most able to understand the feelings of others and are also able to communicate this understanding to them.
2. The three persons who most often demonstrate warm, positive, affectional, unqualified regard for others.
3. The three persons who are most congruent, completely honest, direct, and genuine in what they communicate to others.

In his data analysis, Swan divided the group into two equal halves on the basis of their self-concept scores. (These scores were not known to any of the group members.) Swan then compared the higher half and lower half in terms of the number of times each person was nominated for the three conditions. The results indicated that, for all three conditions, the group members in the upper half were named significantly more often than those in the lower half with regard to the three items. These results support both the human system premises of an underlying unity in personal integration and the premise that the 'conditions' are sufficiently broadly based to extend to recognizable interpersonal relationships in general.

ORGANISMIC INTEGRATION

There were many other studies that my student-colleagues and I did in order to describe high-functioning persons through the use of the human system model. The studies as a whole gave me an opportunity to construct a composite picture of persons high in organismic integration. Here is what I concluded from these studies:

Psychologically integrated persons affirm themselves. They have a core sense of self which they like, respect, and trust. And that makes all the difference. Persons who understand and trust their basic organismic self can listen to their own signals. They do not have the same need to screen, shut out, deflect, or distort signals in a way that characterizes more vulnerable persons. For the integrated person this ability to receive and process the data of their immediate experience results in the optimal receipt of information . . . because they can process and integrate the information more fully as their behavioral subsystems function more congruently, in a harmonized and undistorted rhythm.

This capacity which I have just described, this ability to receive and process the reality data of their world, has portentous effects for the integrated person. Reality data serve as psychological nutrition, fully as important to the psychological organism as food is to the biological organism. This ability to take in and assimilate reality data serves to maintain, to regulate, and to nourish the organism in its transactions with the environment (Seeman, 1983, pp. 233–5).

THE LINK WITH ROGERS' WORK ON CONGRUENCE AND THE FULLY FUNCTIONING PERSON

One of Rogers' abiding interests was in the understanding of positive human potentialities. He showed this interest in many ways, including formulations of such phenomena in his theoretical writings (e.g., 1951) and in separate papers. In this connection, I want to allude here to one paper in particular. In early 1953, Rogers returned from a vacation in the Caribbean with the draft of a new paper in which he envisioned what a person might be like after a successful experience in psychotherapy. He entitled the paper 'The Concept of the Fully Functioning Person'. He summarized his description of such a person as follows:

> He is making use of all his organic equipment to sense, as accurately as possible, the existential situation within and without. He is using all of the data his nervous system can thus supply, using it in awareness, but recognizing that his total organism may be, and often is, wiser than his awareness. He is able to permit his total organism to function in all its complexity . . . He is a fully functioning organism, and because of the awareness of himself which flows freely in and through his experiences, he is a fully functioning person (Rogers, 1963, pp. 21–2).

It may be of interest to compare the two foregoing descriptions of effective human functioning — i.e., Rogers' and mine. You will undoubtedly note the striking similarity between the two descriptions. It may also be useful to remember that my summary was based on 25 empirical studies, while Rogers' was based solely on his clinical experience. Yet the two descriptions are essentially identical in their central emphases, namely, their accent on communication that maximizes awareness of one's self and his or her world. It is, in my view, a tribute to Rogers' clinical wisdom that he could anticipate what extensive research would reveal 30 years after his paper was written.

I want to dwell a bit further on Rogers' paper because there are some interesting sidelights to its existence. First, you may notice the ten-year discrepancy between the completion of the paper in 1953 and its publication in 1963. Rogers had submitted the paper to several journals and had received rejections, along with polite suggestions to write the paper in more traditional ways. The politeness came about because Rogers had become a nationally known psychologist by then. But the paper was too daring and too little dependent on empirical data to be acceptable to conventional editors. It was not until 1963, when Gene Gendlin became editor of the journal *Psychotherapy*, that the paper came into the hands of an understanding editor and was published.

Another interesting sidelight for me was based on the reference list that Rogers had cited in his paper. The paucity of research in the area had resulted in a list of only three references in addition to Rogers' own work. In my early examination of these three references, I noted particularly a reference to Krech (1949). Krech's paper was entitled 'Notes Toward a Psychological Theory'. I looked up the paper and noticed that it dealt with what Krech had called 'dynamic systems'. Since I had by then become interested in systems theory myself, I was particularly interested in the reason for Rogers' inclusion of that particular reference in such

210

a short reference list. I asked Rogers why he had included Krech's paper. His reply was that he, too, was attracted to system theory and indeed had considered casting his paper in a system theory frame, but in the end decided not to do so.

However, for me that view strengthened my own sense of legitimacy in using the human system model to conceptualize organismic integration.

CONCLUSION

This chapter set out on a search for the roots of congruence. What we have found is that when we are at our best as humans we have a harmonious rhythm of connection and communication throughout our organism. It becomes evident, then, that congruence is an integral aspect of organismic integration. The fully functioning person is a congruent person. This congruence involves a directness and harmony, a free flow of communication, within our whole being at all levels of functioning, from biochemical processes up through interpersonal relationships.

The foregoing formulation of congruence may help to explain some of the debates and disagreements that we find in discussions of the meaning of congruence. The use of a human system model helps us to view congruence from a variety of contexts. It is possible, for example, to view congruence from an intrapersonal context where in system terms we are focusing on the person's internal congruence or harmony among the person's subsystems. We may also choose to view congruence within an interpersonal context where we are focusing on the congruity in the interpersonal communication process. Neither context invalidates the other. Each perspective is a part process within the context of the whole. This formulation may obviate the need to decide whether congruence is a within-person process or a between-person process. In my judgment they are both valid perspectives and may be used in multiple ways and from multiple perspectives. It depends on the context within which we are working at any given time.

Finally, I wish here to indicate the centrality of congruence as it relates to psychotherapy process and outcome. I have indicated earlier that the fully functioning person may be defined from a human system perspective in terms of a free flowing and congruent connection and communication. Person-centered theory proposes that the outcome of psychotherapy may be defined in similar terms. But it is also the case, perhaps less noticed, that the process of therapy itself engages those very same elements. As therapists we know that we must remain in *connection* with our clients, and we do so through empathic *communication*. These are the two processes we emphasize as therapists. We thus see that congruence is more than just one of the necessary and sufficient conditions of therapy with clients. It is a broad-based construct that describes who we are and who we may become both as therapists and as persons.

REFERENCES

Angyal, A. (1941). *Foundations for a science of personality*. New York: The Commonwealth Fund.

211

Bohm, D. (1981). *Wholeness and the implicate order.* London: Routledge and Kegan Paul.

Bozarth, J. (1998). *Person-centered therapy: A revolutionary paradigm.* Ross-on-Wye: PCCS Books.

Bowlby, J. (1980). *Attachment and loss: Vol. 3: Loss, sadness and depression.* New York: Basic Books.

Brodley, B.T. (1998). Congruence and its relation to communication in client-centered therapy. *The Person-Centered Journal,* 5(2), pp. 83–116.

Brody, H. (1973). The system view of man. *Perspectives in biology and medicine,* Autumn, pp. 71–92.

Cooley, R. S., and Seeman, J. (1982). Personality integration and maximal use of biofeedback information. *American Journal of Clinical Biofeedback,* 5, pp. 111–22.

Ellingham, I (1999). Carl Rogers' 'congruence' as an organismic; not a Freudian concept. *The Person-Centered Journal,* 6(2), pp. 121–40.

Krech, D. (1949). Notes toward a psychological theory. *Journal of Personality, 18,* pp. 66–87.

Rogers, C.R. (1951). *Client-centered therapy: Its current practice, implications, and theory.* Boston: Houghton Mifflin.

Rogers, C.R. (1956). The necessary and sufficient conditions of therapeutic personality change. Unpublished Counseling Center Discussion Papers, University of Chicago Counseling Center. Subsequently revised and published 1957.

Rogers, C.R. (1957). The necessary and sufficient conditions of therapeutic personality change. *Journal of Consulting Psychology,* 21, pp. 95–103.

Rogers, C.R. (1963). The concept of the fully functioning person. *Psychotherapy,* 1, pp. 17–26.

Ruesch, J and Bateson, G. (1951). *Communication: The social matrix of psychiatry.* New York: Norton.

Scanlan, M. (1997, April). How cells 'talk', subject of Sutherland lecture. *Vanderbilt University Medical Center Reporter.*

Schwartz, G.E. (1983). Behavioral medicine and system theory. *National Forum,* 4, pp. 25–30.

Seeman, J. (1951). Conceptual analysis of client and counselor activity in client-centered therapy. Unpublished Counseling Center Discussion Papers, University of Chicago Counseling Center. Subsequently revised and published 1994.

Seeman, J. (1983). Personality integration: Studies and reflections. Nashville, TN: Counselor Recordings and Tests.

Seeman, J. (1984). The fully functioning person: Theory and research. In R. Levant and Shlien, J. (Eds) *Client-centered therapy and the person-centered approach: New directions in theory, research and practice.* New York: Praeger pp. 131–52.

Seeman, J. (1989). Toward a model of positive health. *American Psychologist, 44,* 1099–109.

Seeman, J. (1994). Conceptual analysis of client and counselor activity in client-centered therapy. *Person-Centered Journal,* 1(1), pp. 15–20.

Swan, A. C. (1970). *Personality integration and perceived behavior in a sensitivity training group.* Unpublished doctoral dissertation, George Peabody College, Nashville, TN.

Wyatt, G. (2000). The multifaceted nature of congruence. *The Person-Centered Journal,* 7(1), pp. 52–68.

212

14   **Authenticity: the Person as His or Her Own Author. Dialogical and Ethical Perspectives on Therapy as an Encounter Relationship. And Beyond.**

Peter F. Schmid

Abstract. *Authenticity essentially is an encounter attitude. In the context of the anthropological meaning of 'person' from a dialogical perspective, it designates a human being as the genuine author of his or her relationships, both to him- or herself (openness) and to other persons (transparency). Being authentic is a precondition to enter dialogue — the way of communicating between persons where the other is truly acknowledged as an Other (in the sense of encounter philosophy), who is opening up, revealing him- or herself. Thus, in an epistemological perspective, it is the foundation of personal and facilitative communication. From an ethical point of view, authenticity is the response-ability which answers the call to respond to another person's needs, whether in therapy, or in any personal relationship. To be authentic is a particular challenge, if we take account of the idea that in practice there is not one (idealistic) 'I-Thou-relationship', but rather that relationships are always embedded in groups, and in society as a whole. This also implies the need for applying judgement to find one's own stance and at the same time acknowledging each as an autonomous being. In this way, the 'We-perspective' of encounter, and presence in the dialectical play of 'being-with' and 'being-counter', is opened up with profound therapeutic, social and political consequences.*

> *This above all: to thine own self be true,*
> *And it must follow as the night the day,*
> *Thou canst not then be false to any man.*
> (Shakespeare *Hamlet*, Act I, Scene 3)

Congruence, as one of the basic therapeutic conditions, has been described many times by Carl Rogers and other person-centred theoreticians.[1] Such descriptions were mainly from a therapeutic perspective and referred to it as a *condition* with a facilitative impact in counselling and similar relationships. From the point of view of personal or dialogical anthropology[2] and ethics, the attitude which Rogers

---

Acknowledgement: I am very grateful to Gill Wyatt and Pete Sanders for their help in making the text understandable to the English reader.
1. E.g. Rogers, 1961, 1970, 1980, 1986; Wood, 1988; Tausch and Tausch, 1990; Thorne, 1991; Lietaer, 1993; Finke, 1994.
2. Footnote 2 appears overleaf.

213

called, among other things, congruence, genuineness or realness, is generally a *fundamental characteristic* of being and becoming a person, and so is much more than a therapeutic attitude or condition. In this chapter, I will consider this view in detail and look at some of the consequences for therapy and human communication in general.[3]

THE HUMAN BEING AS A PERSON — THE UNIQUE 'PERSON'-CENTRED PERSPECTIVE

Whatever other motives might have been important in introducing the term 'person-centred' — it is obvious and clear that this was done consciously and on purpose to denote an anthropology central for the 'person'-centred approach. As described earlier (Schmid 1991, 1998b, 1998c) the term 'person' denotes a specific view of the human being, thoroughly developed and elaborated in the Jewish-Christian tradition and hence in occidental theology and philosophy. It combines two unrenounceable dimensions of human existence: the substantial or individual aspect of being a person and the relational or dialogical aspect of becoming a person. Both of these ways of understanding the human being are contrary, even conflicting, yet it is exactly this tension of autonomy and interconnectedness (or relationality), independence and interdependence, self-reliance and commitment, sovereignty and solidarity, which uniquely characterises the human. Also it can clearly be shown that the meaning of the term 'person' in the original and genuine person-centred context precisely refers to these two dimensions which may be characterised by the catchwords 'actualising tendency' and 'fully functioning person' on the one hand and 'relationship' and 'encounter' on the other hand. Furthermore this anthropological stance, well elaborated by phenomenology and personalistic (or dialogic or encounter) philosophy, is the distinctive characteristic of person-centred understanding, thinking and action.

In 1955 Rogers had already given a process definition to the question 'What is a person?' Already, here, relationality and individuality can be very clearly found as the two characteristics of the person:

> [A] fluid process, potentiality, a continually changing constellation, configuration, matrix of feelings, thoughts, sensations, behaviours. The structure of the process seems configurational, not additive. . . Another way of stating this is that a person is a human process of becoming . . . The person as process seems to me most deeply revealed in a relationship of the most ultimate

---

2. Personal or dialogical anthropology refers to twentieth century encounter philosophy (Martin Buber, Ferdinand Ebner, Franz Rosenzweig, Emmanuel Levinas, Romano Guardini, Paul Tillich, Bernhard Welte, Eberhard Grisebach, Fridolin Wiplinger, Gabriel Marcel, Maurice Merleau-Ponty, Maurice Nédoncelle, Alain Finkielkraut, Frederik J. J. Buytendijk, Michael Theunissen and many others) rooted in the Jewish-Christian tradition and philosophical orientations deriving from it. It is characterised by a view of the image of the human person who from the very beginning of their life as a fellow human being must be understood in a relational context. It also has a commitment to the person-to-person (intersubjective) point of view as opposed to an objectivistic thinking which treats the other in the traditional scientific way as an object.
3. Thus 'authenticity' is used in a wider sense as a basic characteristic of genuinely being a person, not only in its aspect as a therapeutic condition.

and complete acceptance; a real I–Thou relationship. [...] In my experience, the deepest contacts I have with persons reveal them, without exception, to be directional in process, and my experience of that direction is contained in such terms as positive, constructive, creative, toward autonomy, toward maturity, toward socialisation, in the direction of growth, toward greater richness or differentiation (Rogers, 1955, pp. 1–2; cf. also Schmid, 1994, p. 107).

In the substantialistic[4] as well as in the relationalistic[5] conception of the person we find important approaches which render it impossible for a current point of view to regress to earlier conceptions. If the substantialistic approach underlines *what* the person is, then the relationalistic approach accentuates *how* this person has become a person. From the very beginning, the human being is an individual person and from the very beginning he or she is related in personal community with others. It is only through the relationships with other persons that he develops and actualises his being as a person: he becomes a personality. Thus essential elements of the person are both, independence *and* dependence on relationships, sovereignty *and* commitment, autonomy *and* solidarity. Only in the dialectic of both interpretations, not in an 'either–or', but in a 'both–and' does the mystery of the person become accessible to whoever allows himself or herself to become involved in a relationship from person to person. A conception gained from these two perspectives of the person contrasts with a privatistic conception of the human being just as it does with a collectivistic one.

For many years Rogers himself dealt more with the individual aspect of the person in a theoretical sense, emphasising the person as a unique and not-to-be-directed individual in therapy. It was only later that he concentrated more and more on the relational dimension. Furthermore, he did not document this in the structured way he wrote about the substantial aspect of the individual in the therapeutic relationship in his earlier writing. Nevertheless, contact and relationship were a central category of his anthropology from the very beginning (cf. Schmid, 2001c), and the formulation of the 'necessary and sufficient conditions of therapeutic personality change' could never have taken place without it.

To sum it up: the dialectic basic axiom in person-centred anthropology is the actualising tendency as the force of the individual embedded in the interconnectedness, the social nature of the person. Both strands of the axiom form the foundations of the understanding of personalisation — of authentically 'becoming a person' (Rogers 1961).

---

4. The substantialistic (or individualistic) conception of the person was first defined by *Boëthius* (480–525 AD): 'Persona est rationalis naturae individua substantia [the person is the indivisible substance of a rational being]'. Substance derives from 'sub–stare' which literally means 'achieving a standing position from below', which therefore means standing by oneself, being based upon oneself and thus implies autonomy and independence.
5. The relationalistic notion was defined by *Richard of St. Victor* (died 1173 AD) in the tradition of patristic theology: he understood the person as 'naturae intellectualis existentia incommunicabilis [incommunicable existence of an intellectual nature]'. Here, person is not conceived as a sub-sistence, but as an ek-sistence, as coming into being from outside ('ex'), through others, as standing opposite to others. Therefore, a person is he or she who has become himself or herself precisely through others, which implies interdependence, solidarity and responsibility.

AUTHENTICITY: OPENNESS AND TRANSPARENCY

Two of the terms used to describe the way of being and becoming a person are 'genuineness' which mainly refers to the substantial aspect and 'congruence'[6] which also refers to the relational dimension.[7] The term 'congruence' as such shows that there always has to be a relationship before we can make sense when talking about (something or someone) being congruent (with something or someone).

Carl Rogers (1961) prefaces a chapter about genuineness with a quote by Søren Kierkegaard (1849): 'to be that self which one truly is'. A genuine person deeply lives what he or she is: his or her ever-changing organismic experience from moment to moment is exactly — thus genuinely — represented by his or her awareness or consciousness about him- or herself. The person is open to his or her self. Self-actualising tendency and actualising tendency coincide. There is congruence between awareness and organism, self and person. This inner dimension of genuineness referring to the substantial aspect of individuality may be called *openness to oneself*.

It corresponds with an openness to the other. The outer, relational dimension of it is well characterised by the term *transparency* which stands for the correspondence of experience and communication towards others. The person shows him- or herself the way he or she experiences him- or herself in a given moment, not pretending to be different nor consciously or unconsciously showing a façade.[8]

Trust in one's own experiences and being trustworthy, seeing oneself as credible and credibility for others, go hand in hand: experience, its representation and its communication, coincide, are congruent.

The personalistic (encounter philosophical) term for the characterisation described is *authenticity*. To be authentic means to be entitled to acceptance or belief as being reliable, as being real not counterfeit. The Greek word 'auth-éntes' ('autós' = 'self') denotes the 'author', the originator of something, and might describe somebody who does something with his own hand (Duden, 1963). In this etymological view an authentic person is a human being who is the author of him- or herself. Self-authorship, then, is a true characterisation of a person termed 'genuine' or 'congruent' by Carl Rogers — someone who is the author of the symbolisation of his experiences and the author of his communications. Symbolised and verbalised experiences are not second-hand but first-hand. *An authentic person, therefore, is his or her own 'author' in the relationship both to his or her self, and to the others.*

---

6. The Latin word 'congruens' means 'meet together, agree, correspond'; its root may be 'ruere', meaning 'fall, rush', but etymologists are not sure about this. 'Congruent' stands for 'conforming, accordant, agreeable' (Duden, 1963; Hoad, 1986).

7. 'Realness' points to the fact that something is truly (meaning 'real') what its name implies (Lat. 'res' = 'thing, fact'), that what you see coincides with reality, the opposites are counterfeit, unreal, idealistic.

8. Both aspects were already described by Lietaer in 1993 in a somewhat different terminology.

DIALOGUE AS MUTUAL REVELATION AND AUTHENTIC RECEIPT

Communication is both the reason for, and the consequence of, community. In a dialectical process,[9] authenticity fosters encounter and encounter fosters authenticity. Thus authenticity is the foundation for communicating *with* each other instead of talking *about* each other — in other words, to enter dialogue. Dialogue can only occur between authentic persons.

Dialogue is a concept category for a personalistic view of the human being and hence for person-centred anthropology. It requires each person to really see the other person as an 'other'. 'The Other' in an encounter philosophical sense (as the one who cannot be comprehended but empathised with) is crucial for the understanding of the way of relationship called 'encounter' by Carl Rogers. The other person in a communication is not primarily seen as somebody similar to me, as an 'alter me' (to whom I, let's say as a therapist, am simply the 'alter ego'), but as truly another, an absolutely different person, whom I (e.g. as the therapist) encounter as an enigma, being aware of the fundamental otherness of the other, facilitating his process of opening up but in no way directing it. Nor am I the one to comprehend him or her (in the original meaning of 'comprehending' as 'surrounding' or 'encircling' and thus 'taking in' the other person); it is he or she that is the one to open up and to reveal him- or herself. In terms of epistemology it happens in reverse to everyday communication — we do not try to understand the Other by making analogies from us to him or her, by assessing or rating the other, estimating how and who he or she is. Rather we try to understand the Other by opening up to whatever they show, experience, communicate or reveal. The direction goes from the Other to me, not from me to the Other.

This way of relating is truly called an 'en-counter', because the Other also stands 'counter' to me — challenging me and requiring me to change my views and thus myself in accepting and acknowledging him or her and urging me to respond, hence my response-ability (cf. Schmid, 2001a). Because the term 'encounter' in general and in the person-centred approach in particular has undergone inflation, it is necessary to mention here that the essential element of encounter requires that the human being meets a reality which moves him or her deeply. Encounter is not simply an experience, it is an 'experience counter-to' which opposes the affected one. Encounter is an essentially different experience from what an idealistic and subjectivistic understanding (of solely intrinsic development) presupposes, from an understanding of development or fulfilment coming completely from itself. However, it is an alien, an Other, another reality, another person, which or who en-counters my reality, which or who encounters me. This makes up the existential dimension and unavoidability of an encounter.

---

9. 'Dialectical' (from 'dialogue') refers to a way of philosophizing or an art of dialogue which is oriented by a critical consideration of opposites and contradictions thus gaining knowledge and insight. The term is used throughout the article in the Hegelian tradition to indicate a couplet of linked yet contradictory concepts: from thesis and antithesis a synthesis is gained on a new level.

For Martin Buber (1923, 1948, 1951), being a person means communicating oneself: the event of encounter or dialogue actually constitutes the person. In a well-known statement, he says 'All real life is encounter' (Buber, 1923, p. 18). Thus the I is actually constituted *only* in the encounter of the Thou: 'The I becomes through the Thou; becoming an I, I say Thou' (ibid.). He describes encounter as an event in which one 'becomes presence' to the Other. An encounter according to Buber is particularly characterised by authenticity — the 'authenticity of being' instead of the 'breaking-in of seeming', of appearance only. This points to the fact that true revelation is in need of authentic receipt: revelation cannot take place without a personal receiving attitude. Defence, disguise, play-acting, role-playing, the façade of expertism, etc. are obstacles to a person who strives for authenticity — both epistemologically and practically a crucial moment, e.g. for the client's possibilities in therapy.

AUTHENTICITY AS A DIALECTICAL PROCESS IN A PLURALISTIC WORLD

Thinking about congruence implies difference. You cannot reflect on being congruent if you don't experience and consider diversity. If there was no difference there would be no process and progress. But it is not only the difference between me and one other person. While the encounter between the I and the Thou is a main point in Martin Buber's philosophy, Emmanuel Levinas (1961, 1974, 1983) — the Lithuanian encounter philosopher whose ideas are not usually associated with the person-centred approach — develops the focus of the relationship: from 'the Other' to 'the Others'.

Levinas points out that the (relatively) closed relationship of the I-Thou is still a contained (and idealistic) concept. According to his thinking the relationship would be better understood as the 'Thou-I-relationship', because the Other always comes first (phenomenologically, developmental psychologically and ethically).

While Buber stresses the ontological aspect of the encounter relationship, Levinas (1983) is convinced that ethics has to be 'the first philosophy', if we do not want to continue 'egology' (this is how he characterises occidental philosophy until to date). Thus 'diakonia [diacony]' precedes dialogue — 'diakonia' means 'service' as 'therapy' does — so in other words: dialogue is a consequence of this basic conviction and attitude.

Furthermore, if ethics is to be the 'first philosophy' then it is clear that there will be many Others who will bring up the question of whom to trust, i.e. the question of justice. Maybe the friend of my friend is somebody who does seem trustworthy to him but not to me. Each person lives in a world with many Others and therefore has to choose and to judge. He or she has to leave the subjectivistic position of 'mere relating' and to take an objectivistic stance. If the relationship to another person is no longer self-evident when you consider that this person is standing in a context of other relationships, then you cannot limit yourself to a subject-to-subject-relationship. If we can make this step back and out of the relationship it becomes possible for the person to view the different Others from a point which increasingly becomes his or her own point of view, his or her own standpoint. (It should be mentioned that at this stage most people do not get any further in almost all of their relationships.)

This introduces the notion of 'the Third One' — a concept by Levinas which denotes the breaking-up of the dyad. 'The Third One' is a cipher or symbol for the breaking through of idealistic concepts of enclosed relationships.

On this basis, the 'triadic' understanding of relationships becomes crucial for a person-centred understanding of the person. A comprehensive appreciation can no longer concentrate on the one-on-one-relationship alone. On the contrary it has its foundation in an understanding of the human being as always, and from the very beginning, being a member of a group. To be a person in this context means to relate to several significant Others. It implies — and this is especially relevant for counselling and therapy, etc. — not being in a somewhat 'primitive' relationship of 'simply' accepting and being empathic. It further implies deliberately acknowledging and being compassionate — after having gone through the stage of the necessity of judging and evaluating the fellow human beings as described above, it then means to actively open up in an adult way to the mystery of the other anew, trusting him or her and being *impressed* by his or her otherness.

This is the 'hour of congruence': to authentically and deliberately abstain from judgements and 'objective' positions and freshly enter a relationship with what Rogers (e.g. 1986) refers to as 'presence'. At this stage, being authentic is no longer naïve or purely spontaneous, by coincidence, but it is a deliberate step towards the Other and the Others facing them, encountering them face to face. A therapeutic relationship, then, as defined by Carl Rogers, is probably the best description of an encounter relationship of this kind in the literature.

However, it implies much more than probably even Rogers himself was aware. It not only shows the deep roots in philosophy and theology, it also involves the implementation and explication of the existential meaning of personal presence (see below). More than he ever thought, his image of the human is connected with the occidental history of philosophy in general and anthropology in particular (Schmid 1991, 1994, 1996): the question of authenticity is related to the unum-multum problem long discussed in occidental philosophy.[10] Is there ultimately one truth? Is, unity (the unum) the core and the goal to aim for? Or are there many truths? Is plurality (the plurum), variety, multidimensionality the basis of all and the goal to seek? This implies the question whether a person is authentic if he or she is at his or her core (whatever this might be) or is a person authentic if he or she is really in the relationship(s) he or she is in at the moment? The person-centred answer is that in a dialectical way both stances create a process of mutual tension — authenticity is a process term that encompasses unity *and* plurality.[11]

There also is an inherent theological parallel to the Christian image of the

---

10. The nub of the problem is the question: is there a 'universe'? ('Uni-verse' means 'turned to [the] one'.) This question can be seen, for example, in the constructivism debate on an epistemological level: do we grasp (parts of the) reality in the process of recognizing (because reality discloses, reveals itself) and thus strive towards unity or do we (maybe only) create our own realities and thus live in a 'pluri-verse'? Or both?
11. Rogers refers to this with his concept of the 'fully functioning person' who lives the processes he or she is.

human being as an image of God, the Tri-Unite One, being One *and* being Trinity, uniting the substantial and relational dimension in a unique way, so to speak, 'individual' *and* 'group'. In this conception, God is entirely uniqueness *and* community from the very beginning. And he is relating to the community of unique human beings which is founded by him in mutual communication and communion (cf. Schmid, 1998a). Thus, in a Christian theological perspective authenticity also means co-creation: to take part in God's authorship of the world (creation) and his authorship of the relations among human beings.

PRESENCE — PSYCHOPHYSICAL 'BEING WITH' AND 'BEING COUNTER'

Rogers' (1986) description of the therapeutic relationship as being present to the Other seems to be, more than he himself noticed, a basic and comprehensive depiction of a therapeutic encounter relationship. Together, authenticity, unconditional positive regard and empathy constitute *one* human attitude, one fundamental way of being, relating and acting, truly characterised as psychophysical presence.

It is well known and quite often quoted that Carl Rogers (e.g. 1986) in his late years described a phenomenon in therapeutic relationships which he called 'presence'. On close examination of the phenomenon, I suggest that 'presence' is the existential foundation of the basic attitudes of congruence, unconditional positive regard and empathy (Schmid, 1996, pp. 228–44, 1998b, p. 85). From a personalistic view this is not a fourth or even additional core condition — as suggested by Thorne (1985) or Steuri (1992) — the concept comprehensively describes the basic attitudes in an existential way. What Carl Rogers described as authenticity, unconditional positive regard and empathy correspond with presence as understood on a deeper, dialogical–personal level. Presence (in German: 'Gegenwärtigkeit'), in the sense of encounter philosophy, is the existential core of the attitudes. It is further explained by the description of the conditions which themselves were always understood holistically by Rogers, intrinsically connected, a 'trias variable'. Each one of the conditions makes no therapeutic sense without the others. Presence can thus be regarded, in a dialectical sense, as what Hegel calls an 'Aufhebung' of the basic attitudes. The German word 'aufheben' means (1) to preserve, (2) to abolish and dissolve and (3) to supersede, transcend and give new meaning on a higher level. If one takes these meanings together at one and the same time, 'presence' can be understood as an 'Aufhebung' of the basic attitudes: they are preserved as well as dissolved by being superseded and transcended. Hence, encounter is 'more than the variables'. What is essential in the understanding and realization of the person-centred relationship is the transcendence of the single basic attitudes to form a fundamental and extensive, full way of *being* with each other. Thus the source and the goal of person-centred action is personal encounter. Then, presence is not only to be regarded as an altered, transcending state of consciousness, as Rogers (1986) writes, but as a way of being, as 'being in encounter' (Schmid 1996, p. 244; 1998b, p. 85).

Hence, presence is an expression of authenticity, as it is related to the immediately present flow of experiencing. It reflects congruence *and* difference between a person's experiencing and symbolisation and between his or her symbolisation and communication. Presence is an expression of empathy, because, in existential wonderment, it is related to what the Other is experiencing. And presence is an expression of positive regard, as acceptance of myself and personal acknowledgement of the Other, of whatever immediately present feelings he or she is experiencing. These basic attitudes — and presence as their 'Aufhebung' — can thus be understood as *the* encounter condition.

Presence — deriving from the Latin word 'esse' which means 'to be' — means to be authentic as a person; fully myself and fully open; whole; fully living the individual I am; fully living the relationships I am in and the relationships I am. (We are not only *in* relationships, we *are* relationships.) The challenge is, at one and the same time, to be oneself and in relationship. Being able to be touched, impressed, surprised, changed, altered, growing and also being able to stick to my own experiences and symbolisations (instead of taking the experiences, interpretations and stances of the others), to value from within (without judging *the person* of the other), to have one's own point of view. This is what being present means. This is what being authentic means. This is what being a person means.

In the 'way of being with' characterised by the term 'presence', being and acting coincide completely. The person is his or her experiences, the person does what he or she is and is what he or she does — a living congruence of profound impact to those the person relates to.

When a person in need addresses or reaches out to another person, they are asking for a response to their needs. Thus being present means being the response to another person, the response to being addressed by somebody — especially by another person in need. It is this capability of responsiveness from which response–ability evolves. Thus demonstrating the ethical foundation of this way of being and understanding the world. To authentically respond to another person, be it in therapy, be it in any personal relationship, is *the* ethical challenge.[12]

THERAPY AS FACILITATION OF THE AUTHORSHIP OF THE CLIENTS' LIVES

The anthropological and ethical considerations — the human being as a person, both autonomous and relationally interdependent, dialogue as mutual revelation, authenticity as a dialectical process of encounter, presence as 'being with' and response-ability — shed new light upon the therapeutic impact of authenticity. The obviously facilitative aspect of congruence is grounded in the understanding of the human being as a person and in the responsibility which derives from this — as Rogers (1977) put it: congruence begets congruence. Authenticity fosters authenticity, because it 'melts' rigidity and defensiveness in favour of the breaking through of the actualising tendency, of creative individuality and the striving for authentic relationships. In other words: person-centred therapy facilitates the client's wish and need to gradually become (again) the author of his life

---

12. Ethics must not be misunderstand in a moralistic way; it denotes — from a phenomenological and anthropological point of view — the philosophy of the challenge of living in terms of how to live respons-ibly.

Authors know that gaining authorship is a process, not an instant flash of lightning. Therefore authentic people are patient, curious and full of the ability of being astonished and surprised. They know that the task is to *learn* and improve congruence, not to *have* it or not.

There is no authenticity, no presence in relationships to other persons without (at least a minimum of) mutuality. It requires at least some openness, some capability of awareness, of being able to be influenced by the other, of 'psychological contact' (cf. Schmid, 2001c). Person-centred therapy is the kind of encounter relationship which, starting at some point of more or less (even almost complete) impaired mutuality and openness, aims towards full mutuality.

The challenge in unequal relationships — e.g. for the therapist — is to relate to the authentic parts of the other person(s). There is a deep connection between authenticity, on the one hand, and spontaneity and creativity on the other hand. To act spontaneously is the opposite of acting artificially, of acting by copying a model or by acting according to a plan, may this be consciously or not. It is also different from copying oneself: what was helpful in one situation can be inappropriate in another context. Thus the question of the legitimate use of methods and techniques arises (see below). To act authentically always means to act creatively, out of one's inner sources, guided by trust in the actualising tendency. The two 'twin principles' spontaneity and creativity (Moreno, 1969),[13] are inherent to authenticity and essential for person-centred work in general and person-centred therapy in particular.

Authenticity also has eminent bodily aspects: there is no emotion without the body, no thought, no experience. Experiences are always organismic, basically grounded in bodily processes and sensations — and, in the same sense, communication does not exist outside of the bodies involved. Language always has a non-verbal dimension expressed by the body. To be fully present means to be physically there. It is the body which makes it possible that a person can be seen, heard, touched, smelled, tasted. It is the body which makes a person able to see, hear, touch, smell, taste. It is the body of the Other which 'stands counter' to my body, which I can feel and which thus makes the connection between two persons, but which on the contrary also sets the limits between the Other and me. The body is both, the 'incarnation' (the becoming flesh) of what the person is, and the initiator of the 'inspiration' (the becoming spirit) of what the person experiences. Thus becoming a person, always includes incarnation, embodiment. The body both reveals the person and also can hide him or her. There is no authenticity without the body.

This has profound consequences for the understanding of a truly *person-*centred therapy, especially for those who tend to reduce communication to verbal communication and therapy to talking therapy. (On the other hand it is also one-sided and of no use to set the body above the psyche — the respective slogan is that 'the body cannot lie' — or declaring it to be the main road to the understanding of the person or to doing therapy. This simply reduces the person to the body.) Therapists and counsellors who do not pay attention to their clients'

---

13. Jacob L. Moreno, the founder of psychodrama, had already committed himself, ahead of his time, to the concept of encounter in the days of Sigmund Freud and showed many parallels to Rogers' understanding of the therapeutic relationship (Schmid, 1994).

bodies, and their own bodies, fail in facilitating the person as a whole. To facilitate the authorship of the clients' lives always includes the facilitation of their awareness of their body and its paramount importance in both self understanding and communication.

Here it should also be noticed that becoming present always includes dealing with the past, as what made the person become what he or she is, and the future, as what makes the person wish and fear, expect and live up to — but both, past and future, are always embedded in the presence; there is no past or future as such, there is only the present impact of the past and the future, there is only presence in the mode of past and future. This leads to a substantial conclusion: to fully become present by fully becoming authentic might well be a defined goal for psychotherapy and counselling — for the therapist as well as for the client. For the therapist this means to authorise and empower the client by facilitating his or her own struggles for authenticity in the moment-by-moment presence the therapist offers. For the client it means to be the author of his or her own future on the basis of his or her past by living in the moment-to-moment process of presence.

AUTHENTICITY VERSUS METHODOLOGICAL AND TECHNICAL APPROACHES

This goal, discussed in the previous section, is achieved — and this is unique in psychotherapy — by a relationship *person to person* with all its consequences, and not by anything else. In his article: 'The interpersonal relationship: The core of guidance' Rogers (1962a, p. 90) describes the therapeutic relationship in the context of the congruence of the therapist as a 'direct personal encounter with his client, meeting him on a person-to-person basis'. He later emphasised the relationship and the genuineness of the therapist even more, and regarded 'therapy as relationship encounter' (Rogers, 1962b, p. 185). According to Rogers this has precedence over techniques, theory and ideology.

The transparent realness we are talking about implies the renunciation of the use of any preconceived methods or techniques in a therapeutic relationship. Authors prefer new stories to repeating themselves. Authenticity plays a decisive role inasmuch as the therapist is available for the client as a living person and not only in his or her capacity as a therapist. It is crucial for the development of both, client and therapist, that they direct their attention, as free of judgements and interpretations as possible, to the immediate presence of both persons in the relationship. This implies a radical counter-position to expert-oriented approaches (in terms of the contents as well as the process), emphasising that the person as such (and not techniques, methods or skills) is the active change factor. The therapist offers a way of being with the client making possible a process of communication and encounter which moves towards mutuality and dialogue.

A fundamental and principled non-directivity is the logical consequence of an image of the human being which prefers the uniqueness of the Other to standardising diagnosis and acknowledgement to knowledge (cf. Schmid, 2001a). Authenticity means that authors encounter authors and not copies. Authenticity is non-directive, because inherent in it is the notion that only the author of a life can change it. Thus authenticity strictly opposes any expert behaviour, be it in terms of contents and decisions or be it in terms of ways of how to get there, i.e. means, methods and techniques. If authenticity is what therapy is about, the only legitimate 'techné' (the original Greek word which means 'art') is im-media-cy, or im-media-te presence (presence without media), in other words, the encounter person to person. To be precise, therapy is a process to overcome preconceived techniques and methods (which always come in between humans) by making them superfluous.

This also shows that those directions of therapy, theory and practice which concentrate on the experience (and therefore calling themselves 'experiential') reduce the person as a whole to the experience as part of it. Thus they are no longer person-centred but focus only on one aspect of the person ('focusing-oriented therapy' or 'focusing therapy'). They not only pay less attention to the relationship in a dialogical way, and thus miss the essence of an encounter relationship, but also reintroduce the therapist as an expert in terms of directing the process ('process-directional'), even if they limit themselves to process-guiding activities and do not intend to influence the contents (cf. Prouty, 1999; Schmid, 2001d).

THE 'WE-PERSPECTIVE' AND ITS SOCIAL DIMENSION

Being really present is one of the most challenging tasks for human beings. Being true to oneself and being open to others (and not only to one other individual), being authentic in multidimensional relations is a dialectical and provoking ('pro-voke' = 'to call out of') way of being. It neither means pursuing stubbornly or stolidly to 'be always the same', regardless of the relationships the individual is in,[14] nor does it mean to follow the idea of being and behaving completely differently in the various relationships an individual has, continually changing, or being-without-substance.[15]

In regard to therapy, these aspects point to two main misunderstandings of congruence. First, the idea of 'anything is okay as long as it is honest or true' (which in reality, in groups for example, often turns out to be ignorant, even brutal) ignores the relational dimension: there is no congruence *except* in relationship, no 'congruence as such', on its own. The second misunderstanding is to hold the position of 'If I am with you I am completely identified with you and everything you say and do is okay'. This ignores the substantial dimension (and is a major misunderstanding of empathy by ignoring the 'as-if' perspective; cf. Schmid, 2001b).

In this respect, being authentic is particularly a problem when facing more than one person, e.g. in a group. As mentioned above, the person lives in more than one relationship, with more than one 'Other'. Thus the 'We-perspective' is the truly and genuine dialogical perspective.

---

14. 'I am what I am and I don't give a damn, how I am perceived or what effects my being with others may have' — a position easily to be found with 'beginners' of therapeutic experience, especially in groups, or fanatics of the ego.
15. 'I am what you want me to be; I am what I am made by others; everything that is true *here* may be false *there*.'

Even in one-to-one therapy 'the Third One' (as the metaphor for all others, relationships and the external world) is always present: be it the subject talked about, the persons and relationships talked about, the context of the therapy, or the world as such.

The 'We' overcomes the duality of the pair, of the either–or, of the contradiction, of the thinking according to the principles of linear causality; it opens a new level of plurality, of variety, of as-well-as, of being 'whole' (and thus 'healing' — both are etymologically and from a holistic perspective related to 'holy'). This is often expressed in terms of religion or mysticism, because it expresses deep personal experiences: what Buber calls the 'sanctification [the making holy] of everyday life', what Hycner (cf. 1989, pp. 94–5) calls 'the sanctifying presence of the therapist in therapy'. Less solemnly it might be expressed as being to do with the experiences of becoming more whole, of the coming together of split-off or alienated parts of the person, or it might be called 'mystical' as Rogers (1986) does. But this must not be mixed up with 'mysterious' in the sense of 'irrational' or 'esoteric'. It is nothing more or less than the very experience of growth itself, of gaining authorship of one's own life, of personalisation, of becoming a person. And personalisation is never a matter of the individual, nor is it a matter of a single relationship, it is always a matter of a multidimensional being in relations.

The We-perspective stresses the importance of the group. Usually people live in groups; the relationship of two, the pair, is a special case of a group, always embedded in other groups. The group is the 'normal place' of living, the primary locus of life. People depend on groups from the very beginning of their life: the family, groups of friends, groups at the work place, etc. It is in groups where we learn to be authentic and where it really is the task to be authentic. Therefore groups are highly rated and valued in person-centred therapy. It might even be said that they are *the* 'original' therapeutic setting and it can be shown that Carl Rogers historically, psychologically, philosophically and practically was concerned with groups from the very beginning of his work, although he dedicated most of his academic writings in the earlier years to the one-to-one-therapy (Schmid, 1996).

Taking the human seriously as a social being results in a re-evaluation of the indication for single and group therapy. Out of the fundamental understanding of the human being in his or her social relations, as a person in the group, out of the realisation of the fact that working on conflicts is best done where conflicts originate, namely in groups, the question is: when will the group be the chosen therapeutic place and when will the individual therapeutic relationship — as a special and especially protected relationship — be indicated? Looked at in this way, individual therapy should only be chosen when special protection is needed or some other specific reason calls for it. The person-centred approach is a deeply social, and thus, a group approach. This is contrary to how it is usually regarded because of its historical development and the group is considered to be a central aspect in the future of the approach. This also refutes the 'pathology' of over-emphasising individual therapy, e.g. in German-speaking countries, where it is particularly in evidence in training programmes, as opposed to those in Anglo-American countries (ibid.) which emphasise group or community.

THE POLITICAL DIMENSION OF AUTHENTICITY

Thus the political significance of authenticity becomes obvious. Groups are smaller segments of the society. They are the interface of the person and the society. Here a social and political dimension of authenticity becomes obvious. Authenticity is a challenge for solidarity and autonomy. The task is not only to be authentic in intimate relationships and in therapy, but also in everyday life, in society and politics.

It was not by coincidence that Carl Rogers found that the more he dealt with and valued congruence, the more he got interested in groups, large groups and intergroup communication, in intercultural subjects, in social and political questions, such as his peace-facilitating efforts.

The challenge to be an authentic person definitely reaches beyond the individual. The ultimate questions are: 'Who are you? Who am I?' These questions always transcend the immediate situation (in therapy, in a partnership, among friends, in a group). At a closer look, they turn out to be the question: 'Who are we — now and beyond this situation?' (cf. also Wood, 1988, p. 109).

This has profound consequences for the person-centred approach itself. It suggests a paradigm shift lies ahead *within* the approach, which started during the later work of Carl Rogers. The more we understand the social and political implications, the more the person-centred approach faces a challenge to itself. If ethics and the underlying image of the human being are taken seriously it becomes obvious that the approach needs further development towards a truly social approach.

In respect of an ethically founded anthropology — the step from the individual to the person, from relationship to encounter, will be made as a change from the view of the person–centred relationship as an I–Thou–relationship to the view of a We–relationship as well, and therefore arriving at a social therapy. Then the I will not only be found as a response to a Thou, but the I will also be a response to a We. Then the approach will consequently be seen as a social approach. Sociotherapy, besides psychotherapy, will be ranked highly in the frame of an overall therapeutic point of view. Such an overall therapeutic perspective would include the communities in which the human being lives. (Schmid, 2001e)

The human society (starting with parts thereof) has to overcome the one-sided position of only stressing the (individual) dimension of unity as well as the one-sided position of 'whatever you like' and of 'anything goes'. It will have to enter the necessarily dialectical stage of the tension between unity and plurality (cf. also O'Hara, 1998). Once this is achieved, authenticity will be the only possibility to live as a person in a globalised, confusing and technical world. Authenticity is the very opposite of alienation. Authentic persons challenge others to become authentic because they themselves are challenged by really accepting the others as they are.

It is to the great merit of Carl Rogers that he described this for the theory and practice of therapy and similar relationships. It is his legacy to us now to authentically implement the essence of it into all fields of life.

REFERENCES

Buber, M. (1923). *Ich und Du*. Heidelberg: Lambert Schneider, 8th ed. 1974; orig. 1923.
Buber, M. (1948). *Das Problem des Menschen*. Heidelberg: Lambert Schneider, 4th ed.1982; orig. 1948.
Buber, M. (1951). *Urdistanz und Beziehung: Beiträge zu einer philosophischen Anthropologie I*. Heidelberg: Lambert Schneider, 4ed. 1978; orig. 1951.
Duden, K. (1963). (Ed.) *Etymologie: Herkunftswörterbuch der deutschen Sprache*. Mannheim: Dudenverlag, 7th ed.
Finke, Jobst (1994). *Empathie und Interaktion. Methode und Praxis der Gesprächs-psychotherapie*. Stuttgart: Thieme.
Hoad, T. F. (1986). (Ed.) *The concise Oxford dictionary of English etymology*. Oxford: Clarendon.
Hycner, R. (1989). *Zwischen Menschen: Ansätze zu einer Dialogischen Psychotherapie*. Köln: Edition Humanistische Psychologie.
Kierkegaard, S. (1849). *Sygdommen til Døden: En christelig psychologisk Udvikling til Opbyggelse og Opvækkelse*. Kopenhagen: Reitzels, 1849.
Levinas, E. (1961). *Totalité et infini : Essai sur l'extériorité*. Den Haag: Nijhoff.
Levinas, E. (1974). *Autrement qu'être ou au delà de l'essence*. Den Haag: Nijhoff.
Levinas, E. (1983). *Die Spur des Anderen: Untersuchungen zur Phänomenologie und Sozialphilosophie*. Freiburg: Alber.
Lietaer, G. (1993). Authenticity, congruence and transparency. In Brazier, D. (Ed..), *Beyond Carl Rogers*. London: Constable 1993. pp. 17–46 (see also chapter 3 by Lietaer in this volume).
Moreno, J. L. (1969). The Viennese origins of the encounter movement. Paving the way for existentialism, group psychotherapy and psychodrama. *Group Psychotherapy*, XXII, 1/2, 7–16.
O'Hara, M. (1998). Person-Centered and Experiential Therapy in an age of cultural transition. *Person*, 1, pp. 5–14.
Prouty, G. (1999). Carl Rogers and Experiential Therapies: A dissonance? Manuscript.
Rogers, C. R. (1955). Some personal formulations. Manuscript.
Rogers, C. R. (1961). *On becoming a person: A therapist's view of psychotherapy*. Boston: Houghton Mifflin.
Rogers, C. R. (1962a). The interpersonal relationship: The core of guidance. *Harward Educational Review*, 4,32, pp. 416–29.
Rogers, C. R. (1962b). Toward becoming a fully functioning person. In Combs, A. W. (ed.), *Perceiving, behaving, becoming: A new focus for education*. Washington D. C.: Association for Supervision and Curriculum Development, 1962 Yearbook, pp. 21–33.
Rogers, C. R. (1970). *On encounter groups*. New York: Harper and Row.
Rogers, C. R. (1977). *On personal power: Inner strength and its revolutionary impact*. New York: Delacorte, 1977.
Rogers, C. R. (1980). Client–centered psychotherapy. Kaplan, H. I., Freedman, A. M. and Sadock, B. J. (Eds.), *Comprehensive textbook of psychiatry, III,* Vol. 2, Baltimore, MD: Williams and Wilkins, 3rd ed. 1980, pp. 2153–68.
Rogers, C. R. (1986). A client–centered/person–centered approach to therapy. In Kutash, I. L. and Wolf, A. (Eds.), *Psychotherapist's casebook: Theory and technique in the practice of modern times*. San Francisco: Jossey–Bass, pp. 197–208.
Schmid, P. F. (1994). *Personzentrierte Gruppenpsychotherapie: Ein Handbuch. Vol. I: Solidarität und Autonomie*. Köln: Edition Humanistische Psychologie.
Schmid, P. F. (1996). *Personzentrierte Gruppenpsychotherapie in der Praxis: Ein Handbuch. Vol. II: Die Kunst der Begegnung*. Paderborn: Junfermann.
Schmid, P. F. (1998a). *Im Anfang ist Gemeinschaft: Personzentrierte Gruppenarbeit in Seelsorge und Praktischer Theologie. Vol. III: Beitrag zu einer Theologie der Gruppe*. Stuttgart: Kohlhammer.
Schmid, P. F. (1998b). 'Face to face': The art of encounter. In Thorne, B., and Lambers, E. 1998, pp. 74–90.

Schmid, P. F. (1998c). 'On becoming a person-centered approach': A person-centred understanding of the person. In Thorne, B., and Lambers, E. 1998, pp. 38–52.

Schmid, P. F. (2000). Souveränität und Engagement: Zu einem personzentrierten Verständnis von 'Person'. In Rogers, C. R. and Schmid, P. F., *Person-zentriert: Grundlagen von Theorie und Praxis* (4th ed). Mainz: Grünewald, pp.15–164. Original edition published 1991.

Schmid, P. F. (2001a). Unconditional positive regard — a dialogical perspective (working title). In Bozarth, J. and Wilkins, P. (Eds.), *Rogers' Therapeutic Conditions, Vol. 3:Unconditional positive regard*. Ross-on-Wye: PCCS Books.

Schmid, P. F. (2001b). Empathy — a dialogical perspective (working title). In Haugh, S. and Merry, T. (Eds.), *Rogers' Therapeutic Conditions, Vol. 2: Empathy*. Ross-on-Wye: PCCS Books.

Schmid, P. F. (2001c). The therapeutic relationship — a dialogical perspective (working title). In Wyatt, G. and Sanders, P. (Eds.), *Rogers' Therapeutic Conditions, Vol. 4: Contact and perception*. Ross-on-Wye: PCCS Books.

Schmid, P. F. (2001d). The necessary and sufficient conditions of being person-centered: On identity, integrity, integration and differentiation of the paradigm. In Watson, J. (Ed.), *Proceedings of the 5th ICCCEP, Chicago 2000*. Ross-on-Wye: PCCS Books.

Schmid, P. F. (2001e). Encountering a human being means being kept alive by an enigma (E. Levinas): Prospects on further developments in the Person-Centered Approach. In Andrade, N. and Autunes, S. (Eds.), *Proceedings of the 4th ICCCEP, Lisbon 1997*. Lisbon: Universita Católica Portuguesa.

Steuri, H. (1992). Editorial. *Brennpunkt* 32,2.

Tausch, R. and Tausch, A. (1990). *Gesprächspsychotherapie: Hilfreiche Gruppen- und Einzelgespräche in Psychotherapie und alltäglichem Leben*. Göttingen: Hogrefe, 9th ed.

Thorne, B. (1985). The quality of tenderness. Norwich: Norwich Centre Publications.

Thorne, B. (1991). *Person-centered counselling: Therapeutic and spiritual dimensions*. London: Whurr

Thorne, B. and Lambers, E. (1998). *Person-centred therapy: A European perspective*. London: Sage.

Wood, J. K (1988). *Menschliches Dasein als Miteinandersein: Gruppenarbeit nach personenzentrierten Ansätzen*. Köln: Edition Humanistische Psychologie; American orig.: manuscript.

15 Congruence: A Synthesis and Implications

Gill Wyatt

My intention in this final chapter is to draw together some of the many different themes within this volume to attempt to create a synthesis, generating a whole-picture view of congruence encompassing three levels. These are 1) a 'multilevel process' (Ellingham, Chapter 6, p. 114) of congruence within the person, 2) a relational congruence involving the processes between persons and 3) a socio-politico-ecological congruence recognising the processes within groups. I hope to communicate something of the interconnectedness of these different processes as each effects all others.[1] The gain from this more holistic and universal concept of congruence is that it moves the person-centred conceptualisation of theory and philosophy away from a dualistic, mechanistic paradigm to a more accurate approximation of the complexity and inter-relatedness within and between humans, society and the natural world. I believe this will provide the basis for a concept of congruence that can generate a person-centred theory of health and mental health of the individual, the society and the natural world.

PERSONAL CONGRUENCE

The term 'personal congruence' is used to describe the whole-person multi-level process concept of congruence. Rogers (1957, 1959) cited experience and awareness as the two processes which may or may not be congruent, and in other writings (Rogers, 1954, 1961,1980), he adds a third process: the therapist's expression or communication. He frequently used terms like 'deny' and 'distort' originating from a mechanistic dualistic paradigm and at the same time used terms such as 'organism' and 'process' from a more organismic paradigm.

Several theorists have developed Rogers original theory in an attempt to achieve the complexity required to more accurately explain human experiencing — Gendlin on experiencing (1962); Wexler on cognitive processing (1974); and Greenberg's three-level information processing model (Greenberg and Van Balen 1998, p. 165). Ellingham argues that Gendlin, Wexler and Greenberg, although attempting to be more process orientated and hence more holistic and organismically based, are still operating in the 'Cartesian duality'. He offers the

---

As this chapter grew out of my editing of the book, my intention was to acknowledge the work of contributors as they influenced my writing. I apologige if I have omitted any recognitions.
[1] The structure of my synthesis evolved from Jules Seeman's human system model (Chapter 13).

development of Whitehead's evolutionary process of consciousness model by Cassirer and Langer (Ellingham, Chapter 6, p. 114) to move the conceptualisation of experiencing — and hence congruence — towards the organismic paradigm.

Whatever model is used, personal congruence needs to encompass all of the levels of processing and functioning possible within a person, and needs to be holistic — including body, mind and spirit. Such a model will embrace the physiological (neuro-bio-chemical), diffuse and undifferentiated sensations, all emotional-cognitive processing, and of course, behavioural and communication processes. Open connection and communication between all of these different processes within a person (Seeman, Chapter 13) is required if congruence is to be achieved. I believe this requires the development of a non-hierarchical system akin to a human ecological model where human psychology is placed within this larger 'field'. Psychological processes will then co-exist, equal and inter-related; not higher or lower within the processes of the larger 'field'.

The implications for the future

Where would such a concept lead us? Next I highlight some of the further theory development and research opportunities that arise out of a whole-person multi-level process conceptualisation of congruence.

The therapists's values and intent
The therapist's values and intent are part of this multi-level process concept of congruence. They will play a part within the therapist's emotional-cognitive processing which will effect their behaviour and communication.

The therapist's theoretical and philosophical coherence. The therapist's values and intent partly arise from their theoretical and philosophical stance. As the degree of personal congruence results from the coherence between the multi-levels of the system so a harmony is required throughout a therapist's person-centred philosophical stance. This means that therapist congruence cannot be seen in philosophical or theoretical isolation otherwise there is a risk that it will be misunderstood and used to defend ineffective practice (at best) or, unprofessional and even unethical practice (at worst). A therapist must see congruence as an integral part of person-centred theory and therefore working together with other person-centred principles (see among others, Bozarth Chapter 12 and Haugh Chapter 7). If there is a tension between different principles, then dialectical examination should bring about a more complex conceptualisation. This means there needs to be coherence between the concept of congruence, the other 'necessary and sufficient conditions', the growth tendency, personality theory, and process of therapy.

The therapist's Intent embedded within the conditions. There can be no separation or inconsistency between congruence and the philosophical position of person-centred therapy. By very definition a therapist's congruence must therefore be facilitative, non-exploitative, non-intrusive, non-dominant rather than causing the client any harm, being directive, becoming the expert and interfering with the client's own self direction. Thus the person-centred therapist values, and intends to be facilitative using, all six of the therapeutic conditions. The therapist intends that all are present, rather than focusing on only one therapeutic condition at a time. In order for congruence to be congruence, it needs empathy and UPR. There can be no congruence in isolation, Lietaer explains: 'empathy is always implicitly carried by the therapist's congruence' (Lietaer, Chapter, 3, p. 41), and Bozarth says congruence '. . . can be identified as the therapist's presence in client-centred therapy.' The characteristics of this presence are UPR and EU (Chapter 12, p. 196). Bozarth stresses that congruence arises out of a therapist's capacity to experience unconditional positive self regard.

The development of a person's potential

As Haugh states, congruence is '. . . a development of the human potential for experiencing' (Haugh, Chapter 7, p. 127). In a whole-person multi-level conceptualisation of congruence, this development of human potential can now occur at *all* of the different levels of processing, naturally including consciousness, emotional-cognitive processes, physiological processes, and behavioural processes. Unless a person is fully functioning there will be a discrepancy between their potentiality and their actuality. Our society does appear to favour scientific and intellectual styles of thinking, and processing rooted in an individualistic, 'domination over nature' world view rather than the knowledge and wisdom arising from an ecocentric world. Here we are both a part of, and of the whole. There is a connectedness within 'the great web of life' (Neville, 1999). Within this world view, sensations, emotions, being in tune with nature, different types of consciousness and the spiritual dimension take on a greater importance. For the human system and the eco-system to be in balance we need to draw together the best of these two world views. We must both individuate and develop our autonomy *and also* honour our inter-relatedness with people and connection with the natural world. We need technological and scientific advances that enhance the natural world rather than seek domination over it. A human being needs to balance and connect their intellect, rationality, *and* their body awareness, emotions and intuition.

Incongruence

In Rogers' discussion of incongruence he states that incongruence develops as a result of the discrepancy between the 'self as perceived and the actual experiencing of the individual' leading to an 'incongruence between self and experience' (1959, p. 203–4). The person either distorts the meaning of the experience or denies it into consciousness. With a whole-person multi-level conceptualisation of congruence, incongruence can now arise between any two processes within the system and once there is an incongruence between any two processes, all other processes will be effected. Such would be the consequence of a multi-level process system.

Vanaerschot, in developing Gendlin's theory of experiencing, explores the idea that it is only when a person *completes* their process of experiencing (from the diffuse and undifferentiated experience to arriving at some explicit meaning 'that needs to be put the test') that they are then fully free for the 'fresh and rich' experience in the present (1997, p. 144). Previous experiences that have not been completed may interfere with this process. 'Experience is then structure bound, the present situation or certain aspects of it evoking only an already formed experience pattern with a fixed unchangeable and repetitive structure' (ibid.) This is akin to the idea of 'unfinished business' and how our history and memory provide a filter through which we experience. Hence our potentiality becomes a limited actuality. Within a whole-person multi-level process concept of congruence a similar rigidity or limitation could take place within any of the processes already mentioned. The consequence of seeing incongruence (and congruence) as this whole person multi-level process is that person-centred theory would then have the tools to develop a conceptualisation of health. Incongruence, then, 'causally reduces general health' (Tengland, Chapter, 10, p. 171) and can be further developed into a person-centred psychopathology (Tengland ibid.; Speierer 1990, and Biermann-Ratjen, 1998). This would be different from the traditional psychiatric approach in that it would be centred in the respectful, understanding of the client's phenomenological experience. Viewing incongruence within the context of relational and societal systems also gives us a pathology of groups and of our socio-political and ecological domains.

The connection between personal congruence and relational congruence

The processes within personal congruence will influence the processes of relational congruence. What is the connection and communication that takes place between the therapist and the client? My experience is that a person's presence has an effect on me, how they express themselves and how they communicate has an effect on me. Their expression and communication comes from the quality of their presence and the quality of their presence will be determined by who they are and their degree of integration and maturity. Hence, although a person is a separate entity, their connectedness to others allows no person to be seen in isolation.

The therapist's integration and resulting presence
Congruence as a whole person multi-level concept is then synonymous with the integration and maturity of the therapist. Mearns identifies this as 'one of the distinguishing features of the person-centred approach ... the emphasis it places in the counsellor's use of self' (1994, p. 17). Rogers as early as 1939 mentioned the importance of the therapist's understanding of self and insight into his own personality. Ever since, there has been agreement within the range of person-centred therapy (client-centred therapy, experiential and process-directed psychotherapies) concerning the importance of the integration and psychological maturity of the person-centred therapist. For person-centred therapists, the development of maturity is a life long task (see Merry, Chapter 11 and Leijssen Chapter 9).

The degree to which a therapist is integrated will have several effects on their presence: (1) how they express themselves and how the client receives them — contingent upon this is their ability to step into the client's world (as a whole person — kinaesthetically, emotionally and cognitively) and their ability to stay rooted and centred in their own experiences, including their experiences of their client and of themselves (See Greenberg and Geller, Chapter 8); (2) it will determine the level of relationship the therapist is able to enter into with the client — echoed in Mearns idea of 'working at relational depth' (Mearns 1997); and (3) it will determine the clarity of their presence and minimise contaminants from their own life situation including unresolved issues.

Bozarth has highlighted the significance of unconditional positive self regard in determining the fullness and quality of a therapist's presence (Bozarth, Chapter 12). Previously I (Wyatt 2000) have referred to 'therapeutic presence as arising out of the personal presence (authenticity) of the individual and their therapeutic intent (holding the therapist conditions to support the self-directed forces of the client)'. Lietaer identified personal presence as a part of transparency (Chapter 3). Personal presence becomes the 'where' from which the therapist's expression and communication arises. To be fully present requires 'full attention in the moment', and 'to have developed a level of psychological maturity' (Greenberg and Geller, Chapter 8, p. 143), bringing the person of the therapist to the therapeutic relationship. The wholeness of the person-of-the-therapist meeting with the client creates an opportunity for encounter within the moment. Within every moment there is the possibility for each moment to be created anew and within that unique meeting there is the possibility for change and healing for therapist and client. Schmid eloquently expresses this presence, this 'full way of being', as being the transcendence of the conditions as separate entities — that these entities are 'preserved as well as dissolved by being superseded and transcended' (Schmid, Chapter 14, p. 220).

RELATIONAL CONGRUENCE

How does the congruence of the therapist and the client develop during the therapeutic relationship? How does the congruence/incongruence of the therapist and the client effect the other? How does the presence, the behaviour and the communication of one person effect another? These questions are germane to the concept of relational congruence. Grafanaki (Chapter 2) in reviewing the current and past research on congruence concluded that very little research had examined the relational nature of congruence, and that 'appropriateness and timing of congruent responses had been overlooked' (ibid. p. 32). Also the client's experience during moments of counsellor's congruence or incongruence have not been adequately considered (ibid. p. 33) or the important effect client's play in helping their counsellors be facilitative to them.

In recent years there has been growing attention to what is appropriate for a therapist to express, and when and how to express it (Lietaer, Chapter 3; Brodley, Chapter 4; Haugh, Chapter 1; Greenberg and Geller, Chapter 8). In acknowledging the relational nature of congruence these questions remain significant. What the therapist expresses, when and how they express it will influence how the client receives the therapist response i.e. they may experience interest, warmth or understanding as opposed to intrusiveness, being directed or patronised. This, in part, explains why Rogers' (1959) condition 6 is so crucial. The issue of what is appropriate therapist expression must now be decided *within* the relationship. This will arise out of the interaction between therapist and client, the quality of the therapeutic relationship, where they are in the therapeutic process and what is happening for both the therapist and the client. Similarly Greenberg and Geller

233

explain

> The appropriate response arises out of the in the moment interaction of person, situation, and experiencing, it requires the therapist being open, empty and receptive to this in the moment, then in touch with their own experiencing from their own self and their experience in relation to the client's experience, therapist's experience and responding arises out of the therapist's authentic centre (Chapter 8, p. 141).

One of the gaps in this volume is the influence of client incongruence on the condition of relational congruence. Incongruence is discussed in several of the chapters in relation to whether a therapist is being incongruent or congruent and the effect of that on the therapeutic relationship. However, the significance of the client incongruence has not been discussed in relation to it's impact on therapist congruence. Reporting the Wisconsin research programme with clients who had a diagnosis of schizophrenia, Rogers and Gendlin (Rogers and Stevens, 1967) tentatively concluded that therapist congruence and expressivity became ever more important, especially with uncommunicative clients. Is the implication that therapists need to be more expressive depending on client incongruence? Warner (2000), in writing about clients with 'fragile process' advocates very sensitive, genuine empathic following with clients with this type of incongruence (which might imply less therapist expressivity). This is an area, if researched further, would strengthen the standing of person-centred therapy in mental health professions.

What the therapist conveys will include both their intended congruent communication and behaviour *along with* that which they might not intend to communicate to their client. The sensitive client may pick up what the therapist is not intentionally communicating. This may be material at the edge of the therapist's awareness, the therapist's own limited patterns of experiencing, or indeed any ambiguity within the therapist's experiencing. The possible effects on the client are manifold, but in my view are unlikely to facilitate the client in their own growth process. In a worst case scenario the resulting behaviour of the client may then reflexively effect the therapist, thus bringing about a further decline in the therapists congruence, empathy and UPR.

The therapist's intent is to experience congruence, empathy and UPR for the client, their presence and expression will then communicate this to the client. What will the client experience as a result? Whether the client perceives (to some degree) the therapist's UPR and empathy will depend on the client's incongruence and whether their pattern of experiencing limits the fullness of the potential experience in that moment. This is just the start of a process; the way the client will now be within the therapeutic relationship will partly arise from how the client experienced the therapist and this, in turn, will effect the way the therapist now experiences the client, and so on ad infinitum. Of course this reflexive pattern might be positive or negative. The negative scenario would lead to a diminishing level of relational congruence between therapist and client.

To prevent this 'creeping incongruence' the therapist will need to be aware of what is happening between her and the client. At first she may have only an undifferentiated experience that something isn't quite right and decide to self reflect or seek supervision. With this reflection she may gain clarity regarding her experience in response to the client, and her own incongruence which played a part. She may then be willing to talk about her experience of what had been happening in the relationship with the client. The maturity of the therapist will determine the depth and the degree to which she can work with these relational issues, which are arising from the rigidity or limited patterns of experiencing of therapist and/or client. How and when the therapist discusses the relational processes will determine how the client experiences this. The outcome is likely to be more favourable if the therapist is sensitive to the client's availability — is he open to hearing, or too vulnerable, or focused on something unrelated? The therapist takes responsibility for her experience by using 'I' language — speaking about her experiences and what they mean to her as opposed to making evaluative or judgemental interpretations (Brodley, Chapter 4). She discloses her experience affirmatively even if the content of what she is expressing is difficult. She communicates 'comprehensively', a term coined by Greenberg and Geller referring to 'saying it all' rather than the edited highlights (Greenberg and Geller, Chapter 8, p. 136–40). The therapist needs to check how the client experiences what she has said and be non-defensively willing to reconsider or learn from the client what her part was in this relational process.

There is disagreement within the person-centred community regarding the place for the expression and exploration of what I am calling ' relational processes'. Some practitioners (Brodley, Chapter 4; Bozarth, Chapter 12 and Haugh, Chapter 7) advocate a more conservative approach meaning only expressing such 'relational processes' when the client directs the process to this, or in order that the therapist regains their empathy and UPR. Lietaer (similarly Wyatt, Chapter 5 and, Greenberg and Geller, Chapter 8) adopts the position that this relational interactive process shifts the process between therapist and client from one in which the therapist is a mirror or alter ego, to one in which there is 'more a dialogue, . . . an authentic mutual encounter' (Lietaer, Chapter 3, p. 45).

The more traditional client-centred therapists emphasise the therapist putting their 'self' aside, that their 'self' is only used with regards experiencing empathy and UPR for the client (Bozarth, Chapter 13). Their concern arises from the danger that the therapist's self, their expression and their needs will become directive and thus interfere with the self-directive forces of the client. Schmid, Lietaer and Wyatt suggest it is the authenticity of the therapist, the therapist being centred within their authentic personhood that allows the therapist to encounter the client. This leads to freer therapist expression including focusing on the relational processes within the therapeutic relationship.

It is my experience that when I am truly authentic, whatever I say will have empathy and UPR for the other embedded within it. There can be no direction or harm to the client. The tension between the focus on the self or on the other is transcended. Schmid explains that Buber emphasised the 'I-thou' meeting because the 'I' is only created through the meeting with the 'thou'. Drawing from Levinas' work, Schmid suggests that the 'I-Thou' is better conceptualised as 'thou-I' to move away from an ego-centric view towards being relational (Chapter 14, p. 218). There can only be dialogue in the meeting between two different people. It is the very 'otherness' of the other that calls forth 'me' in response; hence the relational nature of dialogue and encounter. Here is offered a mutual co-existence between the individuality of a person and the relational nature between two persons. The individuality of the therapist is not sacrificed in the service of the client, rather the dialectical tension between the individualistic aspects and the relational aspects is transcended with the authentic meeting between client and therapist.

Therapists need to have the ability to focus on their experiences arising from who they are, enabling them to be fully present in the encounter. They then need the ability to shift the focus solely to the other (when the other calls forth this response), and then be able to shift to the relational context as and when the relationship calls for this attention. This flexibility and the ability to know what is required, develops from experience and through the therapist's developing maturity, which will include an openness to unconscious knowing as well as conscious knowing. When there is a sufficient level of congruence between the multi-level processes within our personal congruence, then our behaviour and action is authentic and more likely to be trustworthy.

SOCIO-POLITICO-ECOLOGICAL CONGRUENCE

So far I have only addressed the relational nature of congruence between two people. Levinas opens the 'dyadic' relationship by introducing the concept of the 'Third One'. As Schmid explains, this concept opens up the closed dyadic relationship to include 'the other', to there now being a 'We' (Schmid, Chapter 14, p. 219). He points out that even within the therapeutic relationship 'the Third One' is present by the people mentioned, by the therapy context and the larger cultural, global context. (p. 225).

What is the significance of extending the idea of our inter-relatedness from one 'other' to 'all others' to 'We' within the groups that we live? This, and the holistic view of congruence, raises more questions than answers at this time. Does the actualising tendency operate as part of the broader concept — the formative tendency, and then beyond into a universal directional tendency? How would a person behave if they acknowledge their relationship to the 'others' in any group they belong to? Are there multi-level processes within these groups, and can there be congruence and incongruence between these processes? What would congruence or incongruence look like within organisations, governments, nations? What would societal or global congruence look like?

In extending this exploration to the natural world we might ask what the relationship is between humans and the natural world? Can, for example, pollution, and the resulting climatic changes, be the outcome of the incongruence between humans and the natural world; or the destruction of forests; or the extinction of so many species; or genetic modification?

Holding the dialectical tension between the self and the 'other' (between our individualistic nature and our relational nature) was difficult enough. What of the tensions between the self, 'the other', 'We' and the natural world. Culture and society 'can be thought of as mediating between planet and individual' (Neville, 1999, p. 71). Neville suggests that culture can be congruent or incongruent with the planet and I would add, cultures can also be congruent or incongruent with the individual. An ideal world could be described as one where there would be a congruence between the individual, the groups and society within which we live, and the ecological system. As a therapist and as a person, I experience anxieties as a result of my incongruence at the personal level, the relational level, the group and societal level, and at the global and level of the natural world — as will my client. Sometimes what will be called for is in-depth exploration and healing within me; sometimes the need will be to focus on a relationship; sometimes I will need to take action within a group voicing the incongruence I think I am witnessing, calling for reflection and for the group to find 'right action'; similarly within my community, my society and the natural world. Rogers' focus shifted from the therapeutic relationship to groups, to large unstructured groups and conflict resolution within and between cultures. As we embrace a whole view concept of congruence, our focus has to extend out beyond the self and our immediate relationships to include our society and the natural world. When we witness the distress and alienation within and between people, our societies and the natural world, what authentic response is called forth from us?

REFERENCES

Bozarth, J. D. (1998). *Person-centered therapy: A revolutionary paradigm*. Ross on Wye: PCCS Books.
Biermann-Ratjen, E.-M. (1998). Incongruence and Psychopathology. In Thorne B. and Lambers, E (Eds.), *Person-centered therapy. A European perspective*. London: Sage, pp. 119–30.
Gendlin, E.T. (1962). *Experiencing and the Creation of Meaning*. Illinois: Northwestern Univ. Press, 1997.
Greenberg, L. and Van Balen, (1998). Theory of Experience Centered Therapy. In L. Greenberg, J. Watson & G. Lietaer, (Eds.). *Handbook of Experiential Psychotherapy: Foundations and Differential Treatment*. (pp. 28–57) New York. Guilford Press.
Mearns, D. (1994). *Developing Person-Centred Counselling*. London: Sage.
Mearns, D. (1997). *Person-Centred Counselling Training*. London: Sage.
Neville, B. (1999). The Client-Centered Eco-Psychologist. *Person-Centered Journal* 6(1), pp. 59–74.
Rogers, C.R. (1954). Some Hypotheses Regarding the Facilitation of Personal Growth. *Paper presented at Oberlin College*, Ohio, USA.
Rogers, C.R. (1957). The Necessary and Sufficient Conditions of Therapeutic Change. *Journal of Consulting Psychology*, 21, 95–103.
Rogers, C.R. (1959). A Theory of Therapy, Personality, and Interpersonal Relationships, as Developed in the Client-Centered framework in Koch S. (Ed.), *A Theory of Therapy, Personality and Interpersonal Psychotherapy*. New York: McGraw Hill, pp. 184–256.
Rogers, C.R. (1961). *On Becoming a Person*. London: Constable and Company, (1984).
Rogers, C.R. and Stevens, B. (1967). *Person to Person: The Problem of Being Human*. London: Souvenir Press.
Rogers, C.R. (1980). *A Way of Being*. Boston: Houghton Mifflin Company.
Speierer, G.-W. (1990). Towards a specific illness concept of CCT. In Lietaer, G., Rombauts, J. and Van Balen, R. (Eds.), *Client-Centered and Experiential Psychotherapy in the Nineties*. Leuven: Leuven University Press, pp. 337–59.
Vanaerschot, G. (1997). Empathic resonance as a source of experience-enhancing interventions. In A. C. Bohart & L. S. Greenberg (Eds.), *Empathy Reconsidered*, pp. 141–66. Washington, DC: APA.
Warner, M. (2000). Person-Centred Therapy at the Difficult Edge: a Developmentally Based Model of Fragile and Dissociated Process in Mearns, D. and Thorne, B. (Eds.) *Person-Centred Therapy Today*. London: Sage, pp. 144–71.
Wexler, D.A. (1974). A Cognitive Theory of Experiencing, Self-Actualization, and Therapeutic Process. In Wexler, D.A. and Rice, L.N. (Eds.), (1974) Innovations *in Client-Centered Therapy*. New York: John Wiley, pp. 49–116.
Wyatt, G (2000). *Presence: Bringing together the core conditions*. Paper presented at ICCCEP Conference in Chicago, USA.

Index of Authors

238

Contributors to this volume

THE EDITOR

Gill Wyatt. I am the Director of Person-Centred Connections, an organisation committed to extending the understanding and application of the Person-Centred Approach. I have both managed, designed and tutored on BACP accredited Diplomas in Person-Centred Counselling at postgraduate and undergraduate levels for the last 15 years. I practice in Nottingham as a BACP accredited counsellor and UKCP registered psychotherapist supervisor, facilitator and consultant. My current interests include: congruence and authenticity, groups and group-centred facilitation, aspects of spirituality and energy work, and the nature of power. It is becoming increasingly important for me to find ways of living more authentically in all areas of my life — work, relationships and within the larger contexts of my community, the society within which I live and the environment.

CONTRIBUTORS

Barbara Temaner Brodley has been a client-centered therapist for over forty-five years. She received her Ph.D in clinical psychology and human development at the University of Chicago and was on the staff of the counseling center there, founded by Carl Rogers, for seven years. She is in private practice, teaches client-centered therapy at the Illinois School of Professional psychology and is clinical consultant to the Chicago Counseling and Psychotherapy Center. She also teaches client-centered to training groups in Europe.

Jerold D. Bozarth, Ph.D is Professor Emeritus of the University of Georgia where his tenure included Chairperson of the Department of Counseling and Counseling Psychology, and Director of the Person-Centered Studies Program. He was Editor of the Person-Centered Journal and is currently on the editorial board of numerous journals. Dr. Bozarth has been a consultant with Person-Centered Training Programs in England, the Czech Republic, Portugal, and Brazil. He has participated widely in international presentations and written over 300 professional articles and book chapters. His book, *Person-Centered Therapy: A Revolutionary Paradigm*, is in its second printing with PCCS Books.

Ivan Ellingham After meeting Professor C. H. Patterson when completing a diploma in counselling at the University of Aston in the 70s, I went to study with him at the University of Illinois gaining a PhD in counselling psychology in 1984. Two highlights of my time in the US were attending the La Jolla Program and being introduced to the writings of Susanne Langer by another of my teachers, Michael Piechowski. The further development of person-centred theory remains an abiding interest, alongside my work as counselling psychologist in the NHS and tutor on two person-centred counselling diploma programmes. I live in rural Hertfordshire with my partner, Derryn Thomas, our two dogs and seven cats.

Shari Geller is currently completing her Ph.D in Clinical Psychology at York University in Toronto, Ontario. Her dissertation research is focused on therapists' presence in the psychotherapy encounter. She is also a practising psychotherapist and her approach to therapy and life is holistic in nature and involves an integration of Eastern and Western perspectives. She is also a trained CranioSacral therapist and incorporates her knowledge of the body's role in illness and healing into her therapy practice. Shari has been a student and practitioner of Buddhism and meditation for over 12 years.

Soti Grafanaki, Ph.D is an Assistant Professor in the faculty of Human Sciences at Saint Paul University in Ottawa, Canada. She teaches counselling skills and supervises students in Individual Pastoral Counselling. She has been trained as a counsellor and is a Chartered Psychologist with BPS. Her doctoral research examined client and counsellor experience of congruence during helpful and hindering moments of person-centred therapy. Findings of this project have been presented at various international conferences and in counselling journals. She is involved in projects that study narrative processes in psychotherapy she is also conducting a study on Spirituality and Leisure, funded by the Social Sciences and Humanities Research Council, Canada.

Leslie Greenberg, Ph.D is Professor of Psychology at York University in Toronto, Ontario. He is the Director of the York University Psychotherapy Research Clinic. He has co-authored texts on Emotion in

Psychotherapy (1986); Emotionally Focused Therapy for Couples (1988); Facilitating Emotional Change (1993) and Working with Emotions in Psychotherapy (1997). He recently co-edited Empathy Reconsidered (1997) and the Handbook of Experiential Psychotherapy (1998). Dr. Greenberg is a founding member of the Society of the Exploration of Psychotherapy Integration (SEPI), a past President of the Society for Psychotherapy Research (SPR) and is on the editorial board of a number of psychotherapy journals. He conducts a private practice for individuals and couples and trains people in experiential and emotion focused approaches.

Sheila Haugh is a person centred counsellor/psychotherapist, supervisor and facilitator, a core staff member with the Institute for Person-Centred Learning and an Associate of Psychology Matters. A BACP registered practitioner and a UKCP registered psychotherapist, she has over 20 years experience as a counsellor/psychotherapist in various settings, including work with young people and the terminally ill. Having been a facilitator on BACP accredited courses for 10 years, she has, more recently, been involved in the training of psychotherapists both in England and on the Continent.

Mia Leijssen is professor at the Katholieke Universiteit Leuven, Belgium where she teaches client-centred/experiential psychotherapy, counselling skills and professional ethics for psychologists. She is also coordinator of a three-year part-time postgraduate training programme in client-centred/experiential psychotherapy and has a practice in individual and group psychotherapy.

Germain Lietaer studied as a post-doctoral fellow with Carl Rogers at the Center for the Studies of the Person in La Jolla in 1969-1970. He is a full professor at the Catholic University of Leuven and teaches client-centred/experiential psychotherapy and process research in psychotherapy. He is also a staff member of a three year part-time postgraduate training programme in client-centred/experiential psychotherapy at the same university. Professor Lietaer has published widely: He is chief editor (with J. Rombauts and R. Van Balen) of Client-Centered and Experiential Psychotherapy in the Nineties (Leuven, Belgium: Leuven University Press) and co-editor (with L.S. Greenberg and J. Watson) of the Handbook of Experiential Psychotherapy (New York: Guilford, 1998).

Tony Merry has been involved in the PCA for over twenty years. Currently, he teaches undergraduate and postgraduate courses in counselling and counselling psychology at the University of East London. He has authored or co-authored a number of books, chapters and articles in aspects of client-centred counselling and psychotherapy, including *Learning and Being in Person-Centred Counselling*, published by PCCS Books.

Peter F. Schmid, Univ. Doz. HSProf. Mag. Dr. Born in 1950; Associate Professor at the University of Graz, Styria; teaches at European universities; he is a person–centred psychotherapist, practical theologian and pastoral psychologist; and founder of person-centred training and further training in Austria, co-director of the Academy for Counselling and Psychotherapy of the Austrian 'Institute for Person–Centred Studies (IPS of APG)'. He is a Board Member of both, the World Association (WAPCEPC) and the European Network (NEAPCEPC) and has published many books and articles about anthropology and further developments of the Person–Centered Approach.

Jules Seeman received his PhD degree at the University of Minnesota. In 1947 he was appointed to the university of Chicago Counselling Center and worked there with Carl Rogers until 1953. In that year he moved to George Peabody College to take a position as director of the doctoral programs in clinical and counselling psychology. He remained at Peabody/Vanderbilt on a full-time basis until his retirement in 1985. Since then he has continued to teach part time and to continue in counselling and consulting work. Throughout this academic career he remained active in research and research supervision.

Per-Anders Tengland took his Ph.D at the multidisciplinary Department of Health and Society at Linköping University. The title of his thesis is *Mental Health: A Philosophical Analysis*. He has also written various articles on subjects related to philosophy and mental health. Lately he has taken an interest in methodological questions to do with the measuring of mental health and of the outcome of psychotherapy. He has recently been appointed to a position as lecturer at the Department of Public Health at Malmö University, and he also teaches jazz music at Malmö Academy of Music, Lund University.